# Spanish H...

## The History of Spanish Pistols & Revolvers

### By Gene Gangarosa Jr.

MW01091665

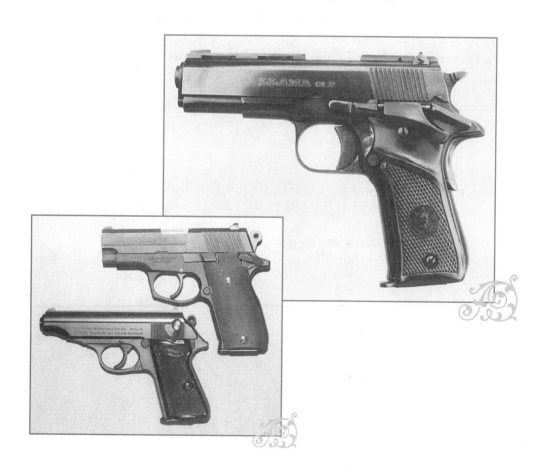

**STOEGER PUBLISHING COMPANY**

**Title:** *Spanish Handguns: The History of Spanish Pistols & Revolvers*

**Editor:** *William S. Jarrett*

**Cover Art Design:** *Ray Wells*

**Book Design And Layout:** *Lesley A. Notorangelo/DSS*

**Project Manager:** *Dominick S. Sorrentino*

**Electronic Imaging:** *Lesley A. Notorangelo/DSS*

Published by Stoeger Publishing Company
17603 Indian Head Highway
Accokeek, Maryland 20607

ISBN: 0-88317-223-2
Library of Congress Control No.: 00-135096
Manufactured in the United States of America

Distributed to the book trade and to the sporting goods trade by
Stoeger Industries, 17603 Indian Head Highway, Accokeek, MD 20607

# Foreword

*D*uring most of the 20th century, Spanish automatic pistols and revolvers have provided a rich and fertile ground for collectors and enthusiasts of all kinds. As a result of the many wars fought during that violent and bloody century, Spanish pistols have been widely distributed throughout the world. For that reason, it makes sense for collectors and shooters traveling in Spain to be aware of these weapons and how they operated. Indeed, automatic pistols made in Spain offer a tremendous variety. Spanish-made copies of the FN Model 1903 alone involve hundreds of roughly similar handguns made by scores of manufacturers. As a result, those who set out to study and collect these guns will never suffer for lack of interesting discoveries and observations.

While Spain's automatic pistols have earned a dubious reputation as being inferior copies of original Browning, Walther and other advanced designs, the Spaniards have made some genuine advancements in design of their own. The Astra "tubular" pistols, particularly the Models 400 and 600, have successfully handled powerful pistol cartridges in an unlocked-breech (blowback) mechanism—a feat attempted but not achieved, either mechanically or commercially, in any other country. Another example is the Jo-Lo-Ar, the largest and most powerful "one-handed" pistol design ever made, chambering cartridges as large as the 9mm Bergmann-Bayard and even the .45 ACP. Moreover, Spanish service pistols are as well-made as top pistols emanating from other countries, witness such highly regarded examples as the Astra Models 300, 400 and 600, the Star Model B and Model 30, and the Llama Model 82, all weapons of unexcelled design and workmanship. Nearly all Spanish automatic pistols of current or recent manufacture—including the Astra Models A-75 and A-100, the Llama Minimax 45, and the Star Models BM, PD, 31, Firestar and Ultrastar—offer qualities and features that make them competitive with the best American, German or Italian pistols. Even the much-maligned .32 caliber pistols of the Ruby or Eibar type, while admittedly made of softer steel than the top-quality pistols of foreign manufacture, are more than adequate to contain the relatively modest pressures of the .32 ACP round for which they were chambered.

Add to these positive elements the fact that, for the most part, Spanish-built automatic pistols are relatively inexpensive compared to, say, Walther handguns (it's possible to buy several Spanish pistols for the price of a single Walther). This makes it possible for persons of modest means to enter the field of collecting handguns coming out of Spain. With such a tremendous variety and quantity existing in the field of collectible automatic pistols, even the most determined and well-heeled collector will find great satisfaction in this endeavor for years to come.

# About The Author

*G*ene Gangarosa Jr., a teacher and technical writer, lives in Florida with his wife and two children. His long association with firearms of all kinds began with his service in the U.S. Navy as a helicopter rescue crewman operating in the Pacific Ocean. Since 1988, he has written more than 200 articles about firearms for such publications as *Shooter's Bible, Guns, Guns & Ammo, Gun World, Combat Handguns, Petersen's Handguns, Sportsman's Gun annual* and *Handgun Testfire*.

Gangarosa is also the author of several books, all published by Stoeger Publishing Company: *P38 Automatic Pistol: The first 50 years, Modern Beretta Firearms, FN/Browning: Armorer to the World, The Walther Handgun Story, Complete Guide to Classic Handguns, Complete Guide to Service Handguns, Complete Guide to Classic Rifles* and *Complete Guide to Modern Rifles*. His next work–*Heckler & Koch: Armorer For The Free World*–will be published soon by Stoeger Publishing Co.

# Table Of Contents

# Chapter 1

## Early Developments

Since ancient times, Spain has been a land where skilled people have worked metal into useful—and often dangerous—shapes. As far back as the Punic Wars, when Romans fought the Carthaginians two centuries before Christ's birth, Spanish swords had already gained a reputation for deadly efficiency. Almost 2,000 years later, Spain was one of the first European nations to become involved in the development and manufacture of firearms, especially handguns. Between 1492 and 1588, it was indisputably the strongest and wealthiest nation in all of Europe, with Spanish firearms and military tactics as advanced as those of any other country. Beginning with the defeat of the "Invincible Armada" in 1588, however, Spain began a long decline in power and influence, a condition that continues to this day.

The story of Spanish handgun manufacture is, to a great extent, the story of the Basque people who live in the northern part of Spain. From ancient times the Basques have preserved a sense of independence and a national culture and identity distinct from that of the rest of Spain. The Basque country is mountainous, but it is also blessed with fertile soil and abundant mineral resources. From the beginning, Basque iron ore provided the steel for Spanish handguns, while Basque forests supplied the wood for the stocks of these weapons. At the turn of the 20th century, the Basques were producing almost all of Spain's iron. The country's steel industry was largely concentrated in this area as well. This process of industrialization lent an importance to Spain wholly out of proportion to its size. While the Basque region comprised only four of Spain's 48 provinces, its income accounted for about a third of the nation's entire economic activity.

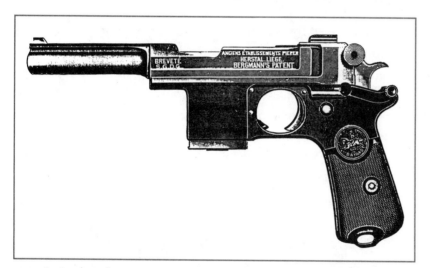

In its day, the Bergmann-Bayard pistol was a large, efficient military-type pistol. The illustration was reproduced from the Bayard company's manual.

The Campo-Giro Model 1913-16 pistol pictured is ready to fire. The hammer is fully cocked and the safety lever on the frame is pushed forward and down. The oval-shaped hole in the slide exposes the slide cross-bolt used in disassembling the pistol for cleaning. (Photo by Ron Waters)

As early as 1863, the manufacturing firm of Orbea Hermanos (founded in 1859 in Eibar) invented a gas-operated automatic revolver that qualifies as one of the early ancestors of the automatic pistol. A piston located beneath the barrel tapped off a small amount of the gas generated by the burning powder, enough to operate the mechanism. It ejected the empty cartridge casing, cocked the hammer, and rotated the cylinder to bring up the next shot. As British gun authorities Ian Hogg and John Weeks note: "It [this process] certainly reflects a great deal of credit on its makers and firmly establishes Eibar as the most likely candidate for the birthplace of the automatic pistol."

## Early Revolvers

In 1863 the Spanish armed forces laid down a requirement for its officers to carry a revolver as part of their basic military equipment. Specifications included a centerfire cartridge ignition system, acceptable weight and length parameters, and a recommendation that American-made revolvers (made by Merwin, Hulbert & Company or Smith & Wesson) meet all these requirements. In October 1884 a revolver manufactured by Orbea Hermanos received royal approval as standard issue for Spain's armed forces. This Smith & Wesson-type revolver already had a double-action trigger mechanism only four years after the American gunmaker had introduced that system in its own revolvers. This whole scenario demonstrated how quickly Spanish manufacturers could evaluate useful innovations created elsewhere and incorporate them into their own products, often with slight modifications aimed at suiting Spanish tastes more efficiently. It also illustrates a peculiarity of contemporary Spanish law: Mechanical devices patented in other countries received a relatively long period of protection—

In this cutaway view of the Bergmann-Bayard pistol, note the flat leaf mainspring located in the hollow of the grip, also the magazine located in front of the triggerguard.

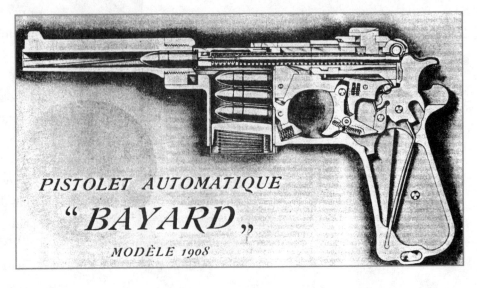

PISTOLET AUTOMATIQUE "BAYARD" MODÈLE 1908

In this view, the Campo-Giro Model 1913-16 pistol is shown with its hammer fully cocked, but the manual safety lever is pushed back to its safe setting. Unlike the earlier Model 1913, where the safety was applied only with the hammer at half cock, the manual safety lever on this pistol type could be applied with the hammer cocked or uncocked. (Photo by Ron Waters)

typically 17 years—but a mechanical device patented in Spain must be produced in Spain within three years, else it could be copied by Spaniards without fear of patent infringements. This loophole enabled Spanish manufacturers to get an earlier start by "borrowing" various desirable features of foreign firearms than was legally permissible elsewhere.

Partially as a result of this policy, Spain had become by the late 1880s an important producer of revolvers. In 1889, for example, manufacturers in Eibar and the surrounding region produced 56,370 revolvers. By 1893 more than 325,000 had been built. Orbea Hermanos, the largest of Spain's handgun firms, employed 406 workers, followed by Garate, Anitua y Cia, with 264 employees. These and other companies were producing military-style revolvers and various patterns of personal-defense revolvers, including pocket types of the famous "Velo Dog" pattern. While the quality of these revolvers was open to question in some instances, there's no doubt that in numbers produced and distributed to various regions of the world, Spain had become by 1900 a significant handgun manufacturer on the international scene.

# *Charola y Anitua*

Early on in its development, Spain had also become deeply involved with the automatic pistol. A Spanish-made automatic pistol—the Charola y Anitua—which appeared in 1897 was one of the first true automatic pistols developed anywhere. Like many Spanish handguns since, this early automatic pistol owed much to a foreign design, in this case the seminal Mauser Model 1896. Also known as the C/96, or the "Broomhandle" (because of its strange grip), this model was a product of the Mauser-Werke factory in Oberndorf, Germany. Though better known for its world-famous bolt action rifles, Mauser's Model 1896 pistol became a great success as well, with over a million built in Germany between 1895 and 1937. It featured a non-detachable 10-round magazine located in front of the triggerguard. It was loaded from the top of the open action (by means of stripper clips), a loading system found also in the Charola y Anitua pistol, whose locking mechanism was also apparently inspired by the Mauser pistol. While it fired only a tiny 5mm cartridge using a 36-grain bullet, the Charola y Anitua weapon incorporated a modified Model 1896-style locked breech (designed around a heavier and faster 86-grain bullet), probably because the Spanish designers were uncertain at this early stage of automatic pistol design how strong this mechanism needed to be. Thanks to its internal mechanical affinities, the Charola y Anitua's overall outward appearance greatly resembled that of the Mauser Model 1896, although the

Like other military pistols of that era, the Bergmann- Bayard could be fitted with a detachable shoulder stock, doubling as a holster when not attached to the rear of the gun. The illustration was taken from the Adolf Frank (ALFA) company catalog of 1911 (printed in Hamburg, Germany).

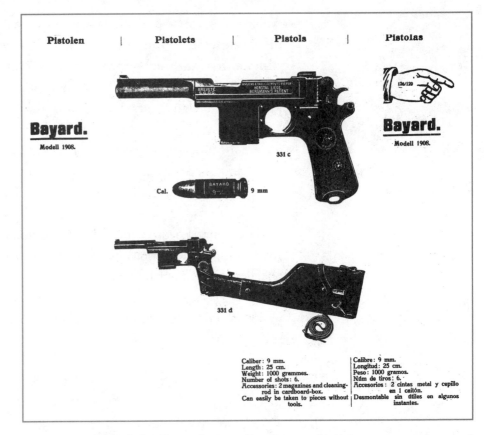

curved profile of the Spanish Pistol's grip made it more attractive and easier to hold than the Mauser's ugly "Broomhandle."

Because of its smaller and far less powerful (5mm) cartridge, the Charola y Anitua's dimensions were even less than the so-called "Bolo Mauser" (the smallest of the Model 1896 variants). For example, the Charola y Anitua was only 9 inches long, an inch shorter than the Bolo Mauser. Barrel lengths were 4.1 inches and 3.9 inches, respectively. Also, the Charola y Anitua's unloaded weight was only 20 ounces, whereas the Bolo Mauser, with its massive bolt and receiver assembly, weighed 37 ounces unloaded (see Appendix for detailed descriptions of ammunition used in Spanish handguns). Regrettably, as with so many other Spanish pistols, the Charola y Anitua's production history is obscure. After being made in Spain until at lest 1900 by its parent company—Anitua y Charola—the manufacture of the pistol and its special 5mm ammunition shifted to an unknown company in Belgium. Production of this model ceased by 1914 at the latest.

With more than a century having elapsed since their introduction, Charola y Anitua pistols are uncommon today. Many were converted in Mexico to fire the widely available .25 ACP caliber ammunition instead of the scarce 5mm round. The Charola y Anitua pistol also found a favorable reception in Russia prior to the 1917 Revolution. Following complaints about the low power of the 5mm cartridge, Anitua y Charola later developed a new version made to fire a larger 7mm round, sometimes with a detachable magazine. Although Spanish manufacturers returned to the Mauser Model 1896 design in the late 1920s and early 1930s, Charola y Anitua's pistol must be regarded as a dead-end in pistol design. It does demonstrate, however, that Spain was looking into the automatic pistol as early as John M. Browning's involvement, and several years before such pistol-making stalwarts as Beretta, Colt and Walther entered the scene.

# Mars

After neutral Switzerland and tiny Belgium, Spain was the third military force to adopt an automatic pistol as military standard. The model chosen was the Bergmann-Bayard Models 1903 and 1908, or the so-called "Mars." Designed by Louis Schmeisser, this powerful and efficient pistol first appeared in 1901. A locked-breech adaptation of earlier blowback designs, it fired a relatively powerful 9mm cartridge, making it suitable for military use.

By 1903, its manufacturer—the Theodor Bergmann firm in Germany—had the Mars model in limited production and available for testing. A number of countries showed an interest, including the United States, Britain

Spanish manufacturers contributed many Velo-Dog revolvers to the international trade, particularly prior to World War I. The revolver at top left is a Crucelegui Hermanos model; the one in the upper right-hand corner is likely one of the Velo-Brom models made by Retolaza Hermanos of Eibar. The illustration is from the 1911 ALFA catalog.

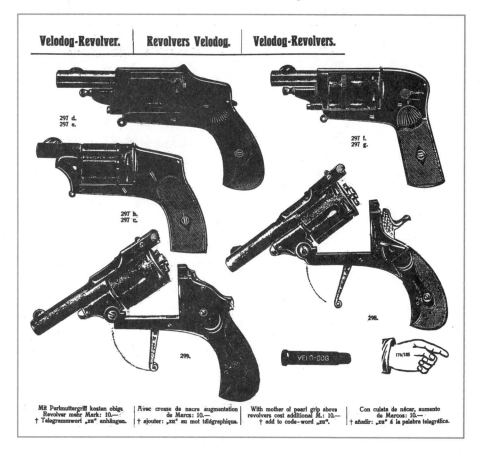

| Velodog-Revolver. | Revolvers Velodog. | Velodog-Revolvers. |
|---|---|---|

| Mit Perlmuttergriff kosten obige Revolver mehr Mark: 10.— † Telegrammwort „zu" anhängen. | Avec crosse de nacre augmentation de Marcs: 10.— † ajouter: „zu" au mot télégraphique. | With mother of pearl grip above revolvers cost additional M.: 10.— † add to code-word „zu". | Con culata de nácar, aumento de Marcos: 10.— † añadir: „zu" á la palabra telegráfica. |

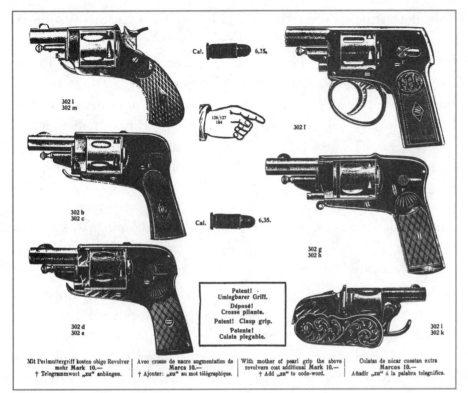

| Mit Perlmuttergriff kosten obige Revolver mehr Mark 10.— † Telegrammwort „zu" anhängen. | Avec crosse de nacre augmentation de Marcs 10.— † Ajouter: „zu" au mot télégraphique. | With mother of pearl grip the above revolvers cost additional Mark 10.— † Add „zu" to code-word. | Culatas de nácar cuestan extra Marcos 10.— Añadir „zu" á la palabra telegráfica. |

and Spain, which purchased a small number for field trials in 1904. The Spaniards were so impressed with this strong, well-made pistol that a military commission (the *Comisíon de Esperiencas de Artilleria*) recommended its adoption. On September 5, 1905, Alfonso XIII, the king of Spain, decreed that the Bergmann pistol be adopted in preference to other early automatic pistol designs, including one under development by Don Venancio López de Caballos y Aquirre.

Immediately after the Spanish approval of the

Revolvers of the Velo-Dog style appeared in some of the more popular Browning-designed cartridges usually found ion small automatic pistols. Revolvers made for the 6.35mm Browning (.25 ACP) round included a model made by Retolaza Hermanos (right, middle), one made by Francisco Arizmendi y Goenaga with a conventional triggerguard (top right), and Crucelegui's Brong-Petit (bottom left).

Bergmann pistol, however, a complication arose having nothing to do with any inherent fault in its design. Because the Bergmann firm was involved in the manufacture of a machine gun, it lacked sufficient factory space to produce these pistols in large quantities (Spain's initial order was for 3000 pistols). Bergmann therefore contracted production of the Spanish order to the Schilling company in nearby Suhl. But the firm of Heinrich Krieghoff bought out Schilling soon after and promptly repudiated all previous contracts made by Schilling. This left Bergmann with no means of fulfilling the highly prestigious contract with the Spanish armed forces. In 1907, after a brief and ultimately fruitless attempt to set up production in the Bergmann factory, the company sold its manufacturing license for the Mars pistol to Anciens Établissements Pieper (AEP) of Liége, Belgium.

Prior to the beginning of series production in Belgium, the Spaniards made a few changes in the Mars design to make the pistol more suitable for use by the military. These changes included improvements in the interruptor mechanism (to ensure that only one shot would be fired for each pull of the trigger) and modifications to the manual safety device. In addition, the magazine release was made larger and easier to operate. AEP also made a few changes of its own and incorporated them in those Mars guns built under contract in Spain. These changes included a slightly shorter barrel—102mm (4.0 inches) as opposed to the original 104mm—and a slight reduction in

The Campo-Giro pistol, Spain's first indigenous military automatic-pistol design, used the powerful 9mm Largo cartridge introduced in the Bergmann-Bayard series. It dispensed, however, with the Bergmann-style locked breech in favor of a powerful recoil spring wrapped around a long barrel. This feature gave the Campo-Giro a unique "tubular" appearance akin to a water pistol. (Photo by Ron Waters)

the overall length from 252mm (9.92 inches) to 250mm. AEP also changed the rifling from a 4-groove, right-hand twist to a 6-groove pattern with a left-hand twist. In addition, AEP increased the Mars' magazine capacity by a round, from five rounds to six. The grip was slightly larger and more angular, replacing the curved, revolver-style handle on the original Bergmann pistol with one more befitting an automatic pistol. Finally, AEP modified the pistol's construction, with the barrel extension becoming an integral part of the barrel rather than machining it as a separate piece. This last change made the pistol easier to make but also raised the overall weight from 910 grams (32.1 ounces) to 1015 grams (35.8 ounce).

This AEP-built pistol became known as the "Bergmann-Bayard" in honor of the Belgian improvements and in recognition of Bergmann's commitment to produce the lion's share of these pistols. [*The origin of the word "Bayard" is AEP's company trademark: a mounted knight above the word*

Spanish gunmakers copied the Nagant revolver (top left) and Smith & Wesson's hinged-frame patterns (bottom left and right). All three guns come from the 1911 ALFA catalog.

*"Bayard"*] Like the competing Mauser Model 1896, which vaguely resembled it in external appearance, the Bergmann-Bayard pistol was available with a slot in the rear portion of the frame designed to accept a detachable shoulder stock. A Spanish royal decree, dated November 1909, established this modified Mars pistol as the *Modelo 1908*, or Model 1908, which became the official name used by AEP as well. The "Bergmann-Bayard" nickname has, however, made a more lasting impression among collectors. The Spanish acceptance of the Bergmann-Bayard pistol made great copy for AEP, which had this to say about it in the Model 1908 manual:

*"In support of the quality and precision of the Bergmann-Bayard Model 1908, the best argument we can advance must be that the Spanish government has chosen the Bergmann-Bayard (improved Mars pistol) for arming its officers, subsequent to exhaustive tests with all available pistols on the market today. This must be the finest recommendation that any pistol can come by."*

The Spanish contract was fulfilled by AEP in 1910 and during the next four years it went on to make other 9mm Bergmann-Bayard pistols, incorporating such Spanish modifications and changes as an enlarged grip and a magazine housing built to facilitate magazine removal for reloading (requested by the armed forces of Denmark in 1911). The pistol also enjoyed limited commercial sales and was adopted by the Greek armed forces in 1913. With the German conquest of Belgium in 1914, sales and production stopped at AEP; still, the pistol remained in production in Belgium from 1922 until 1935.

The Mars/Bergmann-Bayard 9mm pistol used in Spain and elsewhere was a large, powerful weapon. The quality of its manufacture was high, and the gun possessed a strong, well-engineered design capable of handling the powerful 9x23mm cartridges without difficulty. Its locking mechanism for the breech and its sturdy, simple lockwork further enhanced the pistol's rugged durability. The trigger pull was fine, and the gun's precise single-action firing mechanism produced excellent accuracy by most pistol standards. The ease of loading proved a major advance over the Mauser system. The magazine remained fixed in the gun and reloading was made possible via stripper clips only. Under the Bergmann system, by contrast, the shooter could reload the magazine by keeping it in the pistol and loading clipped ammunition through the open breech, as in the Mauser. Or he could remove the magazine from the pistol and reload it one round at a time (as with most modern automatic pistol designs). The location of the magazine release in the forward edge of the triggerguard was fast and convenient for both right-handed and left-handed shooters without fear of accidental release. Placing the magazine ahead of the triggerguard—rather than in the grip or handle portion of the frame, as is more common today—enabled designer Louis Schmeisser to make the pistol more manageable for shooters with small hands while still having access to a large, powerful cartridge.

The AEP company's literature also stressed the many modern safety features of the Bergmann-Bayard design: 1) The exposed hammer, which indicated immediately whether the gun was ready to fire; 2) The manual safety lever, which could be applied with the hammer cocked or uncocked; 3) A spring safety that retracted the point of the firing pin into the front face of the bolt and held it there while the action was open for reloading. Even though the Bergmann-Bayard pistol lacked a loaded-chamber indicator or magazine safety, the action stayed open when the last shot was fired. Maintenance was easy, as indeed it must be in any weapon intended for serious military use. To expose the lockwork, the large pin located just below the manual safety lever (on the left side of the frame) was depressed and slid off the cover plate held in place by the pin.

During this early stage of its development, a few weak points in the make-up of the automatic surfaced. These included an undersized rear sight and an awkward manual safety lever. Before firing, the shooter pushed the safety back and down, like cocking the hammer. Even for a right-handed shooter, the safety lever and hammer were stiff, and the motion required to manipulate them awkward, thus favoring shooters endowed with large hands. The sights were a mixed blessing. The front sight showed up reasonably well, but the rear sight was too small, a problem shared by nearly all pistols made in that era (and by more than a few even today). The 9mm Bergmann-Bayard was also large and inappropriate for concealed carry. The low magazine capacity was also a legitimate complaint, with the slightly larger Mauser pistol holding nearly twice as many shots.

Each of the 3,000 Bergmann-Bayard pistols under Spanish contract bore serial numbers beginning at 1001 and ranging up to about 5000, suggesting that commercial production lots interrupted deliveries to Spain. In addition to AEP's standard "Bayard" and Belgian commercial markings, the Spanish pistols bore an added military acceptance stamp on the receiver, resembling an upside-down "Y" set in a circle. [*For pictures and a discussion of this and other stampings and proofmarks involving Spanish pistols, see the Appendix*] Early issues featured

Revolvers of the Velo-Dog type also appeared in the popular 7.65mm (.32 ACP) cartridge. The revolver at top right is by Crucelegui Hermanos. The other model shown is Retolaza Hermanos' famous Velo-Brom.

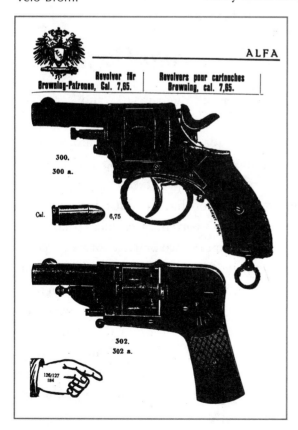

checkered hardwood grips instead of the hard rubber ones (marked "Bayard") found on commercial pistols made by AEP. By 1911, the Spaniards had begun putting hard rubber grips of their own design onto the pistols. This work was done at an arms factory at Oveido (*Real Fábrica de Armas Portátiles de Oveido)*, the same Spanish government arsenal that made prototypes of the first Campo-Giro pistol in 1904 (see below) for the Spanish armed forces. Spain used the 9mm Bergmann-Bayard pistol briefly until better ones became available. Its design, while strong and efficient, did not exert much influence on later pistols. Today, despite its continuing use in Spain and in Denmark (until 1945), the Bergmann-Bayard pistol is quite rare and highly sought after by collectors.

The Bergmann-Bayard pistol's importance in the Spanish handgun story was not a reflection of its limited acceptance and use. Its distinctive cartridge—a bullet 9mm in diameter, but with a longer cartridge casing (23mm long as opposed to 19mm for the Parabellum)—became the standard round for Spain's armed forces pistols for decades to come. In fact, the 9x23mm pistol cartridge became better known in many circles by its Spanish title—the 9mm Largo—than by its original name: the 9mm Bergmann-Bayard. The 9mm Bergmann-Bayard/9mm Largo round, firing a 124-grain bullet at a muzzle velocity of around 1300 feet per second, is by pistol standards on the same order as the 9mm Parabellum and .38 Super (see also the appendix).

# Spanish Commercial Models: The "Velo Dog"

Other important Spanish handguns of the late 19th and early 20th centuries were strictly commercial ventures made for purchase by civilians in search of handguns used primarily for self-defense but also for their novelty or collector value. Among them were the various Spanish revolvers of the period, which fit into several types or patterns. The smallest were called "Velo Dogs," after the first revolver of that type introduced in 1894 by Galand, a French manufacturer. These revolvers consisted of small lightweight models, about five inches long, that fit into a trouser or jacket pocket for a measure of protection. The cylinder capacity was typically five or six shots. For optimum concealment and ease of drawing, the hammer on these revolvers was often concealed at the rear of the frame, and the trigger typically folded up beneath the cylinder when not in use. A few models with conventional exposed trigger and triggerguard were also available. Although Belgian and French manufacturers also made copies of the Velo Dog (with ammunition made by American companies), its most prolific production took place in Spain where a bewildering variety of brand names appeared.

The revolver shown on the bottom right of this 1911-vintage ALFA catalog page clearly indicates the automatic ejection system then used in top-break revolvers. Note the "Smith & Wesson System" and "American Style" nomenclature. ALFA also offered genuine Smith & Wesson revolvers costing between 111 and 170 Marks compared to 11.20 to 32.50 Marks for the poorly-made Spanish copies.

Originally, most of the Velo Dog revolvers used a small, lightweight 5.5mm centerfire cartridge slightly less powerful than a .22 or .25 (see Appendix for details). Later on, to derive more life from the design, some models fired the more popular Browning cartridges. Those Velo Dogs made to fire .25 ACP or .32 ACP cartridges sometimes bore a "Brow-" prefix (e.g., *Browreduit*) indicating the change in caliber from the traditional 5.5mm Velo Dog round. Copies of the Spanish-made Velo Dog included guns from *Cruceletgui Hermanos of Eibar*, a specialist in this genre. The Crucelegui brothers sold Velo Dog revolvers under a bewildering variety of brand names, including Bron-Sport, Brong-Petit, C.H., Le Brong, Puppy and Velo-Mith. Following the initial manufacture of a Velo-Dog copy in 1900, Crucelegui kept these revolvers in production for a remarkably long time, making the switch to other cartridges such as the .25 ACP (6.35mm) and .32 ACP (7.65mm). Unlike most Eibar-based handgun manufacturers, the Crucelegui brothers never converted their plant to the manufacture of automatic pistols. Production of Velo Dog type revolvers kept the Crucelegui company busy until it failed in 1925 on account of worsening economic conditions following World War I.

Another important Velo Dog manufacturer was Francisco Arizmendi. Its revolvers were marked with the "FA" or "FAG" logo and were copied and sold widely by Arizmendi. For example, they appear in both the 1911 A.L. Frank (ALFA) catalog of Hamburg, Germany, and in special long-barreled models exported to Austria-Hungary prior to the outbreak of World War I (gun control laws in Austria prohibited short-barreled handguns in the mistaken believe that people would stop carrying concealable handguns). Ironically, Austria-Hungary's heir to the throne, Archduke Franz Ferdinand, was assassinated in June 1914 by a Serbian nationalist, Gavrilo Princip, who ignored this law and fired the fatal shots from a short-barreled FN pistol, an event that led directly to World War I. Although Arizmendi made many

Holsters with built-in magazine pouches were common among European service pistols. The holster issued with this Campo-Giro model is unusual in that the spare magazine holder appears on the holster flap rather than the main body of the holster. (Photo by Ron Waters)

revolvers in the Velo Dog pattern, the company soon added a long line of automatic pistols (see Chapter 3) designed to supplement and eventually replace the aging Velo Dog copies.

Retolaza Hermanos also made Velo Dog-type revolvers with folding triggers under the brand names *Brompetier, Puppy, Velo-Brom and Velo-Mith.* The Brompetier and the similar Velo-Brom, both intended for sale in France, had French markings on their manual safeties, an unusual device for a revolver, but one used frequently in Spain. The Brompetier had a conventional round barrel, but the Velo-Brom's featured an octagonal cross-section. The calibers available included .25 ACP and .32 ACP (Brompetier) and .5.5mm or 8mm Lebel (Velo-Brom). These two models became highly popular, especially in France; indeed, Retolaza did not stop making them until the pressure of producing a version of the "Ruby" automatic pistol (see below and in Chapter 2) caused the company to drop all other handguns from its product line in 1915. Meanwhile, Retolaza's Velo-Mith demonstrated how much competition small revolvers were receiving from automatic pistols. This model used two Browning-designed pistol cartridges—the .25 ACP and .32 ACP—while the front portion of its barrel was flattened, giving the revolver a profile similar to that of FN's popular Model 1900 pistol (also designed by John Browning). As with the "Puppy" brand name, used by at least four other Spanish manufacturers, the Velo-Mith name proved popular as well among other Spanish firms in the revolver business (notably Crucelegui Hermanos and Ojanguren y Marcaido in Eibar and Garate Hermanos of nearly Ermua).

Perhaps the most interesting Velo-Dog variation was the Dek-Du made by Tomás de Urizar from 1905 to 1912. Holding am impressive 12 cartridges in its cylinder, this model was available in 5.5mm Velo Dog and 6.35mm Browning (.25 ACP). Although it weighed 14 ounces, the Dek-Du was still only 4.7 inches long. Its high capacity was a definite asset, because the Velo-Dog design did not lend itself to rapid reloading, even by revolver standards. Other Velo Dog-type revolvers made in Spain included the popular *Bron-Grand* (made by Fernando Ormachea from 1906 to 1915 in .25 and .32 calibers), the *Brow* (made by Ojanguren y Marcaido in .25 and .32 calibers), the *Browreduit* (made by Salvator Arostegui in .25 caliber), the *Cantabria* (made by Garate Hermanos in several calibers, all the way up to .32 ACP), the *L'Éclair* (Garate, Anitua y Cia: 5.5mm), and the *Puppet* (Ojanguren y Vidosa).

Spanish manufacturers did not confine themselves to copies of the Velo Dog, however. Larger revolvers also appeared, most of these based on Smith & Wesson products. The most popular copy was a double-action model with a hinged frame introduced originally by Smith & Wesson (Springfield,

Massachusetts) in 1880. To open the action for unloading and reloading, a latch was raised at the top of the frame, just behind the rear sight, causing the barrel to drop. This raised the rear end of the cartridges in the cylinder, throwing them clear as the barrel reached its downward limit. Smith & Wesson patented this unloading system as its "Automatic Ejector." This type of revolver featured an exposed hammer spur, making it possible to cock the gun for single-action firing where greater accuracy was desired. The double-action mode was reserved for short-range, rapid-fire emergency work. Spanish copies of this durable revolver included models made by the following gunmakers: Crucelegui, Garate, Anitua y Cia, Orbea Hermanos, and Antonio Errasti (whose "Smith Americano" model appeared in .32 S&W, .38 S&W and .44 calibers). These guns, with their proven design and low cost, proved highly popular in Asia, Africa, South America and Europe. Large numbers of these Spanish revolvers were used in World War I by Allied nations (see following chapter). A less common Spanish copy was Smith & Wesson's hinged-frame model with concealed hammer. Called the "Safety Hammerless" model when it appeared in 1887, it was popularly referred to as the "Lemon Squeezer," because of the safety located in the rear of the grip. The slightly more complicated internal mechanisms of this model led most Spanish revolver manufacturers to turn down this design.

A few years after the Smith & Wesson Military & Police model revolver was introduced in 1899, Spanish manufacturers began to copy it as well. This so-called "Model M&P" differed from the company's earlier automatic ejector pattern (see above). After depressing the cylinder latch and swinging the cylinder to the left, the chambers were emptied by pressing an ejector rod at the front of the cylinder, hence the gun's alternate designation: "Hand Ejector." Spanish copies of this model type made prior to 1936 included the following:

*"Alfa" line (made by Armero Especialistas Reunidas of Eibar)*
*A similar model from Benito Guisasola*
*Orbea Hermanos in various calibers*
*The "Militar y Policia" from Ojanguren y Marcaido*
*The "Oscillante" by Antonio Errasti*
*The S.A. (from Suinaga y Aramperri)*
*Several models from Trocaola, Aranzabal y Cia ("T.A.C.")*

Spanish manufacturers offered numerous caliber choices in this type, including .32, .38, .44 and even .22 rimfire variations. The Military & Police model remains a popular point of departure with Spain's surviving handgun manufacturers even to this day (both Astra and Llama still copy

The unusual grips on this Campo-Giro pistol are made of checkered aluminum with a Soviet-style star emblem. Though some 1916-type pistols used aluminum rather than earlier buffalo horn grips, the star is almost certainly a later addition from the Spanish Civil War. (Photo by Ron Waters)

it). The Colt Police Positive, a contemporary of Smith & Wesson's Hand Ejector, also made its share of Spanish copies, some of which served in the French armed forces during World War I.

Other important early Spanish revolver variations were the various Nagant copies. Based on a Belgian design adopted by the Swedish and Russian governments for military use in 1887 and 1895, the Nagant was a sturdy weapon, albeit slower to reload than the Smith & Wesson revolver designs. The best known among them was Francisco Arizmendi y Goenaga's F.A.G. model. Made in 7.62mm Nagant or the 8mm Lebel caliber favored by the French, this handgun enjoyed large-scale production and considerable use in Africa and South America. It also appeared in the 1911 ALFA catalog. Production there did not stop until the start of World War I, causing Spanish manufacturers to discontinue nonmilitary products and concentrate instead on Allied handgun orders.

## The Automatic Pistol

As important as revolvers were to Spanish manufacturers prior to World War I, an increasing amount of attention was directed toward the newly popular automatic pistol. Because of their comparatively flat profiles and their use of relatively powerful smokeless powder cartridges, automatic pistols quickly supplanted revolvers for many purposes—especially when talented designers like John Browning had sorted out the design's initial shortcomings. Undoubtedly the most important early commercial automatic pistol emerging from Spain was the Star Model 1908. Based loosely on Mannlicher's highly regarded Model 1901, the Model 1908 became the first product of Bonifacio Echeverria, a company founded in 1905 and which later played a major role in Spain's handgun story.

Star's Model 1908 featured an open-topped slide exposing much of the barrel's upper portion and sides. The rear portion of the slide consisted of a breechblock with raised wings. It was serrated so that shooters could grasp the slide with their fingers as an aid when cocking the pistol. In addition to a top-mounted extractor, a prominent spur hammer was located at the rear end of the frame. In these respects, the Star Model 1908 bore marked resemblance to the earlier Mannlicher model. This earliest Star pistol differed from its Mannlicher inspiration, however. Instead of a fixed magazine like the Mannlicher, it featured a detachable box magazine for loading. It fired the 6.35mm Browning Auto (.24 ACP), which had attained a meteoric rise in popularity ever since its introduction by Colt and FN during the period 1905-1906. Boniofacio Echeverria's small (4.5-inch), light (less than 16 ounces unloaded) automatic pistol proved popular and firmly established the brothers Bonifacio and Julian Echeverria in the business of making automatic pistols. The firm continues today, making it one of only three Spanish handgun manufacturers to remain in production to the present.

# The Campo-Giro Pistols

While the guns described above made major contributions to the Spanish handgun story, the most respected and prestigious early Spanish pistols were the various models designed by Don Venancio López de Caballos y Aquirre, Count of Campo-Giro, who was also a Lieutenant Colonel in the artillery. Campo-Giro's pistol-designing career began around 1900, but his first designs did not appear in public until 1904, when one of his pistols received Spanish patent number 34798. This early Campo-Giro pistol was first made in small quantities by the Spanish arms factory at *Oveido Real Fábrica de Armas Portátiles de Oveido*. It then appeared in field trials with Spanish troops but was considered lacking sufficient development to receive serious consideration as a service pistol. Nevertheless, its appearance established Don Venancio as a serious pistol designer. His 1904 model had a locked breech and a wire shoulder-stock which could be detached and screwed into a threaded hole at the rear end of the grip. The caliber was a 7.65mm type, the exact cartridge remaining in some doubt, the most likely candidates being the 7.65x22mm Parabellum (.30 Luger) or another round developed for one of the early Bergmann models.

Following the Spanish government's decision to use the 9mm Largo round (9x23mm Bergmann-Bayard) for its armed forces pistols, the Count of Campo-Giro reworked his pistol design in an effort to make it more acceptable to the military evaluators. His long service in the Spanish army and his many contacts in the government served him well as he developed the prototypes for what became the first armed forces pistol made in Spain. The first change the Count instituted was to chamber the modified design in 9mm Largo caliber. In 1911, the factory in Oviedo produced 25 such pistols, calling them the Modelo 1910. Finally, on September 12, 1912, after extensive testing, a slightly modified version of this pistol—the Modelo 1913—received government acceptance.

The Count then approached the up-and-coming firm of Esperanza y Unceta in Eibar with a request to build this pistol for the Spanish army on a partnership basis. The company, sensing the business potential of this arrangement, relocated in early 1913 from its previous network of small workshops in Eibar to an enlarged, modern factory in the nearby city of Guernica.

The Campo-Giro Model 1913-16 added a second grip screw to the bottom of the frame and relocated the magazine release to the bottom left side of the frame. Note also the lanyard loop at the heel of the frame, a feature typical of Spanish military pistols. (Photo by Ron Waters).

*Chapter 1*

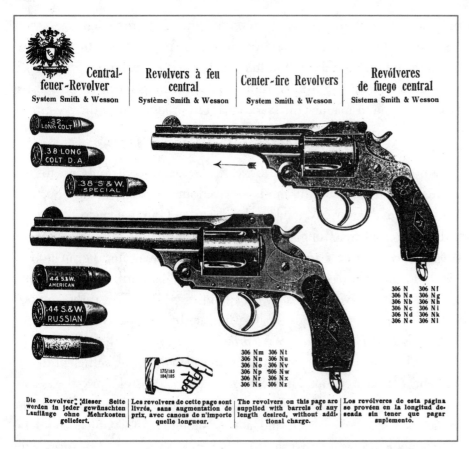

| Central-feuer-Revolver | Revolvers à feu central | Center-fire Revolvers | Revólveres de fuego central |
|---|---|---|---|
| System Smith & Wesson | Système Smith & Wesson | System Smith & Wesson | Sistema Smith & Wesson |

.32 LONG COLT

.38 LONG COLT D.A.

.38 S & W. SPECIAL

.44 S & W. AMERICAN

.44 S. & W. RUSSIAN

.44 S & W.

175/183
184/185

| 306 N | 306 Nf |
| 306 Na | 306 Ng |
| 306 Nb | 306 Nh |
| 306 Nc | 306 Ni |
| 306 Nd | 306 Nk |
| 306 Ne | 306 Nl |

| 306 Nm | 306 Nt |
| 306 Nn | 306 Nu |
| 306 No | 306 Nv |
| 306 Np | 306 Nw |
| 306 Nr | 306 Nx |
| 306 Ns | 306 Nz |

| Die Revolver dieser Seite werden in jeder gewünschten Lauflänge ohne Mehrkosten geliefert. | Les revolvers de cette page sont livrés, sans augmentation de prix, avec canons de n'importe quelle longueur. | The revolvers on this page are supplied with barrels of any length desired, without additional charge. | Los revólveres de esta página se provéen en la longitud deseada sin tener que pagar suplemento. |

These Smith & Wesson copies from the Spanish trade are probably Garate, Anitua or Orbea Hermanos models.

In November 1912, while Campo-Giro continued to tinker with the design, the Spanish army placed an initial order for 500 Modelo 1913 pistols. With the locking mechanism for the breech having been eliminated, the pistol became a simple unlocked-breech (blowback) design. To absorb some of the energy generated by recoil, Campo-Giro added a recoil buffer to the frame in the form of a small but powerful coil spring that fit into an L-shaped piece of metal. This arrangement was then attached to the front end of the locking lug located underneath the barrel. To further reduce the force of the slide as it recoiled into the frame, the recoil spring and mainspring were both strengthened. These powerful springs did much to lessen the force of the slide upon recoil. The buffer, meanwhile, helped cushion the shock to the frame as the slide returned to its forward position. This arrangement worked remarkably well and proved much easier to make than any breech-locking mechanism.

With delivery of the first production pistols to the Spanish army in 1913, a potential problem arose. Whereas the new pistols eliminated the breech-locking mechanism, they differed in several minor details from the pistol contracted for in late 1912. The question then arose as to whether the Count of Campo-Giro was, in fact, delivering the pistol the Spanish military wanted. To resolve this matter, a new military committee was formed to examine the pistol. Official approval was granted on October 27, 1913, followed by delivery of the first batch of Modelo 1913 pistols (serial numbers 1-15 and 51-515) on June 23, 1914. A second shipment of 480 pistols (numbered 516-995) arrived from the factory on August 17, 1914. Esperanza also released 340 additional Modelo 1913 pistols (serial numbers 16-50 and 996-1300) to the commercial market. In all 1,300 Modelo 1913 pistols were made before production ceased in late 1914.

The Campo-Giro pistol used by the Spanish armed forces was quite large—9 1/3 inches (237mm) in length and weighing 33 ½ ounces (unloaded). Fully loaded, the pistol carried eight rounds in its detachable box magazine. Barrel length—6 ½ inches (165mm)—gave the pistol a greater muzzle velocity than the earlier Bergmann-Bayard pistol with its shorter 4-inch barrel. The difference lay in the placement of the magazine. By placing the magazine more to the rear, the Campo-Giro version had a longer barrel, hence a higher muzzle velocity. More importantly, it made possible the use of a relatively long, powerful recoil spring. Given the pistol's blowback mechanism, this was a necessity.

Even after the Spanish government expressed its approval of the Modelo 1913, the Count of Campo-Giro continued to refine his pistol design. Slight changes to the frame contours eliminated the Modelo 1913's uneven, "stepped" frame, which had been wider in front of the grips than it was at the back of the frame. In addition, the magazine release was repositioned from behind the triggerguard to the bottom of the grip. The grip pieces themselves were now held more securely in place by two screws each instead of a single retaining screw on each side (as in the Modelo 1913). Further modification to the manual safety allowed it to operate whether or not the

Bonifacio Echeverria's first pistol, the Star Model 1906, also appeared in ALFA's pre-war product line. Note the distinctive open-topped slide with raised circular cocking bosses at the rear, plus the cross-bolt safety button above and behind the trigger. Echeverria's Star-series pistols retained this open-slide configuration until the 1920s, when the company replaced them with pistols modeled on the Colt Model 1911.

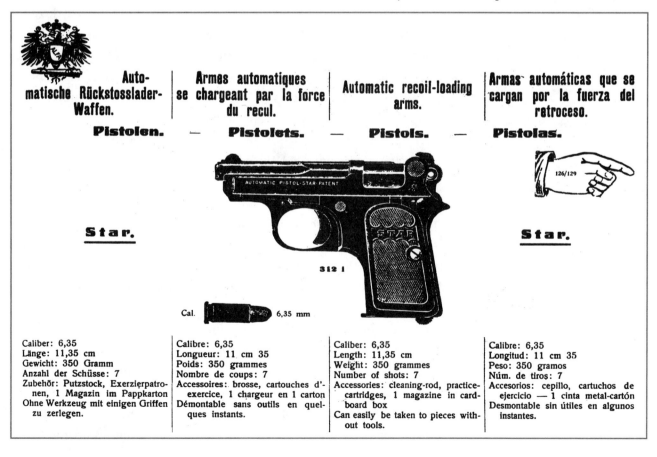

| Auto-matische Rückstosslader-Waffen. | Armes automatiques se chargeant par la force du recul. | Automatic recoil-loading arms. | Armas automáticas que se cargan por la fuerza del retroceso. |
|---|---|---|---|
| Pistolen. — | Pistolets. — | Pistols. — | Pistolas. — |
| Star. | | Star. | |
| Cal. 6,35 mm | | | |
| Caliber: 6,35 | Calibre: 6,35 | Caliber: 6,35 | Calibre: 6,35 |
| Länge: 11,35 cm | Longueur: 11 cm 35 | Length: 11,35 cm | Longitud: 11 cm 35 |
| Gewicht: 350 Gramm | Poids: 350 grammes | Weight: 350 grammes | Peso: 350 gramos |
| Anzahl der Schüsse: 7 | Nombre de coups: 7 | Number of shots: 7 | Núm. de tiros: 7 |
| Zubehör: Putzstock, Exerzierpatro-nen, 1 Magazin im Pappkarton | Accessoires: brosse, cartouches d'-exercice, 1 chargeur en 1 carton | Accessories: cleaning-rod, practice-cartridges, 1 magazine in card-board box | Accesorios: cepillo, cartuchos de ejercicio — 1 cinta metal-cartón |
| Ohne Werkzeug mit einigen Griffen zu zerlegen. | Démontable sans outils en quel-ques instants. | Can easily be taken to pieces with-out tools. | Desmontable sin útiles en algunos instantes. |

*Chapter 1*

hammer was cocked, whereas the safety on the 1913 model could be applied only when the hammer was half-cocked.

The pistols incorporating these changes, as adopted by the Spanish army in late 1915, were known as the Modelo 1913-1916. They represented the final contributions of the Count of Campo-Giro, who died in 1915. Although the Count did not live to see it happen, the Modelo 1913-1916 became by far the most successful Campo-Giro pistol. Spain's armed forces procured 13,178 of this model, and Esperanza y Unceta sold another 447 through commercial channels before production ceased in 1919. Serial numbers were not a continuation of the Modelo 1913 range, but began at 1-9 for commercial sale. Other serial numbers reserved for sale on the open market included a run of 146 pistols (numbered 2429-2573 and 2579), another run of 101 pistols (numbered 3575-3675), and an additional 104 pistols in the 7576-7679 serial number range, 62 more (numbered 8039 to 8100) and a final batch of 25 pistols (numbered from 12101 to 12125). All other Modelo 1913-16 pistols—those that were distributed to the Spanish armed forces—had serial numbers ranging from 10 up to 13625.

Most Campo-Giro pistols had a rust-blue finish, made by placing a solution on the steel parts and allowing them to rust. Unceta's workers then immersed the parts in boiling water, turning the red rust (ferrous hydroxide) into black ferric oxide. This process was repeated until the steel parts attained the desired appearance. Though time-consuming and labor intensive, this rust-bluing process produced attractive results. The Unceta company continued its use until 1957, decades after most manufacturers had switched to the cheaper salt-bluing method. Several small parts, notably the hammer and trigger (also the magazine release on 1913 models and the safety lever on the 1913-16), were given case hardened finishes, while even smaller parts—notably the grip screws and firing pin—were heated until they took on a blue color, a process known as fire bluing. A few commercial models also sported an ornate, silver-plated and engraved finish. The grips on most early models were made of checkered buffalo horn, with checkered wood coming into use later on, often retrofitted to early guns sent out for repair. The engraved models were usually fitted with white synthetic grips resembling pearl. Still other Campo-Giro pistols were refitted with checkered metal grips of aluminum or steel.

Disassembly of Campo-Giro pistols proved more difficult than was acceptable in a military handgun. The process included removal of the magazine, drawing back the slide to clear the weapon of all ammunition, then cocking the hammer. The grips were generally removed next, mostly to prevent damage during the later stages of disassembly. With the firing pin depressed, a screwdriver was placed into the groove on the right side of the slide-retaining bolt. The bolt was then pushed out (from right to left). Once the retaining bolt was removed, the slide could now be drawn fully to the rear while the slide cap was rotated a quarter turn. By carefully controlling the pressure exerted by the recoil spring, the slide could then be eased forward slowly. With the bolt mechanism exposed, it was removed from the back of the slide, which was then lifted off the frame along with the recoil spring. The barrel and two-piece buffer assembly could now be lifted out of the frame. In Spain, both the Campo-Giro 1913 and 1913-16 models saw rather limited use. Once the Model 1921 pistol (Astra Model 400) came into service beginning in 1922, it rapidly replaced the Campo-Giro pistols.

During the desperate days of the Spanish Civil War (1936-1939), Campo-Giro pistols of both 1913 and 1913-16 vintage were returned to service. Once that conflict was over, however, they went back into storage at various Spanish military facilities. In 1959-1960 and again in 1965-

The revolver shown at bottom, left (arrow) was made to resemble an automatic pistol. It was probably of Belgian make, though it strongly resembled Zulaica y Cia's "Revolver Automatico" (1905-1914).

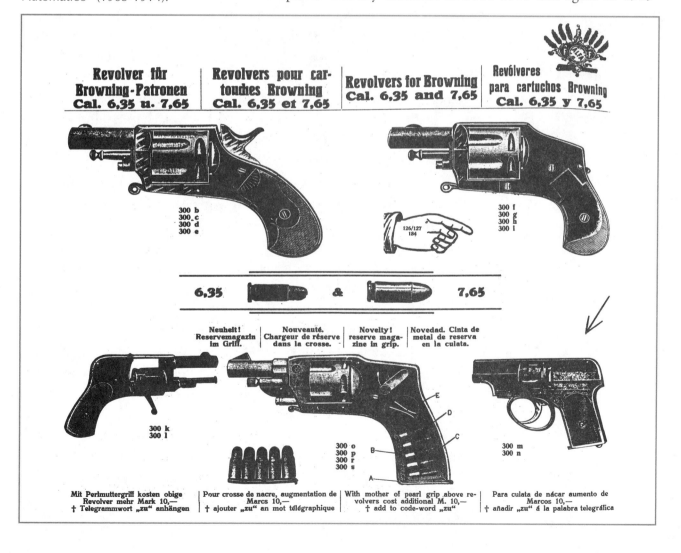

*Chapter 4*

For added reliability, Ruby-type pistols used an exposed extractor, visible here as a long, thin steel strip located behind the ejection port in the slide.

1966, firearms salesman Sam Cummings of Interarms bought up the remaining stocks of Campo-Giro pistols and sold them through his company. These pistols are now considered quite valuable among Spanish pistol collectors, with Modelo 1913s in near-mint condition bringing nearly $3,000 and similar Modelo 1913-16s selling in the $1,500 range at this writing. From a collector's point of view, a genuine Campo-Giro pistol should bear matching serial numbers on the frame, trigger, magazine release, bolt, slide-retaining bolt, slide, barrel, ejector and grips.

The Campo-Giro was also important in the establishment of the Esperanza y Unceta firm. The forerunner of today's *Astra Unceta y Cia*, one of three Spanish handgun companies remaining in business, Esperanza y Unceta gained a measure of respectability in the eyes of the Spanish government. Although the number of Campo-Giro pistols made by Esperanza y Unceta was relatively small compared to the company's total handgun production, being chosen to produce the country's official service pistol conferred immense prestige—and increase sales—for the firm. While it was more than adequate as a service pistol, its large size made it unsuitable for concealed carry, which was another increasingly important niche for automatic pistols in the early years of the 20th century. To service this growing market, pistol manufacturers in Spain began to produce smaller 7.65mm (.32 ACP) caliber copies of the Colt and FN Model 1903 pistols around 1905. The most notable prewar 7-shot Eibar model was the Victoria model, also a product of Esperanza y Unceta. After its introduction in 1911, more than 60,000 Victoria pistols were made by the time the company relocated in 1913 to Guernica (where the Campo-Giro pistols were made). Even after Esperanza y Unceta switched to the 9-shot Models of 1915 and 1916 during World War I, several 7-shot versions of these pistols remained in limited production. They were smaller, handier and therefore better suited to concealed carry and personal defense. Another important Spanish 7-shot .32 caliber pistol copied from the Colt or FN Model 1903 during the prewar period was the Titanic produced by Retolaza Hermanos.

In 1914 Gabilondo y Cia introduced the *Ruby*, a Model 1903 copy designed for police and military personnel who liked its enlarged 9-shot magazine, longer grip and lanyard loop. The Ruby was already a moderate success in Spain and the Americas when World War I broke out in Europe. As the most important Model 1903 copy, the Ruby became extremely important to the Spanish handgun story during the war years. Gabilondo y Cia's introduction of the Ruby pistol in 1914, its adoption by the French armed forces in 1915, and its subsequent history are such an important topic as to deserve a chapter of its own, which follows.

# Chapter 2

---

# The "Ruby" Models, World War One–Present

## Introduction

round 1905, Spanish handgun manufacturers in Spain began making a series of guns based on the design of the FN Model 1903 pistol or the similar (but slightly smaller) Colt Model 1903 pistol, both versions of the same design by John Browning. The Spanish copies, however, employed an internal hammer concealed inside the slide and frame. Also, the barrels on these Spanish copies were attached to the frame by means of several raised ribs machined on the barrel's underside and locked into corresponding grooves machined into the frame. The recoil spring traveled into a hole drilled in the frame beneath the barrel. Almost without exception the early Spanish Model 1903 copies chambered the 7.65mm Browning (.32 ACP) cartridge. The 6.35mm (.25 ACP) caliber was added shortly afterwards. These pocket-sized pistols, which were intended for personal protection, resembled the Colt model more closely than the larger, but mechanically similar FN pistol, a holster-sized pistol designed for military and police issue. As events transpired, though, the distinction between pocket and holster guns soon became blurred and Spanish manufacturers later made both types of guns.

Despite the similarities, these Spanish copies (or clones) also differed in important respects from the refined and elegant FN and Colt Models of 1903. The Spanish pistols were never as well made and lacked some of their more sophisticated features, notably the grip safety. The manual safety lever on most Spanish Model 1903 copies was almost always located midway on the frame (just behind the trigger). In addition to locking the trigger, it also doubled as an aid in disassembling the pistol, i.e., by holding the slide open after it was pulled all the way back. In the first edition of their classic textbook, *Pistols of the World*, Ian Hogg and John Weeks commented that the Eibar-style safety catch that was introduced with the Spanish Model 1903 copies "became a large, bulbous, ribbed item, which always looks as if it were made by the blacksmith's apprentice while the blacksmith was out." Few Spanish manufacturers ever even attempted the task of recreating the more efficient, but harder to produce, Browning-style grip or manual safeties.

# Part I: Spanish Military Handgun Production During World War I (1914-1918)

In early 1914, shortly before World War I began, the Spanish manufacturer Gabilondo y Urresti (now called Llama Gabilondo y Cia) created a sturdy automatic pistol called the Ruby, which ultimately became the most famous of all the Model 1903-type pistols emanating from Eibar and other nearby Spanish cities (in fact, the term "Ruby" has come to be applied generically to the whole lot of them). The original Ruby pistol produced by Gabilondo was slightly over six inches long and weighed about 23 ounces. Intended at first for export to North and South America, it fired the increasingly popular 7.65mm (.32 ACP) cartridge, invented by John M. Browning and introduced with the FN Model 1900 pistol (also a Browning creation). Unlike earlier pistols in this caliber, the Ruby magazine held up to nine rounds, making it a "high capacity model" by the standards of the day.

From the start, Gabilondo designed the Ruby for military and police service, most notably the inclusion of a lanyard loop found at the bottom of the left side of the grip. While rather small and underpowered for a military pistol even then, the Ruby had considerable potential. Because this pistol became so widely copied, all pistols of this type eventually came to be known generically as the "Ruby-type" or "Eibar-type pistols.

In early 1915, Gabilondo y Urresti submitted samples of the Ruby to representatives of the French armed forces, who had been at war now for several months. The French, hard-pressed for handguns, uncharacteristically looked to foreign companies in the United State and Spain to make up the shortfall. Spanish guns held an advantage over American-made guns, however, because they were easier and cheaper to obtain. In May 1915, after at least two series of tests, the French accepted the Gabilondo pistol as their standard weapon and called it the

The extensive line of .32 caliber pistols inspired by Gabilondo's Ruby pistol included (left to right) tiny 6-shot vest pocket models like the "Venus" made by Tomás de Urizar; slightly larger, but still pocketable 7-shot compact pocket pistols like this Alkartasuna; standard 9-shot military models favored by the French and other armed forces in World War I; and finally, the extended-barrel models, some of which had lengthened slides to match while others, like this "Naval" model made by Victor Bernedo, used a standard-length slide with a protruding barrel.

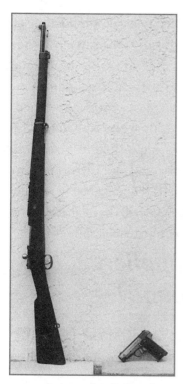

Among the Ruby pistol's claims to fame is its size and handiness, which were far easier to bring to bear than a standard infantry rifle of the time. The Spanish Model 1893 Mauser rifle (left), placed next to the Gabilondo Ruby pistol (right) dramatically illustrates this point.

*Pistolet Automatique, Type Ruby.* Under the agreement, Gabilondo was to deliver 10,000 pistols per month to the French army. By August—one year after the war began—France raised its order to 30,000 per month, and still later increased it to a whopping 50,000 pistols a month.

While it was a larger operation by Spanish standards, Gabilondo could not possibly meet even the lowest of these production figures, so it invited other Spanish manufacturers to help produce pistols under this contract. Gabilondo's original plan encompassed four other companies, all located in the city of Eibar: 1) Armeria Elgoibaressa y Cia, which marked its Ruby-type pistol "Lusitania" in honor of the ocean liner sunk by the Germans; 2) Echealasa y Vincinai y Cia; 3) Hijos de Angel Echeverria y Cia; 4) Iraola Salaverria y Cia. Gabilondo's plan was to produce 10,000 Ruby pistols per month on its own, while each of the other four companies would contribute 5000 pistols per month. All pistols would then be sent to Gabilondo, who would in turn send them to the French. The idea was for Gabilondo to oversee the entire arrangement and assert quality control measures as necessary. The French contract stipulated all pistols must be chambered in the 7.65mm Browning cartridge (called .32 ACP in the United States). [*For information about the ammunition used in Spanish automatic pistols, see Appendix.*] The magazine capacity was set at nine rounds, giving the pistols an unusually long grip relative to the barrel and slide length. The guns made for the French (and later the Italian armed forces) had a blued finish and checkered hardwood grips.

The terms under which the four subcontractors were to supply guns to the Gabilondo firm for final shipment to France are extremely interesting. Firearms expert J. Howard Mathews, whose efforts to uncover the mysteries of the Spanish gun trade between the mid-1920s and early 1950s remain a classic in this difficult field, discovered two agreements between Gabilondo and its four subcontractors: First, if a Gabilondo subcontractor failed to supply Gabilondo, the prime contractor, with 5,000 pistols in a given month, the subcontractor must pay a fine to Gabilondo for each pistol not delivered. On the other hand, should a subcontractor supply Gabilondo with more than 5,000 pistols in a given month, Gabilondo would buy from that subcontractor each pistol delivered over the monthly quota at the going rate—an arrangement that plainly encouraged quantity over quality. Nevertheless, the early Ruby-type pistols made under this five-company arrangement proved satisfactory to the French military.

As questionable as these initial arrangements now appear, the whole business of supplying military handguns for export soon lost complete control. The French continued to clamor for more handguns, as did the

Italians later on in 1915 once they realized that domestic production of pistols could not meet the demands of a world war. Consequently, other manufacturers located in Eibar and the surrounding towns in the Basque region joined what Ian Hogg later called a "gold rush" of official purchases. Some of these companies negotiated their own deals with the French, setting their own prices, while others worked directly with Gabilondo. The result was general confusion, making it next to impossible to determine exactly how many guns were made by a given company. In addition to Gabilondo and the original four subcontractors, as the table below reveals, other Spanish handgun manufacturers are believed to have made guns between 1915 and 1918 under French contracts.

# Table 1. Wartime Spanish Pistol Suppliers to the French and Other Allied Countries

| COMPANY | | BRAND NAME |
|---|---|---|
| Acha Hermanos y Cia | later called Domingo Acha | |
| José Aldazabal | later called Aldazabal y Leturiondo | Imperial |
| Alkartasuma* | | |
| Arizaga | | |
| Francisco Arizmendi | | |
| Arizmendi y Goenaga | | Ideal |
| Armera Elgoibaressa* | located in ElgoibarLusitania | |
| ArrizabalagaRepublic | | |
| Arrostegui | | |
| Azanza y Arrizabalaga | | Reims; Modelo 1916 |
| Martin Bascaran | | Martian |
| Beistegui Hermanos* | | 1914 Model |
| Berasaluce Arietio-Aurteña y Cia | | Allies |
| Vincenzo (Victor) Bernedo | | |
| Gregorio Bolomburu | Suspected to have supplied pistols in the wartime period, though the precise chronology of his products remains uncertain. | Regina |
| Cobra Model | Manufacturer unknown, but construction details suggest wartime manufacture. | |
| Echave y Arizmendi | | Model 1916 |
| Echealaza Y Vincinai y Cia | | |
| Hijos de A Echeverria | | |
| Bonifacio Echeverria | | Izarra |
| Erquiaga y Cia* | Later Erquiaga, Muguruzu y Cia | Fiel |
| Antonio Errasti | | |
| Esperanza y Unceta | | Astra, Brunswig, Victoria |

(Continued on next page)

| COMPANY | | BRAND NAME |
|---|---|---|
| Fabrique d'armes de Guerre de Grande Précision | | Jupiter, Precision |
| Garate, Anitua y Cia | | |
| Isidro Gaztañaga | | Destroyer, Indian |
| Hijos de Calixto Arrizabalaga | | |
| Industrial Orbea | | |
| Iraola Salaverria* | | |
| Lepco Model | Manufacturer unknown but construction details suggest wartime manufacture. | |
| Lobo Model | Manufacturer unknown, but construction details suggest wartime manufacturer. | |
| Mitrailleuse Model | Manufacturer unknown, but construction details suggest wartime manufacture. | |
| Militar Model | Manufacturer unknown, but construction details suggest wartime manufacture. | |
| Modesto Santos | Sometimes marked Les Ouvriers Réunis | Action |
| Oyez Model | Manufacturer unknown, but construction details suggest wartime manufacture. | |
| Pocket Model | Manufacturer unknown, but construction details suggest wartime manufacture. | |
| Retolaza Hermanos | | Liberty, Military, Paramount, Retolaza |
| San Martin y Cia | Located in Elgoibar | Vencedor |
| Societa Espagñola de Armas y Municiones | S.E.A.M. | Silesia |
| Torpille Model | Manufacturer unknown, but construction details suggest wartime manufacture. | |
| Vilar Model | Retolaza Hermanos(?)—Similar to Liberty Model | |
| Urrejola Y Cia | | |
| Tomás de Urizar | | Trust |
| S.A. Royal Vincitor | Sales agency for M. Zulaica y Cia | |
| Wolf Model | Manufacturer unknown, but construction details suggest wartime manufacture | |
| M. Zulaica y Cia | | |

*Indicates companies formally subcontracted with Gabilondo

Those companies that are not marked with an asterisk probably made their own arrangements with the French (except for Modesto Santos, who worked for a French company, Les Ouvriers Réunis, and acted as a sales agent to the French government). Other companies may also have been involved in this lucrative wartime business. Records are difficult to come by, particularly after Spain had suffered through its own Civil War 20 years later. It's estimated that Gabilondo alone may have produced as many as 250,000 to 300,000 Ruby pistols for the French. Ironically, while a

While Gabilondo may have been the main wartime supplier of the Ruby-type pistol to the French armed forces, many other manufacturers also participated. The "GU" marking in an oval near the rear of the frame (top) was added, probably by the French, to conform to a matching logo on the magazine floorplate (bottom). Many magazines of Ruby-type pistols from various companies did not interchange freely.

number of Spanish companies continued to produce Ruby-type pistols up until the Spanish Civil War, Gabilondo quickly dropped its own Ruby pistol and concentrated instead on other designs once the French and Italian orders had been canceled at the end of World War I.

Aside from Gabilondo y Urresti, the most important wartime manufacturer of Ruby- to Eibar-type pistols was Esperanza y Unceta, now known as Astra Unceta y Cia. Founded in July 1908, this company began production in 1911 of a .32 caliber pistol similar to Gabilondo's "Ruby" design (accepted into French service four years later). Initially, Astra's pistol, named the "Victoria" or Model 100, featured an external (exposed) hammer that was visible at the back of the slide, and a short grip with a seven-shot magazine. Early in the production run, Astra eliminated the exposed hammer in favor of a concealed one. Astra made further changes in 1915 to the Victoria pistol so that it conformed more closely to the Ruby design adopted by the French. These changes included a longer grip (making possible a larger nine-round magazine), and checkered wooden grips in place of commercial horn or hard rubber grip pieces. As a result, the pistol became known as the Model 1915 (or Model 1916), later renamed the Model 100. Astra produced about 150,000 such pistols for the French and smaller numbers for the Italians. Like Gabilondo, Astra dropped its own .32 caliber Ruby-type pistol in 1918 and concentrated instead on other designs after business with the French and Italian business had dried up. Astra did, however, keep the .25 caliber versions of its Eibar pistol (see below).

Estimates of total wartime production of Ruby- or Eibar-type pistols for the Allied forces range up to a million pistols or more. French records indicate that their purchasing commission alone received 709,775 such pistols by war's end. A French army inventory taken in 1920 revealed 580,000 .32 pistols on hand, almost all of which were of Spanish origin. From these figures it appears that Spanish pistol manufacturers came close to meeting their monthly quotas as requested by the French. No reliable figures for Italian wartime use have come to light but are thought to have been considerably less than the French orders. Contemporary accounts of Eibar and the surrounding Basque towns suggest that the entire region worked day and night forging, filing and assembling automatic pistols and revolvers to satisfy the Allied armies' insatiable demand for handguns. [*For slide markings of the Ruby-type pistols used in World War I, see the Appendix.*]

Ruby- or Eibar-type pistols remained in production in Spain until the mid-1930s and were exported throughout the world, primarily for the civilian market. In addition to the French contract pistols (7.65mm Browning/.32 ACP caliber) with nine-round magazines, blued finish and checkered walnut grips, the manufacturers also introduced numerous variations on the basic Ruby design to suit different customers—especially for civilian sale—before, during and after World War I. A major variation was in the production of Ruby- or Eibar-type pistols in 6.35mm (.25 ACP) caliber which, in light of the smaller cartridge, had reduced dimensions considerably compared to the 7.65/.32 caliber versions. It was more like a clone of the tiny FN Model 1906 vest pocket pistol rather than the larger Model 1903 service pistol. Some Ruby- or Eibar-type pistols in .25 caliber—notably the Astra Model 200 (also called the Model 1924 or Firecat)—became famous in their own right, enjoying long, successful production runs. In fact, some descendants of these .25 caliber Ruby copies have outlasted the .32 caliber versions to this day.

The standard barrel length for a .32 caliber variant (approx. 3.5 inches) represented another variation in the Ruby- or Eibar-type pistols. A small number of these pistols did, however, have lengthened barrels extending past the front edge of the slide. Still another variation concerned the firing mechanism. Most of these pistols used a standard semiautomatic system in which a single pull of the trigger fired only one shot. But a few Ruby- or Eibar-type pistols used a selective-fire mechanism. In this process a switch on the slide is raised as far as possible, holding the sear out of contact with the trigger mechanism and allowing the shooter to empty the magazine with a single pull of the trigger. Even before 1944, when fully-automatic weapons became illegal for private citizens to own in Spain, the difficulty in controlling them when firing on the full auto setting reduced their utility and caused Spanish gunmakers to manufacture relatively few of them. These machine pistols did, however, see some military use in World War I and later in Asia (particularly China) and during Spain's Civil War of 1936-1939.

Regrettably, some Eibar-type pistols made to fire semiautomatically (one shot for each pull of the trigger) were known to fire in full automatic fashion by accident. The main cause was parts breakage resulting from improperly hardened parts. Early Spanish pistols, particularly the war-era Ruby copies, frequently broke down because of parts that were too soft. Heat treatments designed to

The Ruby-type pistols sometimes had a large "French" rivet added to the slide, just above the safety lever. It helped prevent pressure from the holster when pushing the safety into its fire position during holstering—a condition which on poorly-made Ruby copies sometimes caused an accidental discharge.

*Chapter 2*

# Table 2. Important Basque Barrel Manufacturers

| RIFLING COMPANY | RIFLED PISTOLS ASSEMBLED BY | PISTOL NAME |
| --- | --- | --- |
| *Faustino Artiagoita* | Acha | Looking Glass |
| | Aquirre | Le Dragon |
| | Azpiri | Colon |
| | Bartra y Azpiri | Avion |
| | Gaztañaga | Destroyer |
| | Ojanguren | Apache |
| *Echave y Arizmendi\** | Bascaran | Martian |
| | Santos | El Cid |
| *\*Echave y Arizmendi also made complete pistols of its own* | | |
| *Teodoro Elcoro* | Beistegui | Libia and BH |
| *Teodoro Isarra* | Bolumburu | Bolumburu, Rex, Regina |
| | Salaberrin | Regent, Etna, Invicta, Protector, |
| | Mendiola | Tisane, Unis, Vainqueur |
| *Mendizabal y* | Aldazabal | Aldazabal, Barranco and A.A.A. |
| | Apaolozo | Acier, Comprime and Triumph |
| | Arizmendi | Singer, Walman and Ydeal |
| | Arrizabalaga | Campeon, Especial, Sharp, S[h]ooter |
| | Errasti | Errasti |
| | Retolaza | Destructor, Gallus, Liberty, Military, Paramount, Stosel, Titanic |

lend these parts sufficient hardness called for expensive equipment which the smaller manufacturers could not afford.

The slide serration pattern found on the Ruby- or Eibar-type pistols were either vertical or curved; but the curved pattern (created on a lathe) was much more common in the early years of Spanish production. This pattern was, and remains, less attractive than the parallel lines, whether vertical or diagonal, but the curved slide became quite popular and synonymous with "cheap Spanish pistols." While most Spanish gunmakers settled quickly on either a vertical or a curved pattern, some companies varied their use of the slide-serration pattern from pistol to pistol. This variation is particularly noticeable in pistols marketed by the Antonio Errasti company, whose factory was simply a place where pistols were assembled and whose individual parts were derived from a network of suppliers operating outside their homes or in small shops. The factory collected all these subcontracted parts and performed the final assembly. Many of these so-called "factories" did not possess the proper facilities for rifling their own gun barrels; instead, they had this critical component made elsewhere. The following table indicates some of the most important barrel markers located in Eibar and the surrounding region.

The author shot this 2.1-inch five-shot offhand group at 25 feet, using Winchester ammo and a 73-grain FMJ bullet similar to the then standard military round.

Each small supplier received payment based on the quantity of parts sent to the factory. This piecework system of manufacture also explains in part why so many early Spanish pistols were made of steel that was too soft. Workers armed only with simple hand tools could shape soft steel parts much easier and faster than they could with parts made of harder steel. The softer the metal, the faster it deformed under the stress of firing. This curse of improperly-hardened steel began to stigmatize Spanish handguns during the wartime Ruby contract. The bad reputation that ensued has continued to plague Spanish pistols, despite the absence of any foundation for it even today. Make no mistake, modern Spanish handguns are very well made.

The magazine capacity of Ruby (Eibar-type) pistols also varied widely, depending on the customer and how the gun was to be used. Among the .32 caliber versions, the standard magazine capacity was set at nine rounds. The relatively long grip associated with a 9-round magazine, however, compromised concealability in what was otherwise an extremely compact design. As a result, several manufacturers, notably Unceta (Astra), offered a compact version that held seven (or sometimes six) rounds, with a corresponding reduction in the grip length. This also reduced the gun's height, making it small enough to fit in a pocket. In fact, the earliest Eibar-type

The smaller 7-shot versions of the Ruby can be decently accurate. The author fired this offhand 1.4-inch group of five shots from 25 feet using the famous Winchester 60-grain Silvertip hollowpoint (STHP) with a 60-grain expanding bullet.

*Chapter 2*

The Spanish were not the only ones who made small 7.65mm (.32 ACP) caliber pistols for issue to armed forces personnel. The Germans issued huge quantities of such pistols, notably the Walther Model 4.

pistols—including Astra's Victoria model—featured compact 7-shot magazines that enhanced concealability. For such use, the gun's concealed hammer further facilitated pocket carry by eliminating a possible source of accidental firing or victimization, such as catching or snagging on pocket lining. A smaller number of these pistols incorporated a high-capacity magazine that typically held 12 or more rounds. Naturally, the grip had to be lengthened to accommodate a high-capacity magazine. Few such monstrosities were made and are quite rare today. Occasionally the manufacturer combined the high-capacity magazine with other special features, such as fully-automatic fire capability and/or an extended barrel.

The Ruby and its various copies were easy to manufacture, enabling Spanish manufacturers to sell them at a price which the French and Italians found most attractive. The famous Beretta company, in addition to making many well-known firearms of its own, has at various time acted as a distributor for other companies. One of the pistols they carried was Esperanza y Unceta's "Victoria" (7-shot .32 caliber) model, which sold in 1914 for 37 lire. By contrast, Beretta's own Model 1915, which was also a .32 caliber pistol (but with an original design), cost 65 lire in 1918. This price differential made quite a difference to someone trying to survive on a soldier's pay.

The Ruby or Eibar-type pistol was not the only Spanish pistol design used by the French during World War I. The Bonifacio Echeverria company, which held the "Star" trademark, contributed an original design—the Mannlicher-inspired Model 1914—as well as a Ruby clone called the *Izarra* (the Basque word for *star*). While it fired the same .32 caliber cartridge as the Ruby and its many copies, the Model 1914 was a completely different

After World War I the 7-shot Ruby-type pistol (bottom) was made in greater quantities than the 9-shot military model (top) as the commercial markets began to take over. This actually marked a return to the prewar days, with 7-shot models appearing several years before Gabilondo introduced the 9-shot Ruby in 1914.

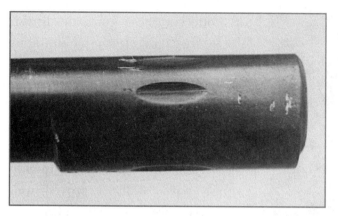

The Ruby pistols are easy to fieldstrip for cleaning. With the slide locked at the rear with the manual safety, enough barrel is exposed for the shooter to rotate and unlock the barrel lugs from the matching grooves in the frame. The barrel can then be moved forward, freeing it from the rest of the pistol. In most cases, the barrel is built up at the muzzle portion, as shown, to offer a more convenient grip for the shooter.

design, including an open slide that exposed the barrel for much of its length. Star's Model 1914, which also appeared in a slightly larger variant, was often called the *Star Military*. A strongly-built weapon of surprisingly high quality, it was fitted and finished as well as many modern handguns. It also had a more positive safety than the Ruby-type pistols, featuring a safety catch that appeared on the right side of the slide toward the rear. By rotating this safety catch to its "on-safe" position, a solid steel block was placed between the hammer and the firing pin. The manual safety later adopted on the French Model 1935 automatic pistols strongly resembled this unit. The Echeverria company contributed about 23,000 .32 caliber Model 1914-type pistols, along with another 10,000 or so Ruby-type Izarra pistols, to the French war effort. So impressed were the French with the quality of these two pistol types that Bonifacio Echeverria, president of the company bearing his name, received a medal from French President Poincaré as a gesture of his country's appreciation.

Other handguns made by Spain for the Allies in World War I included some large revolvers in .455 Webley caliber for British use. On November 5, 1915, the British let out contracts to two companies—Garate, Anitua y Cia and Trocaola, Aranzabal y Cia, both located in Eibar. These Spanish-made revolvers closely resembled Smith & Wesson's double-action, top-break models introduced back in 1880 in .32 S&W and .38 S&W calibers, and a year later in the heavier .44 caliber. The British War Office bestowed its official nomenclature on both products, setting forth strict dimensional standards. Each revolver had to be 10 inches long, with a 5-inch barrel and a capacity of six .455 Webley Mark II (smokeless powder) cartridges in the cylinder. Its weight was 34 ounces unloaded. Mindful of Spain's reputation

The rear end of the barrel has raised ribs that lock into corresponding grooves machined into the inside of the frame.

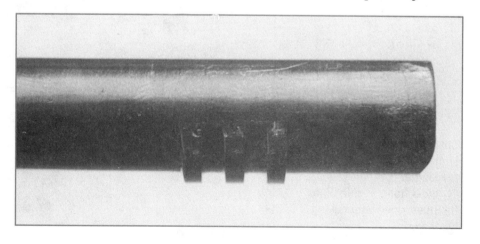

*Chapter 2*

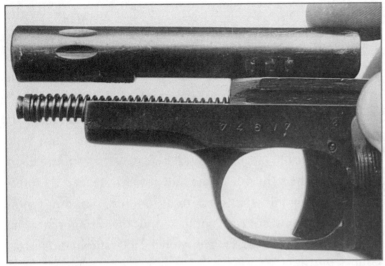

This view, with the slide separated from the frame, indicates the relationship between the barrel and the recoil spring, along with the integral guide rod, beneath it. The recoil spring also powers the manual safety catch, holding it firmly in the safe or fire position once the gun has been assembled and tension is on the spring.

for producing cheap guns, the British War Office set forth voluminous quality-control stipulations, including a final inspection and proofing at Enfield Arsenal, where each gun had to pass close inspection before any payments were made.

As a result of this strict quality control, both revolvers proved well made, serviceable and useful. Their narrow grip offered a secure, comfortable hold, even for small-handed shooters. And the smooth, wide trigger made double-action shooting at close range quick and easy (despite the heavy trigger pull). When distance to the enemy demanded accurate shooting, the revolver's wide, checkered hammer cocked easily by thumb for more precise single-action shooting. Smith & Wesson's top-breaking action operated ambidextrously, with the shooter grasping both sides of the latch and pulling straight up. This was in contrast to the Webley-style cylinder latch which, while it opened the action for loading and unloading in the same manner, lay on the left side of the frame, thus favoring right-handed shooters. The .455 Webley round provided good stopping power by handgun standards, certainly far better then the Ruby and other small .32 ACP caliber automatic pistols (see the Appendix for information on the .32 ACP and .455 Webley cartridges). Despite their large overall size, heavy double-action trigger pull and badly undersized rear sights, the performance of these Spanish revolvers in British service was at least adequate. By 1917, the

British had received approximately 45,000 of these weapons. Meanwhile, production of their own superior weapon—the Webley Mark VI—had reached the point where the British War Office canceled the Spanish and other foreign arms contracts. Accordingly, on November 15, 1923,

A Ruby-type pistol is completely field-stripped into its major components (top to bottom): slide, barrel, recoil spring, frame and (at left) magazine. Note the eight "witness holes" drilled into the magazine for checking its contents.

This Gabilondo-made Ruby, which served in the French armed forces during World War I, also served with the German armed forces in World War II. It was finally captured by an American soldier in 1945, as this document attests.

Britain declared both Spanish revolvers obsolete, although their official use had stopped well before then. The War Office spent the final months of 1921 catching up on the tremendous backlog of paperwork that had accumulated during the war before disposing these surplus weapons.

During World War I the Italian firm of Antonio Errasti made a copy of the Model 1889 "Bodeo" revolver in 10.4mm for Italy's armed forces. This weapon resembled the Model 1889 so closely that it is distinguishable only by its markings. A simple weapon to make, the Bodeo was well suited to Spanish production techniques. Errasti, which later merged with Euliogo Arrostegui and Arizmendi y Goenaga, had by war's end made about 200,000 of these revolvers, a sizable contribution indeed to the Italian war effort. Meanwhile, Orbea Hermanos, one of Spain's premier handgun manufacturers (see Chapter 1), made its Model 1916 revolver to fulfill military orders from Italy. A more modern design than the relatively primitive Bodeo, this large revolver, which was almost identical to the Garate and Trocaola guns built for the British, closely resembled Smith & Wesson's double-action, top-break revolver. To make this revolver more attractive to the Italian, Orbea Hermanos chambered the Model 1916 for the Italian 10.4mm service cartridge rather than the .455 round favored by the British. Interestingly, one version of the Orbea Hermanos revolver, in automatic-pistol fashion, included a safety lever on the left side of the frame, just beneath the hammer.

On February 6, 1917, the French government signed a contract with several Spanish firms for new revolvers to supplement the automatic pistols already in use. For France, still desperate for more arms following three years of warfare, 1917 was in many ways the most difficult year, with army morale down to the point where some units mutinied. In fact, the French military left it up to Spain as to which revolver model they would supply. All they asked was that the revolvers be chambered for the French 8mm revolver cartridge. This policy was in contrast with that covering automatic pistols, in which guns supplied by various manufacturers must conform to the Ruby design.

A French document (dated October 2, 1917) spelled out in detail the specifications and standards for revolvers built under the armed forces contract, as follows (in part):

# Part 1, General Conditions of Furnishing

...The vendor must deposit [two sample revolvers of each type proposed to be sold to the French government for armed forces use]. These arms will be sent to the Reception Commission at Bayonne which will have them sent to the Small Arms Service of the Technical Section of the Artillery. They will only be accepted after having been examined by this service and, if necessary, modified according to its instruction, before proceeding with the sale. One of the two sample revolvers of each type proposed to be sold to the French government for armed forces use will then be forwarded to the Commission to serve as a standard for comparison during the receipt trials. The other will be saved as model-type [i.e., what the British called a "sealed pattern"].

# Part 2, Conditions for Receipt

...The arms will be presented to the Reception Commission in unbroken lots of 1000...The arms presented for receipt shall be the same, in all particulars, to the model-type offered and accepted. All parts, except the grips, shall be of steel. The chambers of the cylinders...must be able to receive, up to the rim, and without a great deal of play, the regulation cartridge for the Model 1892 revolver...made by the Société Française de Munitions...The [barrel bore] shall have a diameter of 8.00mm on the lands and 8.30 on the grooves, with a tolerance of 0.03mm plus or minus for each dimension. The barrel shall be screwed sufficiently tightly to the frame. The front and rear sights, placed very exactly in the center plane of the arm, must remain visible to the firer whatever is the position of the hammer. The cylinder shall turn with a light rubbing on its axis. The extractor shall be

In addition to the Ruby-type automatic pistols (bottom), Spanish manufacturers also supplied several hundred thousand revolvers to the Allied armies, including a copy of Smith & Wesson's hinged-frame model in .455 Webley caliber (made by Garate, Anitua y Cia) for British use (top).

pulled back freely by its spring and its rod shall run without too much play in its lodging. The clearance between the cylinder and the barrel shall not be as great as 0.45mm (0.0177in), without descending to around 0.15mm (0.0059in) when the chamber is in its most forward position. The chambers of the cylinder must align exactly with the axis of the barrel, and remain held, without play, in their successive positions by the cylinder stop or sear bar. The firing pin protrusion from the recoil plate shall be 1.7mm (0.067in) minimum and 2mm (0.079in) maximum, when the hammer is down. The protrusion shall be nil when the hammer is in the rebounding position [thus avoiding the possibility of an accidental discharge of the gun when the shooter's finger is off the trigger]. The sear, in its smallest part, must have a thickness of at least 0.6mm (0.024in). All the parts of the lockwork must be heat treated and must have an elasticity and a resisitance to wear necessary to their functioning and to their maintenance. The [wooden] grips shall be checkered and solidly seated in the frame.

*Proof firing:* each revolver, after a detailed examination, shall undergo proofs of function and of firing 6 shots. The firing shall be done on a paper target, placed 15 meters (49.2 feet) from the firer; all the points of impact shall be contained in a square 40cm (15.75in) on each side. The impacts on the target must be very round, with no trace of ovalization [i.e., keyholing, indicating defective rifling].

*Examination after firing:* The different parts of the arm, examined after firing, shall show no defects nor mutilation of any sort.

*Verdict of the Commission:* If the proportion of arms not satisfying all the conditions of receipt (examination before and after firing, proof firing) is greater than 10% of the lot, the entire lot can be refused for good, and the cancellation of the sale proposed to the Minister. If this proportion is equal to or less than 10%, the arms which are inadmissible but judged capable of being repaired on the spot can be presented again, with the subsequent lot or after a delay determined by the Commission and the vendor together. The arms not accepted after a second examination will be rejected for good. In any case, and whatever may be the proportion of

*Chapter 2*

The Garate, Anitua y Cia revolver was a large, powerful handgun. In British service it was given the name Pistol, Old Pattern, Number 1, Mark 1.

refusals during the first presentation, each arm received only after the second examination will undergo a uniform decrease in value of one peseta, representing the cost of the additional testing. The proportion of 10% fixed above for the refusal of a complete lot may be lowered by the Commission to 5% when the revolvers of the lot are affected by one or more grave defects which the commission judge to be capable of compromising the functioning of these weapons when placed in service. If the defects appear to be repairable, the lot in its entirety shall be returned to the vendor, to be reworked by his labor during a time established by the Commission and the vendor together. If at this second test the proportion of the arms presented which still have the grave defects which motivated the reworking is still greater than 5%, the lot shall be rejected for good. In the opposite case, every arm of the lot satisfying the required conditions shall be accepted, but with the depreciation of one peseta mentioned above. No special condition is imposed on the manufacturer/vendor on the subject of the provenance of the steels to use; it is, however, recommended to them in their own interest, to conform as exactly as possible to the information furnished them by the Commission of Bayonne concerning the types of steel most suitable for the manufacture of the different parts of the weapon.

***Special Conditions:*** The revolvers shall be delivered postpaid to the Artillery Park next to Bayonne. The present provision of Spanish weapons will benefit from the imposition of temporary admission. It will then be free of the payment of duties until the operations at Bayonne are terminated [which happened with the end of the war in November 1918]. These duties, for all the arms accepted, shall be the responsibility of the French government. The arms rejected shall be returned to Spain by the furnisher at his cost without payment of duty, and the proof of exit shall be furnished

The Garate, Anitua y Cia-made revolver could be fired either double action, using the trigger to cock the hammer, or single-action, with the hammer cocked back to the position shown.

to the Artillery Park at Bayonne [this requirement for specific documentation of failed weapons leaving the country, combined with the separate requirement that each Spanish manufacturer mark his weapons with a separate and sequential set of serial numbers, ensured no tricks would be attempted such as passing off rejected guns as new ones, and so on]. The ammunition necessary for the trials shall be furnished at the expense of the French nation.

*Method of Payment:* The payment of the sum of the sales shall be made by the French Consul at Saint-Sebastian, in proportion to the deliveries, upon receipt of the Receiving Commission at Bayonne.

As is so often the case, this original documentation is rich in detail and offers several points to ponder. First: No such detailed specifications have yet come to light involving the "Ruby" automatic pistols. This suggests that the French procurement of Spanish automatic pistols, having started earlier, was far less organized than the revolver order. Second: some details set forth in these revolver specifications suggest the French had already identified specific problems with the "Ruby" pistol and its various clones and sought to avoid them in the revolver order. Note, for instance, the specific requirements set for *sear thickness, heat treatment of the firing lock, the use of quality steel, and easy maintenance.* These specifications suggest that the French had learned the hard way (referring to the Ruby automatic-pistol program) that Spanish manufacturers could produce guns of adequate quality, but only if they were held strictly accountable for the quality of the product.

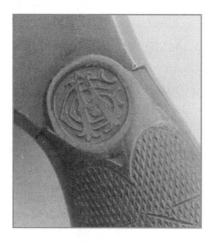

The stylized GAC monogram (for Garate, Anitua y Cia) appeared on the British-issue revolvers. Its resemblance to the world-famous Smith & Wesson monogram was no accident. Spanish manufacturers frequently led customers into thinking they were getting the American product, not this inferior copy.

Orbea Hermanos made a revolver modeled after the Smith & Wesson Military & Police revolver (now the Model 10) for French armed forces contracts made during wartime. At the same time, Garate, Anitua y Cia, having finished its British wartime revolver order, copied Colt's New Service revolver for the French. The numbers involved were huge, one estimate citing 485,280 revolvers patterned after the side-opening Colt and Smith & Wesson copies. While this figure, covering only 18 months, seems an unbelievable accomplishment, bear in mind that the firms involved included Eibar's largest handgun manufacturers. The revolvers made were, moreover, well-tested types of the sort for which these firms had already accumulated extensive experience. These and other factors, combined with

*Chapter 2*

The Garate, Anitua y Cia revolver is unhinged by lifting the checkered bosses (in front of the hammer) straight up.

the smell of French gold, resulted in round-the-clock production at Eibar, where handgun production rose from 682,535 automatic pistols and revolvers in 1916 to 708,551 in the following year. Contrast these impressive figures with the production of only 69,395 revolvers and no automatic pistols in the same city back in 1893. Contemporary accounts from the period 1915-1918 describe the air quality in the little city in the Basque hills as filled with smoke, day and night, from the fires of countless forges, each turning raw steel into rough handgun-shaped lumps, which workers then filed into shape. Virtually every home had one or more family members armed with files, performing subcontracted piecework for one factory or another. Never before had business been so good, and never again, not even in the desperate days of the Spanish Civil War 20 years later, would Eibar experience anything like this bustle of activity.

While the hard-pressed French were ordering Spanish automatic pistols and revolvers, Romania, yet another combatant on the Allied side, ordered the TAC Model 1914, a product of Trocaola, Aranzabal y Cia similar to the .455 caliber revolver being made concurrently for the British. The Model 1914 chambered the .44 S&W centerfire cartridge—the forerunner of the more famous .44 Special—which was popular in South America as well. Serbia also received Spanish-made weapons, and the Greeks, who fought on the Allied side from 1917 to 1918, ordered several thousand Ruby copies (Bascaran's "Martian" models). Ordering pistols from a single source, as the French did, eliminated many of the problems inherent in producing large numbers of similar but not identical sources from 50 or more different manufacturers. The Greek armed forces, being much smaller than the French, did not require such enormous quantities of munitions, so their supply situation presented far fewer difficulties.

# Part II: Between the World Wars (1919-1939)

Following World War I, the Ruby pistols proved remarkably long-lived. Part of the reason for their success in the postwar period lay in the rise of new nations in Central and Eastern Europe. In need of arms, but with little money to buy them, small countries like Yugoslavia and Finland turned to surplus markets awash in low-cost wartime arms in order to equip their own forces until something better was available. Coupled with the pressing

The "broad arrow" between the two "D's" on a revolver made by Garate, Anitua y Cia is a British government stamp.

need for weapons was the urge among Frenchmen to dump their huge stocks of Ruby pistols in favor of more modern designs. When Finland bought 9000 Ruby-type pistols (Model 1919) from France, it established that small country's preference for semiautomatic pistols as opposed to the more common ex-Russian Model 1895 Nagant revolvers. These one-time French pistols served the Finns as front-line weapons until 1923, when most were replaced with 7.65mm Parabellum (Luger) pistols bought from DWM in Germany. A number of similar Spanish pistols—mostly in 6.35mm (.25) and 7.65mm (.32) calibers—also sold in large numbers on the Finnish commercial market during the period between the wars.

Yugoslavia's armed forces also imported large numbers of ex-French, war-era pistols of Spanish make. Later on, VKT (*Voino Teknichki Zavod*, or Armed Forces Technical Factory) began making slides (or possibly complete pistols) of the Ruby type. These were marked with Cyrillic lettering which, in translation, read: "PISTOL 7.65mm. FVTZ 1923." Yugoslavia's adoption in 1923 of a modified and enlarged FN Model 1910 pistol—the Model 1922, of which Yugoslavia bought 60,000—quickly ended further experimentation with the Ruby design. Italy's armed forces, constantly short of handguns and other modern weapons, also kept their wartime-era Ruby pistols in limited use between the wars. Several thousand that remained on hand in 1940 were sent to Finland (see below) to aid that country in its struggle against invading Soviet forces.

# Part III: From World War II to the Present– Evaluating and Collecting

Here a Garate, Anitua y Cia revolver is shown with its frame partially unhinged. The sturdy frame's locking extensions are clearly visible.

Ruby pistols were widely used during World War II, notably by the French Resistance forces and to a lesser extent by Finland, Italy and Yugoslavia. Even the Germans pressed into service considerable numbers of Ruby-type pistols; these weapons were, after all, widely available. They also used the 7.65mm/ .32 cartridge, which was a perennial favorite in

*Chapter 2*

The Garate, Anitua y Cia revolver's frame-locking mechanism, while very strong, left little room for a rear sight. This remains one of the less desirable features copied from the original 1880-vintage Smith & Wesson.

Germany as a police and military standard round. Despite its low cost (suggesting poor quality), the Ruby- or Eibar-type pistol possessed several desirable characteristics, which helped make it at least an adequate, if not inspired, handgun choice for military and police service or civilian self-defense. A soldier could, for example, easily maintain a Ruby- or Eibar-type pistol in the field, an important attribute for a military weapon. Removing its barrel for cleaning was especially easy and convenient. Once the weapon was cleared—by first removing the magazine from the grip and then pulling the slide back to unload the firing chamber—the safety was placed all the way forward on its safe setting. The slide was them pulled all the way to the rear until the safety catch locked it open. The slide's position exposed enough of the barrel's forward portion so that a shooter could then rotate it, unlocking the barrel ribs from the grooves in the frame and withdrawing the barrel from the front of the pistol. Once removed, the barrel was easily cleaned. This was absolutely essential at a time when most ammunition used corrosive primers. If not quickly attended to, these contaminants could rust a barrel bore within hours after firing.

The Garate, Anitua y Cia's frame is shown fully unhinged, automatically lifting clear, then ejecting the empty cartridge cases.

The front sight of a Garate, Anitua y Cia revolver consisted of a razor-thin hemisphere pinned to the barrel

Another positive point in favor of these pistols—those in the military version with a magazine capacity of nine rounds—was their ability to hold more ammunition than virtually all other handguns of the time, most of which held only six rounds (the U.S. Model 1911 automatic pistol had a seven-shot magazine). Among the Ruby's contemporaries, only the 10-shot, .32 caliber Savage automatic pistol made by Savage held more shots. While most military pistols in that era fired more powerful cartridges, the heavy, low-powered Ruby and its copies had in their favor less recoil than competing standard service pistols, which generally promoted accuracy. Still, the Ruby pistols remain quite accurate even today, holding their own against, among others, the Walther Model 4, which served a similar mission for Germany on the other side of the line during both world wars.

Finally, the huge and lucrative handgun business carried on by the French and Italians undoubtedly played a large part in preserving Spain's neutrality during World War I on a pro-Allied basis. It was simply good business for all concerned for the Spaniards to sell these pistols in enormous quantities to the Allied powers. In the meantime, considerable sympathy for Germany was expressed by the Spanish government during World War I. Indeed, some Spanish Germanophiles put great pressure on their government to take a more active role in helping Germany. What if, for example, Spain had allowed German submarines to refuel in Spanish ports, as they repeatedly requested. The desperate submarine war of 1917, which came close to cutting off England's supply route to and from the United States, might well have turned out disastrously for the Allies. The sheer volume of

The serial number on this early revolver made by Garate, Anitua y Cia (along with Trocaola, Aranzabal y Cia) appears at the front of the grip. Some 45,000 revolvers of this type were supplied to the British.

wartime business with nearby France served, however, to keep Spain's pro-German leanings at bay. Unfortunately, Spain's neutrality during World War II took a pro-German bias instead, as described in a later chapter.

Regrettably, the Ruby- or Eibar-type pistols suffered from various weaknesses and shortcomings. The pistols were single-action only,

The Garate, Anitua y Cia revolver produced decent accuracy, though not up to Webley standards. The author fired this 2.2-inch double-action offhand group from 25 feet. Note how the double-action trigger pull placed the shots up and to the right.

The Garate, Anitua y Cia revolver is definitely at its best when fired in the single-action mode, cocking the hammer before each shot. The author grouped five shots into a 2.6-inch pattern at a distance of 75 feet.

which meant that the hammer had to be cocked before firing. Since the hammer was concealed within the slide, it could be cocked only by retracting the slide, and this made it difficult for soldiers to determine their pistols' state of readiness. Accidental shootings occurred frequently to the point where "hammerless" (actually, concealed hammer) automatic pistols gained a bad reputation in military circles. Many soldiers also reported trouble concerning the manual safety. On some .32 caliber Ruby-type pistols, the amount of reach required for a right-handed shooter to thumb back the safety to its fire position was more than many shooters could manage (ironically, the Eibar-type safety was more ambidextrous than almost all other early safety designs; left-handed shooters could operate the safety with their trigger fingers). When using the similar but smaller .25 caliber pistols, however, operating the safety catch proved much easier. With the manual safety catch kept all the way forward on the safe setting, and with the chamber unloaded, the slide will bring up the first round from the magazine. Then, as the slide is pulled back, the manual safety locks the slide open all the way to the rear. This prevents the gun from firing in the shooter's moment of need. In short, this combination of single-action operation and the idiosyncrasies of the manual safety system made these pistols slower into action than later designs. Many contemporary handguns—notably the British Webley Mark VI revolver and the U.S. Model 1911 automatic pistol—were faster into action and more convenient to operate by virtue of a better design.

Another problem occurred when the safety was applied. It operated only on the trigger, locking it, with no effect on the hammer whatsoever. With the hammer cocked, a severe blow to the pistol could conceivably dislodge the hammer from its cocked position and cause the pistol to fire uninten-

tionally with possibly fatal results. Using several dozen contractors made the interchangeability of parts virtually non-existent. Even the magazines on Ruby-type pistols did not interchange among pistols made by the various companies. As a result, they had to be marked on the bottom with the initials of the company to make it clear as to which Eibar-type handgun it belonged.

Despite these problem areas, many a soldier's life

 Although British armed forces stopped using the Garate, Anitua y Cia revolver (top) shortly after World War I ended in 1918, they kept using British-made revolvers of essentially similar configuration, such as the World War II era Webley Mark IV (bottom).

was saved by one of these sturdy little pistols in cases where a rifle was too long and clumsy to bring into immediate action. In this simple formula—easy and rapid accessibility—lies the very essence of a handgun designed for military combat. Despite the low esteem in which these guns are now held—and indeed were held by the French even in their time of greatest need—the Ruby pistols were there when little else was available. With all the problems noted above, mostly the result of low standards of manufacture amongst the many subcontractors, the Ruby-type pistols generally provided passable if uninspired service. Nevertheless, as Ian Hogg and John Weeks point out in their book:

*In fairness it must be said that not every "Eibar" pistol was cheap and nasty; many reputable firms owe their start, or at least their subsequent well-being, to the "Eibar" pattern of pistol, and produced quality weapons right from the start. But, regrettably, it is true that in this particular product, the shoddy outnumbers the good by a wide margin.*

At least, the Ruby and its many copies gave the Spanish handgun industry worldwide exposure and recognition. These guns have been observed literally from Chile to China and all points in between. Unfortunately, this widespread distribution proved a mixed blessing. While the many handgun manufacturing companies in the Basque region of Spain made tremendous profits from the "Ruby"-type pistols, it was ultimately these same guns, perhaps more than any other, that gave the Spanish handgun industry a bad name, one which it has not altogether overcome even to this day.

*Chapter 2*

# Chapter 3

## Early Designs, 1900-1936

While many students of Spanish handguns associate Spain's early automatic pistol development between 1900 and 1936 solely with "Eibar" or Ruby-type automatic pistols, the industry actually developed many other different pistol designs during that period. Some proved quite innovative and clever, for which the designers in that era can take credit. Among the problems they faced was an inherent one—namely, how to load an automatic pistol. Many early automatic pistols, notably the Mauser C.96 and the Steyr Models 1907 and 1912, made use of fixed magazines into which an entire magazine load of cartridges was stripped *en bloc* by means of a stripper clip. Moreover, being integral with the gun, these magazines could not be removed without tools. The chief disadvantage of this fixed-magazine arrangement, on the other hand, was its slow reloading process, particularly in cases where the special stripper clips unique to that model were not available. As a result, by the advent of World War I the detachable magazine had replaced the integral fixed magazine in most automatic pistol designs.

## The Radium (Gabilondo) Magazine Project

Being well aware of these problems, Gabilondo became the first designer to attempt a compromise. Sometime between 1910 and 1915, the company (then known as Gabilondos y Urresti) made a small .25 caliber pistol, called the *Radium*, whose magazine design was unique. What Gabilondo attempted was to combine the best features of both fixed and detachable automatic pistol magazines. Radium's version, similar to the fixed-magazine design, stayed in the pistol at all times but, in this design no special stripper clips were needed to load. Instead, the shooter simply pushed the grip plate down, sliding it far enough out of the way so that it depressed the magazine follower and exposed the interior of the magazine. Up to six rounds of ammunition were inserted into the magazine. The grip was then pushed back into position and the magazine spring was activated, repositioning the cartridges for feeding. With the magazine charged and the grip back in position, the firing chamber was loaded simply by working the slide. Once it was fired, the Radium operated in the conventional manner.

This clever mechanism may have worked satisfactorily in a small pistol designed for pocket carry and emergency self-defense, but it proved more difficult to manufacture. It was also less rugged than the detachable magazine used on the Ruby pistol, which Gabilondo introduced in 1914. When the French army awarded Gabilondo a huge contract in 1915 *(see Chapter 1)*, the company dropped the Radium project and concentrated instead on making the Ruby pistol for the more lucrative military business abroad. Once the war had ended, Gabilondo never revived the Radium, and no other gun manufacturer has reportedly attempted to create its own variation of the design.

## Arizaga's Pinkerton, Mondial & Warwink Pistols

When Gabilondo elected not to reintroduce its Radium pistol following World War I, an Eibar-based company formed by Gaspar Arizaga introduced its own clever solution to another problem common among automatic pistol magazine designs. Compared to the highly visible ammunition supply found on revolvers, the magazines used on automatic pistols—both fixed and detachable—were partially concealed. This made it almost impossible to determine how much ammunition was in the pistol without opening the action or partially disassembling the weapon. To

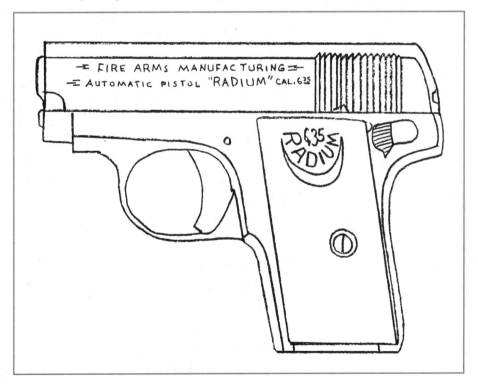

Gabilondo's Radium used an innovative integral magazine, one that remained in the gun while reloading but was easily accessed by pushing down on the sliding right grip plate.

---
**49**

*Chapter 3*

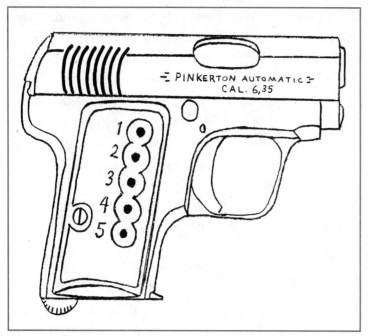

The Pinkerton built by Arizaga had a clever see-through grip design. It allowed the shooter to check the magazine contents at a glance, an idea not revived until the ASP pistol of the 1970s.

address this problem Arizaga created a pistol call the *Pinkerton,* which allowed the shooter to ascertain at a glance how many cartridges were left in the pistol. What Arizaga did was to drill five holes, all numbered, into the right-hand grip, making the contents of a magazine easily apparent. Arizaga went out of business during the Spanish Civil War, but this clever concept reappeared in the 1960s under the aegis of Armament Systems and Procedures (ASP), which created a much-modified Smith & Wesson Model 39 pistol. The ASP grips were made of a translucent plastic material which, in the spirit of Arizago's *Pinkerton* pistol, effectively revealed the magazine's contents.

Another Arizaga product, the *Mondial,* was a typical example of the Spaniards' skills at copying the outward appearance of a well-known foreign gun while at the same time simplifying its manufacturing process—and, in some instances, actually improving on the foreign design. While Arizaga's .25 ACP caliber Mondial outwardly resembled the American-made Savage pistol, the company also produced a similar pistol, the *Warwink,* in .32 ACP, one of Savage's main pistol calibers. Despite their outward resemblance to the Savage, both the Mondial and Warwink were simple Browning-type blowback pistols that proved easier to build than the Savage model with its rotating-barrel locked breech.

## Garate, Anitua y Cia's La Lita

Garate, Anitua y Cia, maker of Spain's first automatic pistol, the tiny *Charola y Anitua,* also made a copy of a famous foreign design. Its *La Lira* pistol, built around 1910-1914, was a close rendition of the Austrian-made Mannlicher Model 1905, but with two distinct improvements: First, it replaced the Mannlicher's integral, fixed magazine with a detachable unit; and second, the La Lira fired the ubiquitous .32 ACP (7.65mm Browning) cartridge instead of the proprietary 7.65mm Mannlicher round. Because of the Mannlicher's graceful curved grip, a matching curved magazine was called for. In the early stages, Garate made the magazine release integral with the magazine itself, rather than placing it on the frame as was more common. The pistol was also marketed as the *Triumph,* with its magazine release repositioned to the frame in the usual manner. The La Lira would doubtless have done well had not World War I intervened. But with the war in progress, Garate curtailed production of this promising design to concentrate on military projects *(see Chapter 2)*, building a Ruby clone (Eibar-type) automatic pistol for the French and a .455 caliber hinged-frame revolver for the British armed forces.

# FN Model 1903/1910 Hybrids and Model 1910 Copies

Other examples of Spain's penchant for making pistols that looked like one thing, but which were in actuality quite different, were the *Alkar Standard*, the *Colonial*, and the *Longines*. All three, while mechanically pure copies of the FN Model 1903, featured slimmed down slides configured to resemble the FN Model 1910. The Alkar Standard, Colonial and Longines offered their manufacturers the best of both worlds: the tried and tested Model 1903 design combined with the marketing appeal of the more modern Model 1910. The Alkar Standard was pocket-sized whereas the Colonial and Longines models were much larger, holster-sized service pistols. Production of the Alkar Standard stopped when its manufacturer's factory burned down in 1920; but the Colonial and the Longines proved fairly successful. The Longines, for example, was the only product of the *Cooperativa Obrera* (or Worker's Cooperative) of Eibar, providing its members with a good living. Only in Spain were hybrids of the Models 1903/1910 made. In this case, two foreign designs were adapted and modified to suit their own purposes. The *Bufalo* and *Danton* pistols, made by Gabilondo between 1919 and 1933, also resembled the John Browning-designed FN Model 1910. While they did place the recoil spring around the barrel in the manner of the Model 1910, Gabilondo replaced its striker ignition arrangement with an improved concealed hammer. The Gabilondo pistols also had a different type of grip safety (protected in Spain under patent number 62004 dated 1919) in place of the Model 1910 design used by FN.

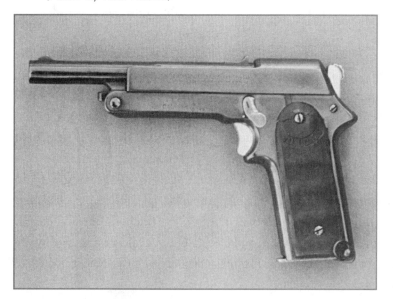

An innovative and successful Spanish model: the Jo-Lo-Ar. (Photo by Ron Waters)

The Bufalo and Danton pistols, which proved highly successful for Gabilondo, were much improved over the Ruby pistol that had gained great fame for the company, not to mention lucrative sales during World War I. Gabilondo made numerous variations on the basic design, including those in .25 ACP (Danton only), .32 ACP and .380 ACP caliber, plus a choice of seven-, nine- or twelve-round magazines. The Bufalo, which was produced from 1919 to 1925, was first, followed by the Danton (protected under patent number 70724 of 1925). The various Danton pistols—marked "War Model" on the slides—probably received no official large-scale orders from armed forces, but they were without question privately purchased by soldiers from various countries as personal weapons. The Bufalo-Danton series proved highly popular; with one sales agency (located in Barcelona) selling 100 Bufalo pistols a day, mostly to mail-order houses in the United States. Gabilondo discontinued this series in 1933 once its newer "Llama" line of Colt Model 1911 copies *(see below)* began to enjoy some success.

The Gregorio Bolumburu firm, located in Eibar, also made an interesting Model 1910 clone, called the *Rex*. Similar to the FN pistol in external appearance and internal workings, it also had a loaded-chamber indicator on top of the slide. This useful feature was one which the Belgian-made original never had despite its high quality. The markings on the Rex were cleverly designed to resemble those of a Belgian pistol, rather than one made in Spain. Obviously, the poor reputation of Spanish-made arms—a legacy of the many cheap turn-of-the-century revolvers and the Ruby automatic pistol—had begun to spread.

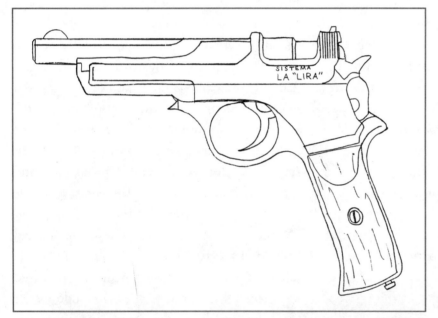

The La Lira pistol made by Garate, Anitua y Cia combined Mannlicher's attractive design with a detachable magazine and a commonly available and successful cartridge—two assets the graceful Mannlicher lacked.

Still another close copy of the FN Model 1910 came from Unceta y Cia, makers of the Astra pistol line. In 1926 the company created its Model 700 Special featuring an FN Model 1910-type slide that was flattened along the sides but with the same Eibar-style thumb safety (and no grip safety). The pistol's elongated grip held a standard 9-shot magazine, but an extended-capacity magazine was optional. Protruding slightly from the bottom of the grip, it would hold an additional three rounds. Specifications included the following: **Caliber:** 7.65mm Browning/.32 ACP. **Overall Length:** 6.3 inches. **Barrel Length:** 3.7 inches. **Height:** 4.9 inches (unloaded: 26 ounces). **Features:** Choice of grip pieces made from hard rubber, Astra logo, grip pieces made of checkered walnut.

Unceta y Cia, as the company was now known, had high hopes for this new pistol. An advertisement (translated for the U.S.) read as follows:

*There is undoubtedly an opening for an accurate cheap Automatic Pistol designed on scientific lines, machined on the interchangeable system and guaranteed by a manufacturer of high repute. The new "ASTRA" Model 700 Special combines these essentials together with extraordinary accuracy that will appeal to all classes. In addition, this pistol possesses a simplicity of action and easy replacement that has never ever before been attained. We offer the "ASTRA" Model 700 Special with the fullest confidence that it will maintain, in its own way and upon its merits, the reputation of this firm, which has been built on excellence and durability.*

Advertisements for the Model 700 Special also appeared in Finland where Spanish pistols proved quite popular between World Wars I and II. Unceta y Cia sold the Model 700 Special on the open market because the gun lacked appeal to government and military bodies, despite its high-capacity magazine and lanyard loop. Unceta ultimately sold only its initial production run of 4,000 Model 700 Specials (serial numbers 400001 to 404000). Because of the limited demand for these pistols, production ceased once the 4,000 units were completed in 1917. Nevertheless, the Model 700 Special, with its interesting design and durability, was as good a handgun as the more successful Gabilondo-made Danton, which it strongly resembled.

## Spanish Clones of the Mauser Model 1896

One of the most admired pistols of the early 20th century was Mauser's Model 1896 (or C.96). First tested in 1895 and introduced commercially in 1896, this well-made gun saw widespread use, causing several Spanish manufacturers to express their admiration for it by making copies. Commonly referred to as the "Broomhandle Mauser" because of its skinny grip, the Mauser Model 1896 included an integral magazine holding 10 rounds (reloading via a stripper clip). Among this model's most desirable features was its powerful, flat-shooting 7.63mm cartridge, commonly known as the .30 Mauser *(see the appendix for detailed information on ammunition used in Spanish handguns)*. The lightweight bullet (ca. 86 grains) produced a high initial muzzle velocity of around 1,600 feet per second, offering excellent range, accuracy and penetration by handgun standards. Another popular feature of the Model 1896 involved the attachment of a shoulder stock, which clipped onto a groove cut into the back of the grip and doubled as a holster. Taking advantage of this feature—along with the long-range adjustable rear sight which Mauser usually equipped for this pistol—a shooter armed with a Model 1896 could engage his targets with reasonably accurate and effective fire at ranges up to 200 yards or so.

Though it resembled the famous Model 1910 pistol from FN externally, the Longines pistol, in its internal workings, was nothing more than a Browning Model 1903 copy. The arrow indicates the 1903-type location of the recoil spring (it's not wrapped around the barrel as in 1910-type pistols).

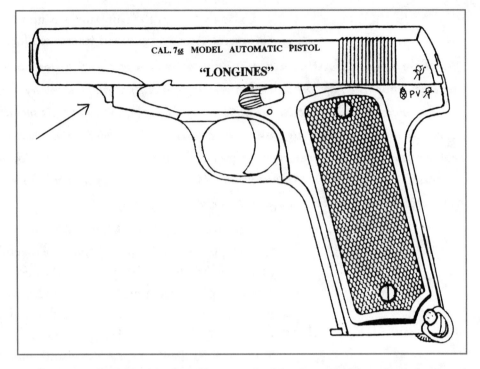

By the end of World War I, Mauser had built several hundred thousand Model 1896 pistols (including approximately 138,000 in 9mm Parabellum caliber). And while military sales were disappointing to a company that sold its bolt-action service rifles by the millions, the Model 1896 was bought in large numbers as a private-purchase item, often by soldiers seeking a powerful and versatile sidearm that was easily portable as well. Following World War I, major restrictions placed on German arms manufacturers by the Treaty of Versailles (1919) gave Spanish, French, Belgian and Czech gunmakers a golden opportunity to expand their market shares.

One firm eager to expand its product line beyond the usual .32 caliber Ruby was Beistegui Hermanos, who decided to make a Model 1896 copy of their own. The result, named the *Royal* or *Azul*, appeared in 1926 and closely resembled its Mauser ancestor in external appearance. It was about the same size and fired the same ammunition, but it differed somewhat in construction. For example, the bolt on the Royal had a rounded cross-section as opposed to the Mauser's square-shaped bolt. This allowed Beistegui's factory workers to turn the bolts on a lathe—a much less costly method. The barrel was made as a separate unit from the barrel extension and then heat-shrunk into place. By contrast, the barrel and barrel extension on the Mauser were forged and milled as one integral unit. The Royal also used two large screws to connect the parts of the mechanism, whereas the Mauser had no screws, relying instead on intricate machining to allow all its parts to interlock precisely. Barrel length options included 5¹/₄, 6¹/₄ and 7¹/₈ inches. Magazine capacities included a 10-shot box and, later, a 20-shot box, both detachable from the receiver by means of a release catch on the right side of the magazine housing.

The changes Beistegui made in the design of the Royal—especially compared to its German counterpart—were much easier to manufacture, enabling the Royal to sell for a lot less money than the German pistol. In 1931, a selective-fire version was added to the line, giving shooters the option of firing a single shot for each pull of the trigger (i.e., semiautomatic fire) or continuous firing until the shooter released the trigger or the gun ran out of ammunition (i.e., fully automatic fire). The finish on the Royal was appallingly poor, and the quality of its metal, which was excessively soft, left much to be desired. Even though it was aggressively marketed by Eulogio Arostegui (as the semiautomatic Azul and fully automatic Azul MM31 or Super Azul) and by Zulaica y Cia (as the Royal in semiautomatic or fully-automatic versions), it was never regarded as highly as the Astra Model 900 series pistols *(see below)*.

# Astra's Model 900

Unceta y Cia also took advantage of German's weakened position following the war by introducing its own copy of the C.96, called the *Astra Model 900*. Like the Beistegui Hermanos product, Astra's Model 900 closely resembled the C.96. It was about the same size and had a heavier barrel, making it slightly heavier overall. Internally, the Astra differed from the Mauser as well. Whereas Mauser made its barrel and barrel extension as a single unit, requiring extensive and costly machining, Astra made its barrel separately, then screwed and heat-shrunk it into the barrel extension. The return spring was placed in a channel drilled into the receiver in front of the magazine well and just beneath the barrel. The Mauser's barrel return spring, by contrast, was located within the bolt mechanism. Also contrary to the Mauser was Astra's decision to pin the lockwork in place in the frame, rather than making it a separate and removable module as Mauser had done. Astra's lockwork was also

The Jo-Lo-Ar (top) in 9mm Largo saw service in Peru and in Spain itself during its Civil War of 1936-1939. It was a good-sized pistol, as large as the Astra Model 1921 (Model 400) shown below. (Photo by Ron Waters)

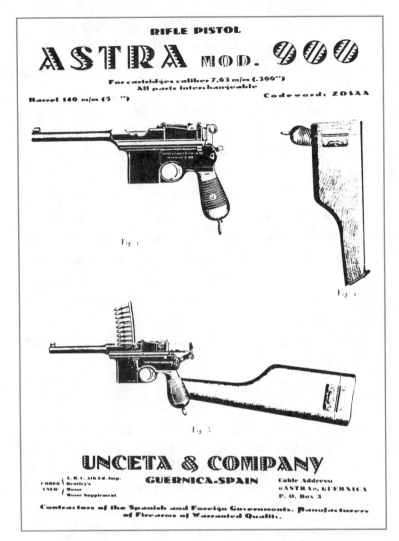

In the manner of the Mauser Model 1896 which inspired it, the Astra Model 900 had a fixed magazine loaded from 10-shot stripper clips carried in a hollow wooden holster that doubled as a shoulder stock for more accurate shooting. (Photocopy courtesy of Astra-Unceta y Cia)

completely different in its configuration than the Mauser's, hence none of the parts would interchange. Since the Model 900's lockwork was not removable, Astra added a cover plate on the left side of the frame so that it would slide off easily while gaining access to the pistol's firing mechanism.

Workers at the Unceta factory lavished great care on each Model 900, carefully fitting the parts by hand. Numerous parts had their own serial numbers to indicate which gun they belonged to. The parts included the following: frame, rear sight components, bolt, barrel extension, locking block, sideplate, two frame crossbolts, magazine parts, and grips. The inner portions of the frame and sideplate were jeweled to help retain a thin film of lubricating oil around the lockwork. The painstaking rust-bluing process used in finishing most of these guns—some of which were engraved and chrome, silver or even gold-plated—gave the flat sides of the frame a beautiful reflective sheen.

The Model 900 was indeed a durable and beautiful gun. Improved versions were equally successful for Astra and posed serious competition even for Mauser. This obvious quality enabled Unceta y Cia to keep the Model 900 and its variants in production for many years. In fact, the company did not sell its last Model 900 variant until 1960, well beyond the demise of the C.96 in 1937 and Beistegui's production of its Mauser clones in 1934. [*For additional information about the Model 900, see chapters 5, 6 and 7.*]

## *Arizmendi and the Boltun Pistol*

Francisco Arizmendi of Eibar was also well aware that a pistol resembling a famous and well-respected foreign model would most likely sell in quantity. His response to this awareness was the *Boltun*, a pocket pistol made in both .25 ACP and .32 ACP calibers. Resembling the *Pieper* pistol (made in Belgium), the Boltun was much simpler and less expensive to produce in quantity than its foreign inspiration. Whereas the Pieper's

The odd shape and angle of the Jo-Lo-Ar's hammer makes thumb-cocking exceedingly difficult. The slide lacks the retraction serrations found on most automatic pistols, forcing the shooter to rely almost completely on the cocking lever when preparing this single-action pistol for firing. Note also the pistol's exposed extractor. (Photo by Ron Waters)

barrel hinged at the front of the receiver, thus raising its breech end for loading, the Boltun had a fixed barrel. And whereas the Pieper was expensive to manufacture, forcing its Belgian armsmaker to cease production in the 1920s, the Boltun cost Arizmendi much less to produce. It also rode to success behind the Pieper's international reputation. Interestingly, all Boltun pistols had markings (in French) on their manual safety—"FEU" for fire and "SUR" for safe. The combination of French safety markings and English slide markings helped to obscure the Spanish origins of the Boltun pistol. Indeed, by the 1920s the reputation of guns from Spain had sunk so low that, aside from some of the Star and Llama pistols, few Spanish handguns bore prominent markings to indicate their country of origin. Either they contained no clue of Spanish origin whatsoever, or there was a tiny "SPAIN" or "MADE IN SPAIN" inscription appearing in some inconspicuous location on the pistol where it remained unnoticed save by the most diligent observer.

In all fairness, not all of Arizmendi's efforts were the result of copying the products of others. The company also designed an original loaded-chamber indicator for use in automatic pistols. This clever device contained an empty firing chamber that allowed the extractor to lie flush with the right side of the slide. A groove machined into the upper portion of the indicator was aligned with a matching groove on the slide top. When the firing chamber was loaded, the extractor would protrude slight from the side of the slide and the indicator groove on the slide top would lean slightly to the left, out of line with the grooved slide. The Arizmendi firm used this loaded-chamber indicator in their other automatic pistols, notably the *Ideal, Singer* and *Walman* models.

## Gaztañaga's Destroyer and Super Destroyer

Another set of pistols to consider in this category of copycat Spanish gunmakers was the *Destroyer* and *Super Destroyer* produced by Gaztañaga in the mid-1930s. Beginning in 1913, original Destroyer models were more or less standard copies of the FN Models 1903 (in 7.65mm) or Model 1906 (in 6.35mm). During World War I, Gaztañaga was one of many manufacturers to join the bandwagon in supplying guns to the French. The postwar 7.65mm second model Destroyer, which was introduced in 1919, was a close copy of the sleek FN Model 1910. Its recoil spring was placed around the barrel and a manual safety lever was located at the rear of the frame in FN fashion (rather than above the trigger). In place of the Eibar-type safety lever on the frame slightly above the trigger, Gaztañaga inserted a large disassembly catch on the frame of the second model Destroyer. The function

AUTOMATIC PISTOL DANTON CAL. 765 (32)
PATENT 70724 TESTED

DANTON

G

Gabilondo's Danton proved a worthy successor to the Ruby, which had proven a commercial success during World War I.

of this disassembly catch was to hold back the slide so the shooter could fieldstrip the pistol more easily. Also in common with the FN Model 1910 were the fine vertical slide serrations for cocking the Destroyer, as opposed to the curved serrations found on most inexpensive Spanish pistols. Later, in the 1920s, Gaztañaga modified the second model Destroyer pistol by dispensing with the disassembly catch altogether. This led to still another pistol, called the *Surete* (French for "Safety"), which closely resembled the FN Model 1910.

In 1933, Gaztañaga reorganized and became Gaztañaga, Trocaola y Ibarzabal. The partners soon dropped the Gaztañaga line of pistols and introduced a new model, the *Super Destroyer*. The inspiration for this 8-shot, .32 ACP caliber gun, at least in its external appearance, was the famous German-made Walther Model PP. Like many pistol manufacturers since, Gaztañaga envied Walther's success and set out to create a competitor to the Model PP.

Mechanically, the Super Destroyer was identical to Gaztañaga's earlier FN Model 1910 copies. Nevertheless, the company went to considerable lengths to make the Super Destroyer resemble the Walther PP instead. Though an inch shorter and several ounces lighter, the Super Destroyer's slide and frame contours closely resembled the PP's. Even the styling of the pistol's logo on the grip and its streaming banner near the top of the grip resembled the well-known Walther emblem. The Super Destroyer's slide-mounted safety catch and pushbutton magazine release were also similar to those of the PP. When the safety catch on the Super Destroyer was applied, it did not decock the hammer in the same manner as the PP's safety, where the shooter simply locked the firing pin instead. The Super Destroyer also lacked the PP's advanced double-action trigger mechanism. Moreover, the Super Destroyer, like the earlier Gaztañaga pistols and the Model 1910 on which they were based, had a muzzle bushing secured with pressure exerted against it by a recoil spring mounted around the barrel. Disassembly of the Walther pistol, on the other hand, was (and remains) controlled by a more sophisticated hinging triggerguard. Despite these criticisms, the Super Destroyer was a well-made gun that enjoyed a considerable, albeit brief, success at replacing Gaztañaga's line of older Eibar-type and Model 1910-type pistols. The Super Destroyer sold well for a few years within Spain itself, thanks to the marketing abilities of Gazañaga and Trocaola y Ibarzabel. The highly respected export firm of José Cruz Mugica (see Chapter 5) undertook Super Destroyer exports to foreign countries, handling this account until the onset of the Spanish Civil War forced the company to close its factory in July 1936.

# The Bernedo Automatic Pistol

An especially innovative Spanish automatic pistol design created between World War I and the Spanish Civil War was a handy pocket pistol manufactured during the 1920s by Vincente Bernedo y Compañia of Eibar.

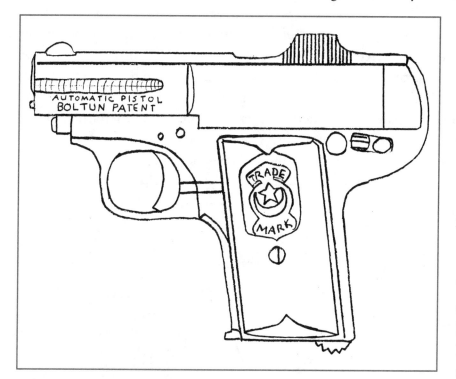

The Bolton pistol made by Arizmendi resembled externally the well-regarded but expensive Pieper pistol made in Belgium. Simpler construction and lower labor costs enabled the Spaniards to sell this gun for less than the Belgians could.

The *Bernedo* pistol, as it was known, made barrel removal for cleaning, maintenance or replacement an easy task in an age when virtually all ammunition used corrosive chemicals in the primer. Even a few hours' neglect after firing could turn the bore of a rifled firearm to rust. In the Bernedo design (Spanish patent number 69952 in 1920), a small spring-loaded pin located in the frame retained the barrel. The slide was cut off at the top and side to expose all but the bottom part of the barrel. Removal of the pin allowed the shooter to lift the barrel out of the frame. Since the manual safety no longer had to double as a slide lock to aid disassembly, as was common in Eibar-style pistols, Bernedo used a manual safety catch at the rear of the frame, similar to that found in FN pocket models. Less than five inches long and weighing only 10.3 ounces, the 7-shot Bernedo was a handy little gun. It failed to prosper, however, because it competed against a host of lower-priced Eibar-type pistols based on the FN Model 1906. As a result, the Bernedo company went out of business around 1929.

# The Sharp-Shooter and Jo-Lo-Ar Pistols

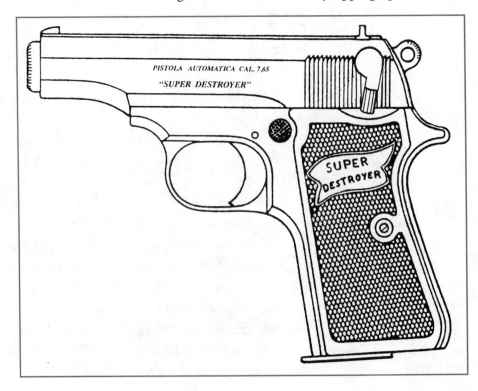

While the designs covered so far in this chapter have displayed ingenuity and creativity, the most innovative Spanish pistol design of the pre-Spanish Civil War period was by far the *Sharp-Shooter* and a related model, introduced several years later, called the *Jo-Lo-Ar*. This pistol, first patented in Spain in 1917 (patent number 68027), went into production sometime around 1919 or 1920. Its original version, the Sharp-Shooter, had a conventional triggerguard but no extractor (spent cartridge casings were expelled from the firing chamber by residual gas pressure, much like some modern Beretta pistols). Shooters utilized a tipping barrel that was opened by a latch on the frame, similar to that found in the modern Beretta Models 21 and 86. In the Sharp-Shooter, the slide was drawn back far enough to separate the front of the breech (the "face") from the rear end of the barrel. The safety catch was then rotated all the way past its "safe" setting, causing the rear end of the barrel to rise. This enabled the shooter to clean the barrel from the breech and rear end, or to load a cartridge. For the barrel to swing up in this manner, the slide had to be cut away on top, completely exposing the barrel (except for its sides and bottom). Unlike other automatic pistols, there were no serrations for slide retraction on the rear portion of the Sharp-Shooter's (and later the Jo-Lo-Ar). That's because the first round from the magazine could be loaded by tipping up the barrel.

The secret for the accuracy of the Llama Model XI "Especial" is, in part, the large square notch in the rear sight, a remarkable innovation for a gun of this age.

PISTOLA AUTOMATICA CAL. 7,65
"SUPER DESTROYER"

SUPER DESTROYER

Gaztañaga's "Super Destroyer" strongly resembled the popular (but expensive) Walther Model PP. Upon disassembly, however, it proved simply another FN Model 1910 clone.

*Spanish Handguns*

The Bernedo pistol was a clever design at a time when such guns were most rare in Spain. Unfortunately, the pistol cost more to make than did the many Ruby clones emanating from Eibar during the 1920s, forcing the Bernedo out of production.

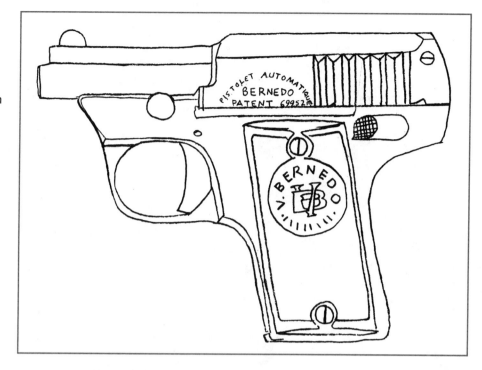

In 1924 firearms dealer and inventor José de Lopez Arnaiz appeared at the Arrizabalaga offices with a design for a chambering/cocking lever, or *palanca*, that he wanted the company to buy. Arnaiz had already received Spanish patent number 70235 (dated September 12, 1919) for this device. It was screwed onto the right side of the slide, and when pulled to the rear by the shooter—using the first two fingers of the shooting hand—it loaded the firing chamber of the automatic pistol and cocked its hammer. Though Arrizabalaga balked at a royalty arrangement with Arnaiz, they did agree to modify some Sharp-Shooter pistols by adding the Arnaiz-designed cocking lever. Because the standard triggerguard on the Sharp-Shooter interfered with the operation of the cocking lever, Arrizabalaga further modified the design by cutting away the triggerguard. The modified pistol was also given an external extractor, which Arrizabalaga had planned to incorporate into the Sharp-Shooter design anyway. The resulting pistol was the Jo-Lo-Ar, which was first tested at the *Banco de Pruevas* (Proof House of Spain) on September 15, 1924 in .380 caliber. Sales of the Jo-Lo-Ar helped supplement those of the Sharp-Shooter model.

The cocking lever designed by Arnaiz allowed one-handed cocking, enabling shooters to carry the pistol with the chamber empty—always the safest way to carry an automatic pistol—and still be capable of instant loading by using the shooting hand only. Several one-handed automatic pistols appeared both before and after the J0-Lo-Ar, but this model proved the most successful in terms of numbers produced and extent of service. One

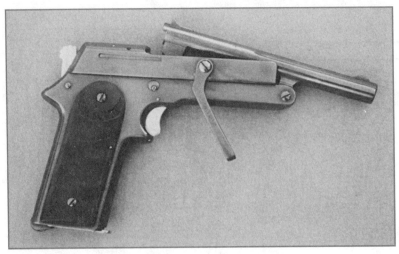

The Jo-Lo-Ar's barrel tips up at the rear, or breech, end. This allows the shooter to load the firing chamber, a system revived in some modern Beretta automatic pistols. (Photo by Ron Waters)

reason for this success was that Arnaiz had made the cocking lever on the Jo-Lo-Ar long enough to provide shooters with solid purchase with the trigger and middle fingers of their shooting hand. Because it was so small, this part exerted insufficient leverage to permit its use with any caliber beyond .25 CAP. The Jo-Lo-Ar's long cocking lever afforded better leverage, however, making slide operation comparatively easy despite the stiff recoil spring required for use with .32, .380 and 9mm Largo caliber pistols.

A refreshing change from the usual Ruby copy, the Jo-Lo-Ar proved durable, reliable and accurate. Both Arrizabalaga and later Ojanguren y Vidosa sold the pistol, the later company adding an "OV" marking impressed into the grip. Most Jo-Lo-Ars had their dates of manufacture marked beneath the left grip (the latest date reported thus far being 1930). The fact that almost all Jo-Lo-Ar pistols included a distinctive Spanish proofmark, nicknamed the "walking lion," on their slide and frame (discontinued in 1929) confirms 1930 as the year in which production ended. Jo-Lo-Ar pistols appeared in production quantities in .25 ACP, .380 ACP, and 9mm Largo calibers, along with a few .45 ACP caliber versions. The 9mm Largo was the first to go into production with just under 2,000 produced in the initial manufacturing run. Its 4mm conversion unit for low-powered indoor shooting—the

The Jo-Lo-Ar featured the palanca, or cocking lever, developed by José de Lopez Arnaiz. It is visible here in its extended position beneath the frame. To retract the slide, the shooter grips the lever with his index and middle fingers. (Photo by Ron Waters)

Germans call this *zimmerschutzen*—was popularized in many pre-World War II pistol models, notably the Walther PPK. One Jo-Lo-Ar in 9mm Parabellum, reported by an American collector, is almost identical to the 9mm Largo version. Along with the .32 caliber version, these pistols were most common and have held up surprisingly well over the years.

Initially, the 9mm Largo proved too strong for the original design, which was based on the .380 frame. After reports of cracked barrels, production in this caliber was halted until a slightly larger version *(see below)* was designed. The rare .25 caliber Jo-Lo-Ar, numbered in the 10000 to 11000 serial number range, had only a 3-inch barrel, with earlier versions being fairly large, holding 9 rounds in the magazine. Because it was too large to compete with other compact guns in this pocket-pistol caliber, Arrizabalaga switched to a slightly smaller 8-shot version, followed by an even smaller 6-shot model, all in .25 ACP caliber. The Jo-Lo-Ar's 8-shot .32 ACP caliber version also had a short barrel (3.8 inches), which protruded only slightly beyond the front of the frame for an overall length of slightly under 6.5 inches. The enlarged .380 caliber version had a 4.1-inch barrel, with an overall length of 7.25 inches. It also had a slightly longer grip than the .32.

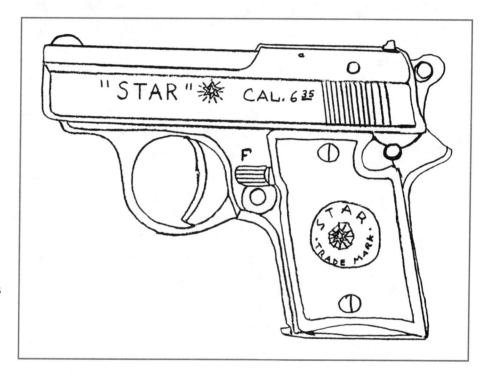

The 6.35mm (.25 ACP) caliber Star Model E was yet another Spanish pistol based on a foreign design, in this case Walther's Model 9.

The 9mm Largo version, once it had been enlarged to handle the much bigger, more powerful Spanish service cartridge, measured almost 8.5 inches overall. These beefed-up 9mm Largo caliber Jo-Lo-Ar models had series numbers in the 4000 range and up. The .45 ACP version—the largest Jo-Lo-Ar of all—had a 7-shot magazine and an overall length of just over 9 inches. In the short-barreled .32 and .380 caliber versions, the rear sight consisted of a simple notch and groove arrangement, while the longer-barreled 9mm Largo caliber had a raised rear sight located on the rear end of the barrel to allow more precise aiming.

These Sharp-Shooter/Jo-Lo-Ar-type pistols offered many positive features. For the calibers in which Arrizabalaga made it, this was a strong, heavy weapon. For example, the largest (9-shot) .25 ACP version weighed

The cocking lever on the Jo-Lo-Ar pivots freely and moves out of the way as the slide recoils. Note the pistol's triggerguard, which was cut away so the cocking lever could function freely. (Photo by Ron Waters)

about 24 ounces unloaded, the .32 ACP weighed about 27 ounces, and the 9mm Largo version was almost 40 ounces—or as heavy as a Colt Model 1911. The rare .45 ACP Jo-Lo-Ar's weight was 46½ ounces, which helped reduce recoil in all but the 9mm Largo and .45 ACP versions. Several shooters in modern times have stated that Jo-Lo-Ar accuracy is very good by automatic pistol standards. During recoil, the one-hand cocking lever swung up and out of the way during recoil, thus posing no threat to a shooter's hand. And because the barrel could be tipped up for easy access, these pistols were usually well-maintained. Even today, most Sharp-Shooters and Jo-Lo-Ars still boast good barrels. Their exterior finish, however, was poor to begin with, so surviving specimens generally show considerable external wear. Among the negative features of the Jo-Lo-Ar design were a trigger pull that was too light, and an awkward hammer whose odd shape, excessive length and angle to the frame made cocking difficult. The cocking lever itself made holstering difficult, and its loose attachment to the slide (necessary to prevent sharp blows to a right-hander's knuckles) caused many of these cocking levers to break loose and became lost.

Jo.-Lo-Ar pistols in 9mm Largo and .380 calibers saw official service in Peru, with an estimated 1000 to 1500 of the former sold to that country's military force and a smaller number of .380 caliber models going to the police, from whence came many of the pistols of this type now known to exist in the United States. The Portuguese also bought a quantity for their use, along with larger numbers of the standard Sharp-Shooter. Initially, Spanish officials remained aloof, preferring the Astra Model 1921 (Model 400) and Star Model A *(see below)*. Republican soldiers are known to have pressed 9mm Largo caliber Jo-Lo-Ar pistols into service during the Spanish Civil War as conditions grew desperate. Gene Lovitz, a Jo-Lo-Ar authority, wrote in 1973 that an estimated total production of this model, in all calibers, reached some 30,000, with even more of the conventional Sharp-Shooters having already been sold.

Ultimately, despite its original design and clever, innovative features, the Jo-Lo-Ar pistol could not compete with the flood of cheaper Ruby copies or Eibar-type pistols being mass-produced by competing Spanish handgun companies. In 1930 or 1931, Señor Arnaiz tried to interest Star Bonifacio

Echeverria in Jo-Lo-Ar's one-handed cocking lever in an attempt to revive this flagging design despite a worldwide recession in the late 1920s and early 1930s. Even at that early date, Star had become one of the few giants of the Spanish handgun industry, which explains why Arnaiz had offered that country his cocking-lever design. Unfortunately, Star was unimpressed, stating that a one-hand cocking lever was unnecessary. As a result, after a production run of only six years, production of the Jo-Lo-Ar was halted. And with it went the one-hand lever. Nevertheless, the Jo-Lo-Ar remains a highly respected gun. Several manufacturers, notably Beretta and Norinco, have incorporated some of its features into their own modern pistol designs. Indeed, the Jo-Lo-Ar, more than most Spanish pistols, enjoys a considerable following among collectors in the new century.

## The Llama Line (Gabilondo y Cia)

With sales of its Danton pistol beginning to slow, Gabilondo started looking for a new pistol line. The result was the Llama series introduced in 1931. Its inspiration was the Colt Model 1911, regarded by many as John M. Browning's finest handgun design. Llama pistols made by Gabilondo in larger calibers—including the 9mm Parabellum, 9mm Largo, .38 Super, .40 S&W and .45 ACP—all have a locked breech based on the Colt model. Llama pistols available in the smaller calibers, notably .22 Long Rifle, .32 ACP and .380 ACP, generally dispensed with the locked breech. They are simple blowbacks, yet they still resemble shrunken Model 1911s.

The first Llama-series pistol to enter series production was Gabilondo's Llama Model IV. This full-sized pistol, which fired the 9mm Largo (9mm Bergmann-Bayard) cartridge, was adopted in 1903 by the Spanish armed forces. Closely resembling the Model 1911 (as do all Llamas), the Model IV differed from the famous Colt by doing away with the Colt grip safety, which was designed to prevent the pistol from being fired unless the shooter had a firm hold on the pistol. Opinions as to the value of this device differ widely. Some Llama pistols have one, many do not. Perhaps the most interesting feature of the Llama Model IV was its firing chamber, which allowed the gun to fire not only the standard 9mm Largo cartridge but also

Gabilondo's Llama Model IV was chambered for the 9mm Largo cartridge. Note the missing thumb safety, while the gun's Model 1911-style grip safety remains intact.

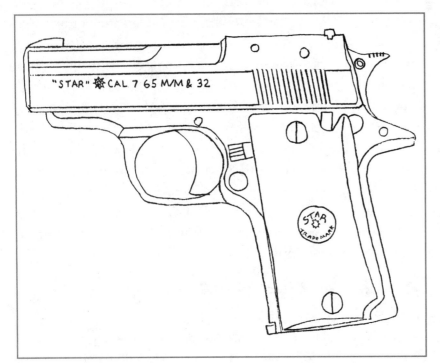

"STAR" ✳ CAL 7 65 M/M & 32

STAR TRADE MARK

The 7.65mm (.32 ACP) caliber Star Model H was powerful for its compact size and proved popular with high-ranking officers and other soldiers who demanded a lightweight or concealable handgun.

the 9mm Parabellum and 9mm Steyr rounds as well. Llama advertised this as the "tolerant chamber" in competition with Astra's Model 400, which offered the same universality in terms of its ammunition. Gabilondo's great success with the Model IV enabled the company to introduce variants such as the Model VII (a .38 Super version without grip safety) and the Model V, which also chambered the .38 Super cartridge with English-language markings for sale to the lucrative U.S. market.

Gabilondo's Model I, which was introduced in 1933, measured only 6.3 inches long, firing 7.65mm (.32 ACP) ammunition from an unlocked (blowback) breech. The Model II was identical to the Model I except that it fired the 9mm Corto or Short (.380 ACP) round. The magazine capacity was reduced by one. Because it fired this slightly larger cartridge, Gabilondo phased out the Models I and II in 1936 in favor of the Model III, which resembled its predecessors but with a locked breech similar to the Colt M1911. Having a breech-locking mechanism in such a small-caliber pistol, plus its all-steel construction, made the Model III a pleasant weapon to shoot.

The most interesting of the early Llama Pistol series was the Model XI "Especial," which remained in production without change until 1954. It was among the first Spanish pistols ever made to chamber the 9mm Parabellum round, which was already well on its way to worldwide prominence by the mid-1930s (thanks to the simultaneous introduction of numerous well-made pistols from various countries made to fire it, including the Polish VIS "Radom," the Finnish Lahti L-35 and the Belgian FN High Power, all introduced in 1935). The Llama Model XI could hold up to 8 rounds in its magazine while retaining its unusually sleek and graceful design with an overall length of 7.6 inches. Other specifications included: **Barrel Length:** 4.9 inches; **Width:** 1.3 inches; **Height:** 5.2 inches; **Weight:** 31 ounces unloaded.

Compared to earlier Llama pistols, the Model XI departed the most from Colt's M1911 design. The Llama pistol featured instead a curved backstrap without grip safety, vertically ribbed wooden grips, and a rounded hammer, making it more like the Russian Tokarev and FN High Power pistols. Still, the mechanical affinities remained strong, with the Model XI's locking mechanism and controls—a manual safety lever, slide stop and magazine release—remaining virtually identical to those of the Model 1911. Gabilondo's designers did, however, succeed in eliminating the somewhat troublesome plunger tube (located between the manual safety and slide stop) of M1911-type pistols. The Model XI saw considerable use in the Spanish Civil War and later became a popular export item. Sold both by Gabilondo and a shotgun dealer named José Cruz Mugica, the Model XI became widely known in Europe and Asia for its 9mm Parabellum chambering, excellent handling qualities and attractive styling. Oddly enough, though, the Model XI remains extremely scarce in the United States.

## The Esperanza y Unceta (Astra) Line

In 1920, after its success in selling military-type .32 caliber pistols to the French and Italians during World War I, Esperanza y Unceta introduced its smaller .25 ACP caliber Astra Model 200. A close copy of the Browning-designed FN Model 1906, this new pistol was essentially a shrunken version of the Model 1903. As a result, the Astra Model 200 might have been just another one of Spain's many Browning copies, except that an exceptionally high standard of manufacture was set by Esperanza y

Gabilondo's decision to chamber the Llama Model XI "Especial" (top) in 9mm Parabellum caliber instead of the longer 9mm Largo cartridge allowed the company to make the Model XI a slimmer, more graceful Model 1911-style pistol than the competing Star Model A (bottom).

*Chapter 3*

Unceta—a rarity in Spain at the time. The first 40,000 Model 200 pistols—now known as the "First Variation" by Astra handgun collectors—had no grip safety but did include a loaded-chamber indicator atop the slide and ahead of the rear sight.

In 1926, after Esperanza y Unceta became known as Unceta y Cia, the so-called First Variation pistol was replaced by a "Second Variation Model 200" (serial number 270000). This version retained the loaded-chamber indicator and also added a grip safety to the rear of the frame along with a magazine disconnect safety. As a result, the pistol could not be fired—even when a round remained in the firing chamber—after the magazine was removed from the grip. The inclusion of the grip and magazine safety devices was somewhat unusual in Spain at the time, most likely because Spanish pistols could not be fired, even when a round remained in the firing chamber, once the magazine was removed from the grip. The inclusion of the grip and magazine safety devices was somewhat unusual in Spain at the time, most likely because Spanish pistols were lacking in such expensive refinements. Actually, it was not surprising since both of the FN pocket-sized pistols—the Models of 1906 and 1910—had also kept these two safety features. Series numbers on the Second Variation ranged from 270000 to 318500 (late 1920s to 1934); 50001 to 506000 (1934 to 1943); 526461 to 526550 (1936, but held in storage, unsold, until 1945); and from 648601 to about 660000 (1947-1949). The interruptions in the numbering sequences occurred because Unceta y Cia, which produced other pistol models, had a company policy to number most of its pistols in continuous series.

The Model 200, or "Third Variation," featured a new type of loaded-chamber indicator, a kind of signal pin that protruded from the rear of the slide whenever there was a round in the firing chamber. This new indicator design represented an improvement over the other variations because it could be felt more easily in the dark. Serial numbers on the Third Variation

Echeverria developed the Star Model I by lengthening the barrel and grip of the Model H to create a slightly larger and better-shooting pistol for open holster carry by military and police users.

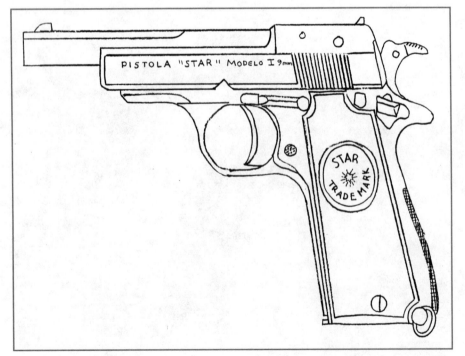

PISTOLA "STAR" MODELO I 9mm

STAR TRADE MARK

In common with other pistols of the Model 1911 type, the Llama Model XI "Especial" can be carried with the hammer fully cocked and the manual safety pushed up to block the sear.

ranged from about 660000 to 663300; again from 678001 to 710000; and 722001 upwards to about 750000. This placed Third Variation production in the period 1949-1958. The final, or "Fourth Variation," Model 200 pistol, (serial numbers beginning 750000, c. 1958) had raised front and rear sights, straight slide serrations, and flutes milled into the rear portion of the slide (compensating for the added metal used to build up the sights). The grips on these Fourth Variation pistols (those sold to the U.S.) were often marked "FIRECAT" on the bottom portion. Serial numbers ranged from 750001 to 779850 (1958 to 1962), after which the block was interrupted by the production of other pistol models. Fourth Variation Model 200 production resumed later (serial number 860001 to 898475) during the period 1962-1967. With the backing of Unceta y Cia, which by 1920 had become a dominant force in handgun manufacture in Spain, success for the Model 200 was assured. When the company finally stopped production of this model in 1967, sales had reached about 234,105.

## *Bonifacio Echeverria (Star)*

Star pistols differed considerably in design from the typical Eibar-type pistol. Once World War I ended, Star decided to expand the company's business by diversifying its pistol line rather than relying on its aging wartime models. Just as Gabilondo did some ten years later, Star settled on the Colt Model 1911 as the most promising basis for future development. The company's first postwar model, which appeared in 1920, was called the *Modelo Militar* (Spanish for "Military Model"). Similar to the M1911-style breech locking system, this pistol bore traces of earlier Star/Mannlicher influences with its cocking bosses and safety on the rear of the slide—also in the shape of the hammer. Chambered in 9mm Largo, the Modelo Militar's chief marketing outlet was clearly the Spanish armed forces, which were experiencing problems with the Campo-Giro pistol and needed a replacement. Though the Modelo Militar competed unsuccessfully in its tests against the Astra pistol (which became the Model 400), the Spanish Guardia Civil, the nation's chief paramilitary force, expressed approval of the Modelo Militar. After a few changes had been made, the Models 1921 and 1922 (Model A), and eventually the Model B *(see Chapter 4)*, were introduced.

In addition to Star's experimentation with large-caliber pistols suitable for armed forces use, the company also tried to replace its early .25 and .32 caliber Mannlicher-inspired compact handguns with more modern types. The .25 ACP caliber (Model E) began production in 1932 and continued until 1941. In typical Spanish fashion, it took its inspiration from a foreign design, Walther's Model 9, which Star then modified to suit its needs. First, the Model E borrowed Walther's open-topped slide, frame-mounted manual safety lever and compact dimensions, adding an external hammer and a lengthened grip tang. The latter was intended to protect the shooter's hand from the sharp bottom edges of the recoiling slide. While these changes did nothing to help the Model E's appearance compared to the sleek Model 9, they did make the Star Model E an easier—and safer—pistol to shoot. Substituting an external hammer for the tiny striker on the Model 9 also increased the Model E's reliability. Walther's vest pocket pistol had an undersized striker spring that became weakened over the years, eventually failing to crush the primer of chambered cartridges and causing misfires. In contrast, the Model E, with its prominent spur hammer and powerful mainspring, could be relied upon to hit cartridge primers with enough force to ignite them.

The Model H series, introduced in 1934, bore a striking resemblance to the Model E, but

The resemblance of the Llama Model IV (top) to the U.S.-made Model 1911A1 (or Government Model) is obvious in this view. A modern stainless-steel version of the M1911 appears below.

In testing for accuracy, the Llama Model XI "Especial" scored high (2.2 inches at 50 feet) for an elderly pistol. It also functioned flawlessly with modern hollowpoint ammunition, which even some modern Model 1911-type pistols can't do.

with enlarged dimensions to accommodate larger cartridges, such as the .32 ACP. The Model HN, which had the same design, chambered the slightly larger .380 ACP cartridge instead. The manual safety catch on these pistols consisted of a lever located on the frame behind the trigger and above the magazine release button. The latter, in typical Colt Model 1911 fashion, was mounted at the rear end of the trigger-guard. In the interest of keeping this gun as small as possible, no slide stop lever was provided.

Following their introduction in 1934, the Models I and IN proved almost identical in mechanical function and appearance to the Model H, but with longer barrels and larger grips with arched rear grip straps in the manner of the M1911A1. In keeping with Spanish military and police practice, a lanyard loop was added to the left corner of the frame. The manual safety was relocated to the rear of the frame, and a slide stop was also added in the same manner as the M1911. The Model I, which fired the .32 ACP cartridge, held nine rounds in the magazine (two more than the corresponding Model H). The Model IN, meanwhile, used the .380 round.

The I series pistols were developed by Star for police work, while the Models I and H both saw service with Spanish police. The larger Model I series pistols found favor for providing open carry on a holster, with the shorter-barreled Model H serving as a concealment arm. The Model H also proved highly popular with high-ranking officers in various European armies, especially the Germans, who liked its small size, light weight and relatively powerful .32 ACP cartridge. Even at this early date, though, a feeling arose at the Star factory that .32 and .380 caliber pistols, resembling as they did the outward appearance of the Colt Model 1911, would compete more successfully with the well-made Llama series made by Gabilondo. Thus, while the Model H and I-series pistols saw widespread service in the Spanish Civil War, they were discontinued shortly afterward (1941). In their place came the Model S, to be covered in a later chapter.

# Chapter 4

# Spanish Service Pistols, 1921–1945

The Campo-Giro's reign as Spain's standard service pistol was brief indeed. In 1919, complaints about the pistol's fragility and difficult disassembly prompted the Spanish armed forces to issue a call for a new service pistol. Their decision, however, did not affect the 9mm Largo or Bergmann-Bayard round as the service standard cartridge. The response was both swift and expected. Two widely respected guns—the Astra Model 400 and the Star Model A—were selected in 1920 and remain highly regarded both by shooters and collectors alike. During the next decade, various Spanish military, paramilitary and police forces chose several other automatic pistols as service sidearms, firmly establishing three manufacturers—Unceta (Astra), Gabilondo (Llama) and Echeverria (Star)—as the key players in Spanish handgun development.

Spanish Army trials for the Astra (Esperanza y Unceta) and the Star (Bonifachio Echeverria) took place in late 1920 and early 1921. These tests, considered rigorous by the standards of the time, included an 800-round

This early example of the Model 1921 wears the hard-rubber grips with the EU log.

The right side of the same early Model 1921 pistol (serial number 8552) displays the many small parts left white and highly polished, rather than blued.

endurance and reliability test, accuracy testing, and harsh-conditions testing. There were, in addition, function firing with both underpowered and overloaded ammunition, and comparison measurements of all parts before and after firing 1000 rounds to determine if the pistols had stayed within manufacturing tolerances. The testing commission worked quickly and efficiently. In September 1921 the Spanish army tentatively adopted the commission's first choice. The Astra (Esperanza y Unceta) was selected as the *Pistola de 9 millimetros modelo 1921* (9mm Model 1921 pistol) to replace the Campo-Giro Model of 1913/16. This decision was confirmed early in October 1921 by royal decree.

# Unceta (Astra) Model 1921/Model 400

Actually, the Astra was only the first of many official adoptions of this pistol. In October of 1922, Spain's *Carabineros* (a branch of the national police force charged with guarding the country's borders and operating its customs houses) also standardized the Esperanza y Unceta pistol. A month later, the Spanish prison service adopted it, followed by the Spanish navy (September 24, 1923) and air force (July 11, 1931). The official Spanish orders were impressively large. The Spanish army alone took over 35,000 Model 1921 pistols prior to 1936 and another 28,000 thereafter, while the Carabineros ordered about 11,700 and the navy another 1,650. During the Spanish Civil War, the semiautonomous government in the Basque region bought another 14,800 with which to equip its armed forces *(see Chapter 6 for a detailed coverage of the Spanish Civil War)*. Following war's end in March 1939, the Model 1921 pistol remained in service as the handgun standard of Spain's armed forces until 1946, when Unceta y Cia (Astros) discontinued its production. During that 25-year production run, some 106,175 pistols were built. Its replacement—the Star pistol (Echeverria)—took several years to bring production up to adequate quantities; hence, the Spanish armed forces did not finally relegate the Astra Model 1921 pistol to the reserves until 1950.

In addition to the Model 1921 pistol, Esperanza y Unceta offered the Astra Model 400 for commercial sale. In this guise, the pistol generated several large-scale orders from important foreign armed forces. In 1930, an order of 842 Model 400 pistols—marked "MARINA DE CHILE" on the forward portion of the slide with serial numbers from 36359 to 37200—went to the Chilean navy. Another order for 6,000 guns (serial numbers 92851 to 98850) were sold to Nazi Germany in 1941. Colombia, Ecuador and France also order Model 400 pistols for their armed forces. These contracts, however, came from dealers who bought pistols direct from the factory; therefore, no records are available for specific serial numbers of guns sent to these customers, though most likely smaller numbers were involved than those cited above for sales to Chile and Germany. Sales continued to be filled from factory inventory until 1951, five years after production had stopped. Numerous civilians also purchased Model 400

Unceta's excellent Model 1921 pistol (bottom) replaced the Campo-Giro Model 1913/1916, which it resembled (both were produced by the same company).

AMMO!

AMMO!

EXTRA MAGAZINES

AMMO!

# ASTRA MODEL 1921
(Commercial Designation Model 400)

## SPECIFICATIONS
Caliber: 9mm Bergmann Bayard (9mm Largo)
Finish: Blued Steel
Barrel: 5.9 Inches
Overall: 8.7 Inches
Magazine: 8 Rounds

Caliber 9mm Bergmann Bayard
(Spanish Designation: 9mm Largo)

EXTRA MAGAZINES

Unceta's excellent Model 1921 pistol (bottom) replaced the Campo-Giro Model 1913/1916, which it resembled (both were produced by the same company).

pistols. Stoeger Arms Company imported Model 400 pistols to the U.S. during the early 1930s, and during the 1960s the Spanish armed forces sold their reserve stocks of surplus Model 1921 pistols to Interarms. Obviously, large numbers of these pistols remain in use today.

While it was based on the earlier Campo-Giro service pistol, the Model 400 was also heavily influenced by FN's Model 1910, particularly in its barrel bushing and barrel retaining system. Among other distinctive features of the Model 400 were a prominent bottom magazine release and both grip and magazine safeties. Like the Campo-Giro, the Astra Model 400 fired the 9mm Large (Bergmann-Bayard) cartridge (with eight rounds in the magazine). This was a large pistol with the following specifications: **Overall length:** 9.25"; **Barrel length:** 5.9"; **Height:** 5.5"; **Width:** 1.1"; **Weight (unloaded):** 31 ounces. Later on, Model 1921 pistols generally wore wooden grips. Early military production and most commercial Model 400s had checkered hard rubber grips with an "EU" logo prior to the 1926-1931 period and a "UC" logo thereafter. Other grip materials used in this 400 series included horn, plastic and smooth (i.e., uncheckered) wood. The EU and UC logos also appeared on the forward portion of the slide top. Unlike all other large-caliber handguns, the Astra Model 400 did not have a breech-locking mechanism; instead, it used a pure blowback system like most small-caliber automatic pistols. Thanks to a long and powerful recoil spring, made possible by quality construction and an above-average barrel, the Model 400 pistols have held up surprisingly well over the years.

Like the earlier Campo-Giro pistol, Unceta y Cia numbered its Model 1921/400 pistols in their own separate serial number range. Although the total number manufactured was 106,175 complete pistols, the serial numbers run from 1 only to 105175. This seeming discrepancy is explained by the fact that, when Unceta built 1,000 pistols for the Spanish navy, it used a duplicate serial number range *(see below)*. Collectors will recognize

The Astra Model 300's heel-mounted release, (seem here from below) is pushed from left to right to unlock the magazine from the pistol grip. Other pistols made by Unceta, notably naval-contract Model 1921s (400s) and the later Model 600, used the same system.

several Model 1921/Model 400 variations. Pistols made prior to Esperanza's leaving the partnership in 1926 were marked on the top rear portion of the slide, as follows:

**ESPERANZA Y UNCETA**
**GUERNICA ESPAÑA**
**PISTOLA DE 9m/m**
**MODELO 1921**

These early Model 1921/Model 400 pistols also had an EU company logo on the top forward portion of the slide, just behind the rear edge of the front sight, and also on the checkered hard-rubber grips for pistols sold through commercial channels. Model 1921/400 pistols made *after* 1926 bore the following slide inscription:

**UNCETA Y COMPAÑIA**
**GUERNICA ESPAÑA**
**PISTOLA DE 9m/m (38)**
**MODELO 1921 (400)**

The later Model 1921/Model 400 pistols had a substituted UC company logo (instead of an EU) on the top forward portion of the slide. The same UC logo appeared on the hard rubber grips of Model 400 pistols sold commercially (Model 1921 pistols secured by military contract generally used checkered wooden grips devoid of a company logo). Because of the overlap of production and the company's understandable reluctance to scrap perfectly usable parts, the earlier EU- and UC-marked slides and grips were more or less interchangeable until around the 43500 serial number range, which was attained in 1931.

The earliest pistols bought by the Spanish armed forces generally lacked proofmarks. Instead, they were given a Spanish army acceptance mark—a Y-shaped insignia in a circle—that was struck on the left side of the triggerguard. Originally, these early army pistols sported checkered hard rubber grips with the EU log, although checkered wooden grips without company markings were often fitted to these early pistols destined for armories and depots for repair. Other early Model 1921 pistols—those sent to the Eibar proofhouse *(Banco Oficial de Pruebas)* between July 18, 1923 and December 14, 1929 for commercial sale—had a rampant lion proofmark stamped in various places on the pistol. These included the portion of the barrel that shows through the ejection port for spent cartridge cases (also called the barrel hood), the left rear grip tang and the left rear portion of the slide. The year of production also appeared occasionally on these pistols. Later Model 1921 pistols—the ones accepted into Spanish government service between 1939 and 1942—also lacked the commercial Eibar

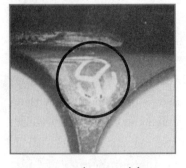

An early armed forces acceptance mark, resembling the letter Y inside a circle, was used during the Spanish monarchy and continued into the Republican regime.

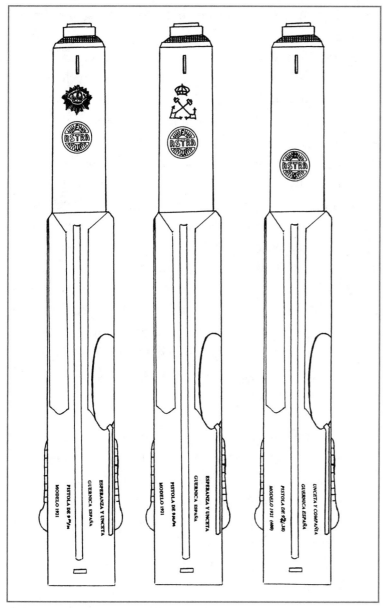

Variant slide markings on Model 1921 pistols include (left) Carabinero purchases with a large crown-and-sunburst emblem just behind the rear sight; (center) naval-contract model with a crown and crossed-anchors emblem; and (right) dual-caliber slide markings found on later pistols made after Juan Esperanza left the partnership in 1926.

proofmarks. The armed forces acceptance stamp, which remained in the same place as before (the left side of the trigger-guard), now resembled a flaming bomb with the letter "I" in the middle. The commercial proofmark on Model 400 pistols made for open-market sales to civilian buyers between December 14, 1929 and the end of production in 1946 resembled a flaming bomb with the letter "P" in its center. This commercial proof-mark appeared on the barrel hood, on the left rear of the slide, and again on the left rear of the frame. On pistols made from late 1929 to the end of production, an Eibar House Proof also appeared on the left grip tang. On Model 400 pistols proofed between December 14, 1929 and July 9, 1931, this proofmark resembled a crown atop a shield marked with a capital letter X, along with the letters P.V. stamped on the side. The current Eibar proof—a knight's helmeted head complete with visor and plume atop a shield emblazoned with the letter X—appeared on pistols proofmarked after July 9, 1931, together with a one or two-letter code indicating the year of proof. The third and final mark, which appeared on the left grip tang at the rear of the frame, was introduced in 1927 to replace the old P.V. mark. The year codes were an A in 1927 and a Q in 1946 (the final year of Model 400 manufacture), with an asterisk appearing above the letter(s). This so-called "trio" or "triad" of proofmarks and year codes were stamped vertically (rare) or, as was more common, horizontally. [*For a more complete discussion of marks used on Spanish pistols, see the Appendix*].

Model 1921 pistols, those made for the *Carabineros*, had a large "crown-inside-a-sunburst" emblem in front of the EU company logo on the top forward portion of the slide. Most of these pistols, which had been purchased by the official Spanish government early on and accepted into service between 1923 and 1926, lacked commercial proofmarks. Chile's

*Chapter 4*

naval order for 842 pistols made in 1930 bore commercial proofmarks (introduced in Eibar on December 14, 1929) resembling a letter P inside a flaming bomb. Also included were a five-pointed star and the legend MARI-NA DE CHILE in front of the EU company logo on the front slide (serial numbers beginning at 36359 and ending at 37200). The Chilean navy kept its Model 400s on hand until the 1980s, becoming the longest run of Model 400s serving in an official capacity (often in reserve) anywhere in the world.

The Model 1921 pistols made for the Spanish navy between 1924 and 1935 featured an unusual bottom magazine release. It was introduced in the Astra Model 300 pistol in 1923 and later in the company's Model 600 as well. Model 1921/400 pistols equipped with the naval-type magazine release appeared in five serial number lots: 28901-29800; 42801-42850; 43001-43100; 43601-43950; and 46101-46400. All but the 42000 series were actually sent to Spanish naval units where they served during 1924-1925, 1930, 1933 and 1935. Unceta y Cia released the 42000 serial number pistols with the naval-type magazine release for commercial sale in 1932. Altogether, the company made fewer than 2,000 of the Model 1921 pistols, with 1,650 going to Spain's navy. Their scarcity has made these pistols highly desired by collectors.

Model 400 pistols under contract with A.F. Stoeger were much scarcer than even the rare naval model. Although Stoeger had begun importing Model 400 "Super Power" pistols as early as 1932, with that company's special markings did not appear until the 1934-1936 period. These special-order pistols bore the following marking (atop the slide) in place of the Unceta address:

**A.F. STOEGER INC., NEW YORK**
**SUPER POWER, .38 CALIBER**

The first batch of Model 400 pistols ordered by German's armed forces were sent to the Germans in two separate shipments in late 1941. The first shipment of 4,500 pistols (serial numbers 92851 through 97350) arrived in France on October 18, 1941; and the final shipment of 1,500 guns (serial numbers 97351 through 98850) went to France on November 11. [*The history of these pistols is covered in detail in Chapter 7*] Unceta also manufactured a variety of experimental pieces for its Model 400 series. These included pistols with different calibers—low-powered 4mm training cartridges, 7.63mm Mauser, 7.65mm (.30 Luger), and 9mm Parabellum ammunition. Other variants featured target-shooting versions with enlarged front sights and adjustable rear sights, fancy engraved presentation pieces, extended 16-shot magazines, and pistols fitted for detachable shoulder stocks. These models were all experimental in nature and none was produced in anything beyond prototypical quantities.

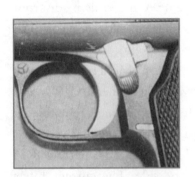

To fire, the manual safety on the Model 1921 had to be pushed forward and down before the pistol could be fired.

By pushing the Model 1921's manual safety lever on the Model 1921 up and back, the pistol's firing mechanism was immobilized.

Bonifacio Echeverria's Star Modelo Militar's slide and frame was a throwback to earlier Star pistols. Note the spur hammer with a vestigial hole in its center. (Photo by Ron Waters)

The Model 400 had many strong points which, in its heyday, made the pistol a popular and efficient military sidearm. A well-made and sturdy handgun, it remains capable of excellent accuracy. In fact, shooters firing Model 1921/400s have won a number of pre-World War II shooting matches involving service pistols. Even today a Model 400 in good condition and with proper ammunition can outshoot virtually every modern service pistol. Despite the concerns of many that a blowback or unlocked-breech pistol would lack the strength to withstand the battering forces of a high-powered military pistol cartridge, Spanish authorities actually stepped up the powder charge of the 9mm Largo cartridge. This occurred around 1930, well after the Model 1921's introduction, once the Spaniards had recognized the pistol's inherent strength.

Among the Model 400's few weak points was its high price. It cost a lot to manufacture, an expense the factory naturally passed on to the consumer. During World War II, Germany, for one, paid considerably more for Model 400 pistols than for its own Parabellum (P08) and P38 service pistols. The Model 400 also suffered from an unusually stiff trigger. The sights, like most contemporary military pistols, were undersized; and the near-vertical grip angle, while loved by some, was detested by others. Also, the pistol's strong recoil and hammer springs made its slide more difficult to retract when cocking and loading the pistol, making it next to impossible for anyone with weak hands to operate. These powerful springs also made

During the 1930s, Stoeger imported limited numbers of Astra Model 400 pistols into the U.S. This advertisement appeared in the company's 1932 catalog.

# PISTOLS

### "SUPER-POWER" MODEL CALIBRE .38
#### Using the .38 Automatic Cartridge.

Declared the Ordinance Model by law for Spanish Army, Navy and Carabine. Has triple safety, and after firing the last cartridge, the breach remains open. Equipped with wide Patridge sights and grip safety.

Specifications: Number of Shots, 8; overall length, 8 ¾ ; length of barrel, 6"; height, 4¾"; weight with magazine, 2 lbs. 4 oz.; walnut grips; blue finish only. Factory ballistic data: muzzle velocity, 1280 ft. seconds; muzzle energy, 448 ft. lbs.
Price . . . . . . . . . . . . . . . . . . . . . . . . . . . . . . . . . . . . . . . . . . . . . . . . . . . . . . . . . . . . . . . . . . . . . . . . . . . . . . . . . . . . . . . .$27.50

*Chapter 4*

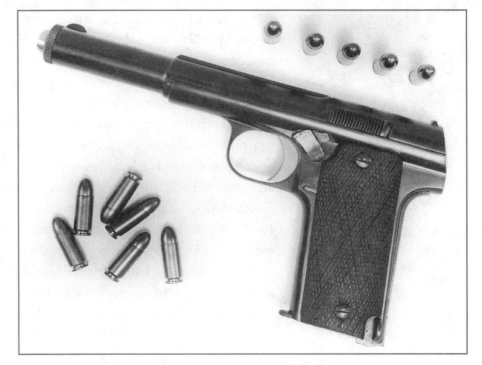

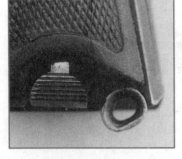

In honor of its oftentimes official service, the Model 300 included a lanyard loop at the bottom rear (heel) of the frame. The grooved control in front of the loop is the magazine release.

disassembly more difficult than desired, especially when in the field. Moreover, the concealed hammer (hidden within the slide) made it impossible to tell at a glance whether or not the pistol was cocked and ready to fire. In addition, recoil was more lively in the Model 400 than in competing pistols with locked breeches, such as the Star Model A. For the same reason, the Model 400's vigorous ejection of spent cartridge casings, which could send ejected brass flying with considerable force, represented a real hazard.

Stories abound about how the Model 400 could handle a variety of 9mm and .38 caliber pistol cartridges other than the 9mm Largo for which it was designed. But most of these aging pistols may prove unreliable or even dangerous with anything other than the 9mm Largo ammunition. As a general rule, it is extremely unwise to fire a gun with ammunition other than that for which it was designed. Fortunately, 9mm Largo ammunition is widely available, making the Model 400 a remarkably efficient and powerful weapon. It is, in fact, enjoying a resurgence of popularity in the U.S., thanks in part to the recent import of large quantities of military surplus pistols from Spain, Chile and elsewhere. More importantly, the 9mm Largo ammunition for which Astra designed the Model 400 is now imported in quantity. Although it may look a little odd, and despite its operational idiosyncrasies, the Astra 400 is still a viable defensive handgun. Considering its excellent workmanship, sterling reputation as an efficient fighting pistol, and the many variations available, the Model 1921/400 remains one of the most popular Spanish handguns for collectors of all types.

# Bonifacio Echeverria (Star)

Bonifacio Echeverria, which produced two handgun designs for the French during World War I, was at work on a more advanced model when the war ended. The company then proceeded to choose instead the Browning-designed Colt Model 1911 as the basis for the future development of its "Star" brand handguns. Adopting the Model 1911-type design proved a brilliant move. The reputation of this excellent handgun was well-established and secure following its extensive use by U.S. forces in World War I. Good as it was, there was room in the Model 1911 for some small changes, mostly in terms of manufacturing improvements. Such efforts bore fruit in Argentina, Poland and the Soviet Union as well as in Spain. Finally, a feature of Spanish patent law established in the early 1900s made it possible for Star to copy the Model 1911's design without fear of lawsuits over patent infringements. A patent applied for in Spain remained in force only if the applicant quickly arranged for the manufacture of the protected product within Spain itself; otherwise, the patent lapsed within three years.

Having settled upon the Colt Model 1911 as the most promising basis for future development, the first postwar model appeared in 1920. Called the *Modelo Militar* (Spanish for "Military Model"), this gun had the same M1911-style breech locking system, and thus it bore some resemblance to the Colt. But traces of earlier Star-Mannlicher influences remained. There was the placement of cocking basses and safety on the rear of the slide, and in the shape of the hammer. Chambered in 9mm Largo, the *Modelo Militar* was clearly intended for the Spanish armed forces, which were experiencing problems with the Campo-Giro pistol and were already searching for a replacement. Although the *Modelo Militar* failed to compete successfully in its tests against the Astra pistol (which became the Model 400), Spain's *Guardia Civil*, the nation's chief paramilitary force, expressed approval of the *Modelo Militar*. It then requested to Star that it make a few changes in the pistol, a process that led to the Models of 1921 and 1922, the latter receiving the designation *Model A* by which it has since become known.

The Star Model A become one of Echeverria's most successful pistols. It differed from the Model 1921 by eliminating the grip safety found on the Colt Model 1911, and it also

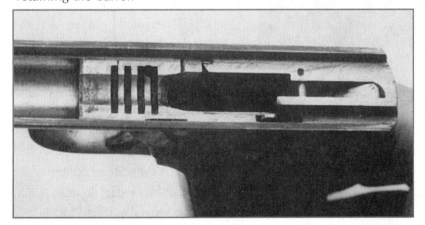

The Model 1921/Model 400 pistols used a rust-blued finish which only affected the outside of the pistol, the interior remaining "in the white." From this inside view of a Model 1921 frame, note the Browning-style locking lugs used for retaining the barrel.

had a distinctive straight backstrap. Aside from that slight alteration to the grip and the absence of a grip safety, the Model A's design differed from that of the Colt Model 1911 pistol only in the caliber it used, the shape of the hammer, a simplified trigger mechanism, mainspring, and an exposed extractor rather than the internal type. Its main specifications included the following: **Overall length:** 8.5"; **Barrel length:** 5.0"; **Width:** 1.3"; **Height:** 5.2"; and **Weight (unloaded):** 35 ounces. It also carried up to eight rounds of 9mm Largo ammunition in its magazine. Because the Spanish Army's adoption in 1921 of the Astra Model 400 pistol did not sit well with the many Spanish government officials who favored a Model 1911-type pistol, the Star Model A was welcomed enthusiastically. Upon its adoption by the Guardia Civil (Civic Guard) in 1922, the Model A enjoyed a long and productive life until it finally went out of production in 1991.

The Model A and the Model 1921 shared many of the same features. When fired with the reliable 9mm Largo cartridge, the Model A was inherently accurate. Its tiny sights made truly accurate shooting difficult; nevertheless, its good balance and relatively heavy weight proved more than adequate for close combat distances. For really precise shooting, though, the Model 1921/400 was a better choice in 9mm Largo caliber. But where the Model A excelled over the competitor at Unceta lay simply in the pleasure it offered when fired. Its locked breech gave less recoil with the powerful 9mm Largo cartridge, and the spent cartridge casings left the pistol with far less force than the Astra Model 400 exhibited. Moreover, the Model A's disassembly procedures, which mirrored those of the Colt Model 1911, were less involved than those of the Model 1921 pistol. All in all, the Model A pistol made an excellent choice for shooters who favored the 9mm Largo round but found the idiosyncrasies of the Astra Mode 1921/400 an annoyance. For this reason, many Spanish authorities favored the Model A, ensuring a long life in Spanish government service—far longer, as it turned out, than the Model 1921.

Despite its heavy trigger and small sights, the Model 1921 displays a high degree of inherent accuracy. Note the commercial designation—"Astra Model 400"—written on the target.

# Other Early Spanish Service Pistols

In addition to the Model 1921/400, Esperanza y Unceta (later Unceta y Cia) introduced yet another pistol for official service—the Model 300—which was simply a Model 400 much reduced in size and chambered for the less powerful 7.65mm (.32 ACP) or 9mm Corto/Short (.380 ACP) pistol rounds. For a further comparison, refer to the following:

| | MODEL 300 | MODEL 400 |
|---|---|---|
| **Length** | 6.3" | 9.25" |
| **Barrel Length** | 5.9" | 4.3" |
| **Height** | 4.3" | 5.5" |
| **Weight (unloaded)** | 22 oz. | 31 oz. |
| **Capacity** | 7 rounds* | 8 rounds |

*A 7.65mm (.32 ACP) caliber Model 300 later raised magazine capacity to 8 rounds*

After Unceta's name changed in 1926 from Esperanza y Unceta to Unceta y Cia, the Model 300 went through a change in inscriptions. Early Model 300s were marked EU on the front portion of the slide, behind the front sight. The same logo appeared on the pistol's hard rubber grips. In addition, Model 300 pistols made prior to 1926, when Juan Esperanza left the partnership, were marked on the top rear portion of the slide, as follows:

ESPERANZA Y UNCETA
GUERNICA ESPAÑA
MODELO 300

After that, the slide inscription was changed to:

UNCETA Y COMPAÑIA S.A.
GUERNICA ESPAÑA

These post-Esperanza Model 300 pistols also bore the company logo UC on the top forward portion of the slide (replacing the previous EU lsunburst company logo). The same UC logo appeared on the hard rubber grips. These company logos and markings were not changed right away, however, because of a substantial parts inventory that had to be used up. As a result, earlier EU-marked slides and grips may appear on some Model 300 pistols made as late as 1929.

Between its introduction in 1923 and the start of the Spanish Civil War, the Model 300 became a popular handgun among Spanish military and police forces, with official orders from the Spanish prison guards (serial

The tiny sights and mediocre trigger of the Model 300 typically combine to defeat the shooter once or twice out of every five rounds as shown. The author adds, in defense of the pistol, that he fired this 5-shot offhand group from 75 feet, rather than the usual 25- and 50-foot distances used with most other pistols described in this book.

numbers 350742-351282 and 351303-351918), the *Carabineros* (serial numbers 353770-353797 and 512055-512184), the Police School in Madrid (serial numbers 364969-365052), the Spanish navy (serial numbers 370969-371151 and 371201-371452), the army's artillery corps (serial numbers 372912-373022), the air force (serial numbers 373051-373056), and finally, the police who represented the province of Bilboa (serial numbers 514551-514675).

Following the victory in 1939 of the Nationalists and the end of Spain's Civil War, additional orders for Model 300 went to various government bodies, including the following nine blocks of serial numbers to the Artillery Park in the city of Valladolid: 525651-526000; 526576-526925; 527626-527975; 528126-528275; 528976-529120; 529125-529329; 529851-530200; 531401-531530; and 531601-531950.

Accuracy with the Model A is no match for the Model 1921, as this offhand group fired from 25 feet demonstrates.

The following six blocks of Model 300 pistols with their serial numbers went to the Artillery Park in the city of Burgos: 516126-526450; 528626-528975; 529501-529850; 530551-530675; 531051-531400 and 531951-532300.

The following nine block of Model 300 pistols with serial numbers as follows went to the Artillery Park in the city of Seville: 526926-527275; 527976-528125; 528276-528625; 529330-529379; 529401-529500; 530201-530550; 530701-531050; 531564-531600; and 532301-532563.

The following two blocks of Model 300 pistols with their serial numbers went to the Artillery Park in the city of Vitoria: 532566-532900 and 532903-533067. An additional shipment of 50 Model 300 pistols, early in the Nationalist regime, went to the police force in the city of Granada: 533069 to 533118. Two blocks of Model 300 pistols with serial numbers 591953-592252 and 592501-592750 went to the Spanish prison guards,

☙ Compared to the Models 1921 and 400 (top), the Model 300 (bottom) was smaller in all its dimensions, including weight, and yet it shared the larger model's rugged reliability.

☙ The Astra Model 300 (top), which was no larger than the 7-shot variation of the standard Eibar-type Browning copy (bottom), was far better made.

*Chapter 4*

In this right-side view, the Model A's resemblances to the Colt Model 1911 are obvious. Changes made to the design include an exposed extractor beneath the slide's ejection port, which actually helped to make the Model A an improvement over the parent model.

supplementing weapons already received during the Republic regime. Finally, the Spanish naval academy received another 80 Model 300 pistols, serial numbered from 592421 to 592500.

Other handguns made by Unceta y Cia and accepted into Spanish government service prior to World War II were the Models 903, 904 and F, all of which were variants of the Model 900, a large pistol based on the Mauser Model 1896. These close copies of the Mauser pistol could be fired one-handed, like a pistol—albeit a large one—with a wooden shoulder stock attached to the rear end of the grip suitably slotted for the fastening hardware. This variant was usually fired from the shoulder, like a small carbine. The prototype Model 904, of which only nine were made in 1933 (serial numbered from 29651-29654 and 29661-29665) and its production version, the Model F (introduced in 1934), differed from the Model 900 (1927 vintage) with its selective-fire mechanism that allowed shooters to choose between single shots for each pull of the trigger or fully-automatic fire at a cyclic rate of 350 rounds per minute. This made the Model F far more controllable in full-auto mode than the earlier machine pistols of the Models 901, 902 and 903 series, whose fully-automatic cyclic rate of fire was a blistering 900 rounds per minute. The Model 900, however, was capable of semiautomatic fire only—that is, one shot per each pull of the trigger. The Model F fired the regulation Spanish 9mm Largo cartridge,

The Star Model A, introduced in 1922, was Echeverria's third M1911-type pistol—and its most successful.

The right-side view of an early Model 300 shows off its graceful lines.

which explained the gun's appeal to the authorities, especially the Guardia Civil, which ordered 1,000 of these pistols. In all, Unceta y Cia made 1,126 Model Fs, serial numbered 29676 and 29276-30800. Of this total, 950 pistols went to the Guardia Civil in June of 1935, serial numbered 29701 to 30650. About 150 more were left in the factory, only to be seized during the Spanish Civil War.

The Gabilondo company, former manufacturers of the World War I era "Ruby" pistol *(see Chapter 2)*, created several pistol designs in the Llama series that saw service with Spanish police and military forces. These Gabilondo pistols, albeit in smaller numbers than the competing Astra and Star products, included the compact .380 ACP caliber Llama Model II pistol. It measured 6.3 inches in length, weighed 19 ounces and held up to eight rounds. The .380 caliber Model II and 9mm Largo Model IV pistols also saw service with various Spanish police organizations during the 1933-1935 period.

In addition to its success in selling the Star Model A to the Guardia Civil, the Bonifacio Echeverria company gained police business in Spain with several smaller pistols in .32 and .380 calibers. There was the aforementioned 7.65mm (.32 ACP) caliber Star Model I pistol, which began a whole line of pistols suited for police work. With its long, exposed barrel and its slide cut away on the upper portion, the Model I was clearly an evolutionary—rather than a revolutionary—design. Locating its manual

Astra's Model 300 pistol became extremely popular with Spanish officials, thanks in part to the pistol's trim shape and compact size.

*Chapter 4*

The rear portion of the Modelo Militar's slide and frame was a throwback to earlier Star pistols. Note the spur hammer with a vestigial hole in its center. The manual safety lever shown is up and to the rear on its safe setting. (Photo by Ron Waters)

Here the Modelo Militar's manual safety lever is pushed forward and down to its fire position. Like all single-action automatic pistols, this model requires that the hammer be cocked before firing. (Photo by Ron Waters)

The Model A (bottom) found favor with numerous Spanish government officials who preferred its handling and appearance (much like the Model 1911) to the odd tubular shape of the Model 1921 (top).

safety lever alongside the left side of the frame (in front of the grip) did not follow earlier Star practice. It was instead reminiscent of the safety system found in the Walther Models 8 and 9 pistols under production in Germany at the time. At 7.6 inches in length and weighing 27 ounces unloaded, the 9-shot Model I was not quite as large as the Model A, and it still required a pistol belt holster to carry effectively. In response, Echeverria introduced a short-barreled version with reduced magazine capacity, calling it the Model H. Like the Model I, it fired the .32 ACP cartridge. Echeverria also made .380 caliber versions—the Models IN and HN, respectively—and all four pistols saw widespread police and some military use in Spain, particularly in the .380 caliber versions. The Models H and HN are still excellent pocket pistols—if there's one to be found! Like early Star pistols, they are scarce and tend to be hoarded jealously by collectors. After Echeverria quit making the H and I series pistols in 1941, they lingered on in Spanish service for a few years. The factory volume of business during World War II at the Echeverria factory delayed the development of a successor indefinitely.

An even more successful Echeverria pistol than the Models H and I was the Star Model D, which prospered primarily because it was smaller even than the Model H and was designed more like the more modern and popular M1911. Introduced in 1930, four years before the Models H and I, it was made in both 7.6mm (.32 ACP) and 9mm Corto (.380 ACP) calibers. This diminutive pistol (5½ inches long) soon received the sobriquet of "Pocket and Police Model" and saw widespread police use, particularly in .380 caliber.

# Chapter 5

# The Early Export Trade (1919 to 1954)

The end of World War I in 1918 did not spell the end of Spain as an important exporter of automatic pistols. In fact, from 1919 to 1936 Spain's pistol manufacturers acquired a worldwide reputation, though not always a wholly favorable one. From China to South America, the sale of inexpensive Spanish pistols enriched dozens of companies that had matured during the lucrative war years. Not until Spain tore itself apart in a violent war of its own did this flourishing business end for a time. In the post-Civil War period the Spanish pistol industry, now reduced to four companies (and later to three), began to rebuild the country's influence and reputation as a pistol maker.

During the period following world War I, the French—and those countries supplied by them—continued to make extensive use militarily of Ruby-type pistols, whose popularity during the 1919-1936 period grew in terms of commercial sales. So many Eibar-type pistols surfaced in France after the war that some Spanish handgun manufacturers marked their pistols in French rather than Spanish or English. In time, several French manufacturers, eager to make their own fortunes at this lucrative business, developed their own automatic pistols, all based closely on the Ruby/Eibar type. Nevertheless, Spain's automatic pistol manufacturers, some of whom had never made pistols until the French contracts came along, were left in a precarious position. Several disappeared virtually overnight, while others managed to prosper, often by diversifying their product lines. Ironically, Gabilondo y Cia, the firm that started the gold rush created by the Ruby pistol, dropped this model from its own line almost immediately after the war in favor of the "Bufalo" and "Danton" models (inspired by the FN Model 1910).

To supplement the compact 7-shot .32 caliber Ruby pistol clones, tiny 6-shot .32s, such as this "Venus" model by Tomás de Urizar, offered shooters an outstanding combination of firepower and concealability.

The 6-shot Urizar Venus, which is not much larger than a modern Seecamp pistol, fits easily in the palm of an average-sized adult hand.

While the wartime 9-shot Ruby types continued to sell (but in far smaller numbers than during the war years), several Spanish pistol manufacturers rediscovered the smaller, 7-shot Model 1903 copies, which first went into production in the 1911-1913 period, before Gabilondo created the Ruby. Not surprisingly, the 7-shot Eibar-type .32 caliber pistol proved more popular among soldiers and police officers than the taller 9-shot military model. The same applied to most civilian gun carriers as well, since the .32 caliber pistol was more compact and easier to conceal in a coat pocket. For example, while Gaztañaga briefly sold a 9-shot pistol (in 1918-1919) made up from parts of wartime manufacture as the "Indian," the company then switched to a 7-shot model, called the "Model of 1916," which was really nothing more than the prewar "Destroyer" models of 1913 and 1914. And Alkartasuna, a firm created during the war specifically to create pistols for the French, also switched enthusiastically to the manufacture of 7-shot pistols following the war.

The table below summarizes other companies who introduced 7-shot compact variations of their wartime 9-shot models in the postwar period.

# Table 1. Early (pre-1936) Post-World War One Compact (7-shot) Ruby Clones (.32 ACP)

| PISTOL NAME | REMARKS |
|---|---|
| Action No.2 | |
| Alkartasuna | |
| Allobrage No.1 | |
| Asiatic | Front and rear sights are concealed in a channel cut into the slide top |
| Azul | Front and rear sights are concealed in a channel cut into the slide top |
| Crucero | Made by Ojanguren y Vidosa |
| Express | Included an FN-style grip safety and manual safety at the rear of the frame |
| Errasti | Made by Antonio Errasti |
| Fiel | |
| Joha | |
| Kapporal | Called M1914 |
| Le Secours | |
| Praga | Named after a contemporary Czech pistol but in no way similar |
| Premier | Called Model 1913, possibly to suggest a well-established product |
| Puppel | Front and rear sights are concealed in a channel cut into the slide top |
| Regina | Straight (vertical) slide serrations |
| Royal | |
| Singer | |
| Stosel | |
| Union Model III | Made for Esperanza y Unceta for export—see text below |
| Vincitor | Called the 1914 model; curved VINCITOR logo on grips |
| Waldman | |
| Walman | |

In the early postwar period, several companies introduced still smaller 6-shot 7.65mm (.32 ACP caliber) Ruby-type pistols. In contrast to the 7-shot pistols, many of which kept their raised military-style sights, these smaller 6-shot guns nearly always incorporated low-profile sights that were sunken into sight channels machined into the top of the slide. This made the pistols even easier to draw from concealment. With their smooth contours and convenient pocket size, combined with the power level of a .32 ACP cartridge, these pistols were the 1920s equivalent of the modern Seecamp pistol. As such, they were considered a highly useful type of self-defense weapon. The table below lists these ultra-compact .32 caliber Eibar models.

## Table 2. Post-World War One Subcompact (6-shot) Ruby Clones (.32 ACP

| PISTOL NAME | REMARKS |
|---|---|
| *Aldazabal* | |
| *Allies* | Introduced 1924; marked with ALLIES logo on hard-rubber grips |
| *Automatic Pistol* | |
| *Bronco* | Called Model 1918; had EA (Echave y Arizmendi) logo on grips |
| *Campeon* | Called Model 1919; used English-language slide inscription |
| *Ca-Si* | Used a sunburst logo on grip tops |
| *Colon* | |
| *Destructor* | Intertwined IS (for Iraola Salverria, its manufacturer) logo on grips |
| *Diana* | Included a grip safety and straight slide serrations with a forward slant |
| *Express* | A hammer or striker used for primer ignition |
| *Jupiter* | |
| *Libia* | Used FN-style thumb safety and grip safety; striker fired |
| *Looking Glass* | Made by Domingo Acha |
| *Lusitania* | |
| *Marina* | |
| *Modesto Santos* | |
| *Omega* | Tied with Venus (see below) for smallest known .32 caliber Ruby variant |
| *Orbea* | |
| *Precision* | Had the same sunburst logo on grips as the Ca-Si (see above) |
| *Princeps* | Fetured a grip safety as well as the standard Eibar-style thumb safety |
| *Regina* | English-language slide markings |
| *Reims* | Used English-language slide markings; AA logo on grip |
| *Roland* | |
| *Selecta* | Echave y Arizmendi, patent #66130 of 1919; some had added grip safety |
| *Singer* | |
| *Titanic* | English-language slide markings; raised front and rear sights |
| *Trust-Supra* | |
| *Union* | |
| *Venus* | Made by Tomás de Urizar y Cia; used English-language slide markings |
| *Veritable Express* | |
| *Ydeal* | Used a striker instead of a hammer for primer ignition |

**PRINCEPS .25 CALIBRE AUTOMATIC PISTOL**

FABRIQUE D'ARMES de GUERRE
PRINCEPS PATENT DEPOSE Nº 21569

PRINCEPS

Of Spanish manufacture; calibre .25; magazine capacity, 5 shots; triple safety; nickel or blue; made of special steel.
Price ..................................................................$12.00

The .25 caliber Princeps model was exported by a Spanish company using a French name, "Fabrique d'Armes de Guerre de Grande Précision." The Princeps represented a slight step up from the usual mediocre quality of such pistols (note the grip safety and the "special steel" in the description). This model also appeared in the Stoeger 1932 catalog.

Most of these pistols had appeared earlier in standard 9-shot models for sale to the French during the war. The postwar introduction of smaller models that were mechanically identical to the wartime pistols, but more compact, represented a sensible adaptation to the shifting market demand. Since the French orders had ended virtually overnight following the Armistice in November 1918, civilian sales assumed greater importance than any future military or police order, if any.

While most of the tiny 6-shot pistols used a hammer to ignite the cartridge, as in the larger models, a few subcompact 7.65mm (.32 caliber) Ruby-type pistols—including the 6-shot *Omega* (made by Armero Especialistas—used a striker instead. Mechanically, these concealment models were identical to the larger 9-shot Ruby-type pistols used during the war. They were simply smaller in outside dimensions. Guns of this type proved surprisingly popular in Spain and the rest of Europe (particularly in Finland, France, Italy and Germany), throughout Central and South America, and in the United States. Many thousands doubtless remain in use, carried in pockets or locked up in drawers.

In the early postwar period, Spanish pistol manufacturers traveled in still another direction; specifically, the ultra-high-capacity .32 caliber pistol. A small number of Eibar-type pistols were available with lengthened magazines holding between 11 and 20 rounds. Immediately after World War I, Esperanza y Unceta briefly assembled the 9-shot *Brunswig* model from war-surplus parts. Then, during the period 1924-1931, while they were making the Model 1921/Model 400 pistol for the Spanish armed forces *(see Chapter 4)*, the company contracted out to a firm in nearby Ermua to build a line of four pistols, called the *Union* series. Models I and II were small .25 caliber types, holding six and eight rounds respectively, while the Models III and IV were in 7.65mm/.32 ACP caliber. The Model III was a 7-shot subcompact model, but the Model IV was a 12-shot monster. Clearly, Esperanza y Unceta made these pistols for export, witness the fact that the company's promotional literature for these models was invariably written in several foreign languages, but never in Spanish. The Union pistols, however, were not as well-made as Esperanza y Unceta's "Astra" line of pistols.

During this period, Esperanza y Unceta also made the Astra-marked "Models 1000" and "1000 Special." Both had 11-round magazines and differed in only a few respects. The Model 1000 Special had a standard-length slide and 4-inch barrel, making it nearly as tall (5.5 inches) as it was long (6.7 inches). As for the Model 1000, its slide and barrel were lengthened, bringing the pistol's overall length to 7.9 inches for a more symmetrical and graceful appearance. The A.F. Stoeger Company once offered this model for sale in the U.S. during the early 1930s. Zulaica's last *Royal* pistol also fit into this category with its 12-round magazine and extended-length barrel and slide (similar to the Astra Model 1000). The Ruby "Plus Ultra" made by Gabilondo y Cia from 1928 to 1933 was another high-capacity monstrosity. It held up to 20 rounds and was available in normal and extended-length barrels, but always with a standard-length slide. Gabilondo built both semiautomatic and fully-automatic versions of this model, which saw the most military service of any high-capacity Ruby copies. The Plus Ultra was used by the private armies of Chinese warlords, the Japanese air force, and volunteers of the International Brigades fighting on the Republican side in the Spanish Civil War. Nevertheless, these high-capacity pistols, regarded by many as curiosities, did not sell well and are today quite scarce.

All of these high-capacity pistols—except for the 20-shot Plus Ultra—stacked their rounds in a single column, making the magazines extremely long and lending the pistols a correspondingly lengthy grip. Except for Gabilondo and its Plus Ultra, Spanish pistol manufacturers at the time did not pursue the expedient of stacking cartridges in a double column, as did the U.S. Savage automatic pistol. They only wanted to use the same milling machinery used in creating the standard 6-, 7- and 9-shot .32 caliber Ruby-type pistols.

The sale of even smaller 6.35mm (.25 caliber) vest-pocket pistols cloned from the FN Model 1906 comprised a major portion of Spain's pistol business between 1918 and 1936. Most of these .25 caliber pistols eliminated the FN-style grip safety and used instead the standard trigger-locking Eibar safety catch located at the midpoint of the frame. The magazine capacity was typically six rounds, as in the smallest 7.65mm models, with either a hammer or a striker used for igniting the cartridge primer.

Table 3, which follows, summarizes the pertinent details of the Spanish .25 caliber pistols.

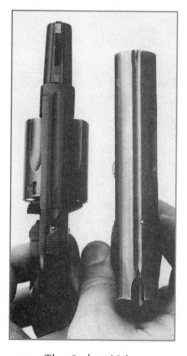

The 6-shot Urizar Venus (left) is even smaller than Smith & Wesson's famous (J)-frame revolver, which is considered the standard by which pocket pistols are judged.

*Chapter 5*

# Table 3: Guide to 6.35mm (.25 ACP caliber) Spanish Pistols made prior to 1936

| PISTOL NAME | MAGAZINE CAPACITY | SLIDE SERRATIONS | SAFETY DEVICE(S) | IGNITION METHOD | OTHER REMARKS |
|---|---|---|---|---|---|
| AAA | 6 | Straight | Eibar type | Hammer | Introduced 1919; knight's-head motif on grip |
| Action | 6 | Straight | FN type on rear of frame and FN-type grip safety | Striker | FN-style grip motif with intertwined MS (for Modesto Santos) |
| Allies | 6 | Straight | Eibar type | Hammer | Marked 1924 on slide |
| Alkar | 6 | Curved | Eibar type | Hammer | Plastic (with company logo) or unmarked checkered wooden grips |
| Alkar | 7 | Curved | crossbolt on frame rear | Hammer | Curved backstrap |
| Apache | 7 | Straight | Eibar type or curved | Hammer | Grip had motif of a bereted Parisian gangster; the slide marking includedthe word "BROWNING" |
| Asiatic | 6 | Curved | Eibar type | Hammer | Grip motif showed a cobra in the grass, head raised and hood flared as if to strike |
| Astra M200 | 6 | Curved | Eibar type | Hammer | |
| Atlas | 6 | Straight | Eibar type | Hammer | Made by Acha Hermanos ; both |
| Atlas | 6 | Curved | Eibar type | Striker | Versions use French slide markings |
| Aurora | 6 | Straight | Eibar type | Hammer | Plastic grips w/ "AURORA" and crown motif |
| Automatic Pistol | Usually 6 | Usually Straight | Eibar type | Hammer | Features vary, as different manufacturers were involved |
| Avion | 6 | Straight | Eibar type on rear of frame in FN fashion | Hammer or striker | Airplane motif on grips ("Avion" is French for "airplane") |
| Azul | 6 | Curved | Eibar type | Hammer | Made by Eulogio Arostegui |
| Beistegui | 6 | Curved | Eibar type | Hammer | "BH" (Beistegui Hermanos) logo on FN-style hard-rubber grips |
| Benemerita | 7 | Straight | Eibar type | Hammer | Called 1918 Model |
| Bronco | 6 | Curved | Eibar type and grip safety | Hammer or striker | Made by Echave y Arizmendi and marked EA on grips |
| Bufalo | 6 | Curved | Eibar type and grip safety | Hammer | "GB" (Gregorio Bolumboru) logo on FN-style hard-rubber grips |
| Bulwark | 6 | Straight | FN type | Striker at rear of frame | Had FN-style grips with "BH" (Beistegui Hermanos) logo |
| Campeon | 6 | Curved | Eibar type | Hammer | Marked 1919 on slide and CAMPEON on slide and grips |
| Cantabria | 7 | Straight | Eibar type | Hammer | Marked 1918 Model on slide |
| Celta | 6 | Straight | Eibar type | Hammer | Has Urizar dragon motif on grips |
| Colon | 6 | Curved | Eibar type | Hammer | |
| Colonial | 6 or 7 | Usually straight | Eibar or FN type | Hammer | Details vary, as different manufacturers were involved |
| Continental | 6 or 7 | Curved or straight | Eibar or FN type | Usually striker | Another Urizar product |
| Cow Boy | 6 | Straight | Eibar type | Hammer | Marked FABRICATION FRANÇAISE ("French made") to disguise its Spanish origins |
| Crucelegui Hermanos | 8 | Curved | Eibar type | Hammer | Had unusually long grip to hold two extra rounds |
| Danton | 6 | Curved | rear of frame but not FN type; grip safety, too | Hammer | Raised sights; marked DANTON on slide and frame; product of Gabilondo y Cia |
| Defense | 6 | Straight | Eibar type | Hammer | French-language markings on slide |
| Demon | 6 | Curved | rear of frame | Hammer | DEMON & devil's-head logo on grips |
| Destroyer Model 1913 | 6 | Curved | rear of frame | Hammer | Marked IG (for Isidro Gaztañaga) on grips |
| Destroyer Model 1919 | 6 | Curved | Eibar type | Hammer | Unmarked grips |
| Dewaf | 6 | Curved | Eibar type | Hammer | Marked MODEL VI on slide |
| Diana | 6 | Straight and angled forward | Eibar type | Hammer | Marked SEAM (Sociedad Española de Armas y Municiones) on grips |
| Douglas | 6 | Curved | Eibar type | Hammer | Made by Lasagabaster Hermanos (LH marking on grips) probably in early 1920s |
| Duan | 6 | Straight | Eibar type | Hammer | |

| PISTOL NAME | MAGAZINE CAPACITY | SLIDE SERRATIONS | SAFETY DEVICE(S) | IGNITION METHOD | OTHER REMARKS |
|---|---|---|---|---|---|
| EA | 6 | Straight | Eibar type | Hammer | Made by Eulogio Arostegui; has hunting-dog motif on grip |
| EA 1916 Model | 6 | Curved | Eibar type | Hammer | Made by Eulogio Arostegui; has rabbit motif on grips |
| El Cid | 6 | Curved | Eibar type | Hammer | Crown logo on grips |
| Ermua Model 1924 | 6 | Curved | Eibar type | Hammer | Acha Hermanos manufacture |
| Ermua Model 1925 | 6 | Curved | Eibar type | Hammer | Ormachea manufacture; distributed by Tómas de Urizar |
| Errasti | 6 | Straight or curved | Eibar type | Hammer | AE (Antonio Errasti) logo and ERRASTI marked on grips |
| E.S.A. | 6 | Straight and angled forward | Eibar type | Hammer | French-language slide markings; intertwined ESA logo on grips |
| Etna | 6 | Straight | Eibar type | Hammer | French-language slide markings |
| Express | 5 or 6 | Straight or curved | Eibar type or FN type | Hammer or striker | Combined French- and English-language slide markings |
| Favorit | 6 | Straight and angled forward | Eibar type | Hammer | Introduced in the 1920s |
| Fiel | 6 | Straight | FN type | Hammer | Slide marking includes a picture of a 25 caliber cartridge |
| Fortuna | 7 | Straight | Eibar type | Hammer | Marked FORTUNA on slide and grips |
| Gallus | 6 | Straight | Eibar type | Hammer | Caliber marking (6.35) on the grips |
| Gloria | 6 | Straight | FN type | Striker | Introduced in 1913 |
| Guisasola Hermanos | 6 | Straight | FN type | Hammer | Combined French and Spanish slide markings |
| Hudson | 6 | Curved | Eibar type | Hammer | English-language slide markings |
| Imperial | 7 | Straight | Eibar type | Hammer | French-language slide markings |
| J. Cesar | 6 | Straight | Eibar type | Hammer | Has Urizar dragon motif on grips |
| Joha | 6 | Straight | Eibar type | Hammer | |
| Jubala | 6 | Curved | Eibar type | Hammer | Has intertwined LE (Larranaga y Elartza) logo, JUBALA and ancient warrior's head logos on the grips |
| Jupiter | 7 | Straight | Eibar type | Hammer | French-language slide markings; seated god logo on grips; introduced in 1920s |
| Kaba Spezial | 6 | Straight | FN type | Striker | Made for export to Karl Bauer GmbH in Berlin, Germany by F. Arizmendi |
| Le Dragon | 6 | Straight | Eibar type | Hammer | |
| Liberty | 6 | Straight | FN type and grip safety | Striker | Most similar to FN pocket model; introduced in 1913 |
| Liberty | 10 or 11 | Straight | Eibar type | Hammer | Extended-length grip to hold longer magazine |
| Libia | 6 | Straight | FN type and grip safety | Striker | |
| Looking Glass | 6 | Straight | Eibar type | Hammer | Introduced in 1920s |
| Marina | 6 | Straight | Eibar type | Hammer | French-language slide markings; naval-style fouled anchor grip logo |
| Marte | 6 | Curved | Eibar type | Hammer | Intertwined EM (Erquiaga, Muguruzu y Cia) grip logo |
| Martian | 6 | Straight | Eibar type | Striker | MB (Martin Bascaran) logos on grips and slide |
| Merke | 6 | Straight | Eibar type | Hammer | MK logos on grips; introduced 1920s |
| Minerva | 7 | Straight and angled forward | Eibar type | Hammer | Introduced in the 1920s |
| MS | 6 | Straight | Eibar type | Hammer | Intertwined MS (Modesto Santos) logos on grips; introduced in the 1920s |
| Olympia | 6 | Straight | Eibar type | Hammer | Grip has caliber marking (6.35) and a picture of a savage wielding a club |
| Omega | 6 | Curved | Eibar type | Hammer | OMEGA markings on grips and slide |
| Orbea | 6 | Straight | Eibar type | Hammer | |
| Paramount | 6 | Curved or straight | Eibar type | Hammer | Caliber marking (6.35) and bird logo on grips or just a PARAMOUNT marking |
| Pinkerton | 5 or 6 | Curved or straight | Eibar type | Striker | Used loaded-indicator holes in grips (see Chapter 3) |
| Premier | 6 | Curved | Eibar type | Hammer | Urizar dragon motif on grips |
| Princeps | 6 | Straight | Eibar type and grip safety | Hammer | |
| Principe | 6 | Straight | FN type and grip safety | Striker | Most similar to FN pocket model |
| Protector | 6 | Curved or straight | Eibar type | Hammer | Caliber marking (6.35) on grips on some variations of this model |

| PISTOL NAME | MAGAZINE CAPACITY | SLIDE SERRATIONS | SAFETY DEVICE(S) | IGNITION METHOD | OTHER REMARKS |
|---|---|---|---|---|---|
| *Radium* | 6 | Straight | rear of frame | Hammer | Belgian proofmarks but made in Spain |
| *Rayon* | 6 | Curved | Eibar type | Hammer | RAYON inscription on the grips |
| *Regent* | 6 | Curved or straight | Eibar type | Hammer | Angry bull marking on grip tops or a crown logo |
| *Regina* | 7 | Curved | Eibar type | Hammer | Crown logo and REGINA on grips |
| *Reims* | 6 | Curved | Eibar type | Hammer | REGINA logo on grips |
| *Renard* | 6 | Curved | Eibar type | Hammer | Caliber marking (6.35) on grips |
| *Retolaza* | 6 | Curved | Eibar type | Hammer | Intertwined RHC (Retolaza Hermanos y Cia) logo on grips |
| *Rival* | 6 | Straight | FN type | Striker | |
| *Royal* | 6 | Straight | FN type | Striker | |
| *Ruby* | 6 | Curved or straight | FN or Eibar type | Hammer or striker | Mmade by Gabilondo |
| *Salvaje* | 7 | Curved | Eibar type | Hammer | Indian head motif on grips; includes the word BROWNING as part of slide inscription |
| *S.E.A.M.* | 6 | Straight and angled forward | Eibar type | Hammer | |
| *Selecta* | 7 | Curved | Eibar type | Hammer | Scalloped slide for lighter weight; intertwined EA (for Echave y Arizmendi) logo on grips |
| *Singer* | 6 | Curved or straight | FN type | Striker | |
| *Sivispacem Parabellum* | 6 | Curved | Eibar type | Hammer | Introduced 1920; SIVISPACEM PARABELLUM occurs on grips and slide |
| *Sprinter* | 6 | Straight | FN type | Striker | Includes intertwined GAC logo (Garate, Anitua y Cia) on grips |
| *Stosel* | 6 | Curved or straight | Eibar type | Hammer | A crown logo appears at the top of some Stosel grips |
| *Tatra* | 6 | Straight | Eibar type | Hammer | "TATRA" on slide written in fancy script; introduced in 1920s |
| *Tisan* | 6 | Straight | Eibar type | Hammer | Caliber marking (6.35) on grips |
| *Titan* | 6 | Straight | Eibar type | Hammer | English-language slide markings |
| *Titanic* | 6 | Curved | Eibar type | Hammer | Slide scalloped above gripping serrations to lighten weight |
| *Tiwa* | 6 | Straight | Eibar type | Hammer | Extended-length barrel on some models |
| *Triomphe* | 6 | Curved | Eibar type | Hammer | French-language slide markings; caliber marking and bird on grips as on Paramount model; made by same company (Apaolozo Hermanos) |
| *Trust* | 6 | Straight and angled forward | Eibar type | Hammer | English-language slide markings |
| *Union* | various | Straight | Eibar type | Hammer | Sold by Seytres, a French gun dealer, but made by or for Unceta y Cia |
| *Unique* | 6 | Curved | Eibar type | Hammer | Model 1924; made by Unceta y Cia but sold in France by Manufacture D'Armes des Pyrénées in Hendaye |
| *Venus* | 6 | Curved | Eibar type | Hammer | VENUS and 6.35 caliber marking on grip tops |
| *Venzedor* | 6 | Straight | Eibar type | Hammer | |
| *Veritable* | 6 | Straight | Eibar type | Hammer | |
| *Vesta* | 6 | Curved | Eibar type | Hammer | Made by Garate, Anitua y Cia |
| *Vesta* | 6 | Straight | FN type; some added grip safety | Striker | Made by Hijos de Angel Echeverria |
| *Victor* | 6 | Curved | FN type | Striker | |
| *Victor* | 6 | Straight | Eibar type | Hammer | Introduced in the 1920s |
| *Victoria* | 6 | Curved | Eibar type | Hammer | Unceta y Cia; introduced 1911; early pistol of its type |
| *Victory* | 7 | Straight | Eibar type | Hammer | |
| *Vincitor* | 6 | Straight | FN type | Striker | |
| *Vite* | 6 or 8 | Straight | rear of frame | Striker | Had English-language slide markings despite its French name ("Vite" means "Fast" in French) |
| *Vulcain* | 5 | Curved | Eibar type | Hammer | English-language slide markings |
| *Waldman* | 6 | Straight | rear of frame | Striker | Slide cut away at rear |
| *Walman* | 6 | Curved or straight | rear of frame | Striker | Some use slide inscription AMERICAN AUTOMATIC PISTOL |
| *Ydeal* | 6 | Curved | rear of frame or straight | Striker | English-language slide markings |
| *Zaldun* | 6 | Straight | Eibar type | Hammer | English-language slide markings |

The adjustable rear sight on the Astra Model 900 is shown in its highest position (to compensate for long-range shooting).

In the United States, the sale of Ruby or Eibar-type pistols used in World War I continued well into the postwar period. As late as the mid-1930s, import houses, including Stoeger Arms, offered new-production Spanish pistols at considerably less cost than competing brands in America. For example, in Stoeger's 1932 catalog a Princeps .25 caliber automatic pistol was priced at $12, compared to $17 for a Colt Pocket Model of similar size and caliber. The Astra Model 400, which had been adopted by Spain as its official service pistol; and which had enjoyed considerable prestige abroad, sold for only $27.50. Others included Colt's Government Model ($36.75), Smith & Wesson's Military & Police Model revolver ($32.50), a Webley British service revolver ($50), and Germany's P08 Parabellum "Luger" pistols, which began at $50. Spanish automatic pistols also proved highly popular in South America, with Spanish copies of the Mauser 1896 selling to Central and South American police forces.

In Europe, Ruby-type pistols remained in widespread use between World Wars. In Italy, Beretta, in addition to selling its own line of pistols, marketed some Spanish handguns, notably Unceta's "Victoria." In France, several companies tried to emulate Spain's success by making Ruby-type pistols of their own. Even in Germany, which was rightly regarded for its high standards in the manufacture of handguns, Spanish pistols had a huge advantage in being noticeably less expensive than German models. To many handgun buyers—Germans and Europeans generally—cost has always been a dominant factor in selection. And, since so many people who buy a pistol never fire it, many of the least efficient Spanish pistols of that period found their way into the homes of satisfied customers with relatively few complaints.

Interestingly, Spain's influence asserted itself most strongly in China, where the Mauser Model 1896 was especially revered. And so, when Spanish manufacturers began offering weapons of similar appearance, and always at a lower price than the German-made original, the Chinese found the combination irresistible. Until the Civil War ended in Spain (1936), the Chinese bought tens of thousands of these Spanish Mauser copies.

As successful as the original Model 90 was (Unceta would ultimately make an estimated 20,776 of them), the successful experience in China soon suggested that Astra might be wise to

Despite being a .32 caliber, the 6-shot Ruby pistol clone (top) was only a little larger than a typical .25 caliber pistol, such as Astra's Model 2000 (bottom), and yet it offered much more striking power.

*Chapter 5*

make modifications to the pistol's basic semiautomatic mechanism of its own in order to increase the market—especially in China and South America. To service this lucrative market, Unceta introduced a modified Model 901 in 1928. It was identical in design and features to the standard Model 900 except for the addition of a fire selector switch mounted on the right side of the receiver. Pushing this selector switch back to the number one position provided one shot for each pull of the trigger. For fully-

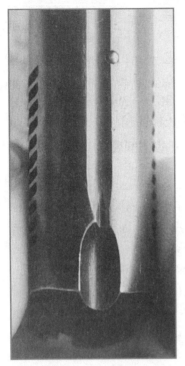

Considering its rudimentary sights, which were designed more for a smooth, snagproof draw than for precise aim, the accuracy of the Venus pistol is all the more remarkable.

The Astra Model 903 had a detachable magazine in 10- and 20-round capacities and a fire selector (for shooting semiautomatic or fully automatic fire). This page from the Unceta owner's manual illustrates the dual functions of the should-stock/holster combination. (Courtesy of Astra-Unceta y Cia)

# ASTRA 903 AUTOMATIC PISTOL

CAL. 7.63 m/m (.300) WITH INTERCHANGEABLE 10 AND 20 ROUND MAGAZINE AND DETACHABLE STOCK. — 160 m/m BARREL (6,3")

The pistol ready for loading from top per clip, with the 20 round magazine placed and the 10 round magazine separated.

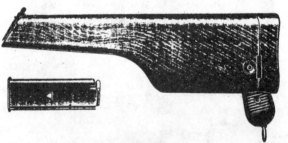

The pistol resting in holster-stock

The pistol with holster attached.

EXCELLENT FIREARM FOR ALL MILITARY AND POLICE SERVICE AND FOR PROTECTION OF PUBLIC INSTITUTIONS, BANKS, ETC., AND ALSO FOR BIG GAME HUNTING

automatic fire, the selector went up and forward to the number 10, firing at a frenetic cyclic rate of 900 rounds per minute. Eventually, the 901 was deemed an impractical weapon, largely because it emptied the magazine too quickly, forcing Unceta y Cia to drop the Model 901 in 1928 after producing only 1,655 pistols. Dissatisfaction with the Model 901 led to the improved Model 902 later that same year. Unceta y Cia had changed from an integral 10-round magazine to a 20-round type. The new model remained permanently attached to the gun and could be reloaded in place using stripper clips, as in the Mauser M1896 and Astra Models 900 and 901. The Model 902 was longer (13 inches vs. 11.4 inches for the Models 900 and 901) and heavier (54 ounces vs. 44.4 ounces for the Models 900 and 901. It was a particularly unwieldy weapon, however, due mostly to the long protrusion of the extended magazine. Nevertheless, Unceta y Cia produced 7,075 Model 902s, more than any pistol of this series save the original Model 900 itself.

The next pistol in Unceta's Astra Model 900 series was the Model 903, which addressed the bulky magazine issue by making its 10-round (20-shot optional) magazine detachable from the receiver. The magazines could now be reloaded either by taking them off the gun or by leaving them in place with stripper clips. Upon its introduction in 1932, the Model 903 might have been a major success for Unceta had not the rising political situation in Spain severely hampered its distribution. Nevertheless, Unceta y Cia sold 3,082 of the Model 903 pistol.

Unceta y Cia next tackled the lingering complaint directed at the selective-fire variations of its Model 900 series pistols. Their cyclic rate of fire (900 rounds per minute) was simply too fast for the average shooter to control; hence there was much wasted ammunition. The new Model 904 resolved that problem by adding a device in the form of a flywheel mounted inside the pistol grip. The result was a reduction of the rate of fire, making the pistol more manageable. This so-called *mecanismo moderator* slowed down the hammer travel, reducing the cyclic rate of fire from 900 rounds per minute to only 350 rounds per minute. Cyclic rates of fire, by the way, assume there's an unlimited supply of ammunition. The actual rate of fire for a belt-fed weapon is invariably

The Venus pistol fires a 5-shot offhand group from 25 feet measuring three inches across, good accuracy for such a small pistol and a tribute to the company's manufacturing standards.

*Chapter 5*

The rear sight on the Astra Model 900 marked in 50-meter increments out to 1000 meters (about 6/10th of a mile). This is not a realistic maximum range with the shoulder stock/holster attached to the frame.

lower than the theoretical cyclic rate for a magazine-fed weapon, because time is inevitably lost while the shooter replaces spent magazines with full ones before resuming firing. Unceta made only a few of these Model 904s before commencing production of the even newer Model F, which combined the rate-of-fire-reducing mechanism with the 9mm Largo round for Spanish government service. Since few other countries could use the 9mm Largo cartridge, no Model Fs were ever exported. The final gun in the Model 900 series—the Model E—reverted back to the 7.63mm Mauser caliber (actually, a 7.62x25mm round) found on all 900-series pistols except the Model F. It also eliminated the rate-of-fire reducing mechanism employed by its predecessor. Unceta y Cia made and exported a total of only 548 Model Es (serial numbers 33789-34336) between 1949 and 1960. Unceta y Cia numbered its Model 900 series pistols separately, making them exceptions to the sequential numbering system to which the company usually adhered.

The growing popularity of Spanish-made Mauser Model 1896 copies—especially among the lucrative China trade—forced Mauser-Werke to add to its own product line. Some of the Spanish weapons fired fully automatically and for that reason were outselling Mauser in several important Asian and South American markets. Mauser also felt compelled to offer a selective-fire version of its Model 1896. The resulting weapon, named the *Schnellfeuerpistole* (Rapid-fire-pistol) or Model 712, went into production in 1932. An improved version—still called the Model 712 and featuring a modified selective-fire mechanism—appeared in 1936. This was a case of

In the foreign gun trade during the 1920s and 1930s, Unceta's Astra Model 900 (top) was almost as famous as the WWI-era Gabilondo Ruby (bottom).

Mauser responding directly with selective-fire mechanism and the use of 10- or 20-shot detachable magazines, all features of Spanish copies that were cutting into Mauser's own sales. The growing popularity of these Mauser copies from Spain attracted the public ire of Mauser-Werke. For example, in the 1932 catalog published by A.F. Stoeger company, the following statement was made in a Mauser advertisement:

*WARNING—The principle postulated by Paul von Mauser in 1896—that the safest type of automatic arm is that with visible hammer—has caused competing firms to market automatics of this type.*

*Recognizing the truth of the old adage that "Imitation is the sincerest form of flattery," certain firms have not scrupled to offer arms which, externally at least, appear to be exact copies in all details of the Mauser. It is needless to emphasize the unreliability of such imitations, as they could not—no doubt for purely manufacturing reasons—be built to incorporate the very points assuring Mauser superiority; namely, avoidance of all pins and screws in the working parts, and monobloc barrel and bolt casing. It is evident that the mechanism of such copies, in which the most important features of the original could not be embodied to the full, is unable in the long run to withstand the heavy stresses set up by the powerful cartridge, least of all in quick or automatic fire. All who desire an accurate, utterly reliable and effective automatic of practically unlimited durability will do well, in their own highest interest, to avoid spurious imitations. The original Mauser Auto-pistol Cal. 7.63mm alone combines unique structural superiority with the extreme accuracy of workmanship necessary to meet without reserve the most difficult and refined arms-technical (sic) problems arising in the functioning of automatic arms.*

In this same 1932 catalog, the cost of a Mauser-made Model 1896 pistol was $75 in its semiautomatic form and $85 in the selective-fire version. By comparison, an MM31 machine pistol made by Beistegui Hermanos sold for only $22. Unquestionably, the Mauser system was far better made than the Spanish gun. One could buy nearly four of the Spanish weapons for the cost of a single Mauser. And yet, in some respects the Spanish weapons were actually superior to the Mauser, notably in their use of rate-reducing mechanisms in later selective-fire weapons made by Astra and Beistegui. This rate reducer made Astra's Model F a far more controllable weapon in automatic fire than Mauser's vaunted *Schnellfeuerpistole*. In the end, Mauser triumphed. Tens of thousands of its Model 712 selective-fire weapon were sold to China, while others became the official pistol of the Yugoslavians from 1933 onward (and in Germany, too, beginning in 1938). Altogether, Mauser-Werke made about 95,000 of these excellent machine pistols before production stopped in 1938.

Whether the fully-automatic Mauser-type machine pistols and their Spanish copies were effective has long been hotly debated. To answer these questions, the U.S. Army's Special Warfare Training Center at Fort Bragg,

North Carolina, conducted tests of the Mauser Model 1932 in the early 1960s to observe just how effective these weapons could be in the hands of experts. Using a Mauser Model 1932, U.S. Army specialists found that accurate fire on man-sized targets was possible at ranges as great as 100 meters (109 yards) in fully-automatic fire and up to 200 meters in semi-automatic fire (in both cases, the shoulder-stock/holster assembly was attached to the frame). In the late 1940s, the Soviets, who also studied and tested the Mauser and Astra weapons in developing their own military handguns, experienced similar results with their Stechkin (APS) machine pistol. In the hand of an expert shooter with extensive experience in this type of weapon, a fully-automatic pistol—especially one outfitted with a detachable stock—can be highly effective. But in the hands of a novice, the same gun merely makes a lot of noise as the bullets scatter wildly. The machine-pistol concept does find support in some military forces, though, which explains why manufacturers keep reviving the concept at various times, most recently the Heckler & Koch Model VP-70, the Beretta Model 93R, the Glock Model 18 and the Steyr TMP. Regrettably, selective-fire pistols have more often than not attracted the attention of individuals and organizations who bought them as prestige items without ever investing the time and ammunition necessary to learn how to handle them properly (hence their bad reputation for poor control). In semi-automatic fire, however,

The Mauser company, feeling the pinch from the competition of the select-fire Spanish copies, felt compelled to introduce a selective-fire version of its own M1896 pistol/carbine, the Model 711, which is shown as it appeared in the A.F. Stoeger Company's 1932 catalog.

---

86

A. F. STOEGER, INC., 509 FIFTH AVE., NEW YORK, N. Y.

## Original Mauser Rapid Fire Pistol

WITH INTERCHANGEABLE TEN AND TWENTY SHOT MAGAZINES AND COMBINATION WOOD SHOULDER STOCK AND HOLSTER

NEW 1932 MODEL

With 5¼-inch Barrel.

**Model 711**
Illustration shows pistol with ten shot magazine inserted and shoulder stock, which also serves as holster, attached.

The Mauser Works now present under the above designation a new autoloading pistol which can function at will as a semi-automatic (shot-for-shot) arm, or by the simple motion of a change-over lever as a FULL AUTOMATIC RAPID - FIRER. It possesses the further novelty of uniting in the same weapon the Mauser "clip" and "detachable magazine" systems of loading.

In its essential structural features the new arm is identical with the universally known and reputed Standard Mauser auto-pistol Cal. 7.63 mm, whose absolutely characteristic points of superiority have assured its sweeping success and unique reputation in all parts of the world.

GENERAL—The new arm integrally embodies the salient characteristics of the Standard Mauser Pistol, namely:

1.—Total avoidance of pins and screws in working parts.

2.—Complete enclosure of mechanism in body.

3.—Grouping of working parts in self-contained assemblies thereby not only affording the most complete protection against corrosive gases, dust, snow and foreign bodies generally, but greatly facilitating cleaning, stripping and maintenance.

The chief parts subjected to severe stress have been considerably reinforced, enabling the arm to stand up without reserve to the racking stresses set up in quick or automatic fire (bursts), no matter how long continued, in which the shots follow each other with machine-gun rapidity. The unsurpassed solidity of its unique construction positively guarantees absolutely uniform and certain functioning even in prolonged automatic fire.

HOLSTER-STOCK—The use of this adjunct is advisable in automatic fire, affording the shooter a firm hold and by reducing the jump inseparable from one-hand use, rendering the firing more effective.

FIRE CONTROL—A change-over lever snapping into two notches on the left hand side of body; it is normally set in notch "N" for single, that is, semi-automatic fire, each shot requiring a fresh pull of trigger. Moved over to notch "R" the function changes to all-automatic, delivering a burst of fire with the utmost rapidity so long as the trigger is held back and there are cartridges in magazine. Releasing trigger interrupts the fire, and with a little practice short bursts of 2 to 3 or more shots can be delivered at will, by quickly pulling and releasing trigger, affording an alternative method of quick fire.

RATE OF FIRE—Including the time necessary for reloading, the practical sustained rate of automatic fire is about 180 rounds per minute.

MAGAZINE—The arm is regularly equipped with a detachable 10-round magazine, which can be interchanged with a "long" magazine holding 20 rounds.

MAGAZINE CHANGING is exceedingly simple and certain. The empty magazine is released by pressing a stud on the right hand side of body, then inserting and securing the full one in place by a single motion. Any number of spare magazines can be carried in leather cases on the belt.

LOADING—Cock hammer and fully retract bolt, in which position it is then held by hammer. Smartly insert full magazine into arm, so that it snaps into place. Ease hammer, releasing bolt, which flies forward, carrying the topmost cartridge into chamber. The arm is now ready to fire.

On firing last cartridge, bolt is held back in its rearmost ("open") position by a projecting stud on carrier, leaving arm ready to reload, and giving the firer Unmistakable warning that this is necessary.

RELOADING, when a fresh loaded magazine is not available, is accomplished—without removing empty magazine—by refilling with two successive clips of 10 cartridges, a valuable advantage in emergency.

UNLOADING—Release and remove magazine and eject cartridge in chamber by gently retracting bolt. Release bolt and lower hammer, if cocked, by pulling trigger.

UNIVERSAL SAFETY LOCK—The arm is provided with the new "Universal" safety lock, by means of which the arm can not only be rendered "safe" whether cocked or uncocked, but—safety "on"— the hammer is lowered with one hand and without the slightest risk by simply pulling trigger.

RELIABILITY—Apart from its unconditional reliability under the worst service conditions, the Original Mauser Quickfiring Pistol has been fully tried out by the severest possible tests with a large number of rounds, without loss of accuracy, malfunction of any kind or ascertainable wear. It is offered in complete confidence as an absolutely first-rate automatic arm, fulfilling to the last iota the most exacting demands with a responsible War, Gendarmerie, Police or Customs department can require in a weapon for the equipment of its officers and subordinates.

WARNING—The principle postulated by Paul von Mauser in 1896 that the safest type of automatic arm is that with visible mechanism, has caused competing firms to market automatics of this type. Recognizing the truth of the old adage that "Imitation is the sincerest form of flattery," certain concerns have not scrupled to offer arms which, externally at least, appear to be exact copies in all details of the Mauser. It is needless to emphasize the unreliability of such imitations, as they could not—no doubt for purely manufacturing reason—be built to incorporate the very points assuring Mauser superiority, namely, avoidance of all pins and screws in the working parts, and monobloc barrel and bolt casing. It is evident that the mechanism of such copies, in which the most important features of the original could not be embodied to the full, is unable in the long run to withstand the heavy stresses set up by the powerful cartridge, least of all in quick or automatic fire.

All who desire an accurate, utterly reliable and effective automatic of practically unlimited durability will do well, in their own highest interest, to Avoid Spurious Imitations.

The original Mauser Auto-pistol Cal. 7.63 mm alone combines unique structural superiority with the extreme accuracy of workmanship necessary to meet without reserve the most difficult and refined arms-technical problems arising in the functioning of automatic arms. It can be recognized by the Mauser trade-mark on left side of frame and marking on top of barrel and right side of frame: Waffenbrik Mauser, Obendorf a. Necker.

PRICE (see opposite page) Model 711 ........................ $85.00
Extra Ten-shot Magazine ............................................. 4.00
Extra Twenty-shot Magazine ........................................ 7.50

A NEW GUN CARRIES A FACTORY GUARANTEE

---

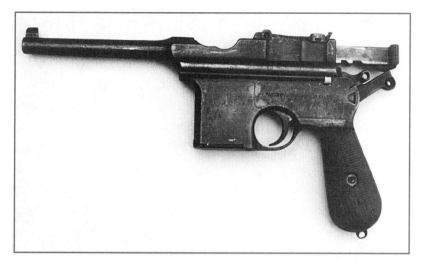

these large pistols in good condition are surprisingly accurate, especially when fired as a carbine with the detachable stock locked in place.

The success of the fully-automatic Royal and Astra Model 903 machine pistols encouraged Bonifacio Echeverria (Star) to develop a selective-fire pistol of its own based on the Colt M1911 copies. The first effort—the *Model 1922(A)*—received Spanish patent number 116,773 on February 11, 1930. It featured a fire selector located on the right side of the slide which, when pushed down, activated the sear trip, preventing the mechanism from resetting itself after a shot was fires. The mechanism continued to fire as long as the trigger was pulled (or, more likely, until the magazine ran dry). Star advertised its new pistol in 9mm Largo, .38 ACP and .45 ACP calibers, discontinuing production of the model in late 1931 in order to build a slightly enlarged version, called the *Model MD*. Caliber choices included the popular 7.63mm Mauser followed by the 9mm Largo, .38 ACP and .45 ACP. Star offered the Model MD in barrel lengths up to 7.9 inches (200mm). Extended high-capacity magazines of 16 or even 32 rounds were also available, as was a clip-on shoulder stock (inspired by the Mauser) attached to the rear end of the frame. Not only did this device produce more accurate shooting, it doubled as a holster when not attached to the gun.

Upon firing the last shot from an Astra Model 900, the bolt remains locked all the way to the rear as shown. The similar-looking Mauser Model 1896 pistol was the first commercially available handgun to incorporate this useful hold-open feature.

Like all early Spanish automatic pistols, the Astra Model 900 is a single-action design. Its hammer must be cocked to allow firing. Note that the manual safety lever (next to the hammer) must also be cocked toward the rear, as shown, for the hammer to move.

The Astra Model 900's serial number appears on the left side of the frame and the bolt as well. This photo indicates serial number 3967 on the bolt.

Because it was lighter and smaller than the Astra Model 900 series and other Mauser copies, Star's adaptation of the Browning-system handgun was not a success in fully-automatic fire. Different versions produced from 1934 on included a rate-reducing mechanism that slowed down the cyclic rate of fire from over 1,300 shots per minute to a more controllable 800 shots per minute. Star received a Spanish patent (number 133,526, dated February 17, 1934) for this device, which proved impossible to fire less than six shots with a single trigger pull, thus making the pistol utterly useless in fully-automatic fire, even with the shoulder stock attached. These Star machine pistols received some novelty sales, but the only military orders came from Nicaragua and Siam (now Thailand). The Siamese even set up a factory in 1938 to produce their own "Type 80" Star machine pistols, but Japan's occupation of Southeast Asia ended this project before it had gotten a proper start. Production by Echeverria of these impressive-sounding but impractical weapons (at least on their fully-automatic fire settings) came to a total of around 8,000 pistols by 1952 when production ceased. The company had much more success expanding its Star line of pocket pistols, following the modest successes of the Models H and I with a smaller gun similar to the Model H. Called the *Model CO*, it was a bit larger than the Model E (.25 ACP) which it replaced. The Model CO was also chambered

The Astra Model 900-type pistols were surprisingly easy to disassemble and maintain, but their Chinese owners rarely bothered. That explains why surplus Mauser Model 1896s and Astra Model 900s coming from China are usually in such bad shape.

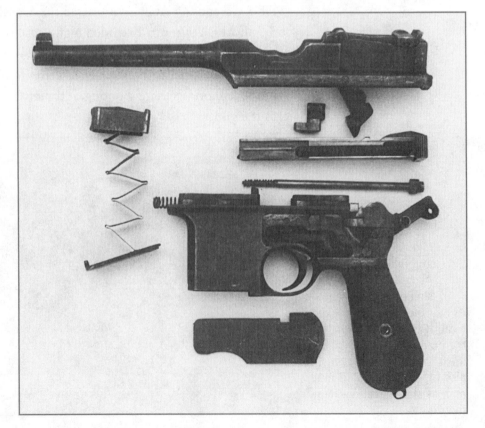

in the .25 caliber cartridge and had the same type of open-slide design and manual safety. Its spur hammer, however, was larger and had a more prominent shape. Introduced in 1941, the Model CO remained in production until 1957.

Another line of pistols, marked "Tauler" on the slide, should be noted. Señor Tauler was an excellent pistol shot who once won a shooting medal in Olympic competition. Later he became a gunsmith and, later still, a gun dealer in Madrid. He also served in the Spanish secret police, using his influence and connections with Spain's official bodies in the days prior to the Spanish Civil War to sell Llama-type pistols made by Gabilondo but marked with his own name. The paramilitary force, *Guardia Civil*, along with Spanish police and customs guards, are known to have contracted with Tauler during the period 1933-1935. The following table delineates the Tauler Lines.

## Table 4: Tauler Pistol Models: 1933-1935

| TAULER MODEL | LLAMA EQUIVALENT | DESCRIPTION |
|---|---|---|
| I | I | 7.65/.32 small pistol with no grip safety |
| II | II | .380 ACP small pistol with no grip safety |
| III | III | .380 ACP small pistol with no grip safety |
| IV | IV | 9mm Largo service pistol (no grip safety) |
| V | VII | Identical to Model IV but .38 Super caliber |
| P | VIII | 9mm Largo service pistol with grip safety |

Of all these Tauler pistols, the most exceptional was the Model II. Similar in size, caliber and general configuration to Llama's own Model II, the Tauler version had an open-topped slide, similar to many Beretta pistols and the Model I and 9 made by Walther. Tauler's Model II had slide serrations that were also angled forward, something which Gabilondo did not use on any of its own Llama-brand pistols until after World War II. The earliest Tauler marking was a heart within a circle, similar to the first trademark Gabilondo used when it introduced the Llama pistol line. Tauler soon switched to another trademark, this one consisting of a dog's head inside a circle. The last Tauler pistols featured an Indian kneeling and drawing a bow. This third trademark (patent number 96,730, dated December 13, 1933), as with all Tauler pistols, had the word 'TAULER" somewhere in the slide inscriptions, its markings all written in English, with no hint of Spanish manufacture aside from the Eibar proofmarks. British firearms

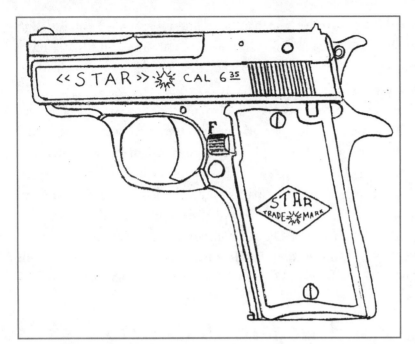

The .25 ACP caliber Star Model CO proved more successful than its Model 1911-style machine pistols and remained in production from 1941 to 1957.

authorities Ian Hogg and John Weeks speculate that Tauler's choice of English-language markings was intended to "convince his customers that they were obtaining genuine American products." In any event, the Tauler line lasted only two years, ending production just prior to the start of the Spanish Civil War. It's likely that Señor Tauler then lost his position with the secret police. Although some Tauler-marked pistols saw use in the Spanish Civil War, the line was never revived after 1935.

Far more successful than the Tauler line was an export house owned by José Cruz Mugica, who also owned a shotgun manufacturing concern located in Eibar. Originally, he contracted with the government of Siam (now Thailand) in the early 1930s to sell a large quantity of pistols to that Asian country. When sales of his pistols to Siam ended with the Japanese occupation of 1941, Mugica continued to export pistols, mostly to China.

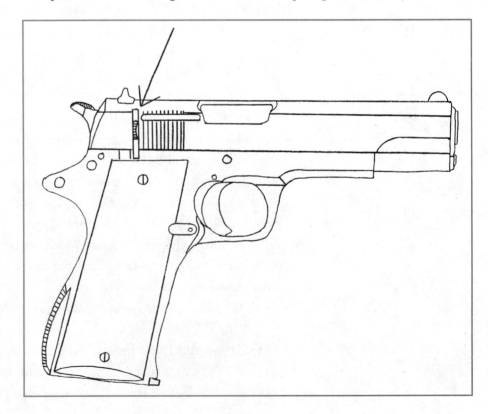

Echeverria's attempt to supply a selective-fire (arrow) "machine-pistol" to the lucrative Chinese and South American trade culminated in the Star Model MD. The pistol proved uncontrollable in fully-automatic fire, however, and the company sold only a few thousand, despite offering them in four caliber choices.

The bulk of his products were Llama models (made by Gabilondo marked with Mugica's company name). The more important models appear in the table below.

## Table 5: Mugica Pistol Models

| MUGICA<br>MODEL | LLAMA<br>EQUIVALENT | DESCRIPTION |
|---|---|---|
| 101-G | X-A | 7.65/32 small pistol with grip safety |
| 101 | X | Identical to 101-G/X-A but no grip safety |
| 105-G | III-A | .380 ACP small pistol with grip safety |
| 105 | III | Identical to 105-G/X-A but no grip safety |
| 110-G | VIII | 9mm Largo full-sized service pistol with grip safety |
| 110 | VII | Like 110-G/VIII but without grip safety |
| 120 | XI "Especial" | 9mm Parabellum caliber service pistol; no grip safety |
| MUGICA | Perfect | Ruby-type pistol in .25 ACP and .32 ACP calibers |

In addition to the Gabilondo pistols, the Mugica firm also handled Gaztañaga's *Super Destroyer* pistols *(see Chapter 3)*. This 7.65mm (.32 ACP) compact model with 8-shot magazine bore a strong resemblance to the highly popular German Walther PP and remained a good seller for Mugica in the brief time (less than two years) it was available. Although Spain's Civil War forced Mugica to suspend operations for a time, he resumed his business after the war. A four-page Mugica pistol catalog published around 1951 offered three Llama pistol models, including the Model 101 in 7.65mm/.32 ACP caliber and the superb Model 120 in 9mm Parabellum caliber. Mugica continued to export Llama-made pistols until Gabilondo revamped its pistol line, taking full responsibility for all of its exports in 1954.

The manual safety lever on the Astra Model 900 (alongside the hammer) must be pushed to the rear to unlock the hammer (right). Pushing the safety lever forward to the frame (below) locks the hammer.

As for Spanish revolvers, they also remained in production during the 18-year period 1919-1937. Prior to World War I, the most popular pattern to copy had been the small Velo Dog and the hinged-frame, double-action copies of the Smith & Wesson model of 1880. After

*Chapter 5*

Spanish-made revolvers, like automatic pistols, most frequently drew on foreign designs for their inspiration. The chief prototypes included top-break, automatic-ejecting Smith & Wesson models, such as the Safety Hammerless or "Lemon Squeezer" (top), the Smith & Wesson Military & Police Model (center), or the Colt Police Positive (bottom).

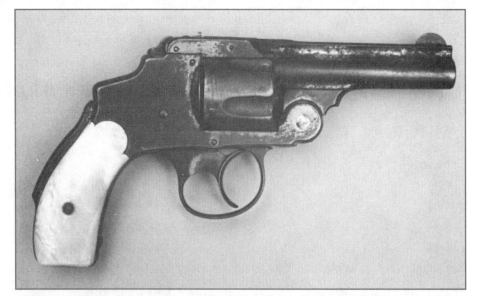

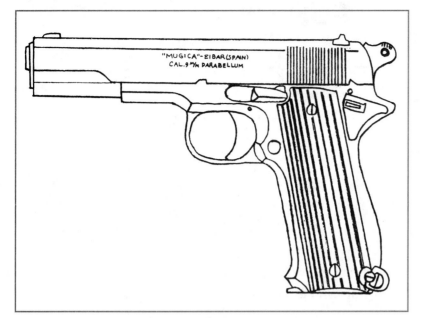

World War I, copies of the Smith & Wesson Military & Police model revolver predominated. The Velo Dog models, chambered for the Browning cartridges popularized by Fabrique Nationale (FN) of Belgium—especially the .25 and .32 ACP—began to appear in larger numbers than the original 5.5mm version. Copies of the Smith & Wesson Hand Ejector M&P-type revolver series included models from such Spanish companies as Armero Especialistas Reunidas, Benito Guisasola, Orbea Hermanos, Ojanguren y Marcaido, Antonio Errasti, Suinaga y Aramperri, and Trocaola, Aranzabal y Cia. Some of these revolvers had appeared before World War I and some were used by the French armed forces during the period 1917-1918. After World War I, the Spanish manufacturers noted above took to the M&P pattern in greater numbers than before, largely supplanting the now outdated 1880 Smith & Wesson top-break, hinged-frame pattern. Caliber choices in the Spanish

Mugica's Model 120 was actually a Model XI "Especial" with different slide markings.

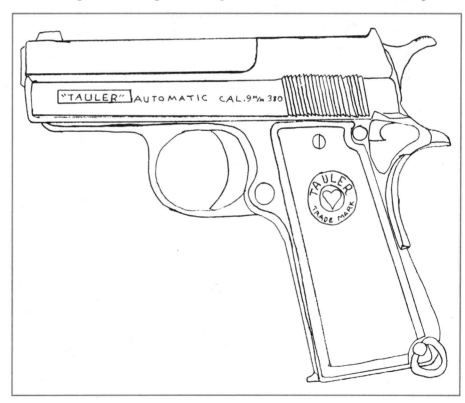

The "Tauler line," though short-lived, went through three variations of slide markings. Tauler's Model II differed from other pistols made by Gabilondo with its open-topped slide and slanted slide serrations.

The most ambitious Spanish revolver copy of pre-Civil War days was undoubtedly the Modelo Militar made by Trocaola, Aranzabal y Cia. This .44 Special caliber revolver was a faithful copy of the Smith & Wesson Triple Lock mechanism, an exceedingly difficult design to manufacture. Note how the ejector rod is locked into the underside of the barrel (source of the third lock).

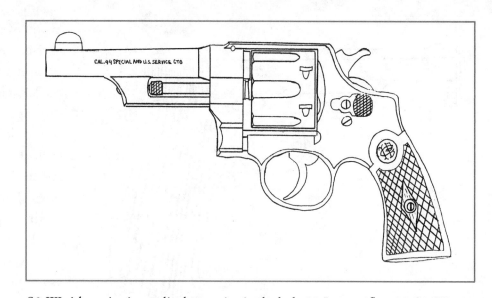

When copying Smith & Wesson or Colt revolvers, some Spanish gunmakers employed unique touches of their own. The T.A.C. Model 333, for example, displays an unusual design for its cylinder latch.

S&W side-swinging cylinder copies included .22 Long rifle, .32 S&W, .32 Long Colt, .38 S&W, .38 Long Colt, .44 S&W Russian, and even one .44 Special model. This last revolver, called the *Modelo Militar*, was a well-made product of Trocaola, Aranzabal y Cia. Interestingly, it copied the "Triple Lock" system used briefly by Smith & Wesson in its .44 Military Model (First Variation) made from 1908 to 1915. In addition to the usual two-cylinder locking points of the Hand Ejector series, This design added a third locking point where the yoke meets the extractor shroud (*see below*) beneath the barrel. Moreover, the Triple Lock design incorporated a protective shroud over the front edge of the ejector rod, making this the first revolver so equipped. Because of the extraordinarily tight tolerances involved, manufacturing this model was so difficult that even Smith & Wesson made only 21,000 or so before eliminating the third lock at the yoke and the extractor shroud in favor of a simplified version. The fact that Trocaola, Aranzabal y Cia felt equal to the task of copying this advanced revolver model several years after its originator had abandoned it says a lot for that Spanish gunmaker.

Following their limited use in WWI, copies of Colt's swinging-cylinder revolvers grew in popularity from the mid-1920s onward. Even so, the Smith & Wesson M&P copies always remained in the majority among Spanish

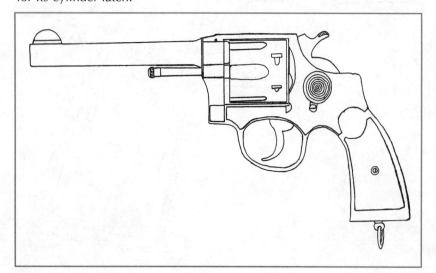

An Astra Model 900 pistol, when maintained in good condition, shoots as well as any combat-type pistol at realistic pistol distances. The author fired this tight 25-foot offhand target group using an Astra in much better condition than the worn specimen shown here.

revolver manufacturers. Garate, Anitua y Cia, Ojanguren y Marcaido (Model 1926) and Trocaola, Aranzabal y Cia (Modelo Corzo and Para Bosino) became the chief Spanish Colt revolver copyists. Calibers of the Colt copies made in Spain included 8mm Lebel, .32 Long Colt and .38 Long Colt. Sensing a need to supply automatic pistols to the French war effort during 1914-1918, Francisco Arizmendi y Cia reintroduced a 7.62mm Nagant caliber revolver called the *Nagans*. An updated version of the pre-1914 F.A.G. model *(see Chapter 1)*, this revolver retained its fixed cylinder (the forward-camming cylinder of the Belgian/Russian gas seal model was then considered too complex and expensive to justify copying it). However, the Arizmendi copy had a 7-shot cylinder, lending some appeal to shooters who were dissatisfied with the 5- and 6-shot cylinders of the more common Colt and Smith & Wesson copies. With the Belgian company that originated the Nagant design having quit the revolver business, and with production of post-1919 Russian Nagant revolvers having been usurped by domestic Red Army orders, the Arizmendi version proved quite successful in commercial sales, thanks to its low price and greater availability.

This group was fired from 50 feet in an offhand position. The target shows that a well-maintained Model 900 pistol can shoot about as well as a modern military handgun.

While Spanish companies in the pistol-making business did not even come close to the output of the giants in the international arms markets—particularly Colt, Smith & Wesson, Mauser, Walther and Fabrique Nationale—the handguns made by Spain companies enjoyed considerable sales in the United States and Central Europe, more still in France and Central and South America, and a great deal in China. The period from 1914 to 1936—especially the earlier years of that period—was indeed a golden age for the Basque gunmakers of Eibar and Guernica. This would all change, however, with the onset of the Spanish Civil War, the subject of the next chapter.

*Chapter 5*

# Chapter 6

## The Spanish Civil War

 ver since 1808, arguments had raged in Spain over how the country should be governed. French forces under Napoleon had invaded the country that year, leaving the Spanish monarchy embattled and discredited. An attempt to restore an absolute monarchy failed, as did a subsequent attempt to create a federal republic with much authority given to the various regions of Spain. Finally, a compromise was reached in 1876 with the formation of a constitutional monarchy. As with many compromises, this one pleased nobody. Conservatives—primarily factions within the military and the Catholic church—felt that this arrangement legitimized political activity which they saw as destructive. The liberals, on the other hand, felt that the constitutional monarchy preserved Spain's status quo, thus oppressing those citizens who lived in poverty and keeping the country primitive and backward. The storm clouds continued to gather.

**Spain in July, 1936**
The line dividing the territory held by the Nationalist rebels and land still belonging to the Republic as of July 21, 1936 appeared as follows: Beginning halfway up the Spanish-Portuguese border, the line ran northeast to the Guadarrama Mountains near Madrid. There it turned southeast to the city of Teruel in Aragon, and then almost due north to the Pyrenees Mountains that separated Spain and France. A narrow strip of land along the north coast of Spain, including the gunmaking provinces of Vizcaya and Guipuzcoa, also remained in Republican hands.

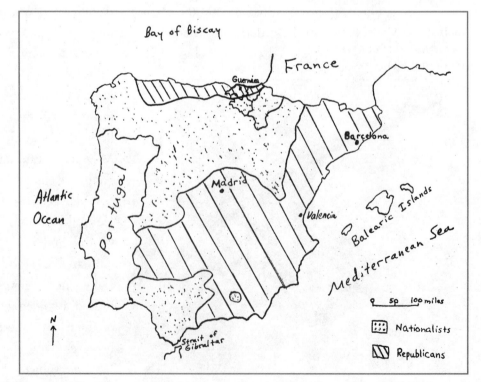

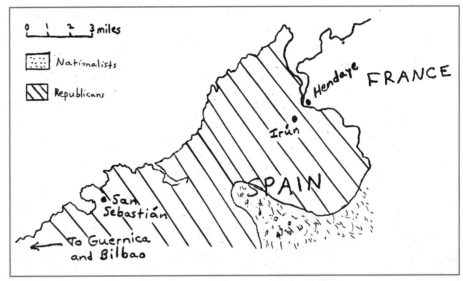

An early goal of the Nationalists was to cut off the northern coastal strip of the Spanish Republic from direct land communications with France, thus making its eventual capture easier. In mid-August, therefore, the Nationalists launched an offensive against the Spanish border town of Irún.

By late August the Nationalists had made significant progress towards Irún.

Irún fell on September 3, 1936 to a small Nationalist force of 1,500 men commanded by Colonel Beorlegui. The capture of this key town cut off northern Spain, which still supported the Republic, from receiving supplies from France via a direct overland route.

In 1898, Spain's humiliation at the hands of U.S. forces in the Spanish-American War focused worldwide attention on the serious divisions and weaknesses within Spain. Even the most patriotic and loyal Spaniards felt forced to admit their country remained only a token of its former power and grandeur. When in 1904 Spain saw a chance to expand into Morocco, located directly across the Strait of Gibraltar in North Africa, she eagerly took the opportunity. It was a decision that led to a bloody and costly war lasting over two decades. In Spain, meanwhile, unrest boiled over into ever more ominous episodes of rebellion and terrorism. In 1909, a riot broke out

The grips on the RE pistol used vertical grooving, similar to a Tokarev pistol.

in Barcelona after the government had called up reservists to join the battle in Morocco. The Barcelona uprising lasted a week, but not before the army had killed 120 people and executed five of the most egregious participants. Barcelona's "Tragic Week" emphasized and reinforced three major problems undermining Spanish society at the time: the demand of working-class people for improved conditions, the question of regional autonomy, and what to do about a war still raging in Morocco. The election in 1910 of José Canalejas as Prime Minister offered some lingering hope that a way could be found to solve Spain's most pressing problems. Unfortunately, Canalejas was assassinated in 1912 by an anarchist, leaving Spain more divided than ever.

All through World War I, Spain remained neutral while Spanish gunmakers made fortunes producing weapons for the French, British and Italians. The Russian Revolution of 1917 further inspired working-class people in Spain to demand a better life. From then on, the anarchist movement grew enormously in strength and numbers. Strikes, takeovers of large estates by force, and even assassinations of politicians and wealthy business leaders were blamed on the anarchists. Encouraged by these events, the hitherto cautious Spanish Socialist party began to espouse extensive reforms, which in early 20th century Spain were little short of revolutionary. In 1917, the army and police crushed a general strike organized by the anarchists and socialists, but from that point on politics throughout Spain became increasingly vicious and desperate, leading finally to all-out civil war 19 years later.

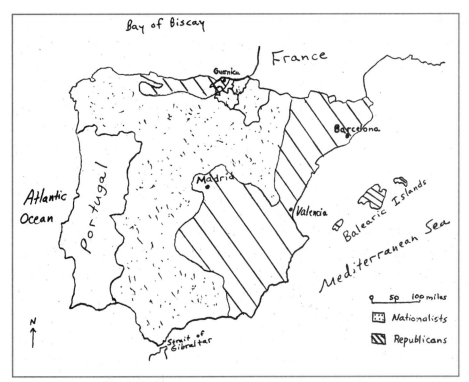

Bay of Biscay

France

Guernica

Barcelona

Portugal

Atlantic
Ocean

Madrid

Valencia

Balearic Islands

Mediterranean Sea

0  50  100 miles

Nationalists

Republicans

N

Strait of
Gibraltar

**Spain in March, 1937**
The situation in March 1937 shows that the Nationalists had made considerable gains in southern and central Spain, and had also isolated the northern coast. The Republic still held firm around Madrid, however.

The depressed economic climate that spread around the world following World War I hit Spain especially hard. The Spanish economy had never been strong even in the best of times and, not surprisingly, proved extremely vulnerable to economic downturns. Another disaster for Spain was the ongoing Moroccan war, which Spain almost lost in 1921 after Moroccan tribesmen had killed 15,000 Spanish soldiers and civilians. With that, the government of Spain fell and was replaced by a group of generals led by Miguel Primo de Rivera. While in some respects generous and magnanimous, de Rivera was unable to solve most of his country's growing problems, although he was able to conclude the war in Morocco, thanks to cooperation with French forces. In an attempt to come to terms with Spain's other difficult situations, de Rivera managed to alienate virtually every group in Spain while pleasing nobody. Finally, in January of 1930, King Alfonso forced the general to resign and then attempted to restore Spain's government and civil life to its former status. It was an effort doomed from the start. When a succession of ministers failed to do what the king demanded, unrest grew. Elections held in 1931 led to a resounding vote of no confidence in the king's efforts, whereupon several regions of Spain, notably the Basque country around Eibar, proclaimed the end of the monarchy and called for the formation of a republic. King Alfonso XIII, realizing he had lost the support of most of the Spanish people, fled the country, after which a republic was established.

Heavily influenced by anarchists and a powerful communist party, Spain's new Republican government, which had ruled from 1931 to 1936, enacted a series of far-reaching economic reforms attacking the power of the Catholic church, large landowners and wealthy industrialists, alienating many conservative elements. These conservative forces began working together, temporarily gaining an electoral majority in the Spanish parliament in 1933. Unrest continued to grow, with extremist parties at both

The pebbled grips on the F. Ascaso were not unlike the modern SIG/Sauer pistol grips

ends of the political spectrum gaining power at the expense of moderate forces. After winning the 1936 election by a very narrow margin, the Republicans promised even more threatening reforms, some of which were actually carried out. Finally, in July 1936, anti-government terrorism culminated in an armed rebellion against the Republic led by high-ranking officers of the Spanish army.

These rebel forces, which came to be know as the Nationalists, consisted of conservative army officers, notably General Francisco Franco. They were, in turn, supported by Spanish troops, including those brought in from Morocco. The war went well for the Nationalist rebels from the outset. Still, in July 1936, the Republican forces remained in control of two-thirds of the country, plus Spain's entire gold reserves and most of the Spanish fleet. They were also better trained and led by experienced military types. The Republican forces, in contrast, were disorganized and wracked by fierce internal struggles that sometimes led to open warfare between their own factions. As a result, the Nationalists quickly conquered large tracts of Republican territory. Wherever the Nationalists gained ground, they initiated brutal reprisals, killing thousands of those who supported the Republic, which then responded with atrocities of its own.

By 1937 the Nationalists appeared on the verge of victory, but a fierce defense of Madrid, aided by large quantities of military forces from the Soviet Union and other foreign volunteers (called the International Brigades), enabled the Republican forces to put off inevitable defeat. During the next two years, the Republican forces launched a number of counterattacks, but the Nationalists, with the help of German and Italian allies, were able to contain further Republican offensives while launching successful attacks of their own. The war dragged on until March 1939, with the Republican forces growing steadily weaker and more dependent on the Soviet Union, while the Nationalists grew in strength and gained large chunks of territory.

One of the areas under Republican control during the early war years was the northern coast of Spain, which included part of the Basque region, including the provinces of Vizcaya and Guipuzcoa. This area held the bulk of Spain's iron and steel production, including the cities of Eibar and Guernica, which contained what was left of the country's handgun factories. The Basques had always felt alienated from Spain because of cultural differences. Since 1876, feelings of alienation and hostility towards the central government in Madrid had grown dramatically. Even the Basques' great wartime prosperity from 1914 to 1918 created the notion among the people of the region that they did not really need Spain's support. Basque

The Nationalist offensive against the Basque provinces, now isolated both from Republican Spain and from officially neutral but friendly France, began in late March 1939. Eibar fell in early April, and with it most of the remaining handgun manufacturers either closed their doors or began making munitions for the Nationalists.

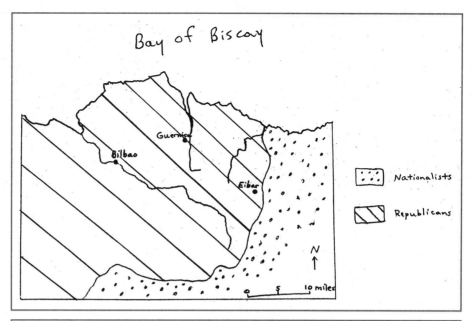

The city of Guernica, and with it the Astra pistol factory, fell to the Nationalists on April 29, 1937. The Basque and Republican governments' plans to evacuate the Astra factory to a point behind the "ring of iron" fortifications surrounding Bilbao fell through, and the Astra factory went to work for the Nationalist side.

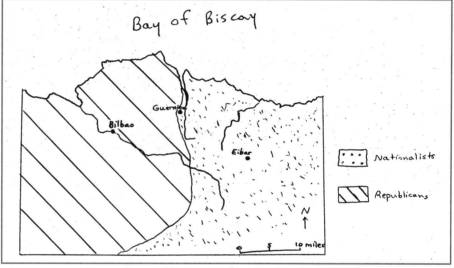

The final Nationalist assault against the Basque separatist movement began on June 11, 1937, and on June 19 Bilbao fell. Thus ended Basque hopes for an independent country.

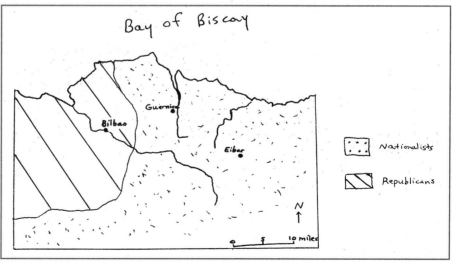

*Chapter 6*

**Spain in late 1937**
By late 1937 the Republic had lost the northern coast and was confined to the eastern portion of Spain. Production of Model 1921 (Astra Model 400) pistol copies for the Republican armed forces was in progress both at Tarassa, near Barcelona, and in Valencia.

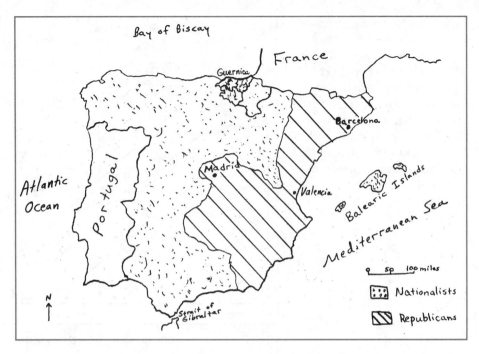

prosperity was tenuous at best, however. The worldwide economic recession during the late 1920s and 1930s greatly affected the region. By 1929, Basque iron ore production was only a third of what it had been just before World War I. The Basques themselves were divided on how best to attain their national goals. Many wanted total independence from Spain, while others preferred a measure of autonomy within a federation of Spanish states. The largest Basque province and the one closest to France—Navarre—opposed the independence movement. Even the Basques who decided to work together for autonomy were divided on strategy. With their strong Catholic background and firm middle-class values, the Basques had little in common with the radical leftists in Republican Spain. Many Basques initially felt that bargaining with the Nationalists instead of the Republicans was a better way to ensure independence for their region; that is, until General Franco, the Nationalist leader, demonstrated his absolute inflexibility and unwillingness to compromise.

Despite the early warning signs, the desire among Basques for an independent nation was so strong that on October 7, 1936, the Basques declared the "Republic of Euzkadi" as their new homeland, electing José Antonio Aquirre as its president. Aquirre quickly pledged his support of the Republican regime in Madrid against the Nationalists. Since the Basques had almost nothing in common with the rest of Republican Spain, their uneasy alliance with the Republicans hinged solely on the hope of gaining autonomy for their region. Indeed, relations between the Basque and Republican governments were never cordial. The widespread reforms and

*Spanish Handguns*

attacks on the old order occurring in other regions of Spain under the republic never took root in "Euzkadi." In short, theirs was a relatively conservative uprising, motivated chiefly by the desire for independence from Spain.

The case of Unceta y Cia—the only handgun manufacturer at the time with significant surviving documentation—is probably representative of the region as a whole. The company, maker of the Model 1921 pistol (Astra Model 400), was unquestionably the largest and most important handgun manufacturer in Spain at the time. Don Rufino Unceta, sole owner of the Astra firm since 1926, had no use for the socialistic program of the Republicans. If enacted in its entirety, it would seriously threaten the prosperity—even the survival—of large firms such as his. Therefore, Don Rufino secretly hoped the Nationalists would win. Like any good businessman in a war industry, however, he did not let his personal beliefs hinder the everlasting quest for profits. Accordingly, he sold his wares to the nearest available customer, which early on was the local Basque militia of the new Euzkadi Republic. Placed under strict Basque government control amounting to military occupation of its factory, Astra reluctantly produced 14,800 Model 1921 pistols between July 28, 1936, and April 27, 1939 (serial numbers 55001-69800). According to company records, however, large numbers of pistols were stolen. In 1937, for example, 100 Model 1921 pistols (serial numbers 69801 to 69900) were "stolen" from the factory itself, and an additional 575 (serial numbers 69926 to 70500) were taken from the army arsenal in the town of Burgos, plus 150 more (serial numbers 70501 to 70650) were pilfered from the nearby proofhouse in Bilbao. These large-scale so-called thefts of 825 pistols were almost certainly "inside jobs" performed on behalf of the Nationalist army.

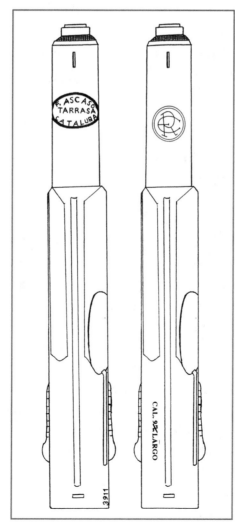

**Astra Model 400 copies of the Spanish Civil War**

*Right:* A converted army facility in Tarrasa, near Barcelona, made about 5000 to 8000 Model 1921 (Model 400) copies, called the F. Ascaso, between 1937 and January 1939 for the Republican armed forces. These pistols had a large oval F. Ascaso emblem stamped on the top of the barrel. On all but the earliest examples, the full serial number also appeared on the right rear portion of the slide. *Far Right:* A converted textile factory in Valencia made for the Republican war effort about 15,000 Model 1921 (Model 400) copies between 1937 and March 1939. These pistols had a large intertwined RE (for República Española, "Spanish Republic") stamped on the top of the barrel, and the caliber marking on the left rear portion of the slide.

In early 1937, the semi-autonomous Euzkadian government purchased several Astra Model 300 pistols. These were identical in design to the Model 1921/400 Spanish army pistol, but considerably smaller. They fired the 9mm Corto (.380 ACP) cartridge rather than the more powerful 9mm Largo round used in the Model 1921 pistol. Although less efficient as a combat handgun, the Model 300 had the great advantage of being far handier and more portable than the Model 1921, and as such it was preferred by high-ranking officers, aviators and the like over the standard pistol. Astra Model 300 pistols known to have been purchased for military use by the government of Euzkadi during the Spanish Civil War against the Nationalists include the following serial numbers *(reading left to right)*:

| | | | |
|---|---|---|---|
| 516154 | 518588 | 518593-518597 | 520464-520466 |
| 520473 | 520479-520481 | 520553-520555 | 520577 |
| 520584-520590 | 520631-520700 | 521001-521013 | 521015-521800 |
| 522001-522100 | 522201-522400 | 522551 | 523200 |
| 52390 | 524400 | 524526-524575 | 524601-524625 |
| 524629-524630 | 524632-525000 | 525201-525404 | 525409 |
| 525489 | 525491 | 525494 | 525497-525498 |
| 525500-525533 | 525539-525548 | 525551-525568 | 525571-525583 |
| 525585-525637 | 525639-525650 | 526001-526015 | |

Unceta y Cia filled this government order with stock on hand rather than making up a production run especially for the order. Originally intended for private sale through commercial channels, these pistols all bear the usual commercial markings and can be traced to their involvement in the Spanish Civil War only by their serial numbers.

The Nationalist rebellion affected the Basque region almost from the first moments of the Civil War. While most eyes were riveted on General Franco's impressive advance in the south of Spain during late July and early August, covering more than 300 miles in only four weeks, another Nationalist army under General Mola was cutting off the Basque provinces of Spain from their counterparts in France. The first Nationalist offensive against the Basques began on August 11, 1936, just three weeks after the Nationalist rebellion against the Republican government began. The towns of San Sebastián and Irún came under heavy air attack, a grim foretaste of what would happen to Guernica less than a year later. When the Nationalists, with a force of only 1500 men, captured Irún on September 3, 1936, the Basques could no longer receive help from their French neighbors. By March 1937, most of the Basque territory—all of Navarre, most of Alava and Guipuzcoa, and some of Vizcaya—was under Nationalist control.

On March 31, 1937, the Nationalists, having been thwarted in their first attempt to take Madrid from the south, embarked on an ambitious campaign to seize what remained of the Basque provinces. Their goal was to bring these hard-working people, with their rich natural resources and important war industry, under Nationalist control. Thus, on April 26, 1937, the Basque city of Guernica came under fierce aerial attack from the Condor Legion, an air group consisting entirely of German aviators and airplanes. These future *Luftwaffe* aircraft appeared over the hapless city and bombed it for nearly three hours. This German air force consisted of four new twin-engine Heinkel 111 and 23 older tri-motor Junkers bombers carrying 100,000 pounds of bombs. When it was apparent that Guernica had no air defense of its own, the German fighters dropped to low level and began strafing groups of people in the little city, whose population of 7000 had at least doubled by retreating troops and refugees from those regions overrun during previous battles. Officially, the Germans were trying to knock out a small bridge over the Mundaca River, but in reality the Germans were experimenting with carpet bombing using incendiary bombs. The fact that the first bombs fell on the railroad station in the middle of Guernica supported the carpet bombing argument despite German denials. Whatever the motivation for the attack, its results were undeniable. The bridge survived unscathed, allowing Nationalist troops to cross over it three days later, but more than two-thirds of the town was demolished and more than a thousand people killed. Amazingly, the Unceta factory, whose location and purpose were unknown by the Germans, remained untouched.

Following Guernica's fall to the Nationalist forces on April 29, Unceta y Cia resumed Model 1921 production for Franco's troops. Between May 3, 1937 and the end of the Spanish Civil War in March 1939, the company delivered 20,300 more Model 1921 pistols to the Nationalists (serial numbers 70651-86000 and 86051-91000). Unceta y Cia also sent several hundred Model 300 pistols to the German Condor Legion. During the Nazi era (1933-1945), German pilots developed a high regard for small pistols, particularly 6.35mm (.25 ACP), 7.65mm (.32 ACP) and 9mm Short (.380 ACP) models. Their flight gear was so bulky that little room was left for the larger 9mm pistols that were then standard issue. The Astra

Llama Model XI "Especial" made by Gabilondo (top) was introduced the year the war began. It saw use with the armed forces, as did .32 caliber blowback pistols of the Ruby type (bottom).

Model 300, with its sleek contours, was not likely to snag on their equipment, while its good striking power, relative to its small size and weight, made an ideal sidearm.

Those Model 300 pistols that went to the Condor Legion during the 1937-1939 period include the following serial numbers (*reading left to right*):

| | | | |
|---|---|---|---|
| 501796 | 502876 | 502935 | 502940-502941 |
| 503006 | 503008-503009 | 503019 | 503158-503161 |
| 503163 | 503165-503168 | 503170-503173 | 503175-503185 |
| 503189-503200 | 503301 | 503331-503334 | 503339-503350 |
| 503355-503360 | 503365-503375 | 503385-503389 | 503395-503399 |
| 503451-503465 | 503476-503490 | 503606-503612 | 503614-503625 |
| 503639 | 503646-503667 | 503676-503678 | 522439 |
| 522444 | 522452 | 522455-522456 | 522471-522473 |
| 522502 | 522526-522529 | 522531-522536 | 523506 |
| 523508-523512 | 523514-523521 | 523526-523534 | 523552-523558 |
| 523671-523690 | 523810 | 523837-523838 | 523840 |
| 524478-524487 | 524495-524500 | 525005-525014 | 525085-525087 |
| 525137-525171 | 525411-525435 | | |

Note that these serial numbers, which were used by the Germans in support of General Franco's Nationalists, overlapped those found on pistols supplied to the Euzkadian government for use against the Nationalists. This overlap illustrates the odd situation in which Unceta y Cia found itself—that of supplying arms to both sides in the conflict. Whether used by the Basques or the Germans, these pistols had been stockpiled in the Unceta factory before the Civil War began. Other pistols used by Spanish Republican forces were those from the Model 900 series. These large pistols (*see Chapters 4 and 5*), which resembled the Mauser Model 1896 "Broomhandle" model, had been exported mostly to China prior to 1936. Enough remained on hand, though, for use by Republican military and police forces (1931-1936) and by elements of the Euzkadian government's armed forces (July 1936-April 1937). Earlier, in August 1931, a Republican military commission had seized 6,184 Model 900 pistols (4,334 completed) along with 600 Model 901s and 2,421 Model 902s (796 completed). Eventually, the Republic decided to retain only a portion of these powerful weapons, buying 600 Model 901s and 750 Model 902s, returning the rest to Unceta for eventual export to China and elsewhere. Most of these weapons were stored in an armory in Madrid when the fighting began several years later and saw combat. Indeed, the Model 1896 Mauser

Broomhandle, which had inspired the design of the Astra Model 900 series, was no stranger to the fighting in Spain. In his novel, *For Whom the Bell Tolls*, Ernest Hemingway describes the slaughter of all the inhabitants in a pro-Nationalist village by a ragtag Republican band. While the account is fictional, it doubtless comes close to the truth about what happened in many small villages throughout Spain between 1936 and 1939. So desperate was the situation in Spain in those wartime years that modern weapons suitable for combat remained in constant short supply, with soldiers on both sides happy to lay hands on whatever they could and worry about spare parts and ammunition supplies later.

The Model F pistol, which was identical to the Model 900 series but chambered for the 9mm Largo cartridge, remained in plentiful supply, however, and consequently saw considerable wartime use. The Model F pistols in the amount of 950 were delivered to the *Guardia Civil* in mid-1935 and went into wartime service a year later in the battle for Madrid. In addition, the Euzkadian government took 150 Model Fs (serial numbers 30651-30800), 44 Model 903s and 2,085 Model 900s (serial numbers 26413-26451, 26453-26475, 26501-26700, 26805-26975, and 29001-29554. In escaping damage to its plant, the Unceta firm was far luckier than most of the handgun manufacturers in Basque territory. For example,

An Astra Model 1921 pistol appears next to a Nationalist poster. (Photo by Ron Waters)

when Eibar, the center of Spanish handgun manufacture, fell to the Nationalists in early April, fierce fighting broke out in the city. Bonifacio Echeverria (Star), the one handgun factory in Eibar that survives today, sustained severe damage, its buildings having been heavily bombed and its pre-Civil War records destroyed by fire. The shortage or, in some instances, the total absence of accurate records of the Spanish handgun industry in the early part of the 20th century is directly attributable to those chaotic and destructive days.

Efforts by the Republic in the center and south of Spain to aid their embattled Basque allies in the north were totally inadequate. The Basque region was nearly 100 miles from the nearest Republican territory. Moreover, the Republican-controlled fleet was cowed by the Nationalist navy, not to mention the German and Italian air forces which were sent to help it.

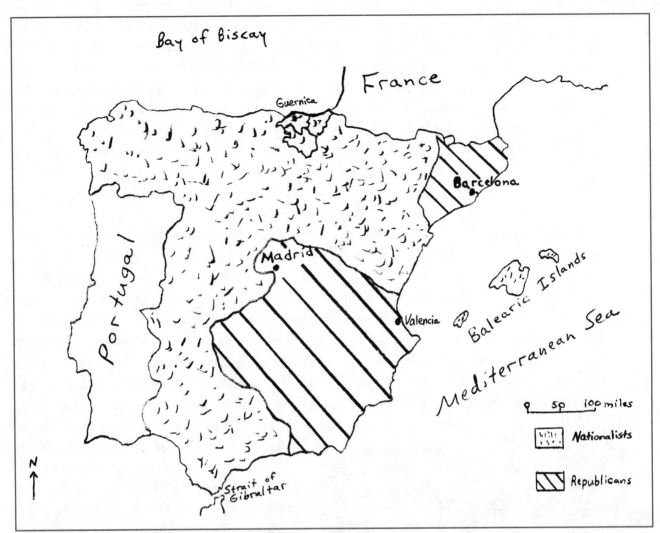

**Spain in July, 1938**

With the Basque north region subdued, Franco's Nationalists turned their attention to separating Catalonia, in northeast Spain, from the rest of Republican Spain. Between July 1938 (shown here) and February 1939, the Nationalists succeeded in this plan. The fall of Tarassa, near Barcelona, in January 1939, deprived the Republican army of the F. Ascaso pistol. Only the RE pistol, made in Valencia, remained in production.

As a result, there was no way to get additional troops or supplies to the Basques. Hoping to draw Nationalist forces away from their ever-tightening stranglehold on Bilbao, the chief city in the region, the Republicans launched two diversionary attacks in other parts of Spain. This strategy worked no better to save the Basques than it did elsewhere. Both Republican drives stalled and the Nationalist recovered quickly without disrupting their attack on Bilbao. Novelist Ernest Hemingway's thesis in *For Whom the Bell Tolls* maintains that the Republicans continued the attack too long, failing to switch to a defensive posture in time because of treachery within their own ranks. In actuality, the Republicans continued the attack too long and failed to consolidate their gains. While no less squeamish about shedding blood than Franco's men, and thus every bit as ruthless, they were far less skilled at making war than their opponents. They were unable to guess correctly that the opportunity to attack had passed. Thus did the diversionary attack bog down and fail to save the Basques.

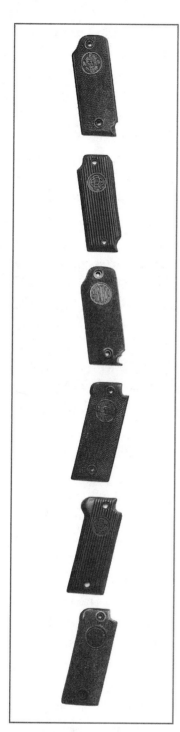

The grips of the standard Model 1921/400 pistols (from top to bottom), as made by Unceta, RE and F. Ascaso, are all fully interchangeable, although their markings and patterns are quite different.

Bilbao fell on June 19, 1937, ending the brief and tragic Basque experiment in autonomy. The Euzkadi Republic set up a government in exile in Barcelona, hoping that Basque desire for self-rule would one day be restored—which, of course, it never was. The iron mines and steel-producing plants in the province of Vizcaya, along with whatever explosives and armaments production remained after the battles, henceforth went to aid the Nationalist cause against the Republicans.

Early in the Civil War, the Republic, having no doubt anticipated the loss to its war effort of the isolated and unfriendly Basque region, made arrangements to produce pistols in other parts of Spain where Republican control was more solid. The standard Spanish armed forces pistol—the powerful and efficient 9mm Largo caliber Model 1921 (Astra Model 400)—was considered a useful and popular, albeit difficult, model for copying purposes. We know of two Spanish workshops in Republican territory where the difficult task of cloning this sophisticated and rather complex design took place. In 1937, workers in Valencia who were sympathetic to the Republican government began making Model 1921 copies, known as the RE (for *Republica Española*, or "Spanish Republic"). The machinery they used was subtly different from the Unceta y Cia setup in Guernica. The rifling of the RE pistol, while it had the same six grooves with a right-hand twist as the Model 1921/Astra Model 400, made a complete revolution in 10 inches (as opposed to 9.4 to 9.55 inches in the pistol made by Unceta y Cia). Obviously, the RE factory had been set up without direct help from Unceta y Cia; rather, the RE technicians reverse-engineered their production machinery by studying Spanish army-issue Model 1921 pistols, then designing and building the machinery necessary to produce that model themselves.

Markings on the RE pistol included a serial number on the right rear grip tang only (with no serial number on the slide), an intertwined RE logo on the top of the barrel, behind the front sight, and the caliber designation (CAL.9MM LARGO) on the left rear portion of the slide slightly above the gripping serrations. A pattern of vertical ribs impressed into the pistol grips helped shooters get a firm hold on the pistol. The grip was made of plastic (with an intertwined RE logo at the top) or wood. The latter were either unadorned, except for the vertical ribbing described above, or they had a small brass medallion with the intertwined RE logo let into the top portion (beneath the upper grip screw). Valencia, located on the Mediterranean cost of Spain in the eastern part of the country, remained in Republican hands until the end of the war, which accounts for the relatively large production of this pistol. Estimates of total RE production go as high as 15,000 pistols.

The second copy of the Model 1921 made in Republican territory was the *F. Ascaso* pistol, named after Francisco Ascaso, a famous leader of the Spanish anarchists. As such, he was responsible for many of the political murders that had poisoned Spanish political life in the late 1920s. After having been deported from Spain by General Primo de Revera in 1929, Ascaso returned to Spain just before the Civil War broke out. Ascaso died in an attack launched by anarchist forces in Barcelona on July 20, 1936. His brother, Domingo, and cousin Joaquín remained important anarchist leaders in the Republic throughout the war, so it was only natural that the pistol would be named after Ascaso. The Republicans utilized a converted armory in Tarrasa (a suburb of Barcelona in the province of Catalonia) to produce the F. Ascaso pistols. The rifling of this RE-type pistol— six grooves with a right-hand twist similar to the "real" Astra Model 400—made a complete revolution in 12 inches, whereas the Model 400 was 9.4 to 9.55 and the RE model was 10 inches.

A Campo-Giro Model 1913/16 pistol is shown with a Republican Poster. Note the communist hammer and sickle emblem in the upper right-hand corner of the poster (Photo by Ron Waters)

Interestingly, two manufacturing shortcuts were made compared to the standard Model 1921 pistol: First, the safety lever on some early F. Ascaso pistols lacked the ability to hold open the slide. Deleting this secondary feature of the safety lever on the Model 1921 enabled the factory to omit machining a notch in the slide of the F. Ascaso pistols, thus simplifying production. This omission, however, made early F. Ascaso pistols more difficult to maintain in the field, since disassembly for cleaning and maintenance was even harder than the already complex procedure used on Model 1921 pistols made by Unceta y Cia. As a result, later F. Ascaso pistols returned to the standard slide design. The second manufacturing shortcut was the use of serrations (straight lines) on the muzzle bushing, rather than the knurling (checkered pattern) cut into the muzzle bushings of standard Model 1921 pistols. Again, as with the slide hold-open feature, F. Ascaso pistols later returned to the standard configuration.

Markings on the F. Ascaso pistol included a serial number on the right rear grip tang and right rear of the slide. An oval "F. Ascaso" marking appeared on the top of the barrel, slightly behind the front sight. Unlike the Astra and RE pistols, the F. Ascaso pistol had no caliber designation. Its pistol grips were made of pebbled plastic, with a circular "F. Ascaso" logo at the top portion of each grip (beneath the upper grip screw). The serial number appeared on the right grip tang and, with the exception of a few early pistols, also bore a stamp on the right rear portion of the slide. These numbers followed the same practice as established with the genuine Astra pistols made by Unceta. Since Tarrasa remained in Republican hands only until its capture by Nationalist troops in January 1939, the F. Ascaso pistol did not stay in production as long as the RE; hence, its production figures were lower (total production amounted to at least 5,000 pistols, but no more than 8,000).

Compared to the Astra original, both the RE and Ascaso pistols were partially the result of manufacturing shortcuts. In addition to the simplified machining (mentioned above) both pistols were given a salt blued finish rather than the more labor-intensive rust blue finish used by Unceta (Astra) in its Model 1921 production. Surviving Republican pistols also indicate less polish and care in their fitting than do the Astra Model 1923Is. The RE and F. Ascaso pistols, however, while not quite meeting the Astra's high standards, were exactly the same size and caliber and equal in function as well. Neither Republican factory took any obvious manufacturing short-cuts, such as eliminating the grip safety or lanyard loop, which one might expect under the same desperate circumstances. What's more, the factories that produced those two Republican copies had to be created from scratch and their workers retrained in the art of pistol manufacture. Viewed in this light—and considering the tremendous stress placed upon the Republican economy—both the RE and F. Ascaso pistols must be considered impressive accomplishments. An Eibar-type .32 caliber copy of the Ruby pistol would have resulted in a far easier manufacturing process under the circumstances, but the Republicans refused to take the easy way out, striving instead to supply their officers with a pistol equal to those used by Spain's prewar armed forces as well as the opposing Nationalists.

In addition to the production of various pistols, both prewar and wartime, cited above, both sides made extensive use of other Spanish hand-guns, including the *Plus Ultra* (1925 to 1933) made by Gabilondo y Cia. It featured a Ruby-type design, but with a much longer magazine that held up to 20 rounds. As a result, this pistol adopted a long, awkward grip shaped to facilitate two-handed firing. The *Plus Ultra* also appeared in both semiautomatic and selective-fire versions, the latter frequently including an extended barrel. Despite its awkwardness, the *Plus Ultra* gained considerable (but short-lived) popularity in Spain during the Civil War, becoming especially popular among the International Brigades serving on the Republican side.

The communist star is engraved into a checkered aluminum Campo-Giro Model 1913/16 grip, probably added during the Civil War. Certainly it was done too crudely to have been a factory job.

The Modelo Militar (top) competed with the Model 1921. Although the latter prevailed, the Modelo Militar attracted enough favorable comment to encourage Echeverria to develop the concept further. This led to a wide range of Model 1911-type pistols.

Other pistols known to have been used in the Civil War were the .380 ACP caliber Llama Model II and the 9mm Largo caliber Llama Model IV. There were also the Tauler products in service with Spanish police, and even the Llama Model XI or "Especial," which chambered the 9mm Parabellum cartridge but was not placed in official use by the Spaniards for years to come. Nevertheless, the use of non-standard ammunition proved no impediment so long as the weapons in question were well-made and of modern design.

Several pistols made by Bonifacio Echeverria, the "Star maker," had already entered official service by 1936 and later saw use during the war. These included the Models A and B (9mm Largo caliber) and the *Modelo Militar* (see Chapter 5). Even Star pistols chambered in nonstandard calibers also saw heavy use (a photograph taken during the war shows a woman on the Republican side carrying a .32 ACP Star Model I pistol or its .380 caliber equivalent, a Model IN, thrust into her belt). The surviving Campo-Giro pistols were also taken out of storage and reissued, as were whatever Bergmann-Bayard (Model 1908) pistols had lasted from the dawn of Spanish automatic pistols nearly 30 years earlier. In a war, handguns of all ages and origins make their way to the front lines. Both guns cited above fired the standard 9mm Largo cartridge, making them especially valuable additions to the war effort despite their age. Another 9mm Largo caliber pistol used during the war and sometimes observed in old photographs was the odd Jo-lo-Ar *(see also Chapter 5)*. Though its makers had failed to sell this pistol to the authorities the first time around, the situation became too desperate during the Civil War for any combatant to turn down a functioning firearm.

As is the case in most wars, pistols played an important, though not crucial, role in the Spanish Civil War. While it is artillery and rifles that win wars, revolvers and automatic pistols occasionally do save the lives of soldiers who either don't have a rifle available or can't bring one into action fast enough because of its size. This advantage enjoyed by pistols helps explain their great popularity in a war zone. It's also the reason why soldiers will go to almost any lengths to get their hands on one. In the Spanish Civil War, more than in mot wars, pistols also served to help maintain order. The shooting of deserters was all too common, especially in the increasingly demoralized Republican armies in the latter stages of the war. Pistols also proved important to the cavalry, which played an important role during some of the offensives. In many areas, mostly around Madrid where trench warfare predominated, and in other cities where extensive house-to-house fighting took place, pistols once again proved highly useful, as they had in World War I.

Spain's economic downturn and the unrest that led to Republican rule and, finally, a civil war, all had a tremendous effect on the Spanish handgun industry. Between 1919 and 1920, many of the factories that had made pistols for the French failed in the recession following the collapse of the lucrative wartime business. Even in the period immediately before the Spanish Civil War began, several handgun firms had already failed due to tightening of export controls under the Republic, increasing foreign competition, and a worsening economic climate. Of the companies which had made such huge profits selling pistols to the Allies during the war, Urrejola had failed by 1925, followed in 1929-30 by Antonio Azpiri,

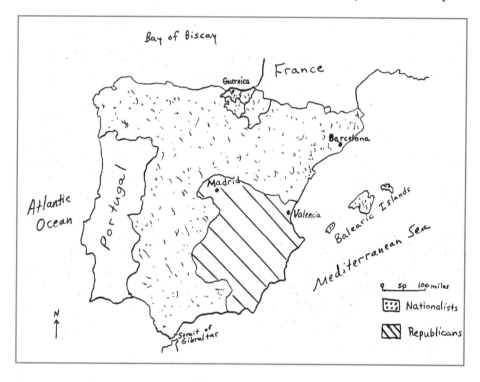

**Spain at War's End (March 1939)**
By war's end in March 1939 the Republican enclave consisted only of the southeast corner of the country. Note that both Madrid and the industrial city of Valencia remained under Republican control.

Berasaluce Arietio-Aurtena, Vincente Bernedo and Martin Bascaran (of "Martian" fame). By then, Spain had joined the worldwide depression afflicting even the most powerful industrialized nations.

With the Republic's rise to power in 1931, the Spanish arms industry fell under stricter government scrutiny than ever before. In August of 1931, an Arms Seizure Commission was appointed by the Republic to take inventory and distribute to government forces all firearms stored in arms factories throughout the provinces of Vuzcaya and Guipuzcoa. The commission also had a mandate to compensate various owners of the firms affected by the seizures. Eventually, the commission's assigned task underwent a change, enabling manufacturers to continue making pistols for commercial sale. The government commission did, however, closely supervise exports, granting licenses on a case-by-case basis. During this period, at least two more manufacturers who had been major players in world War I—Acha Hermanos and Arizmendi—both closed their doors. Thus, even before the Spanish Civil War began, the handgun manufacturing scene in Spain was beginning to change. A pattern developed whereby the smaller workshops were crowded out of business, while a handful of larger firms—Unceta (Astra), Gabilondo (Llama) and Echeverria (Star) among them—not only survived but prospered, thanks in large part to sizable government orders.

One might conclude that the production of Eibar-type pistols would actually have increased during the war, but the available evidence suggests otherwise. Certainly demand for pistols and all classes of firearms rose, but in the Basque region during 1936-1937 the dwindling supply of raw materials, soaring food prices and rampant inflation caused armaments production to fall significantly. To counteract these events, plenty of German, Italian, French and Russian firearms—especially rifles and machine guns—came pouring into the country. Later, following the war, Franco's victorious Nationalist government allowed only four Spanish companies to continue their production of handguns: Bonifacio Echeverria (Star), Echave y Arizmendi (Echasa), Gabilondo y Cia (Llama), and Unceta y Cia (Astra). By government order, all other companies which previously had produced handguns in Spain either went into other product lines or were closed down altogether.

Gabilondo's 20-shot Plus Ultra was used in large numbers by the Republicans' International Brigades. Note the awkwardly long grip, made necessary by the large, high-capacity magazine. The Plus Ultra was also available with a standard-length barrel and in a selective-fire version.

The war totally changed the world of handgun manufacture in Spain. In retrospect, the years 1914 to 1936, particularly during the early years of that period, had been a golden age for the gunmakers of northern Spain. Still, the post-Civil War years saw the four surviving companies produce a wider range of handgun designs together with improved quality. In some respects, it can be said that the Spanish handgun story underwent a renaissance after the Civil War. In the following chapters, we will trace the development of these four surviving handgun companies in Spain, along with the evolution of their product lines.

# Chapter 7

## World War II

A s is so often the case with neutral nations, Spain did a thriving business in World War II on both sides in the titanic struggle that engulfed nearly all of Europe. Mercifully for Spain, which was still recovering from its own recently concluded civil war, the country was spared direct involvement in the worldwide struggle against the Axis powers. France still had a large number of Spanish-made pistols on hand, with the vast majority being the various .32 caliber Ruby models with 9-shot magazines, plus smaller numbers of Star Military models, also in .32 caliber. These sturdy pistols remained in service from September 1939 to June 1940, when France suffered a disastrous defeat at the hands of Nazi Germany, followed by a humiliating occupation. French police forces reconstituted after the defeat and occupation also carried Ruby-type pistols, as did Vichy French police and those military forces that were allowed to exist (until November 1942) in parts of unoccupied France in accordance with the terms of the German peace treaty. Spanish-made pistols issued during World War I also found their way into the hands of French resistance forces in the ongoing struggle between French guerrillas and the German troops until France was liberated in 1944.

The Model 400 saw considerable service with the German armed forces, paving the way for acceptance of the later Model 600.

With the fall of France in June 1940, Great Britain stood alone against Germany for a time. As the Battle of Britain raged on in the summer of 1940, the British feared an invasion of their homeland was imminent. With that in mind, a British purchasing commission received a mandate to buy every type of handgun available that could still shoot. At this desperate juncture, the British were not at all choosy, buying weapons as diverse as Colt

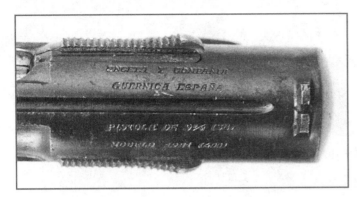

Late-production Model 400 pistols featured a four-line slide inscription.

Single Action Army frontier-style revolvers (in .357 Magnum caliber) from the United States and Ballester-Molina "Hafdasa" Model 1911-type automatic pistols from Argentina. Among these purchases were several thousand handguns from Spain, among them the Star Model A and the Llama Model IX, both in 9mm Largo caliber. Smaller numbers of Llama Model II (.380 ACP) and Star Model B and Llama Model XI pistols (both 9mm Parabellum) were also bought. By contrast, Unceta factory records reveal no sales of the company's Astra-brand pistols to the British armed forces. Apparently the British distrusted Astra's blowback configuration and its strange (to the British) handling characteristics.

When the threat of invasion passed, large numbers of domestic Enfield and Webley revolvers became available, along with imported Smith & Wesson revolvers, which most British military units still preferred over automatic pistols. As a result, Spanish handguns were quickly relegated to secondary duties until they were declared obsolete and sold as surplus following the war. By far the largest customer for Spanish handguns during the World War II period was Germany, which used them extensively. Between 1941 and 1944, the Germans bought several hundred thousand automatic pistols from three of the four Spanish pistol manufacturers still in business. In addition, commercial importers in Germany brought in

Most Astra Model 300s purchased by the Germans used checkered hardwood grips.

The Astra Model 300 (bottom), while seemingly undersized for a service pistol by U.S. standards, was popular with European and Asian countries who routinely issued small pistols to their armed forces personnel. Note the size comparison with the widely distributed Russian-designed Makarov pistol (top).

additional Spanish pistols for sale in what remained of the domestic firearms market. In considering these and other sales of Spanish handguns in Germany, the following manufacturers played important roles.

# *Astra Model 400*

Initially, Unceta y Cia, makers of the Astra pistol series, sent specimens of its pistols in current production to Germany. As business improved, Unceta modified its products to better suit German requirements, culminating in the creation of a new pistol—the Model 600—made in adherence to German requirements. Meanwhile, sales of the Model 400—still the official Spanish armed forces standard service pistol—continued apace. A total of 6,000 Model 400 pistols were sent to the Germans in two separate shipments: 4,500 pistols (serial numbers 92851 through 97350), arriving in Occupied France on October 18, 1941 for distribution to German units, and 1,500 pistols (serial numbers 97351 through 98850) reaching the German authorities on November 11. Spain also sent a large quantity of 9mm Largo (9mm Bergmann-Bayard) ammunition to the Germans. Although this round was developed at the turn of the century by a German manufacturer *(see Chapter 1)*, it was not a standard German army caliber.

These German-issue Model 400 pistols had all the late Spanish marks found on contemporary Model 400 pistols made for use in Spain, i.e., the pistol proof used from 1929 with a letter "P" inside a flaming bomb, the knight's-head, post-1931 House Proof, and the year code ("M" for 1941).

The Model 600 (bottom), which was designed originally for the German armed forces, was slightly smaller than the legendary Model 400 (top).

The magazine release on the Astra Model 600 (top) copied that of the earlier Model 300 pistol (bottom). Since the Model 600 fired the 9mm Parabellum cartridge—a larger and more powerful round than the .32 and .380 caliber ammunition used in the Model 300—it was by necessity a larger gun.

The Germans added no marks of their own to these well-made weapons and accepted the later Spanish proofing process as equivalent to their own. The finish on these pistols was blacker than the usual Spanish production. This suggested that a higher degree of surface preparation, such as polishing, was applied to the metal prior to the rust-bluing process. Apparently Unceta y Cia, in the hope of receiving future orders, set out to make a favorable impression on the fastidious Germans. The strategy worked.

The record compiled by the Astra Model 400 in German service was excellent, with one slight flaw. Because the Germans did not want to depend on a foreign supply of 9mm Largo (Bergmann-Bayard) ammunition, nor to undertake domestic manufacture of this nonstandard round in the middle of a war, they tried to utilize their own stocks of service standard 9mm Parabellum ammunition for the Astra pistols. The German military then discovered what American civilian shooters have since learned: The Model 400 is not wholly reliable with 9mm Parabellum ammunition. And since this round is significantly shorter—by about 4mm—than the 9mm Largo round, a 9mm Parabellum cartridge may not feed reliably into a Model 400 pistol. But even if it does, it might fall too far forward into the chamber for the firing pin to reach it. This distressing result led to a request by the Germans that Unceta develop a new Model 400 that was similar in construction but slightly smaller for optimal performance with the 9mm Parabellum round. This request led in 1943 to the Model 600, which is covered below.

# *Astra Model 300*

The German armed forces during World War II were quite devoted to small blowback-caliber automatic pistols. They found in Astra's Model 300 a handgun that was ideally suited to their needs. Initial deliveries of this pistol to German-occupied France occurred on October 18, 1941, when German authorities in the border town of Hendaye (near the strategic Spanish town of Irun) received 5,500 .380 caliber Model 300 pistols (in addition to the 4,500 Model 400 pistols cited above). These early Model 300 pistols had serial numbers in the following ranges: 533894 to 533900; 533951 to 535000; 535851 to 538651; and 538659 to 540300. A second shipment of five hundred .380 caliber Astra Model 300 pistols arrived in Occupied France on November 11, 1941 (serial numbers 540301 to 540800).

Unceta y Cia kept making Model 300s in .380 caliber for the Germans. The table below lists the various shipments of Model 300 pistols in .380 caliber shipped from the Unceta y Cia factory to the Germans in 1942.

| DATE | QUANTITY | SERIAL NUMBERS |
|------|----------|----------------|
| April 30 | 3,200 | 541801-545000 |
| June 12 | 3,000 | 545001-548000 |
| July 12 | 3,000 | 548001-551000 |
| August 13 | 2,500 | 551001-553500 |
| October 8 | 2,500 | 553501-556000 |
| December 19 | 3,000 | 556001-559000 |

During 1943, shipments of Model 300 pistols in .380 caliber to the German armed forces continued. Pistols delivered to the Germans during 1943 included serial numbers beginning at 559001 and ending at 591800. A final shipment took place on July 21, 1944, when 7,000 pistols (serial numbers 613451 to 613650 and 615801 to 622600) reached German-occupied France only days before advancing Allied armies sealed off the Franco-Spanish border. Thus ended all deliveries of Spanish small arms to the crumbling Third Reich. Unceta y Cia had delivered a total of 63,000 Model 300 pistols in .380 caliber for use by German armed forces.

The Astra Model 600 shares a high level of accuracy inherent to all Astra "tubular" pistols. This 5-shot offhand group, which was fired from a distance of 50 feet, looks more like a 25-foot target fired from a lesser pistol.

The early Model 300 pistols in .380 caliber delivered to the Germans resembled Astra's standard production for Spain's official bodies and commercial sale. The grips were made of checkered hard rubber complete with the "UC" (Unceta y Cia) logo and the caliber marking—9mm & 380—stamped on the barrel hood. These features were commonly found on pistols made for Spanish consumption. When serial number 552000 was delivered to the Germans on August 13, 1942, Unceta had by then changed the configuration of the Model 300 slightly to bring it more in line with accepted German practice. Like any smart company trying to satisfy a steady customer, Unceta y Cia changed the grip material to checkered hardwood and the caliber marking to 9mm Kurz. All but the earliest .380 caliber Model 300 pistols had a *Waffenamt* ("Weapons Office") stamp applied to the right side of the grip tang bearing the number 251 beneath a stylized Nazi eagle. These signified the inspection and eventual acceptance of the Model 300 pistols into German service by the Army Weapons Office set up in Hendaye (Occupied France). The Astra's sunburst logo appeared on the forward portion of the slide, behind the front sight, while the left grip tang displayed the Eibar house proof (a

The Astra Model 600 (bottom) was used by the German armed forces as a supplement to their standard pistol, the P38 (top).

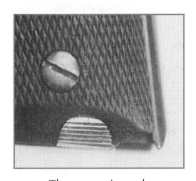

The magazine release used on Astra Model 300 and 600 pistols differed from that of the company's earlier Model 400, in which the release was pushed in from left to right rather than straight back.

knight's helmeted head and shield), the year code (M for 1941, N for 1942, Ñ for 1943 and O for 1944), and the official proofmark for the automatic pistol: a flaming bomb with the letter P inside it. This last mark was repeated on the left rear portion of the slide. The complete serial number for these pistols appeared on the slide (right rear portion) as well as the right rear portion of the frame, above the grip safety.

Unceta's Astra Model 300 in .380 caliber was also produced in .32 ACP caliber, with some 22,390 variants serving in the German military. The first of these arrived in Occupied France on January 5, 1942, consisting of 400 pistols (serial numbers 540901 to 541300). In 1943, however, no Model 300 .32 caliber were shipped to the German, whereupon Unceta y Cia concentrated instead on producing the .380 caliber variant described above. During 1944, some 21,990 Model 300 pistols in .32 caliber were delivered to the Germans in three separate shipments: 10,000 on February 24, another 10,000 on April 1, and 1,990 on July 21, with serial numbers running from 593001 to 615800. The final shipment of .32 caliber Model 300 pistols arrived in France on July 21, 1944, each with checkered wooden grips but without the *Waffenamt* stamp found on most of the later .380 caliber Model 300 pistols sent to Germany. Other markings—including the Astra logo behind the rear sight and the proofmarks and serial numeration—were the same as described earlier for the .380 caliber variant. Ironically, the Germans traditionally preferred .32 ACP to .380 for their medium-frame

Although Unceta's Astra Model 900 pistols (top) were considerably larger than the more efficient tubular designs of the Model 600 (bottom), they were well received by the Germans because of their similarity to the Mauser pistol then in widespread use.

Since Germany's adoption of the popular Luger pistol in 1908, all Star Model Bs made for the Germans had an "08" caliber designation.

pocket automatic pistols, and yet many more of the .380 caliber Model 300 pistols served in the German armed forces during the Nazi era than the .32 caliber variant by a ratio of nearly three to one.

Exactly where and how the Germans used their Model 300 pistols remains a mystery. Firearms researcher Edward C. Ezell and others have maintained that the German *Luftwaffe* (Air Force) was the major customer. While the earlier Condor Legion procurement of Model 300 pistols during the Spanish Civil War is well documented *(see Chapter 6)*, and whereas this small pistol certainly served well as an efficient pistol for air crews, there exist no records to establish firmly any purchases by the *Luftwaffe* during wartime. One place where the sale of Model 300 pistols has been confirmed was in Norway, where the Germans maintained a large garrison defending against a possible Allied invasion or to counter raids by British Commandos. The Model 300s were also used by the Allies serving in Norway to suppress the powerful local Resistance movement, and to support Germany's extensive naval and air force concentrations in that country. Indeed, Norway's geographic location astride the shortest route

The Star Model B pistols shipped to Germany during World War II had four distinct variations in their slide markings.

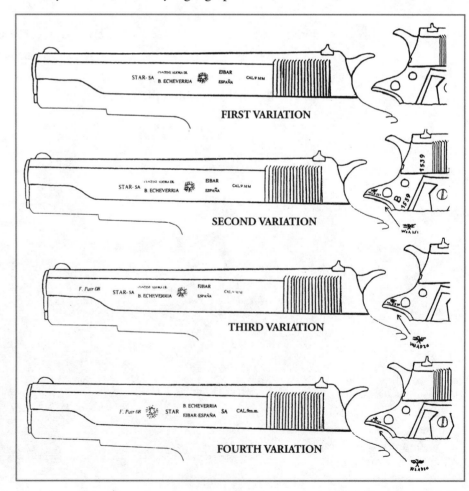

**FIRST VARIATION**

**SECOND VARIATION**

**THIRD VARIATION**

**FOURTH VARIATION**

*Spanish Handguns*

from Great Britain to the USSR made it an ideal place to establish bases charged with the interdiction of Allied shipping. Despite Germany's extensive military and naval presence in Norway, it remained a secondary war theater compared to Russia and France. The use by the Germans of Model 300 pistols in Norway freed up more powerful handguns for use in the primary theaters of war.

# Astra Model 600

In 1943, the German government requested that Unceta y Cia make a version of the Model 400 geared to the 9mm Parabellum cartridge (which was then standard German issue). In response, the company developed the Model 600, which was virtually identical to the Model 400 but slightly smaller, with the following specifications: **Overall Length:** 7.9 inches; **Barrel Length:** 5.2 inches; **Width:** 1.3 inches; **Height:** 5.1 inches, and **Weight:** (unloaded) 35 ounces. Magazine capacity of the Model 600 was eight rounds but it worked only with the 9mm Parabellum cartridge and could not fire the 9mm Largo, 9mm Steyr, .38 Auto, and so on, the way the Model 400 could. Unceta

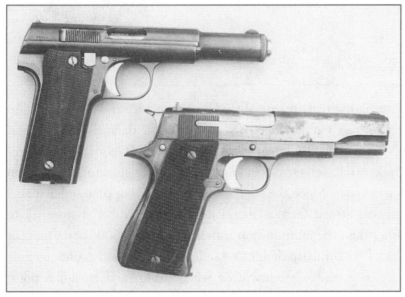

The Germans kept Spanish arms manufacturers busy during World War II. Unceta y Cia supplied its Astra Model 600 (top), while Bonifacio Echeverria sent 27,000 of its Star Model B pistols (bottom) to the Nazis.

developed the "new" design in late 1943 and sent 50 test samples of the modified pistol to the Germans, who accepted it as the *Pistole Astra 600/43*, ordering 50,000 of them. Delivery of the first batch of 2,950 production pistols (serial numbers 51-3000) took place on May 16, 1944, with another 5,000 (numbers 30001-8000) arriving in German-controlled France on June 23. The final shipment of 2,500 Model 600 pistols (serial numbers 8001-10500) arrived in France on July 16, only a week before the advancing Allied armies cut off the overland route between Spain and France. In all, 10,450 Model 600s were delivered to German forces during the Nazi regime. Collectors now identify these guns as the "First Contract."

Another 31,350 Model 600 pistols (serial numbers 10501-41850) had been paid for by Nazi Germany but were never delivered because the Franco-Spanish border had been sealed off. Unceta y Cia rerouted these guns to the Spanish government, which stored them in an arsenal until 1951, when they were sold—a second time—to West Germany. Because

Making the Model B for the 9mm Parabellum cartridge (rather than the longer 9mm Largo round preferred by Spain's armed forces) enabled Star to produce a pistol that was appreciably more graceful than the Model A.

The Star Model B in 9mm Parabellum, while based closely on the .45 ACP caliber Model 1911, is a slimmer and handier pistol because of the smaller cartridge it fires.

these guns were originally intended for German service and are identical to the "First Contract" guns, collectors now refer to them as the "Second Contract." These guns were used extensively by West German police until the late 1960s, when Interarms bought the remaining guns for importation to the United States. Since the Model 600 began as a special order model for the German armed forces, Unceta decided to number it from 01 to 59400. Other than the ammunition it uses, the Model 600 shares most of the features of its similarly designed Model 400. Its good points include excellent accuracy and reliability, even when using modern hollowpoint ammunition favored by knowledgeable shooters who share an interest in handguns for self-defense.

Shortcomings of the Model 600 include its undersized sights and stiff trigger pull. As with Astra's other "tubular" pistols—including the ancestral Model 400 and the related Models 300, 600 and 700 derived from it—the Model 600 with its "hammerless" design bothers people who want a visible hammer that indicates whether or not the weapon is cocked and ready to fire. Also, due to its unlocked breech or blowback construction, the Model 600 has an overly strong recoil spring for containing chamber pressure, resulting in a stiff slide that's difficult for people with weak hands to retract. The stiff recoil spring makes disassembly for mainte-nance and reassembling harder still. Despite

these failings, the Model 600 remains an excellent service pistol—a highly accurate, rugged and reliable weapon capable of defending its owner under the worst conditions.

# Astra Model 900 Series

While the famous Mauser Model 1896—the so-called "Broomhandle"—never won the coveted contract as Germany's standard armed forces service pistol, it saw extensive use in both World Wars as a substitute standard weapon. It was also highly popular as a personal weapon, one which many German and Austrian soldiers bought privately. At the beginning of World War II, the Nazi government took over the large remaining stock of unsold Mauser Model 1932 pistols (commercially designated Model 712), which were the "Schnellfeuer" (selective-fire) version of the Model 1896. Tens of thousands of these powerful 7.62mm weapons went to the Waffen SS, with another 7,800 going to the German air force.

The Model B's grip is well-liked by fans of 1911-type pistols. Note the slight forward extension at the bottom front ("toe") of the grip and the checkered rear gripstrap.

When Mauser quite making its Model 1896 variants in 1937, and with pistols of this type remaining popular, Unceta y Cia took up the slack with its Astra Model 900 series. Germany was sent 1,050 of these new pistols on March 23, 1943 (serial numbers 29555-29600; 29649-50; 29655-29660; 29667-29675; and 32788-33774) to German army headquarters in Hendaye, France, and from there to the German army. Interestingly, those guns with serial numbers in the 29000 range were all built between 1934 and 1935. After that, the Franco government severely restricted the manufacture of such weapons following the Spanish Civil War. Consequently, Astra Model 900 pistols sent to the Germans bear year codes stamped G for 1934 and H for 1935. Because Franco owed so much to the Germans for helping him win the war in Spain, his victorious Nationalist government allowed Unceta y Cia to produce a large run of guns for the *Wehrmacht*. That explains why the later year codes—LL for 1940 and M for 1941—are seen on Astra Model 900s with serial numbers from 32788 on up *(see the Appendix for a fuller discussion of Spanish year codes)*. The serial numbers on all Astra Model 900 pistols appeared on the left side of the frame, above the grooved wooden grip, with two Spanish proofmarks and a year code located on the right side of the frame (above the trigger and slightly ahead of the takedown crossbolt that holds the barrel extension to the frame). The German army received its Model 900 pistols with detachable wooden shoulder stocks hollowed out to receive the pistol when it wasn't clipped to the rear of the frame, thereby turning the weapon into a carbine. The shoulder stock/holster assembly also bore the same serial number (carved on the inside of the lid) as the gun itself.

Model B pistols made under German contract indicate extensive serialization. This early postwar Model B delivered to the West German police in 1952, for example, has a full serial number on the rear of the frame behind the magazine (top) repeating the last three digits on the muzzle bushing (middle), the front of the magazine floorplate (bottom), and the slide stop (right).

Unceta's Astra Model 902 also received its share of business from the German *Wehrmacht*. This model differed from earlier Model 900s with its selector mechanism, offering a choice of semi-automatic or fully-automatic fire at a cyclic rate of about 850 rounds per minute. The Model 902 also had a longer magazine with a 20-round capacity designed to increase the time spent between reloadings. On March 23, 1943, the German forces in France received 13 of these weapons (serial numbers 13160; 13167; 13184; 21519; 22478; 26706; 26711; 26713; 16726-8; and 26731-2) along with 987 Astra Model 903s. The Germans also bought nearly 2,100 selective-fire Astra Model 903s from Unceta, which represented well over half the total production of this type of fully-automatic weapon *(see also Chapters 4 and 5)*. It was, of all the Astra Models, most similar to the Mauser Model 712 *Schellfeuerpistole*. The Model 903 was the first of the 900 series pistols to have a detachable magazine, one that could be reloaded by pushing fresh ammunition from stripper clips into the mechanism, or by detaching the empty magazine from the pistol and replacing it with a loaded one (Unceta supplied the Model 903 with both 10-round and 20-round magazines as standard equipment). On November 26, 1940, Unceta delivered 1,004 of these pistols to Hendaye (Occupied France) for distribution to German army units. These pistols had the following serial numbers: 28972; 28975; 29647-8; and 30801-31800. A final shipment of 1,000 Astra Model 902 and 903 machine pistols went to Germany on March 23, 1943. The 987 Model 903s included in this shipment had serial numbers ranging from 31801 to 32787.

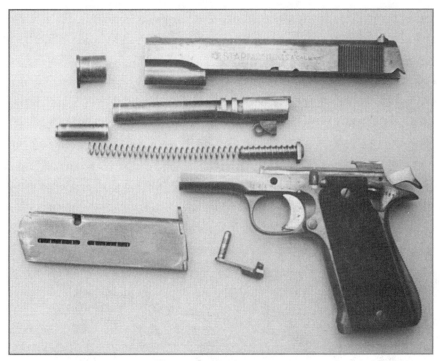

When disassembled, the Star Model B closely resembles the Colt Model 1911.

The German government also ordered 1,510 of Unceta's smallest handgun: the Model 200 pistol in 6.35mm (.25 ACP) caliber. These tiny pistols—numbered 503926 to 503935 and 504501 to 506000—may not have had much military use, but small arms like these proved extraordinarily popular among German soldiers in both World Wars. These little weapons, which served tank crews, flight crews, and high-ranking officers, were often concealed in tunic and pants pockets as hideaway or backup weapons for use in the event of capture. As with many other Spanish pistols bought by the Germans during World War II, they applied no identifying marks of their own on these weapons; but at least a few still have the "Geco" stamp belonging to the Gustav Genschow Company of Hamburg, which imported them into Germany. These pistols can also be identified by serial number. In any event, wartime business proved extremely important to Unceta y Cia. In addition to small-scale British orders in 1940, the company produced a total of 104,450 pistols (Models 200, 300, 400, 600 and 900) for Germany's armed forces, whose purchases comprised the lion's share of the company's sales from 1941 to 1944.

## *Bonifacio Echeverria (Star) Model B*

When it was introduced in 1933, the Star Model B became Spain's first production pistol to chamber the increasingly popular 9mm Parabellum cartridge. Following its use in World War I by the Germans for their Parabellum P08 (Luger) and Mauser Model 1896 ("Red Nine") pistols and MP-18 Bergmann submachine guns, manufacturers in other parts of the world soon came to recognize the extraordinary power which this comparatively compact round could produce. To their credit, Bonifacio Echeverria's designers were among the first foreigners to recognize the potential of this cartridge. The company's Model B combined the mechanical features of the Model A pistol *(see Chapter 4)* with the improved handling features of the 1936-vintage Colt Model 1911A1 and the 9mm

Parabellum cartridge to produce an excellent combat handgun. Even now, many knowledgeable shooters regard the Star Model B as one of the best handguns ever made for military use.

The Model B strongly resembled the Colt M1911A1, except that the Star pistol lacked the Colt's grip safety and was much slimmer and more graceful than the Colt, thanks to its use of the smaller 9mm Parabellum cartridge instead of the .45 ACP round for which John Browning designed the Colt Model 1911. The Germans proved to be one of the most enthusiastic buyers of Star Model B pistols, purchasing 27,000 of this model during World War II alone, plus many thousands later on for West German police forces. Four variations of Star Model B pistols are recognized by collectors

The Model B (right) excels as a military pistol. It actually out-performed the ultra-modern SIG/Sauer P226 (left) in 5-shot offhand groups fired from 25 feet.

as having been purchased during the Nazi era for use by German armed forces. The "First Variation" shipment, consisting of 4,000 Model B pistols, arrived in Occupied France in two separate lots of 2,000 each on May 15 and May 28, 1942. These pistols (serial numbers 210951-214950) had no German markings whatsoever. Aside from their serial numbers, they cannot be distinguished from typical Spanish production.

The "Second Variation" of Star Model B pistols imported by the Germans consisted of 7,999 units shipped to German army headquarters in Hendaye, France, on July 26, 1943, of which 4,000 were intended for German army use, with the remaining 3,999 going to the German navy. Those pistols intended for army use had the same Spanish markings on the left side of the slide as the First Variation pistols described above. These Second Variation guns, however, had a German acceptance stamp added to the right grip tang. It consisted of a stylized eagle over the inscription WaA

The Star Model B and its competing Llama "Especial" both have efficient square-notch rear sights that are larger than the tiny sights found on earlier Spanish pistols.

Unlike the Colt Model 1911, the Star Model B has an exposed extractor, which actually makes the Model B a better pistol than its American ancestor.

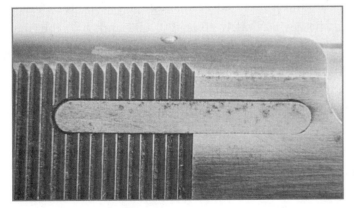

251 (WaA standing for *Waffen Amt*, meaning "Weapons Office"). Second Variation Model B pistols used by the German army had the following serial numbers: 214953-216200; 216251-217502; 222457-222675; 222701-222750 and 223776-225006. Some pistols used by the German navy also had the WaA acceptance stamp, but most did not. Serial numbers on these Second Variation Model B pistols used by the German navy were as follows (reading left to right):

| | |
|---|---|
| *217503-218042* | *218044-218048* |
| *218050-218123* | *218125-219400* |
| *219501-219530* | *219532-219950* |
| *220026-220942* | *220944-221200* |
| *221976-222456* | |

The "Third Variation" of Star Model B pistols during the Nazi era consisted of 5,000 pistols, half of which went to the army and half to the navy. They were delivered to the Germans on May 29, 1944, only a week before the D-Day invasion of Normandy. These Model Bs bore serial numbers 244503-247002 for German army service, and 242003-244502 for the navy. A German caliber designation *(Patr 08)* was added to the slide inscription. The acceptance stamp on the right grip tang appeared as WaAD20. The fourth and last variation of Model B pistols to reach the German armed forces during the war kept the Germanic caliber designation of the Third Variation slide markings, but it moved the company's distinctive starburst logo to a location in front of the factory name rather than behind it as in earlier variations. This shipment of 8,000 pistols (serial numbers 248001-254300 and 254551-256250) reached the German army headquarters in Hendaye on June 6, 1944, the day the Allied armies landed at Normandy.

A "Fifth Variation" of 2,000 Model B pistols (serial numbers 256251-25800 and 260001-260250) was also ordered by the German government and shipped by Echeverria on June 7, 1944. However, it failed to reach the German army because by then the Allied invasion had sealed off the Spanish border. These same guns were later used by the West German police, many of them with an "LPN" stamp on the front gripstrap. These "Fifth Variation" Star Model B pistols are analogous in every way to Unceta's "Second Contract" Astra Model 600 guns, which also failed to arrive in time for Nazi military service but saw extensive police use in West Germany.

*Chapter 7*

# Gabilondo y Cia (Llama)

During World War II, 9mm Parabellum caliber Llama Model XI and earlier Models VIII and IX (sometime rechambered to 9mm Parabellum caliber from the slightly longer 9mm Largo round), as well as .380 caliber Model III pistols, all served in smaller numbers with various armed forces. Unlike the Astra and Star pistols, the Llamas never achieved service standard status but were instead limited- or substitute-standard issue. As such, specifics about their service and serial numbers are far less clear than for the most famous pistols covered in this chapter.

In addition to official orders from the German military, Gustav Genschow AG of Hamburg also imported 6.35mm (.25 ACP) Astra Model 200 pistols from Unceta and 7.65mm (.32 ACP) Llama Model 1 pistols during the wartime years. These pistols were made available for purchase by military personnel for personal use and by civil servants, especially Germans working in occupied territories and foreigners working for Germany.

In common with many versions of the Model 1911, the Model B's trigger features vertical grooves.

# Conclusion

Spain's large production of pistols for the various nations involved in World War II was important if only for the volume of business it generated on behalf of Astra, Llama-Gabilondo and Star. Even more important was the fact that this large-scale production of military-style handguns of advanced design and high quality did much to rehabilitate the reputation of the Spanish handgun industry. Perhaps aware of increased scrutiny by Spain's handgun production, Spain's proofhouses enforced the 1924 proof law rigorously. As a result, the quality of Spanish pistols improved over anything that had been accomplished by the industry up to that time. The Astra Models 300, 400, 600 and 900, the Star Models A and B and the Llama Models I, III, VIII and XI all were made to high standards during the war years. These excellent pistols of high quality workmanship and advanced design gained much more respect than the often questionable Ruby-type pistols of World War I. As firearms authority W.H.B. Smith once reported a few months after World War II finally indeed: "The era of the Spanish booby-trap pistol is over." This improvement in Spanish pistol standards continued after the war and indeed has remained in force to the present day.

# Chapter 8

# Astra (Unceta) Since 1945

n 1946, Unceta y Cia underwent a reorganization that enabled the company to expand its product line to include such industrial products as pneumatic hammers, pumps and textile machinery. However, the company's name change in 1953 to Astra-Unceta y Cia, S.A. indicated that, despite a broader product line, automatic pistols bearing the Astra brand name remained the company's chief source of income, just as it had since the company's founding in 1908. Later, in 1958, Astra-Unceta y Cia received permission from the Franco regime to expand its handgun line, including a series of high-quality revolvers based on Smith & Wesson designs, but with some notable changes.

Unceta y Cia began its postwar production of automatic pistols by continuing the pistol models it had begun before the war. But the company soon modified its entire line of automatic pistols, first by adding exposed hammers to its "tubular pistol" designs and then eventually eliminating the tubular pistols altogether (with one exception: the Model 4000 or "Falcon") in favor of more modern arms based on the various Walther and SIG products, a practice which Astra-Unceta y Cia continues to the present.

The Model 2000 is a small, sleek pistol well-suited for concealed personal protection. Note the Eibar-type safety jut above the trigger, and the pushbutton magazine release on the lower left corner of the frame.

## Model 600

In 1943, Unceta y Cia had modified its successful Model 400 into the Model 600, creating an improved 9mm Parabellum caliber service pistol that satisfied Germany's armed forces, then Unceta's best customer. Once the company realized that the increasingly popular 9mm Parabellum caliber might be a commercial success, it continued production of the Model 600 through 1945, advertising the pistol widely—a necessity since tens of thousands of these pistols had been earmarked for the Germans and were now undeliverable. Thanks to these efforts,

Unceta exported an additional 3,550 Model 600 pistols to various countries during the late 1940s and early 1950s. These sales included the following:

| COUNTRY | DATE | QUANTITY | SERIAL NUMBERS |
|---|---|---|---|
| *Chile* | 1950 | 450 | 43601-44050 |
| *Costa Rico* | 1949 | 100 | 43201-43300 |
| *Egypt* | 1951 | 25 | 42588-42612 |
| *Jordan* | 1951 | 200 | 44301-44500 |
| *Portugal* | 1951 | 800 | 44501-45300 |
| *Thailand* | 1950 | 15 | 43391-43405 |
| *Turkey* | 1949 | 100 | 43001-43100 |
| *Ankara (Turkey) Police* | 1949 | 100 | 43101-43200 |

In the late 1950s Unceta y Cia sold an additional 14,000 Model 600 pistols to West Germany, over and above the 31,350 Second Contract pistols that were never delivered in 1944 but were sent to West Germany following Germany's defeat in World War II. This final Model 600 installment had serial numbers ranging from 45401 to 59400. Total Model 600 production was 59,400, including a run of 15 Model 600s (numbers 43406-43420) all chambered in 7.65mm (.32 ACP) caliber. Although Unceta released only small numbers of Model 600 pistols from its inventory for civilian sale, surplus Model 600s once owned by the West German police have been a mainstay of the used-handgun market in the United Sates. Survivors of the original "First Contract" Model 600 pistols, which were actually used by German forces during World War II (as indicated by the *Waffenamt* stamping on the right rear grip tang), command a collector's

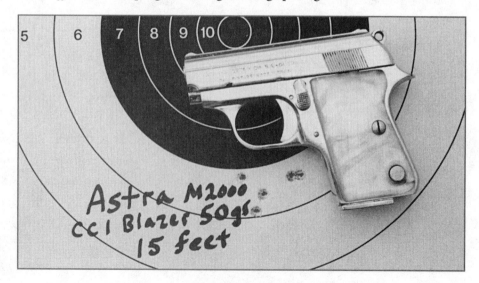

This 5-shot offhand group fired from 15 feet measures 1.1 inches across. The tiny .22 Short or .25 ACP cartridges give the Astra Model 2000 almost no recoil despite its light weight (less than a pound fully loaded).

premium up to 100% for guns in good condition. In 1996, Portuguese navy pistols marked MRP (for *Marinha Republica de Portugal*, or Navy of the Republic of Portugal) on the upper left portion of the slide also became available on the surplus market for the first time. Many of these pistols were in excellent condition.

# Model 700

In 1945 Unceta y Cia created the Model 700—a modified Model 400—for possible adoption by the Spanish armed forces as replacements for the Model 1921 (Model 400) standard service pistol. While the old Model 1921/400 had served well, an updating of its design was deemed necessary. A year later, Unceta sent 20 prototype models of the 9mm Largo caliber Model 700 with concealed hammer for service trials, along with what later became the Astra Model 800 *(see below)* with an exposed-hammer design in 9mm Parabellum caliber. Both Models were "tubular" designs as evidence of the Model 400's influence. The Model 700 differed only in its graceful curved grip backstrap and a new loaded-chamber indicator pin that was accessible by means of a removable rear sight. The weight of the rearmost portion of the slide was reduced and the heel-mounted magazine release was replaced. It now resembled the magazine release on the Model 300 and Model 600 pistols. The Model 700 had the exact same specifications as the Model 1921, so that all shipping crates, holsters and other containers and

Unceta y Cia's Model 800 or Condor pistol closely resembles its predecessor, the Model 600, but with an exposed hammer and repositioned magazine release.

PISTOLA AUTOMÁTICA
**CONDOR**

**ASTRA** *Unceta y Compañia,* S.A.
**GUERNICA** (VIZCAYA) ESPAÑA

accessories already in Spanish service worked efficiently with the new gun. The thumb safety, grip safety, magazine safety and disassembly procedures of the Model 700 were all identical to those of the earlier Model 1921 or 400 pistols, ensuring that soldiers who were already trained to handle the Model 1921 would experience no difficulty in switching to the new pistol.

Unfortunately, this handsome and well-balanced pistol failed to impress the Spanish servicemen who tested it. They felt it didn't offer enough advantages over the Model 1921 pistols already in service to justify its adoption. In particular, the Model 700's disassembly procedure and unlocked breech (blowback) mechanism made it more difficult to shoot than a locked-breech pistol. Following this rejection as the next Spanish service pistol, Unceta decided not to put the Model 700 into series production, feeling that its loss of prestige and a waning interest in the 9mm Largo cartridge (outside of Spain) would limit its sales. Only 19 Model 700 prototypes and one chrome-plated cutaway model were ever made. This regrettable decision deprived the world of what was arguably the best of an excellent breed: the tubular pistols of Unceta y Cia. As it was, the exposed-hammer 9mm Parabellum caliber Model 800, which the company placed into production instead, proved to be an inferior gun.

Unceta y Cia introduced its Model 357 revolver in 1971. Although it was made to fire the .357 Magnum cartridge, the Astra Model 357 also fires the similar .38 Special round. The photo shows the four-inch barrel model. (Photo courtesy of Interarms)

# Model 3000

In addition to marketing the full-sized Model 600 during the early postwar period, and in its attempts to interest Spain's armed forces in a replacement for the Model 400, Unceta found room for improvement in the old reliable Model 300 compact pistol. This model had been discontinued in 1947 after a production run of 171,300 units since 1923, of which nearly half—85,390 pistols in all—had been sent to Germany during World War II. Production of the Astra Model 3000 began in 1946 and represented Unceta's attempt to update the Model 300 by improving the shape of the grip, changing the magazine release (a pushbutton positioned on the left rear portion of the triggerguard) and adding a loaded-

The Model 5000 or Constable (top) owes a considerable debt to German-designed double-action pistols, notably Walther's famous Model PPK (bottom).

chamber indicator. Aside from these slight changes, the Model 3000 boasted the same compact dimensions, solidity and reliability of design that had made the Model 300 a favorite among military and police forces around the world.

Regrettably, times had changed and the Model 3000 never proved popular with military and police forces. The latest vogues in service pistols then were the double-action designs with exposed hammers and the more powerful 9mm Parabellum cartridge. Thus the Model 3000, with its revamped 1920s design and relatively low-powered .32 and .380 cartridges, held scant appeal for the world's police forces and armies. Civilian shooters, however, liked its concealed carry and bought it in the tens of thousands. Because civilian sales became such a significant factor in the early postwar days, Unceta codified and systematized the optional service of embellishing its pistols with special finishes, engravings and fancy grip materials, which it had offered since the early 1900s.

This embellishing service, having taken form in the Astra Model 3000 line, led the company to produce a standard pistol with blued finish and black checkered plastic grips under the name Model 3000. There followed several variants in the Model 3000 lines:

| MODEL NUMBER | QUANTITY | FEATURES |
| --- | --- | --- |
| 3001 | 4,317 | Chrome finish |
| 3002 | 2,433 | Shallow engraving; silver-plated finish |
| 3003 | 1,051 | Deep engraving; silver plating |
| 3004* | 135 | Gold damascene inlaid and engraved |
| 3005 | 142 | Gold plating |
| 3006** | 96 | Extensive engraving; gold-plated finish |

*Unceta sent one of the Model 3004s to General Franco, president of Spain (1939-1975)
** Model 3006 was eight times as expensive as the standard pistol

Although the Model 3000 attracted relatively little interest or demand, Unceta's advertising concentrated on the long-established success of the earlier "tubular" pistols, such as the Models 300, 400 and 600 (which the Model 3000 strongly resembled). Here, in translation, is the introduction (in part) to the owner's manual:

*For many decades now our firm has been producing firearms. Based on experience gathered in this sector, and thanks to ultra-modern manufacturing processes, we have been able to create the Astra 3000 auto pistol, a top model that, through simple but ingenious design, has finally solved technical and ballistic problems to a degree not solved by any other pistol. The Astra 3000 is guaranteed to function consistently without a hitch, even when subjected to continual use under ruthless conditions. The Spanish government appreciated the fine properties of the Astra pistol, subsequent to grueling trials, and issued it to the Army, Navy, Air Force, Guardia Civil, Customs, Border Patrol, Prison Wardens, Government Agents, etc. Many foreign armies and police departments are likewise equipped with [Astra handguns]. Special features: supreme accuracy, excellent pointability, thumb safety which blocks the trigger, grip safety, cartridge indicator (this is an important safety precaution, since the indicator can be seen or felt in the dark when a cartridge is in the firing chamber), and slide stop. The mechanics of the pistol [are] extremely simple, consisting of only a few parts, which greatly facilitates stripping and reassembly. There are no sprung pins or screws. All working parts are in the slide and receiver, protected against corrosive powder gases, dust, dirt and snow. (Translation excerpted from "Famous Automatic Pistols and Revolvers")*

By civilian standards, the Model 3000 was quite successful despite the lack of large military and police orders. Moreover, good war-surplus pistols of similar size and caliber were flooding the markets at the same time Unceta was producing the Model 3000. The two most significant importers of Model 3000 pistols were in West Germany and the United States. The Gustav Genschow Company in Hamburg handled the Model 3000 imports to Germany while the Garcia Corporation brought these pistols into the U.S. Eventually, Unceta sold 44,839 Model 3000 pistols of all types, with serial numbers ranging from 630476 to 648600 (1946-1947); 663201-663250 (1949); 663301-678000 (1950 to 1952); 710001-720500 (1952); 720501-721000 (1955); and 721012-721975 (1956). Unceta discontinued the Model 3000 in 1956 and turned toward the Model 4000.

## Astra Model 2000 "Cub"

In 1954, as part of its policy of updating existing pistols in favor of similar designs with exposed hammers, Unceta introduced the Model 2000, or Cub, subcompact pistol. Its purpose was to supplement and eventually supplant the smallest pistol in its line: the Model 200 Firecat. Though the Model 2000 has not been imported into the U.S. since December 1968 (the Gun Control Act of 1968 requires that a handgun must be at least four inches high with a combined height plus length of at least 10 inches), it remains in production and is still one of Astra's most popular models.

Though not the smallest pistol Unceta has made—the slightly smaller Model 200 holds that particular distinction—the Model 2000 has the following specifications:   **Length:** $4^2/_5$"; **Barrel Length:** $2^1/_4$"; **Width:** $^8/_{10}$ths"; **Height:** $3^1/_3$"; **Weight:** (unloaded) 13 ounces; **Capacity:** 7 rounds in .22 Short caliber; 6 rounds in .25 ACP. The Model 2000 is truly a compact, concealable and eminently portable handgun. The most obvious external difference between it and the Model 200 is that the former has an exposed, rounded hammer visible at the rear of the slide, while the hammer on the Model 200 was concealed within the frame and slide (with the pistol fully assembled and ready to fire). Like the Model 200—and indeed all Unceta-made handguns until the introduction of the Cadix revolver and Constable automatic pistol—the Model 2000 is a single-action design.

In 1980 Unceta y Cia followed the Model 367 (top) with a similar but larger Model 44 chambered for the .44 Magnum cartridge. The stainless-steel Model 44 with a 6-inch barrel appeared in Interarms' 1989 catalog and remained in production until 1993.

Before firing this pistol, the shooter must cock the hammer, either by retracting and releasing the slide or by drawing the hammer to the rear with one thumb over a loaded firing chamber. Unlike the Model 200, which in its later improved versions used manual, magazine and grip safeties (the so-called "Triple Safety" popularized by FN), the Model 2000 design eliminated the grip safety altogether. It does retain, however, the Eibar-type manual safety and magazine safety. In addition to offering the Model 2000 in a choice of .25 ACP and .22 Short calibers, Unceta provides a variety of finishes, including the standard blued finish, which had been a rust-blued process until 1957 and is now a salt blue. Plated finishes include satin nickel and chrome, while deluxe engraved versions are available plated in blued, satin nickel, chrome, silver and gold. In 1994 Astra Sport, S.A. (the modern name for Unceta y Cia) began making a stainless steel version of this model as well.

## A S T R A

.44 MAGNUM

.357 MAGNUM

LARGE frame, big-bore revolvers are an Astra specialty. Workmanship, rich finish and close attention to manufacturing details are on a par with any modern revolver made today. Produced in three big-bore calibers — in the most popular barrel lengths — Astra revolvers offer wide application for sport, personal defense and law enforcement use. Forged steel construction, massive cylinders, magnum sized bolts and recessed chambers (full 360° case-head support) make these some of the strongest available. A unique four-position adjustment for main spring tension tailors the trigger pull to your precise specifications.

*SPECIFICATIONS*
ASTRA BIG-BORE REVOLVERS

| Caliber: | .357 Mag. | .44 Mag. | .45 ACP |
|---|---|---|---|
| Finish: | Blue | Stainless | Blue |
| Capacity | 6-Rds. | 6-Rds. | 6-Rds. |
| Barrel: | 3" - 4" | | |
| | 6" - 8½" | 6" | 6" |
| Overall: | 8½" - 9½" | | |
| | 11½" - 13½" | 11½" | 11½" |
| Weight: | 2¼ - 2½ | | |
| | or 2¾ lbs. | 2½ lbs. | 2½ lbs. |

.357 Magnum with 6" Barrel
Available in Stainless Steel

The controls of the Astra 2000, though typical of an Eibar-style pistol, are somewhat strange to American shooters and may require a period of adjustment on their part. The manual safety, located at the midpoint of the frame, just above the trigger, has to be pushed down for the pistol to fire (after loading the firing chamber and cocking the hammer). Pushing the safety lever up locks the trigger and the slide after it has been fully retracted to the rear. With the slide locked in this manner, disassembly can proceed the same as any Ruby or Eibar-type pistol *(see the Appendix)*. The magazine release is in the form of a pushbutton located at the bottom left side of the frame in the corner of the grip. This location is reminiscent of some Beretta pistols and was later incorporated into the slightly larger Astra Model 4000 or Falcon *(see below)*.

❧ Some early Model 5000 or Constable pistols had ribbed plastic grips similar to the Walther P38s during World War II. The early variation Constable pistols also used a single grip screw and their triggers were white, another trademark of early (pre-1971) guns.

The .22 Short version of the Model 2000 was the first to appear in 1954, followed by the .25 ACP version two years later. By 1967, Unceta had ceased production of the older and smaller Model 200, leaving the M200 Cub as the smallest handgun in the Astra line (which still holds true today). By 1977, Unceta had produced 138,975 Model 2000 pistols in .22 Short caliber with serial numbers in the following ranges: 50001-125000 (1954 to 1962) and 125001-188975 (1963-1977). According to recent Astra catalogs, the company has discontinued the .22 Short caliber Cub, leaving only the 6.35mm (.25 ACP) caliber version in the product line. The .22 Short Model 2000s, by the way, had their own separate serial number range, starting at 5000, except for two ranges of 200 pistols each made in 1982 bearing serial numbers 1262901-1263100 and 1294451-1294650.

The company, meanwhile, numbered its .25 caliber Model 2000s in the same serial number sequence it had used (except the Campo-Giro pistols and

❧ Despite the Model 5000 or Constable's (right) likeness to the Walther PPK (left), the Constable's design reflects an effort to make a better-shooting gun at the expense of some concealability. Note the Constable's extended grip tang and slightly larger grip.

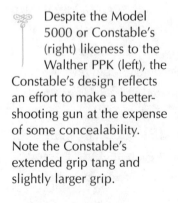

the Models 400, 600, 700 and 900) since starting out as a pistol manufacturer in 1908. Serial numbers for the .25 ACP caliber Model 2000 began at 780001 in 1956, and by 1983 the company had turned out 146,198 .25 caliber M2000 pistols in this serial-numbering sequence. In 1983 a .25 caliber Model 2000 was given serial number 1317025, at which time Unceta switched to a new numbering system—one with an alphabetic prefix or suffix followed by a four-digit number, a system that remains in effect. Interestingly, the highest production of .25 caliber Model 2000 pistols in any single year occurred in 1968 with passage of the Gun Control Act by the U.S. Congress. To extract the last piece of business it could from this lucrative market before it closed

Unceta offered its deluxe finishes and engraving services with the Model 5000 or Constable. The grips in this drawing are wooden but they also came with standard black plastic or white plastic.

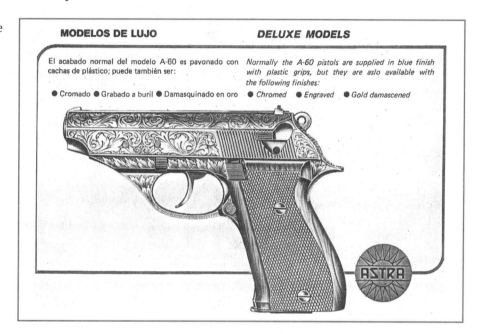

MODELOS DE LUJO — DELUXE MODELS

El acabado normal del modelo A-60 es pavonado con cachas de plástico; puede también ser:

Normally the A-60 pistols are supplied in blue finish with plastic grips, but they are aslo available with the following finishes:

● Cromado ● Grabado a buril ● Damasquinado en oro — ● Chromed ● Engraved ● Gold damascened

ASTRA

forever, Unceta exerted itself mightily. As a result, the firm mad an impressive 31,050 M2000 pistols (serial numbers 938376-940000 and 950001 to 979425). During that period Unceta achieved more than twice the highest production total for one year ever attained before or since.

With no large-scale importation into the U.S. since that time, the Model 2000 is surprisingly not all that uncommon in the American market. In addition to having made several hundred thousand of these pistols under the "Astra" label, Unceta also built an identical pistol, called the Colt Junior (1957 to 1969). A total of 24,775 of these pistols in .22 Short caliber and another 48,300 in .25 caliber were made under this arrangement between Colt and Unceta. Serial numbers on the Colt guns began at "ICC" in 1957, reaching 62475CC in 1967, at which time the serial numbers skipped up to 75001CC, ending at 85600CC. The last of these guns were made just before the end of small foreign pistol importation in December 1968.

*Chapter 8*

The two-screw grip was introduced in 1974 on the Model 5000 or Constable. Continuing use of the one-sided safety did not show through the right side of the slide. In this view the disassembly yoke appears clearly to the left of the serial number on the frame. To remove the slide from the frame, this yoke must first be lowered and held down while the slide is drawn back and up. (Photo courtesy of Interarms)

Production of the Colt Junior was resumed in 1970 at the Firearms International plant in Accokeek, Maryland (now the site of the Beretta USA facility), using imported parts supplied by Astra. A loophole in the U.S. Gun Control Act of 1968 allows the domestic manufacture of small handguns or even the assembly of imported parts for small handguns. Demand for this reincarnated Colt Junior proved lower than expected, however, so that production was halted in 1973.

Meanwhile, Unceta was making a sporting model of the Model 2000, called the Astra Camper. It appeared only in .22 Short caliber with a 4-inch barrel that protruded nearly two inches beyond the front of the slide, The front sight was mounted at the end of the extended barrel, similar to that of the Walther P38. A caliber conversion kit—consisting of an extra slide, barrel and a magazine adapted for rimfire use—made it possible to switch from the centerfire .25 ACP to the rimfire .22 Short round, though Colt dropped this kit from its line in 1965. The company wanted shooters to purchase instead the complete .22 Short caliber Junior Colt, whose sales were lagging far behind those of the more popular .25 caliber model. Demand for both these products—the long-barreled Camper model and the rimfire conversion kit—was limited and few were actually produced. In the perverse world of gun collecting, in which today's lemon becomes tomorrow's rarity, the conversion kits, being rare and sought after, now sell for about the same as a complete pistol.

Despite its diminutive size, the well-made Model 2000 offers excellent accuracy at distances appropriate for pistols of this caliber, type and size. One 5-shot offhand group fired by the author at 15 feet with a .25 caliber Model 2000 measured only 1.1 inches across. Recoil is negligible and

reliability has proven flawless with several ammunition brands tested. The Model 2000 remains competitive around the world, which is why Unceta has elected to keep it in production despite losing the U.S. market. Another variation of the Model 2000 worth consideration is the Model 7000, which is actually a Model 2000

The thumb safety on later Constable pistols imported by Interarms extended all the way through to the right side of the slide. (Photo courtesy of Interarms)

The Model A-50, which Unceta brought out in 1979, bears a strong resemblance to the Model 5000/Constable. The A-50, however, uses a single-action trigger mechanism and a different manual safety arrangement.

chambered for the .22 Long Rifle cartridge and has a magazine capacity of up to 8 rounds. Since this cartridge is longer than the .22 Short and .25 ACP rounds used in the original Model 2000, the grip found on the Model 7000 must be a little wider than the Cub's. In 1972, after the company decided to make this model, series production began the following year at serial number 1080001. The pistol proved popular everywhere but in the U.S., where importation was once again prohibited because the pistol did not meet the minimum size requirement of the GCA. By 1980, the factory had already built 15,000 of these little pistols, but it has since been discontinued along with the .22 Short version.

## Model 4000 "Falcon"

The Astra Model 4000, also known as the "Falcon," represents a further refinement of the tubular pistol concept pioneered by the Model 400 pistol (1921-1946). Introduced in 1956, the Model 4000 differed from earlier pistols of its type with as exposed, rounded hammer at the rear of the slide, much like that of the smaller Model 400. The Model 4000, with its medium-sized frame, is only slightly larger than the Models 300 and 3000. Its specifications include: **Overall Length:** 6.46". **Barrel Length:** 3.9". **Height:** 4.4". **Weight:** 22.9 ounces. **Caliber:** .32 (7.65mm Browning). Unceta once made a .22 Long Rifle version in both standard and extended 7-inch barrel lengths, and there was also a .380 ACP (9mm Browning Short) version, but it no longer remains in production. Early Model 4000 pistols made prior to 1970 had black or brown plastic grips with identifying logos, consisting of (top to bottom) "MOD. 4000," the Astra sunburst, and the word "FALCON" in a Walther-style banner. Standard Model 4000 pistols made since 1970 have featured black checkered plastic grips without company logos or model designations. Astra has offered the Model 4000 in various deluxe finishes, including satin nickel plating (with or without engraving) and silver- and gold-engraved finishes. The first 13,000 of these pistols wore a rust-blue finish before the factory switched (in 1958) to the less expensive salt-bluing process, a cost-cutting measure which virtually all European and American gun manufacturers had adopted decades earlier. The first series production of the Model 4000 in 1956 had serial numbers ranging from 779851 to 780000, reaching 1314602 by 1983. Unceta then switched to the four-digit serial number with an alphabetic prefix (or suffix). The first gun produced with this new numbering scheme as an Astra Model 4000 (serial number A0001) made in 1983. As with the Model 2000, the magazine release on the Model 4000 has always been a pushbutton type located on the left rear corner of the grip. A Model 300-type manual safety, located on the midpoint of the frame above the trigger, pushes up for safe and down to fire.

The design debt owed by Astra-Unceta y Cia's A-80/90/100 pistol series (an A-100 is shown at top) to the SIG P220-style pistols (shown at bottom) is evident in this photo. The most obvious change is the disassembly lever, which was moved to the opposite side of the frame.

While it was large enough to qualify for importation under the GCA, the Model 4000 did not make the required 70 points prescribed by the U.S. Treasury Department's Bureau of Alcohol, Tobacco and Firearms (BATF). To reach 70 points, the Falcon would need target-type grips with a thumbrest on the left side, adjustable target-type sights, and changes in its safety system. Since the pistol was never very popular in the U.S. to begin with, and it was enjoying good sales in its standard configuration in other world regions, Unceta wisely decided not to bother making the requisite changes. In all, the Model 4000 represents Unceta's final pistol with a tubular design, one that proved highly popular, particularly in the Middle East. Even though it has not been imported into the United States since the end of 1968, it remains a fitting tribute to the essential soundness in quality and serviceability of the tubular pistol concept originally unveiled in 1921 as the Model 400.

An important change in the A-60's design was the addition of an ambidextrous safety lever, which made the gun more usable for left-handed shooters.

# Model 800 "Condor"

Interarms was the first importer of the Model A-90 to the United States. Note the unusual combination of decocking lever and slide-mounted safety catch, creating a cluster of controls on the left side, which some shooters found confusing. (Drawing courtesy of Interarms)

In 1946, Unceta sent two types of guns to the Spanish armed forces testing commission for trials to be held that year before selecting a new service pistol to supplant the Model 1921. The exposed-hammer version, while it was also turned down by the army, was deemed by Astra to offer enough potential to justify developing it further as a commercial venture. Its development, however, was a long, drawn-out affair. After building some 30 preproduction samples (1945-1957), the company was able to sort out various details, including the shape of the safety and location of the magazine release. Series production of the standard Model 800 pistol finally commenced in January 1958 with serial number 820001. In its final form, this pistol became available in 9mm Parabellum caliber with an 8-shot magazine. Although a lanyard loop had been supplied on preproduction models, this feature did not appear on standard production models. The magazine release, which had started out identical in appearance and function to those found on the Models 300, 600 and 700, was revised as a pushbutton release located on the left rear corner of the frame, much like the Models 2000 and 4000. The manual safety also evolved throughout this period, eventually becoming a thumb lever similar to that used in the Colt Model 1911 pistol, and in the same location. The hammer was a large, exposed spur protruding prominently from the rear of the slide. A magazine safety and a loaded-chamber indicator were standard, but there was no grip safety.

ASTRA A-90

| SPECIFICATIONS | | | |
|---|---|---|---|
| | Constable | A60 | A90 |
| Finish: | Blue | Blue | Blue |
| Length – | | | |
| Barrel: | 3.5" | 3.5" | 3.75" |
| Overall: | 6.75" | 6.75" | 7" |
| Weight: | 2.5 Lbs. | 2.5 Lbs. | 2.5 Lbs. |
| **DOUBLE-ACTION** | | | |
| WITH ONE MAGAZINE | | | |

PREMIUM forged steel pistols for sport and personal defense . . . from Astra's sleek small frame Constable, large capacity Model A-60 in .380 ACP, to the compact A-90 designed for either 15-rounds of 9mm Parabellum or 9-rounds .45 ACP. All feature an exceptionally smooth double-action and a carefully engineered grip design for maximum control and instinctive aiming. In spite of its multi-round capacity, the A-90 is remarkably compact with a shorter overall length than the Colt Commander. Whatever your requirement . . . size, carrying comfort or big-bore fire power . . . Astra is your answer.

This 1990 Interarms catalog page displays the A-90, the A-60 and the Constable— the very heart of the Astra automatic pistol line. The tiny Model 2000, because of its size, could not be imported legally into the USA after 1968 and so did not appear in Interarms' catalog.

Model 800 finish options included the standard model with it salt-blued finish and black plastic grips complete with P38-style horizontal ribbing, the Astra sunburst logo in the middle, and the world "CONDOR" near the bottom. Fancier models were the chrome plated 801, the silver plated and engraved 802, the silver plated and engraved 803, and the 804 (gold plated and engraved). Because of their extremely high prices and limited demand, only a handful of embellished Model-800 type pistols were built by the factory. The golden Model 804, for example, sold for nearly eight times the cost of a standard blued Model 800 pistol.

The Model 800 proved relatively unsuccessful, never garnering an armed forces order or winning over civilian shooters. Part of the reason for this lack of interest concerned the pistol's unpleasant firing characteristics. Compared to the Model 600 from which it was derived, the Model 800 delivered a sharp, stinging recoil to the shooter's hand, a defect attributed to the pistol's altered grip shape and a recoil spring that was necessarily shorter, hence weaker. The recoil spring, in turn, was the result of opening up the rear of the slide to accommodate an exposed hammer. Naturally, the Model 800, with its tubular blowback design, shared the difficult takedown and reassembly procedures of the Models 300, 400 and 600 that had preceded it. These shortcomings resulted in disappointingly sluggish sales, forcing Unceta to halt Model 800 production in 1968 (serial number 831432) after making a total of only 11,432 pistols.

## Astra Revolvers, 1958-Present

In 1958 Unceta received permission from the government of Francisco Franco to manufacture revolvers, which represented a first for the company. Unceta had formerly built Astra-brand revolvers at a separate plant based in Elgoibar (formerly the home of the first Gabilondo factory), rather than at its home factory in Guernica. All revolvers made thus far by Unceta have followed the Smith & Wesson design made famous by the Military & Police (Model 10), wherein the cylinder opens up to the left side for loading.

The European American Armory (EAA) currently handles importation of the Astra pistol line, including the .45 ACP caliber model with satin nickel finish. Note the location of the disassembly lever, which is blued, on the right side of the frame above the trigger (opposite that of the SIG/Sauer P220-type pistols).

The 9mm Parabellum version of the A-100, which originally held an impressive 17 rounds in its relatively narrow grip, has become less attractive to U.S. gun enthusiasts since 1995, when magazine capacity was limited to 10 rounds. The 17-shot version, however, can still be sold to U.S. police forces.

Once Unceta obtained the necessary authorization in 1958, the company wasted no time entering the revolver field, announcing its *Cadix* series later that same year, with production in full swing by 1960. The Cadix resembled a small-frame Smith & Wesson design, but with two unique features: the ejector rod underneath the barrel had a protective shroud with a pronounced taper, narrowing as it approached the muzzle; and the trailing edge of the trigger-guard was squared off, not rounded. Initial issues of the Cadix were in .22 Long Rifle caliber, but when Unceta saw how successful it was, it expanded the Cadix line to include centerfire models.

The Cadix line included versions in .22 Long Rifle (9-shot cylinder), .32 S&W (6-shot cylinder) and .38 Special (5-shot cylinder) calibers. Barrel lengths were 2-, 4- or 6-inches, leading to a clever three-digit numbering system. The first two digits represented the caliber and the last digit referred to the barrel length in inches. Thus, the Model 222 was a .22LR with a 2-inch barrel; the Model 224 was a .22 with a 4-inch barrel; and the Model 226 was a .22 with a 6-inch barrel. The same system applied to the .32 S&W. With a 2-inch barrel, it became the Model 322; 324 was a .32 with a 4-inch barrel, and the Model 326 was a .32 with a 6-inch barrel. The Model 382 was a .38 with 2-inch barrel. Both fixed and adjustable sights were available. In general, the Cadix was a quality entry into the revolver field and proved popular, especially in Europe. As a result, Unceta kept the Cadix line in production until 1973, even though it was unable to meet U.S. safety standards imposed by the Gun Control Act of 1968.

Unceta's current small-frame revolver—the Model 680—has the same external appearance of the Cadix but with modernized lockwork. Its specifications run as follows: **Caliber:** .38 Special; **Capacity:** 6 shots; **Overall Length:** 6.6"; **Barrel Length:** 2"; **Weight:** (unloaded) 22 ounces. The Astra 680 is almost exactly the same size as a Smith

& Wesson small-frame revolver and comes in both exposed spur hammer and bobbed hammer variants. The Model 680 is also available in a choice of blued carbon steel or stainless steel. In keeping with the current trend of offering maximum firepower in a small-sized package, Astra also makes the Model 680 in a slightly longer and heavier 6-shot .357 Magnum version. Although this versatile revolver design is well-suited to concealed carry and is popular in Europe, Africa, the Middle East and elsewhere, no company imports the Model 680 in the United States at this writing.

In 1971 Unceta introduced a larger revolver, called simply the Model 357. As with other revolvers made to fire the .357 Magnum cartridge, this one can also fire the .38 special (which is 1/8 of an inch shorter). The Model 357 features a transfer-bar mechanism in its firing system, enabling its importation to the U.S. under the safety provisions of the Gun Control Act. This mechanism prevents the frame-mounted firing pin from making contact with the hammer until the trigger has been pulled all the way through the cocking stroke. An intermediate steel component (the transfer bar) then rises into position, transmitting the force of the falling hammer to the firing pin. Much larger and more substantial than the Cadix, the Model 357 once came in a choice of 2-, 3-, 4-, 6- and 8$^1/_2$-inch barrel lengths, though only the 4-inch barrel remains standard at this writing. It has a six-shot cylinder and an adjustable rear sight. The mainspring is adjustable as well, allowing four different tension settings, or allowing shooters a measure of control over the trigger pull needed to fire the revolver. The mainspring is a coil type rather than the leaf-type mainspring used on all Smith & Wesson revolvers from the K-frame size and upwards. Otherwise similar in design to Smith & Wesson's superb Model 19 Combat Magnum, the Astra revolver is made of good-quality materials, plus excellent fit and finish.

In 1980, Unceta followed the Model 357 with its Models 41, 44 and 45 (chambered for the .41 Magnum, .44 Magnum and .45 Colt cartridges, respectively), complete with adjustable rear sights and target-style grips. This powerful line of revolvers has enabled Unceta to compete in most markets with Gabilondo's line of Llama revolvers as well as Colt, Ruger and Smith & Wesson in the U.S. The Astra revolvers remain scarce in America where competition among revolver companies is particularly fierce.

The A-70 (top) appears slightly larger than the Walther PPK (bottom), and yet it must be wider and heavier in order to fire the more powerful 9mm Para-bellum and .40 S&W caliber cartridges compared to the PPK's relatively low-powered .380 ACP cartridge.

## Astra A-100

It's unlikely that any pistol has ever been better suited to law enforcement needs than the A-100, the full featured duty-size member of the dynamic Astra trio. Even though the A-100 is priced below most of the other law enforcement leaders, its impressive list of features includes:
- A selective double/single action;
- Law enforcement-approved de-cocking lever;
- Automatic firing pin block safety to guard against accidental discharge;
- All steel construction;
- New higher capacity staggered magazine;
- Streamlined size and weight.

**CALIBERS:** 9mm, .40 S&W, .45 ACP
**LENGTH:** Overall - 7.5"; Barrel - 3.8"
**WEIGHT:** 34.0 oz
**CAPACITY:** 9mm - 10 plus 1, .40 S&W - 10 plus 1, .45 ACP - 9 plus 1
**FINISHES:** Blue, Nickel, Stainless Steel
**OPTIONS:** SEE CHART ON PAGE 12

NEW FEATHERWEIGHT 9MM IN 1995

## Astra A-100 Carry Comp

Only Astra and European American Armory could improve upon one of the finest pistols in the world... the A-100 compact in size, light in weight, high capacity, and now, a compensator to reduce recoil and muzzle jump. This is the ideal gun for law enforcement or home defence. Why spend hundreds more on the competition basic pistol when you can have an A-100 compensated for less? If you all ready have an A-100 don't worry you can now get an A-100 carry comp conversion kit to fit your pistol.

**CALIBERS:** 9mm, .40S&W, .45ACP
**LENGTH:** Overall - 8.5"; Barrel - 4.3"
**WEIGHT:** 38 oz.
**CAPACITY:** 9mm - 10 plus 1; .40 S&W - 10 plus 1; .45ACP - 9 plus 1
**FINISHES:** Blue
**OPTIONS:** SEE CHART ON PAGE 12

In 1995 Unceta added both a compensator and a lightweight alloy-framed model to its growing line of A-100 pistols, as illustrated in European American Armory's 1995 catalog.

While Unceta has discontinued the larger-caliber variants—the Model 41 in 1985 and the others in 1987—it kept a stainless-steel variant of the Model 44 with 6-inch barrel in production until 1993. The big-bore Astra revolvers—Models 412, 44 and 45—also provided the basis for an interesting custom creation called the *Terminator*. Made by the John Jovino company, this revolver was mostly a Model 44 revolver cut down in size to make it more compact. The barrel length was reduced to $2^3/_4$ inches while enough metal was removed from the large Astra grips to make them fit the same type of Pachmayr rubber grips found on Smith & Wesson K-frame revolvers. The trigger was also adjusted to pull smoother and lighter. And whereas the adjustable rear sight was retained, Jovino smoothed its contours and rounded its edges to make the gun more concealable. White highlights were added to the rear sight to complement the red insert in its front sight. Relatively inexpensive as custom guns go, the Terminator remains the smallest .44 Magnum revolver available. It's difficult to shoot, though, because of its fierce recoil. Most owners opt for the .44 Special cartridge with lighter powder charges. In any event, demand was limited and sales stopped in 1989.

For shooters who like a full-sized .38 Special caliber revolver, Unceta introduced in 1973 its new Astra Model 960. Similar to the Model 357, but with a slightly shorter cylinder, this weapon accepts only .38 Special ammunition. Compared to the small-frame Cadix, medium-frame 960 revolver is considerably larger—$9^1/_2$ inches long with a 4-inch barrel and weighing 40 ounces—and thus is more comfortable to shoot. It also boasts an improved internal safety system; i.e., the hammer cannot reach the firing pin until a transfer bar has been raised into the correct position between the two. This can happen, however, only when the trigger has been pulled all the way through its firing stroke. This change in firing mechanism was created to conform with drop-test safety requirements (same as the Model 357) mandated by the Gun Control Act of 1968. It also makes the Model 960 a

The A-70 (bottom) is much more compact than classic 9mm pistols of similar magazine capacity, such as Walther's Model P38 (top).

safer weapon to use than the Cadix. Thanks to its comfortable shooting characteristics and wide choice of options, the Model 960 has attracted considerable police and commercial sales. It remains in production at this writing (although it is not imported into the U.S.). Another full-sized .38 Special revolver in current production—the Astra NC-6 model—is much like the Model 960, but with a lighter, less robust Model 680-type frame.

The Astra 357 Police revolver is an improved version of Unceta's Model 357. It has a low-profile front, fixed rear sights and a 3-inch barrel for easier draw from a holster. Unceta also supplies the 357 Police Model with a replacement cylinder that fires 9mm Parabellum cartridges, with a special full-moon clip holding six cartridges in the cylinder. This Police model will also fire .38 Special cartridges, making it a highly versatile handgun. It was introduced in 1979 by Fabrique Nationale (FN) as the "Barracuda," with the front of its triggerguard recurved slightly for a two-handed hold. Unceta brought out its version of the Astra 357 Police in 1980 and it has since become a popular police sidearm in parts of Europe (contrary to the popular belief, revolvers have a significant following in European police work). And while FN dropped the Barracuda from its product line in 1987, the Astra 357 Police revolver remains in production at this writing.

# *Astra Constable (Model 5000)*

Around 1961 Unceta y Cia decided to undertake a double-action automatic pistol as an adjunct to the company's automatic pistol line, which was still relying on an aging design dating from the 1920s. The continuing popularity of Germany's Walther Models PP and PPK was a source of inspiration for Unceta's own double-action automatic pistol. Production of prototypes began in 1963, with early examples featuring wooden grips, adjustable sights and an exposed barrel that protruded well beyond the leading edge of the open-topped slide. The first 50 production models (serial numbers 940001 to 940049) left the Guernica factory in 1965. Production lagged at first, with only 2,850 having been made by 1970. But from then on, the "Constable, as it was called, had become quite popular, offering the kind of styling and performance typified by Walther's PPK, plus several features which actually were improvements over the world-famous German competitor. Not since Gaztañaga's Super Destroyer of 1934 *(see Chapter 5)* had a Spanish gun manufacturer created a pistol styled after the popular Model PP. In addition, the Constable's price was considerably less than the

PP's, rendering the Unceta pistol even more attractive. This popularity paid off in increased production until, by 1983, more than 80,000 of these excellent pistols had been made. Although production of Unceta's standard model ceased in 1992, its high-capacity version, the A-60, remains on the market.

The Constable was available in .22 Long Rifle, .32 ACP and .380 ACP caliber versions. Its magazine held 10 rounds in .22, eight rounds in .32 and seven rounds in .380. Overall length (standard model) was 6.5 inches and the barrel measured 3.5 inches (long-barreled models were also available). Height was 4.6 inches and width only 1.1 inches, making the pistol ideal for concealed carry and enhancing its popularity. With an unloaded weight of 25 ounces, the Constable was only slightly heavier than its rival, the famed Walther PP. Its grip was slightly larger and its disassembly was different, too. A separate yoke-shaped disassembly latch was located on the frame above the front edge of the triggerguard. The latch was pulled down while at the same time the slide was pulled all the way to the rear and lifted back and off the frame. The result was the same as the PP with its hinged triggerguard, but following a somewhat different procedure. The slightly larger frame of the Constable—notably its pronounced curve on the rear gripstrap and its long protective grip tang—made it a more pleasant gun to fire, especially for large-handed shooters. The Constable also had a slide release lever, a useful feature typical of full-sized service pistols. Even for shooters who reload before their pistol locks its slide back on an empty firing chamber, the external slide release makes the job of clearing a hammed action much easier (which can be a real problem with PP/PPK-type pistols).

In addition to the A-60, Unceta has made numerous versions of the basic Constable design. The first one—called the Constable I—was produced until the early 1970s, with the Constable II making up the balance of production. The most obvious difference between the two models remains the shaft end of the Walther PP-style manual safety on the Constable I, which did not show through the right side of the slide. The safety shaft on the Constable II **did** show through that side of the slide. Another easy way to tell the Constable apart is to note how many screws secured the plastic grip pieces to the frame. In early pistols, only a single screw, located at about the midpoint of the grip, was found on each side, while later pistols used two grip screws, located near the top and bottom of the grip, to hold each piece in place on the frame. Triggers on early

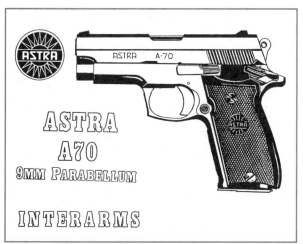

Interarms briefly handled the Model A-70 but dropped it within a year along with the rest of the Astra-Unceta automatic pistol and revolver lines. (Drawing courtesy of Interarms)

pistols were made of highly polished, unfinished steel, while triggers on later Constables were blued to match the frame and slide. The Constable I also included the famous Astra sunburst logo, which was struck on the left side of the slide as part of the pistol's identifying inscription. The Constable II, however, generally lacked this company logo. Internally, minor mechanical changes to the disassembly control, firing pin, barrel, hammer, sear, trigger and frame also differed from one model to the other; but in appearance, dimensions, performance and functioning, they are much the same pistol. Choice of finish included the standard blued model (M5000), a chrome-plated finish (Model 5001), a silver-plated, engraved finish (Model 5002), and a deluxe gold-plated and engraved finish (Model 5004). During the early stages of production, about 2,000 *Constable Sports* made their appearance. This variation (in .22 Long Rifle caliber only) had a 6-inch barrel with a front sight secured to the muzzle end of the barrel by a large nut. A counterweight/front sight combination could be substituted for the long barrel. A large adjustable rear sight, dovetailed into the top of the slide, came standard on this model. All but the earliest Constable Sports utilized a single-action trigger mechanism instead of the double-action trigger employed on the regular Constable.

A special variation of the Constable I was the *Model 500*, which was made with a single-action trigger only, although it kept the slide-mounted safety found on the standard model. Markings on the Model 500 included "MOD. 500" on the left side of the slide, which remains the best way to differentiate it from standard production. Unceta made fewer than 500 of these pistols (1973-1974), although a few turned up in production as late as 1977. This pistol served as the forerunner of the more specialized A-50, a single-action pistol with a design like the Constable. The Model 500 had a frame-mounted manual safety lever but lacked the slide release latch common to the standard constable. A *Model A-50* Sport, introduced in 1950, added a longer barrel with an enlarged front sight, while the Model A-50 (1979) is much more common overseas than in the U.S. via Interarms (Alexandria, Virginia). Demand for this specialized variation could not justify Interarms' efforts and thus it chose to import only the double-action *Model 5000* version. Unceta stopped production of the standard 8-shot Constable model in 1992, concentrating instead on a slightly enlarged version, the *Model A-60 (see below)*. It featured a Constable barrel and slide atop a wider, taller frame with a 13-shot magazine in the grip. Must less expensive than the Walther Models PP and PPK which inspired it—and easier to shoot owing to its slightly increased size—the Constable remains an excellent compact pistol for personal defense.

The engraving on this Model 5000 or Constable has been worked in around the lettering on the slide. In some cases the slide inscription was added after the engraving, thus altering the usual pattern.

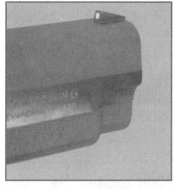

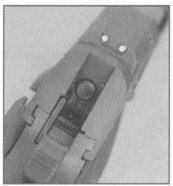

Like most modern combat-type pistols, the A-70 employs three-dot sight highlights, with one dot on the front sight (top) and two on the rear sight (bottom).

# TS-22

Prior to the mid-1970s, Unceta had catered to the needs of target shooters by modifying existing pistols—notably the already accurate Model 400 and Constable—by adding longer barrels, adjustable sights, and the like. In 1978, the company decided to compete in the competitive shooting field with a specialized target pistol, the *Model TS-22* in .22 Long Rifle caliber. After producing five prototype models that year, the company entered into series production in 1979. Though it bears a superficial resemblance to the Constable, the Model TS is actually a new design built for competition. As such, it includes large, anatomical target grips made of smooth hardwood with prominent thumbrests carved into the left grip. The rear sight is not only fully adjustable for windage and elevation, it's also mounted on the projection of its barrel counterweight, which protects the sight from battering caused by movement of the slide—the kind of rapid, violent motion that has spoiled the delicate adjustments of many such sights mounted on automatic pistols. The TS-22 has a 10-round magazine whose bottom portion includes a wooden extension, similar to the prewar Walther Olympia model, that fits flush with oversized wooden grips covering the frame and extending beyond the bottom edge. Because the rear sight is large and bulky, Unceta moved the slide serrations (for loading and cocking the pistol) forward to a point near the leading edge of the slide. Aside from these changes, the TS-22 strongly resembles the single-action A-50 and, like that pistol, includes a frame-mounted manual safety lever, omitting the slide release latch found on the standard double-action Constable. Compared to competition pistols by Erma, Hämmerli, Unique, Walther and other companies, the TS-22 is relatively inexpensive; and yet it remains quite capable of competing in all but the most exacting regimens of competitive shooting.

# Model A-60

After Unceta stopped production of the standard 8-shot Constable model in 1992, it concentrated on a slightly enlarged version, the *Model A-60*. This variant featured a Constable-type barrel and slide assembly atop a taller, wider frame that held a 13-shot magazine. Unlike the Constable, the slide-mounted hammer decocking safety on the A-60 was ambidextrous, its levers mounted on both sides of the slide. The grips are pebbled black plastic (like those of the Smith & Wesson Model 469 and Astra's own Model A-75). This pistol is made in both blued and satin nickel-plated finishes, and in a choice of .32 or .380 calibers, but only the blued-finish .380 caliber models are marketed in the United States. First introduced in 1986,

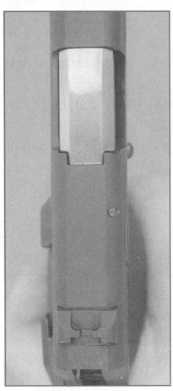

The A-70, like other Astra pistols, has a SIG-style modified Browning breech lock. Instead of barrel locking lugs, it features a large, squared off barrel hood that locks into the rear edge of the ejection port.

the A-60 remains in the Astra lineup at this writing, although U.S. importation stopped when Interarms dropped the Astra line in 1991. Springfield Armory (Geneseo, Illinois) briefly marketed the pistol as its "Bobcat" model in 1992, along with several other Spanish designs from Astra. But plans to import and sell the pistol in the U.S. under this name were stillborn when Springfield Armory went out of business later that year. When European American Armory (EAA) picked up the Astra line in 1993, the A-60 was not among its offerings; hence this well-made pistol with its excellent design remains virtually unavailable to American shooters.

## Models, A-80, A-90 and A-100

As one of the three surviving Spanish pistolmaking firms, Astra Unceta created a pistol to compete in Spain's service pistol trials to be announced in the late 1970s and held in early 1980. The Spanish armed forces required that any new pistol design must not only fire the NATO-standard 9mm Parabellum round, it must incorporate a double-action trigger and a high-capacity magazine. The Astra entry was introduced in 1978 with eight 9mm Parabellum prototypes (serial numbers 1179732 to 1179739) and was given the model designation A-80. Though it did not win the competition, the A-80 showed great promise, thanks to its large, 15-round magazine and modern safety and operating features. When Unceta began selling it commercially in 1981 (serial number 1255676) in 7.65MM Parabellum caliber, the A-80 soon attracted favorable attention from civilian shooters along with various police and security forces. The *A-80* was one of the earliest automatic pistol designs to use a firing-pin safety lock linked to the trigger. It included as well an advanced decocking lever (similar to the SIG P220 type) and incorporated a loaded-chamber indicator in the design. Unlike earlier pistols made by Unceta, particularly the Astra Model 400 and its descendants, the A-80 was easy to disassemble.

In hopes of attracting as much business as possible, Unceta announced the availability of the A-80 in an unusually wide range of calibers, including 7.65mm Parabellum, 9mm Parabellum, 9mm Steyr, .38 Super and .45 ACP. Unceta built 800 pistols in 7.65mm Parabellum caliber (called .30 Luger in the U.S.) with serial numbers 1255676-1256275 (1981) and 1264301-1264500 (1982), with another 1,000 pistols in 9mm Steyr caliber (serial numbers 1306926-1307425 and 1308426-1308925) in 1983. Unceta dropped these two calibers (7.65mm and 9mm Steyr), leaving 9mm Parabellum, .38 Super and .45 ACP as the caliber choices. These three calibers, which represent a wider variety than many pistols are made for, rank among the most popular throughout the world for large-frame automatic pistols. In particular, the A-80 in .45 caliber built a small but loyal following among shooters who sought a double-action .45. That was before the Smith & Wesson Model 645 came on line and the SIG P220 had not yet caught on due to its high price. Unceta's first production run in .45 ACP caliber consisted in 1981 of 500 pistols (serial numbers 1257426-1257925), virtually all of which most likely went to the U.S.

In 1983 Astra introduced a slightly modified pistol called the A-90. While clearly based on the A-80, it had slightly altered controls and its magazine capacity rose to 17 rounds. And while the A-80 featured a heel-type magazine release, the A-90 used a triggerguard-mounted magazine release button. It also had an ambidextrous slide-mounted safety to supplement the decocking lever. After making three .45 caliber prototypes (serial numbers 1308926, 1313105 and 1313106) and one 9mm Parabellum prototype (serial number 1314601), all in 1983, Astra put the A-90 into series production in 1983 at serial number A4995. Unceta kept both the A-80 and A-90 pistols in production until 1989, at which time the parts inventory unique to the A-80 was used up. At that point, the company discontinued further production

Not much of an Astra A-70 is revealed when a PPK is placed atop it, dramatically underscoring the A-70's unexpectedly compact dimensions.

Since many people found the hodgepodge of controls on the left side of the A-90 excessive and confusing, Unceta dropped that model in 1990, creating instead the A-100 by combining the best features of the two pistols; namely, the smooth, flat slide of the A-80 and the magazine release on the triggerguard of the A-90. Interarms briefly offered this refined model—the A-100—in the period prior to European American Armory's taking over importation of the entire Astra pistol line in 1993. The A-80/A-90/A-100 represent Unceta's second line of modern pistol designs, with the PP-inspired Constable and A-60 line being the first. Here the company has displayed once again its superb skill at copying the best features of a foreign design, then reworking them into an attractive new package of superb design and workmanship—and all for a price appreciably lower than the original model on which it is based (in this case the SIG Model P220). Like the SIG pistol, the A-80 and A-100 pistols have a modified Browning short-recoil and a breech-locking mechanism in which the rear end of the barrel fit into the edge of the large ejection port. Upon recoil, a cam beneath the barrel draws the rear end of the barrel down and out of engagement with the slide. The decocking lever (located on the leading edge of the left grip) is another A-80 feature taken from the SIG design, in which the lever is depressed automatically and lowers the hammer (if cocked) safety

*Chapter 8*

onto a notch on the sear, jut short of the firing pin. Once the decocking lever is released, it pops back up into its rest position, leaving the gun ready for a double-action first shot. The only major differences between the Astra A-80 series pistols and the Swiss-designed, German-made pistols of the SIG P220 line favor the Astras. For one thing, they cost much less than any SIG model; and second, they are made of all-steel, which renders them more durable than the lighter SIG pistols.

Until 1995, European American Armory imported the A-100 in three calibers: 9mm (17-shot), .40 S&W (13-shot) and .45 ACP (9-shot). Specifications are the same for all three calibers: **Overall Length:** 7.1"; **Barrel Length:** 3.9"; **Height:** 5.6"; **Width:** 1.4"; **Weight:** (unloaded) 29 ounces. Considering its impressive capacity, the A-100 is remarkably compact, with a surprisingly slim grip. Its width is deceiving, for this is not a large, clumsy pistol. Its width marks the widest spot on the pistol; and its decocking lever, which is actually a small, well-contoured piece, must by necessity protrude slightly from the grip so the shooter's thumb may gain a firm grasp. Also, the barrel on this pistol is relatively short, which increases the accuracy and muzzle velocity compared to longer-barreled pistols. The double-action trigger pull of A-80 series pistols is long and heavy, but smooth. And the single-action trigger pull, though relatively light, allows nearly 10mm of slack before there's enough pressure to fire the pistol. In short, these well-made pistols are quite accurate and utterly reliable.

The A-70 is a single-action pistol that must be cocked before it is fired.

Pistols imported into the United States for sale to civilians since 1995 must by law be limited to 10-round magazines (except for police service, which is exempt from that limitation). Although the A-100 is remarkably compact for a high-capacity pistol, a number of smaller and handier pistols come to mind when considering guns that are limited to 10 shots. While EAA continues to import the A-100 in all three calibers at this writing, its future among civilian shooters in the U.S., particularly in its 9mm version, is in jeopardy. The A-100, on the other hand, is worth serious consideration by any police or military agency which expresses interest in the excellent SIG/Sauer pistols but is appalled by the high prices of these guns. Astra's A-100 offers the same features at an appreciably lower price. While its resale value may be less than a SIG pistol, this applies more to civilian gun collectors than the armed forces, which are interested primarily in performance—an asset the A-100 offers in abundance.

# Model A-70

In 1992, with interest increasing in small, concealable handguns with serious military handgun calibers, Unceta decided to produce the *Model A-70*. Its specifications included the following: **Overall Length:** 3.5"; **Height:** 4.75"; **Width:** 1.2"; **Weight:** (unloaded) 29.3 ounces. The A-70 is almost as compact as a Walther PPK, but it's chambered for the far more potent 9mm Parabellum or .40S&W caliber rounds (as opposed to the .32 or .380 rounds commonly found in the PPK). In competition with Star's Firestar M-43 or M-40, the A-70 also uses a single-action trigger mechanism combined with all-steel construction. In this day of double-action automatic pistols and revolvers, the single-action trigger may seem a step backward. But it has a slimmer frame, simplifying the job of concealment. As with most modern Spanish handguns, the A-70 boasts outstanding workmanship. It was first introduced with a blued finish, but a nickel finish made it debut in 1993, followed in 1994 by a stainless-steel version. The magazine on the A-70 holds up to eight rounds in 9mm and seven rounds in .40 S&W. Unlike the competitive Firestar, however, the A-70 has well-rounded magazine feed lips, which make the gun easier to load without injury to a shooter's fingers. In addition, unlike the Firestar, the magazine release on the A-70 forcefully ejects the magazine from the pistol. It also has no magazine safety, thus allowing a shooter to fire the pistol as a single-shot should the magazine be lost or while reloading. The sights, which are the popular 3-dot system, are well-rounded to avoid catching on a holster or one's clothing. Its sights are large enough for fast, accurate shooting, although the rear sight could be made slightly wider.

The safety mechanisms on the A-70 include an automatic firing pin safety (released only when the trigger is pulled all the way to the rear upon firing), a half-cock notch on the hammer (to keep the hammer off the firing pin should the shooter's thumb slip while thumb-cocking the hammer), and a manual safety that can be locked on with the hammer cocked. The safety lever—up to safe and down to fire—is the same type popularized by the M1911A1, FN High Power and CZ Model 75 pistols. The manual safety lever on the A-70 is fitted on the left side of the gun only, so left-handers are best advised

For a medium-frame automatic pistol intended mostly for concealment, the Model 5000 or Constable is easy to handle and surprisingly accurate. The author fired this 1.2-inch, 5-shot offhand group from 25 feet using the 9mm Short (.380 ACP) Constable shown.

to switch to a different gun. Despite its small size, the A-70 fits the hand comfortably. And thanks to its weight (approximately 30 ounces, and more than 33 ounces with a full magazine), the A-70 is easy to manage even in rapid fire. Its accuracy and reliability are also excellent, even with its heavy military-style trigger pull.

# Model A-75 "Firefox"

The *Model A-75*, introduced by Astra/Unceta in 1993, is essentially a double-action version of the single-action A-70. Its dimensions are the same as the A-70 *(see above)*, except that the A-75's double-action trigger mechanism adds to its width, and its weight (32 ounces unloaded and approximately 35 ounces with a full 8-shot magazine) shows a slight increase over the A-70. The A-75's barrel, which employs an unlocking cam with a different shape, is not interchangeable with that of the A-70. The A-75 also bears more than a passing resemblance to SIG's Model P225 in size, operating system and magazine capacity. However, unlike the lightweight SIG with its alloy frame, the A-75 is available with a steel frame (making it five ounces heavier than the SIG) or with an aluminum alloy frame designed for lightness (23.25 ounces). The A-75 comes in a choice of matte blue, nickel or stainless steel finishes. The magazine release is reversible to suit either right-handed or left-handed shooters. When depressed, it pops the magazine free of the pistol, which is the preferred way for most American shooters.

The A-60, which strongly resembled the Astra Model 5000 or Constable, added an enlarged frame with a high-capacity, double-column magazine.

The safety mechanisms on the A-70 include an automatic firing pin safety (released only when the trigger is pulled all the way back at the moment of firing) and a half-cock notch on the hammer. Both are modeled after the parent A-70. Because of the A-75's double-action trigger mechanism, however, Unceta chose another design: a decocking lever that automatically—and safely—lowers the hammer and then returns up to the firing position when it's released. This system is much like that found on modern SIG pistols in the P220 and P230 series, except that the position of the decocking lever is changed on the A-75 to the left rear portion of the frame. Unlike the A-70, which is built for right-handed operation only, the A-75 has an ambidextrous decocking lever.

The A-70 is surprisingly accurate, as this rapid-fire full magazine target illustrates.

The A-75 shoots well and fits firmly and comfortably in the hand despite its short grip. The grip panels (or stocks, as some shooters prefer to call them) are made of black plastic slightly roughened to feel like sandpaper, and the front and rear grip-straps have heavy checkering to ensure a secure hold on the pistol, even with wet hands. As with the A-70, Astra makes a .40 S&W caliber version, which is identical in size but loses one round of magazine capacity. In 1994 European American Armory unveiled a 9mm A-75 for the U.S. market with a lightweight alloy frame (call the *Featherweight Model*). Its aluminum-alloy frame shaves 7.75 ounces off the standard all-steel pistol weight. The .45 caliber model has the following dimensions: **Overall Length:** 6.85"; **Barrel Length:** 3.7"; **Height:** 5.12"; **Weight:** 33.8 ounces (unloaded). It's only a bit larger than the standard 9mm model and quite compact for a double-action .45 caliber pistol. Thanks to its modern operational and safety features, the A-75 is highly competitive against comparable models from Smith & Wesson and SIG, and yet it is considerably less expensive.

# Closing Comments

Other products related to handguns include a wide selection of replacement grips for automatic pistols made from various smooth and checkered woods. For revolvers, a line of checkered wooden grips, along with Pachmayr and Astra-logo rubber grips, are offered. For the A-75 and A-100, a replacement lightweight aluminum alloy frame is on the market, as

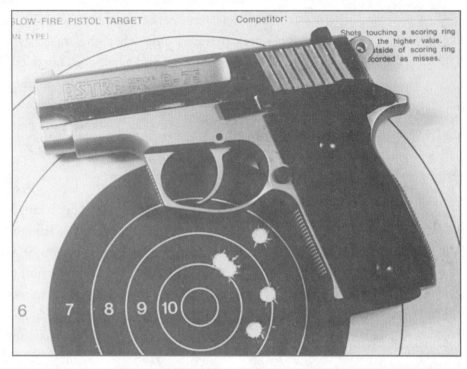

The A-75 shares the same impressive accuracy with the A-70, a tribute to this pistol's excellent workmanship.

The A-75 (top) is essentially an A-70 with a double-action trigger mechanism. Despite the slight increase in bulk, it remains surprisingly compact, as this comparison view with a Walther PP (bottom) clearly shows.

are caliber conversion kits for the Models A-70, A-75 and A-100. This allows owners of 9mm Parabellum versions of these Spanish pistols to be converted to the increasingly popular and more powerful .40 S&W caliber. A longer, threaded barrel with compensator attachment is available for the A-100, as is a left-handed decocking lever. Adjustable target sights and sights with luminous tritium inserts are available for the Models A-70, A-75, A-90 and A-100. Other services include a fully-equipped engraving shop that carries on Astra Unceta's long tradition of embellishing fine pistols with deluxe finishes (high-polish blue, satin nickel, and silver or gold damascene at this writing) and beautiful, intricate patterns engraved by hand into the steel frames and slides of the guns. Once given the model type, caliber and serial number, the company can provide the date of manufacture and the original purchases to whom the factory shipped the weapon following its manufacture. Today, the Astra company is well poised to maintain its significant share of the world-wide military and police handgun market. Its automatic pistols and revolvers feature mature designs that are accurate, reliable and competitively priced.

# Chapter 9

## Echave y Arizmendi, 1945–1970

chave y Arizmendi was only one of four Spanish handgun manufacturers allowed to resume business after the Spanish Civil War but without receiving any Spanish government orders. In the absence of such lucrative business, the company tried instead to make a living by producing some interesting but offbeat models directed toward civilian markets. Accordingly, following World War II, Echave y Arizmendi (the company name was subsequently shortened to "Echasa") shifted its product line to a more Germanic character, placing its hopes on copies of two highly successful German handguns: the double-action Walther PP and the Erma .22 caliber version of the Luger pistol. After pursuing this policy successfully for 23 years, the company failed, through no fault of its own, mostly as a result of legislative action taken in the United States.

### Echasa and the Walther PP Look-alikes

The Walther PP copies made by Echasa went by several different names, including the "Fast" (for South American and European sale) and the "Basque," "Dickson Special Agent" and "Madison" (for sale in the U.S.). Echasa also built a 7.65mm (.32 ACP) version, marked "MODELO GZ—MAB ESPAGNOLA," and a similar "MODELO G" in .22 LR caliber for the French firm, *Manufacture d'Armes de Bayonne* (MAB). Whatever its brand name, the Echasa PP look-alike bore a strong resemblance to the Walther PP, differing only in appearance and to a greater degree in its mechanical features as well. The "FAST", Echasa's initial effort, was chambered in the popular .32 ACP caliber (7.65mm Browning). It was a simple blowback pistol measuring 7.1 inches in length, with a 3.2-inch barrel and a weight of 23 ounces. When this model proved popular, Echasa created various derivative models, adding calibers and a lightweight aluminum alloy frame (as Walther had done with the Model PP) and changing brand names to suit various markets.

Other similarities between the Echasa pistols and the Walther PP included a double-action trigger mechanism and an overall similarity of appearance, that of a sleek, compact and well-balanced pistol. Echasa's pistol, like the Walther, had a spring coiled around the barrel for maximum compactness. Echasa's numbering system makes it easy to sort out the various finishes and calibers that are available. For example, the "Fast" model appeared as the Model 221 (when chambered in .22 Long Rifle), the Model 631 when chambered for the .25 ACP (6.35mm Browning), the Model 761 in .32 ACP (7.65mm Browning), and the Model 901 in .380 ACP (9mm Browning Short). The first two digits in Echasa's numbering system denoted the European or metric caliber, while the third digit indicated the finish. Thus, the final digit 1 indicated a blued finish with black checkered plastic grips. A third digit of 2 (e.g., Model 632) signified checkered wooden grips with a company medallion, while a third digit of 3 (e.g., Model 763) represented the deluxe model, featuring a bright chrome-plated finish with either checkered wooden grips with company medallion or smooth white plastic pearlite grips. Magazine capacities were 10 rounds in .22 caliber, eight rounds in .32 and seven rounds in .380.

✣ Echave y Arizmendi's Model 1916 was a typical 9-shot Ruby clone sold to the French armed forces during World War I. It turned out to be the company's sole foray into the lucrative and prestigious military and police market. The company's subsequent loss of official business haunted the company in the following years and ultimately contributed to its demise.

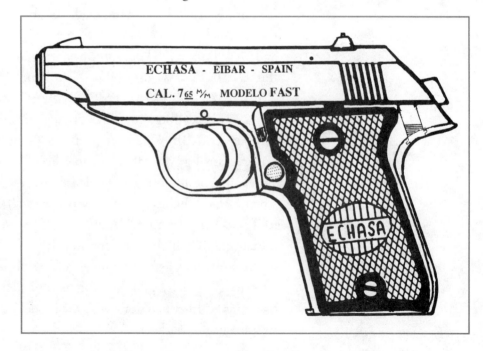

✣ The "Fast" model, introduced after World War II, was the first of Echave y Arizmendi's Walther look-alikes and quickly became a commercial success.

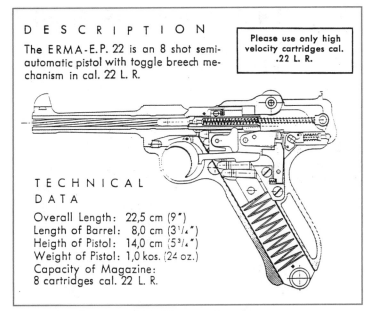

## DESCRIPTION

The ERMA-E.P. 22 is an 8 shot semi-automatic pistol with toggle breech mechanism in cal. 22 L. R.

> Please use only high velocity cartridges cal. .22 L. R.

## TECHNICAL DATA

Overall Length: 22,5 cm (9")
Length of Barrel: 8,0 cm (3¹/₄")
Heigth of Pistol: 14,0 cm (5³/₄")
Weight of Pistol: 1,0 kos. (24 oz.)
Capacity of Magazine:
8 cartridges cal. 22 L. R.

This drawing of the EP-22 shows the inside of the mechanism which the Erma EP and the Lur Panzer shared. (Drawing courtesy of Erma-Werke).

Mechanically, the Echasa pistols differed from the Walther PP in other respects. When disassembling these guns, the triggerguard was not hinged down, as with the Walther pistol; instead, a rectangular disassembly catch on the left grip tang was pushed down, while at the same time the slide moved back to the rear and up. The safety catch on the Echasa pistol was located on the frame between the trigger and the left grip. When applied, it locked the trigger but did not decock the hammer as did Walther's safety lever. In that respect, the Echasa's manual safety catch more closely resembled those found on the Eibar-type pistols of the early 1900s. The double-action mechanism was not identical to Walther's, although it accomplished the same purpose and gave shooters the option of firing the first shot with the hammer down or cocking the hammer for a lighter, more accurate single-action first shot.

The "Dickson Special Agent" model, which was available in .22 LR, 32 ACP and .380 ACP, came standard with a lightweight aluminum alloy-frame. This small pistol's overall length was only 6¹/₄ inches and weighed a mere 10 ounces. A nickel-plated slide was available, but the more common finish was blued. The similar "Madison" model was a minor variation of the

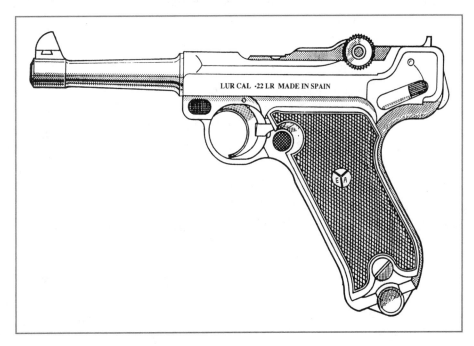

The second major post-war model manufactured by Echave y Arizmendi was the Lur Panzer, a close copy of the Erma EP/LA-22. Note the distinctive EYA company logo on the grips and the markings on the barrel extension.

# HOW TO TAKE DOWN AND ASSEMBLE
## *Figure A.*

Assembly and disassembly procedures 1 thru 4. *(Drawings courtesy of Erma-Werke)*

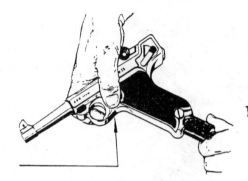

1. Check to ensure the pistol is unloaded. Push magazine catch and remove the magazine.

2. Cock the pistol by pulling the rear toggle link upwards.

3. Push barrel with receiver assembly forward; this will enable the locking bolt to be removed.

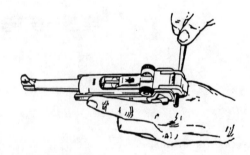

4. Barrel and receiver assembly will now slide backwards on the frame due to spring tension; the receiver axle pin can then be removed.

# HOW TO TAKE DOWN AND ASSEMBLE
## *Figure B.*

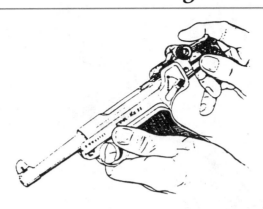

5. Toggle link and breech-block assembly can now be withdrawn from the rear of the receiver.

Assembly and disassembly procedures 5 thru 8. *(Drawings courtesy of Erma-Werke)*

6. Slide complete barrel and receiver out of the frame. The pistol is now dismantled and ready for cleaning.

7. To reassemble, slide in barrel and receiver on the frame.

8. Push slide forward so that the hole remains accessible to receiver axle pin.

*Chapter 9*

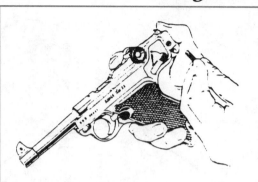

9. Insert the receiver axle pin.

 Assembly and disassembly procedures 9 thru 11. *(Drawings courtesy of Erma-Werke)*

10. Pull the barrel forward against spring tension and at the same time insert the locking bolt, then pull the trigger.

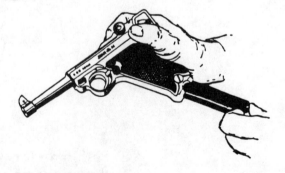

11. Replace the magazine.

same design. Both pistols came into the U.S. under the auspices of the American Import Company from the early 1950s until the end of importation in 1968. Exact production figures are unavailable, because all companies involved have been out of business for many years (although the author has seen serial numbers in the high 50,000s on Dickson Special Agent pistols).

Echasa also made a variant of the Fast version under contract for Manufacture d'Armes de Bayonne (MAB). Its Model G was available in .22 Long Rifle or .25 ACP caliber. The French knew these pistols by the designation *"MAB Espagnol"* (French for "Spanish MAB"). Pistols belonging to the MAB Model G series were available in an all-steel variant or a lightweight aluminum alloy-framed version. The Model G with alloy frame was remarkably light (16 ounces in .32 caliber), whereas the all-steel version in .32 caliber weighed 23 ounces, about the same as the Walther PP.

# *Echasa's Luger Look-alike*

The second postwar flagship of the Echasa line was known as the "Lur Panzer." Based on a design introduced in 1964 by Erma-Werke in Germany (called the AP-22), this pistol fired the .22 caliber LR rimfire cartridge. Like almost all automatic pistols in this comparatively mild caliber, the Lur

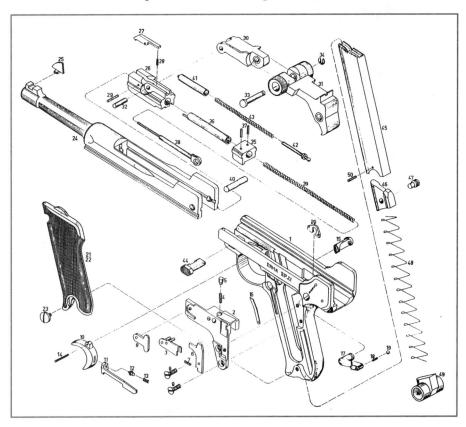

The EP-22's mechanism was quite simple and bore only a slight resemblance—internally and mechanically—to that of the Parabellum (Luger) pistol, despite the striking similarity of external outline. (Drawing courtesy of Erma-Werke)

The Dickson Special Agent model was available in .22 LR, .32 ACP and .380 ACP and came standard with an aluminum alloy frame.

Panzer used a blowback mechanism rather than the Luger's standard locked breech. The original inspiration for this .22 caliber Luger look-alike was a device called the "Kulisch Conversion," which was developed in Germany prior to World War II at a time when severe restrictions had been imposed on German military armaments. The Kulisch Conversion took the form of a simple kit, replacing the standard 9mm caliber barrel and toggle mechanism with lightweight aluminum components designed to function with the lower-powered .22 LR cartridge. By using the Kulisch unit, low-cost training was made possible with the standard service pistol of its time.

To create the EP-22, Erma modified the Kulisch Conversion by moving the return spring to the rear of the frame. The pistol could then use a conventional toggle unit closely resembling one used on the original Parabellum pistol. For marketing purposes, this change in the location of the spring created a more attractive pistol than did the boxy-looking Kulisch kit.

The Lur Panzer closely resembled the Erma pistol inside and out. In fact, it was a virtual copy except for the markings, which took the form of the letters E and A inside a large Y, symbolizing the company name (Echave y

Arizmendi). The Lur Panzer may have been a single-action pistol, but it was significantly larger than its double-action PP look-alike. It was 8.8 inches long overall, with a 4.1-inch barrel and an unloaded weight of 28.3 ounces. Magazine capacity was 10 rounds, and only a .22 Long Rifle version was available. The Lur Panzer remained in production for only a short time and is a scarce commodity today.

## Postscript and Epitaph

Echave y Arizmendi's lack of government business explains why the company reproduced two pistol designs that were so solidly established among civilian gun buyers. Regrettably, Echasa's plan, logical as it was, failed when passage by America's Gun Control Act in 1968 severely limited imports into the U.S. Echave y Arizmendi's best-selling model line—the "Fast" and its variant forms—could no longer be exported, not being tall and long enough in its combined dimensions (i.e., a minimum height of four inches and a minimum combined length and height of ten inches). Sales of the Lur Panzer could not make up the difference: in fact, even the Erma copy has since gone out of production because of insufficient sales. While Echasa also had contacts and sales in Europe and South America, the loss of its lucrative U.S. business proved fatal. After losing its share of the U.S. market, Echave y Arizmendi lasted less than two years. Its collapse in 1970 left only Astra, Llama and Star to continue the Spanish handgun story.

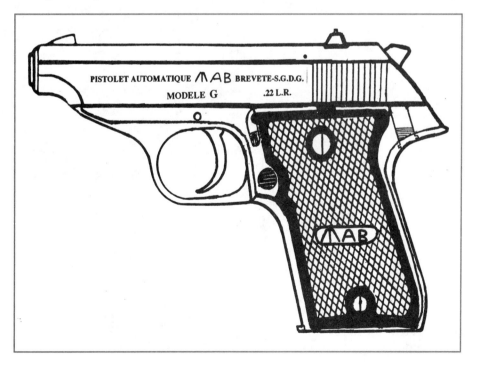

The MAB Model G, a variant of the "Fast" version, fired either a .22 LR or .25 ACP caliber.

# Chapter 10

## Gabilondo (Llama) Since 1945

### The Llama Line: Compact Models

Following World War II, Gabilondo y Cia continued the highly successful Llama line it had introduced during the early 1930s. The popular .380 Caliber Model III (Model 3) remained a mainstay of the line until its discontinuance in 1954, at which time a slightly improved version—the Model III-A—went into production. The chief difference between these two pistols was a grip safety (in Model 1911 style) installed on the Model III-A at the rear of the frame. A less noticeable change was the thumb safety used in the Model III-A. Thought it was still patterned after the Model 1911 type, it had a longer and larger working surface designed to help shooters push the safety down to its fire setting.

Gabilondo's Llama Model III-A remains the company's most important .380 ACP caliber pistol in terms of total numbers produced.

Gabilondo's Llama Model X-A, like all Llama-type pistols, featured an exposed extractor mounted on the slide behind and slightly below the ejection port.

Like the Model III from which it was derived, the Model III-A featured an unlocked breech (blowback) mechanism. Llama also made a locked-breech variation, called the Model 6 (or Model VI), which was identical in outward appearance. It was slightly heavier, though, because of its Browning-style tipping barrel, breech locking system. The Model 10-A (or X-A), which was also introduced in 1954 (and is still in production), while identical to the Model III-A in outward appearance, fires the .32 ACP cartridge. The Model 15 (XV) "Especial" was much the same as the Model III-A, but it fired the .22 Long Rifle cartridge instead. The Model 16 (XVI) added fancy embellishments to the finish of the basic Model 15, but mechanically it was the same gun. The similar Model 19 (or XIX), while still a .380 caliber gun like the Model III-A, had a frame made of lightweight aluminum alloy instead of steel. The alloy frame reduced the weight of the Model 19 by about five ounces, or a total weight of only 18 ounces, but it lost some of the durability inherent with the all-steel model. For those in need of an especially lightweight pistol, however, this weight reduction of slightly over a pound was well worth it. Two of these Llama-type pistols made an appearance in the Mugica line as well. The Model III-A .380 caliber pistol became the Mugica Model 105G, replacing the earlier Llama Model III/Mugica Model 105. By the same token, the Model X-A became Mugica's Model 101G, replacing the earlier Llama Model X/Mugica Model 101.

The 7.65mm (.32 caliber) Llama Model X-A (bottom) bears a strong resemblance to the locked-breech pistols built by Gabilondo, such as the 9mm Model XI "Especial" (top). The smaller, less powerful cartridge enables the Model X-A to use a simple, unlocked breech mechanism.

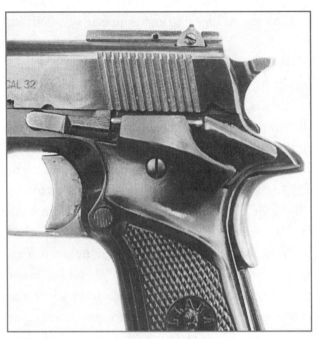

The Llama Model X-A includes a thumbrest molded into the checkered plastic grip.

Early versions of the Model III-A retained the lanyard loop so popular on Spanish pistol designs, suggesting as they did some hope of military acceptance. Later variations of the Model III-A also chose a more civilized configuration, including the addition of a raised ventilated sight rib atop the slide, and contoured plastic grips with thumbrests molded in. As with the Astra and Star firms, Llama-Gabilondo continues to offer pistols embellished with fancy (and costly) finishes, such as chrome, silver and gold, and engraving as well. Variants of the Model III-A pistol remain in production but are no longer available in the U.S. A slightly modified version—the "Llama Micro-max"—appeared in 1997 *(see below)*. Llama continues to produce the Model X-A, but it is no longer sold in the United States. It remains popular, though, in Europe, where the .32 ACP (7.65mm) cartridge still has a wide following a century after its introduction in 1899 by FN and John Browning. In the U.S., pistols armed with the .32 ACP cartridge have traditionally run a distant second to those firing the larger and more powerful .380 ACP. As an example, during the period 1975-1994, U.S. manufacturers produced 2,457,123 pistols in .380 caliber but only 618,266 in .32 ACP, which suggests that the U.S. market for .32 caliber pistols is both smaller and served to a greater extent by imported types, including some of the Spanish

A front view of the Llama Model X-A displays the pistol's Colt-style muzzle bushing and recoil-spring plug.

pistols covered in this book. *(See the Appendix for more information on pistol calibers used in Spanish handguns.)*

The smallest Gabilondo pistol ever made was the Llama Model 17 (or Model XVII), which was also called the Executive Model. It appeared in 1963 and was essentially a Model 15 that had been radically downsized. The Model 17 was indeed a tiny gun, with an overall length of only 4.7 inches, with a 2.36-inch barrel. It weighed only 12.33 ounces and fired a .22 Short cartridge, its tiny magazine holding a maximum of six rounds (a companion pistol—the Model 18 (or XVIII)—used the .25 ACP/6.35mm Browning cartridge). The small size of these pistols certainly contributed to their popularity, but Gabilondo's timing was off. Passage of the Gun

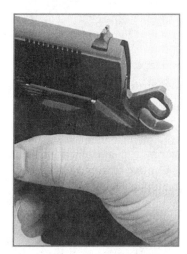

The extended beaver-tail-type grip safety, a mainstay of Llama pistols since the Max-1, makes the Mini-max virtually immune to hand injuries caused by a recoiling slide or hammer.

Control Act of 1968 *(see Chapter 8)* curtailed further importation of this tiny pistol to the all-important U.S. market, forcing the company to stop production only six years after it had begun.

## *The Llama Line: Full-sized Models*

The Llama line of holster pistols based on the Browning-designed Colt Model of 1911 flourishes to this day. The Llama Model 8 (or Model VIII), introduced in 1955, was simply a reissue, with slight modifications, of the company's Model VII pistol. The latter was itself nothing more than the Model IV, which originated the Llama line. Rechambered to fire the .38 Super Automatic cartridge, the Model IV remains popular among sport shooters in North, Central and South America. The design of the Model VIII followed the typical Llama variation on the Model 1911 theme, which included a grip safety with an arched mainspring housing on the lower rear gripstrap, in the fashion of the M1911A1. It also had a plunger tube on the frame—between the slide stop lever and manual safety lever—as in the original M1911 design. The only deviations from the M1911 pistol design were a ventilated rib placed atop the slide and carrying the front and rear sights, along with the flexible lanyard ring so popular with the Spaniards (as it was with any pistols offering even the faintest potential for military or police service).

Gabilondo kept the original Model VIII pistol in production until 1985. Its .38 Super chambering made it a popular pistol in Central and South America, and it even enjoyed some success in the U.S. because of its good

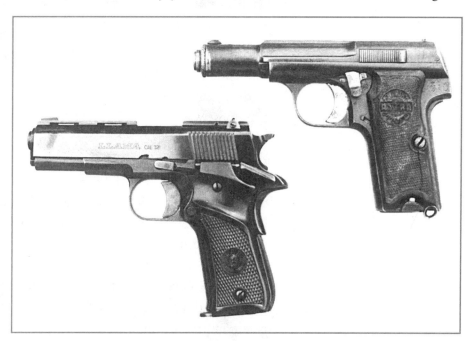

Gabilondo's Llama Model X-A (bottom) has become a modern classic, just as the Astra Model 300 (top) was during the 1920s and 1930s.

quality and modest price. U.S. shooters, however, often displayed a willingness to pay more for a Colt Government Model (civilian variation of the M1911) in the same .38 caliber chambering. The current version of the Model VIII—the Model VIII-C—holds an awesome 18 rounds in its cavernous double-column magazine, which is twice as many rounds as the original Model VIII could hold. Aside from its increased magazine capacity (which comes at the cost of a significantly wider, less manageable grip for shooters with small hands), the Model VIII-C now features checkered neoprene grips similar to other Llama pistols. It lacks, however, the distinctive ventilated sight rib, once common on Llama-brand pistols but which now is preserved only on the small-frame Models III-A and X-A. As with Llama-Gabilondo's recent offerings, the Model VIII-C uses a rounded hammer rather than the M1911-style spur hammer found on virtually all pistols in the Llama line (except the Model XI) up to the early 1990s.

Llama Models III-A, X-A (shown) and XV all employ a rib atop the slide. This 1979-vintage Model X-A, with its sight rib ventilated, presents an elegant touch for such an inexpensive pistol.

The .45 ACP caliber Model IX (sometimes written as Model 9) was introduced in 1936 and remained in production until 1954, at which time Gabilondo replaced it with the Model IX-A (9A), an identical gun except for the addition of a grip safety on the upper portion of the rear gripstrap. Its purpose was to give this pistol an even stronger resemblance to the Colt Government Model that had inspired its design. Later, a ventilated rib was added to carry both front and rear sights. Like the Colt Government Model, the 7-shot Model IX-A was a full-sized handgun measuring 8.5 inches in length with a 5-inch barrel and an unloaded weight of 38 ounces. Its cost was significantly less than the competing Colt Government Model, yet it offered similar features, smooth performance and good quality of material and workmanship. From its introduction in 1954 until 1985, the Model IX-A served as the backbone of the Llama line, inspiring numerous minor variations on the basic Government Model theme, several of which remain in production to this day.

To demonstrate its excellent accuracy, this 5-shot offhand group fired with a Mini-max from 25 feet away measures only 1.1 inches across.

In 1954, Llama reluctantly dropped its strikingly attractive, European-styled Model XI "Especial" 9mm Parabellum service pistol in favor of a modified variant, the Model XI-B, which also fired the 9mm Parabellum cartridge. The Model XI-B differed from its ancestor, however, by reverting to a Model 1911-type appearance, mostly by eliminating the gracefully-curved rear gripstrap on the "Especial" and adding a grip safety at the rear of the frame (the Model XI-B's slide also had a raised and ventilated sighting rib not used on the M1911). Mechanically, the Llama Model XI-B followed the Model 1911's lead, departing still further from that of the company's earlier Model XI "Especial" by restoring a plunger tube between the slide stop and thumb safety. The decision to reinstitute this feature was, in this author's opinion, one of the few weak points of an otherwise superb Model XI-B design.

## Gabilondo Revolvers

Although revolvers were the first product of Gabilondos y Urresti (the parent company to today's Llama-Gabilondo y Cia), the company's production of revolvers did not begin until ten years after World War II ended. The "Ruby Extra," which first appeared in 1955, marked Gabilondo's first entry into the revolver field. Built along the lines of a basic Smith & Wesson Hand Ejector/M&P pattern—but with a coiled mainspring instead of the flat leaf type favored by Smith & Wesson for all but its smallest revolvers—Gabilondo's Ruby Extra series represented the company's economy line of revolvers. Models 12 (XII), 13 (XIII) and 14 (XIV) were all Ruby Extra revolvers. The Model 12 fired the .38 S&W

Although the pistols in this chapter are known as "Llamas," the company name remains "Gabilondo" in honor of the founders. The model shown is a Llama Model X-A.

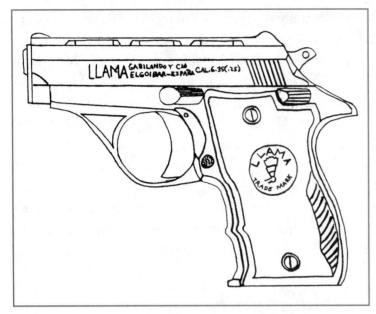

The .25 ACP caliber Llama Model XVIII was an extraordinarily compact pocket pistol. It appeared briefly during the period 1963-1969 along with a companion model, the XVII in .22 Short.

caliber cartridge and had a 5-inch barrel and a square butt, making it suitable for use as a holster gun (though the caliber choice is low-powered for such a large gun). The Model 13 was a more powerful but smaller revolver. It fired the longer .38 Special round, had a more concealable rounded butt, and provided shooters a choice of a 4- or 6-inch barrel. In either length, the barrel on the Model 13 had a ventilated rib, while the Model 13 with its 6-inch barrel added an adjustable rear sight and target grips. The Model 14-—which was available in .22 LR and .32 S&W—came in a wide choice of barrel lengths and sights.

The moderately-priced Ruby Extra line remained in production until 1970. Although the quality of its revolvers was not on a par with the outstanding "Comanche" line *(see below)*, these Ruby Extra guns afforded adequate workmanship and material at an attractive price, which as we have seen was a Spanish specialty. Consequently, Ruby Extra revolvers were a favorite among police forces, particularly among cash-strapped agencies and civilians in Central and South America and throughout the world, and sold widely to civilians (except in the U.S.). Indeed, the Ruby Extra revolvers were for many years the second-most popular revolver line in the Philippines, surpassed only by the Smith & Wesson line.

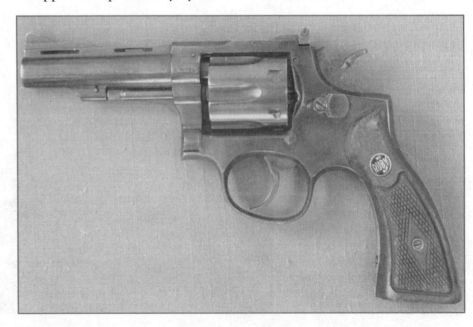

The Ruby Extra revolvers, made from 1955 to 1970, proved popular outside the United States. This Model XIII (13) once served on a South American police force.

The Gabilondo company still makes its Llama line of revolvers (introduced in 1969 with the "Martial") in the company's modern plant in Vitoria, Spain. Their guns continue to be patterned after the highly successful and efficient Smith & Wesson revolvers with their double-action trigger mechanism and yoke-mounted cylinder that swings open to the left side of the frame for reloading. In these respects, the Llama Martial resembles the Ruby Extra Model 12, including its coil mainspring, heavier barrel with a ventilated sighting rib on top, and an adjustable rear sight. The quality

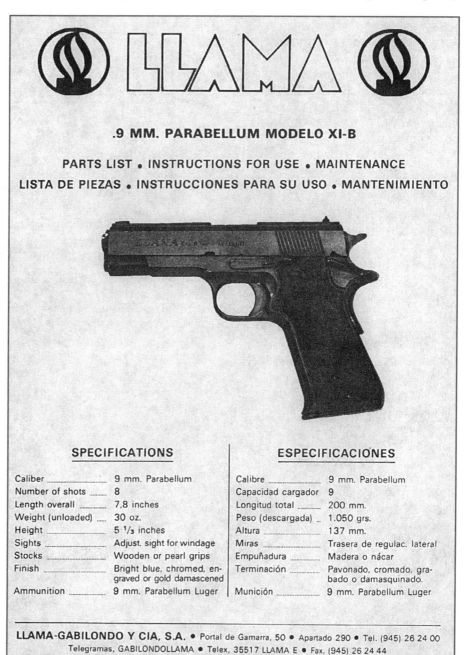

## LLAMA

### .9 MM. PARABELLUM MODELO XI-B

**PARTS LIST • INSTRUCTIONS FOR USE • MAINTENANCE**
**LISTA DE PIEZAS • INSTRUCCIONES PARA SU USO • MANTENIMIENTO**

| SPECIFICATIONS | | ESPECIFICACIONES | |
|---|---|---|---|
| Caliber | 9 mm. Parabellum | Calibre | 9 mm. Parabellum |
| Number of shots | 8 | Capacidad cargador | 9 |
| Length overall | 7,8 inches | Longitud total | 200 mm. |
| Weight (unloaded) | 30 oz. | Peso (descargada) | 1.050 grs. |
| Height | 5 1/3 inches | Altura | 137 mm. |
| Sights | Adjust. sight for windage | Miras | Trasera de regulac. lateral |
| Stocks | Wooden or pearl grips | Empuñadura | Madera o nácar |
| Finish | Bright blue, chromed, engraved or gold damascened | Terminación | Pavonado, cromado, grabado o damasquinado. |
| Ammunition | 9 mm. Parabellum Luger | Munición | 9 mm. Parabellum Luger |

**LLAMA-GABILONDO Y CIA, S.A. •** Portal de Gamarra, 50 • Apartado 290 • Tel. (945) 26 24 00
Telegramas, GABILONDOLLAMA • Telex, 35517 LLAMA E • Fax, (945) 26 24 44
**01080 VITORIA** (España)

The Model XI-B replaced the more graceful Model XI "Especial" with a design similar to the Colt Model 1911 which inspired it.

*Chapter 10*

of fit and finish also represent an improvement over the Ruby Extra guns, but not without a rise in price, reflecting the Llama-brand revolver's higher manufacturing costs. Standard caliber is .38 Special, but Gabilondo has also made a similar .38 S&W caliber (called the "Martial Police"), Model 26 (.22 LR) with a steel frame, a Model 27 (.32 S&W Long), a Model 28 (.22 Long Rifle) with a lightweight aluminum-alloy frame, and a Model 30 (.22 Magnum). Target revolvers included the Model 22 in .38 Special, the Model 29 in .22 Long Rifle, and the Model 32 in .32 caliber. These three models, having been optimized for target-shooting with adjustable sights,

The Llama Martial, introduced in 1969, has since appeared in numerous variations of finish and barrel length, a flexibility that led in part to the model's continuing popularity.

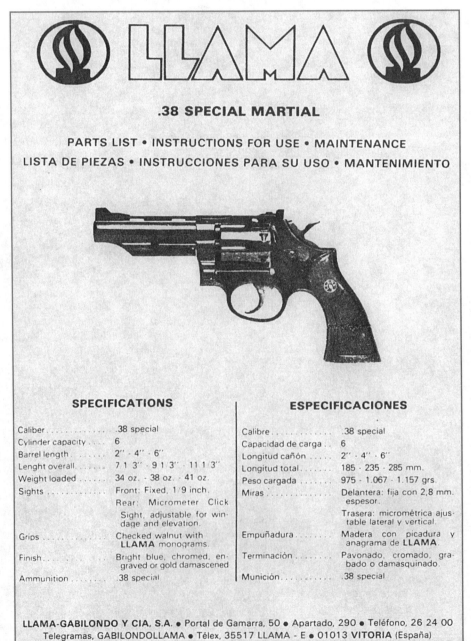

# LLAMA

## .38 SPECIAL MARTIAL

PARTS LIST • INSTRUCTIONS FOR USE • MAINTENANCE
LISTA DE PIEZAS • INSTRUCCIONES PARA SU USO • MANTENIMIENTO

| SPECIFICATIONS | | ESPECIFICACIONES | |
|---|---|---|---|
| Caliber | .38 special | Calibre | .38 special |
| Cylinder capacity | 6 | Capacidad de carga | 6 |
| Barrel length | 2″ - 4″ - 6″ | Longitud cañón | 2″ - 4″ - 6″ |
| Lenght overall | 7 1 3″ - 9 1 3″ - 11 1 3″ | Longitud total | 185 - 235 - 285 mm. |
| Weight loaded | 34 oz. - 38 oz. - 41 oz. | Peso cargada | 975 - 1.067 - 1.157 grs. |
| Sights | Front: Fixed, 1/9 inch. Rear: Micrometer Click Sight, adjustable for windage and elevation. | Miras | Delantera: fija con 2,8 mm. espesor. Trasera: micrométrica ajustable lateral y vertical. |
| Grips | Checked walnut with LLAMA monograms. | Empuñadura | Madera con picadura y anagrama de LLAMA. |
| Finish | Bright blue, chromed, engraved or gold damascened | Terminación | Pavonado, cromado, grabado o damasquinado. |
| Ammunition | .38 special | Munición | .38 special |

LLAMA-GABILONDO Y CIA, S.A. ● Portal de Gamarra, 50 ● Apartado, 290 ● Teléfono, 26 24 00
Telegramas, GABILONDOLLAMA ● Télex, 35517 LLAMA - E ● 01013 VITORIA (España)

The Mini-max (bottom) is one of a series of Spanish clones of the Colt Model 1911, beginning in the early 1920s with Bonifacio Echeverria's Star Model A (top).

grips and the like, frequently had the suffix *olimpico* (Olympic) added to their model designation. As with its automatic pistols, Gabilondo frequently identifies these various Llama revolvers with the model numbers written in Roman numerals. Of these, only the .38 Special Martial model and the Model 26 (XXVI) in .22 LR remain in production at this writing, the others having been discontinued by 1976 to make way for the evolving Comanche line.

The Comanche—flagship of the Llama revolver line—went into production in 1975. It began with the Comanche (.357 Magnum) followed in 1977 by the Comanche I (.22 Long Rifle) with a 6-inch barrel, to be supplemented later that same year by the Comanche II in .38 Special caliber (with a choice of 4-inch or 6-inch barrel). With three popular revolver calibers in hand by 1977, Llama renamed its original .357 Magnum model the Comanche III, which is still in production but is no longer imported into the U.S. The larger .44 Magnum Super Comanche, or Comanche IV, followed in 1978. It was superseded in 1982 by a .357 Magnum caliber version on the same large frame, called the Comanche V. The well-made Super Comanche, which was available with a 4-inch (.357 Comanche V only), 6-inch or 8.5-inch barrel and blued finish only, cost considerably less than the Smith &

The Comanche, flagship of the Llama revolver line since 1975, is now made only in .357 Magnum caliber.

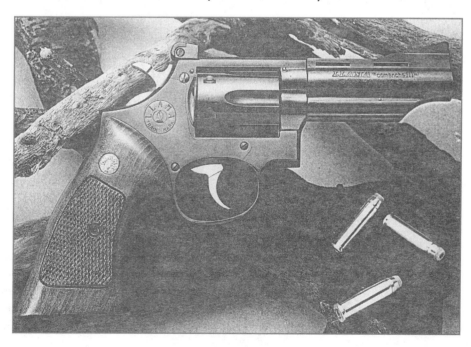

Wesson Model 29, which it closely resembled in size, appearance and features. Nevertheless, the Super Comanche lacked the prestige of its Smith & Wesson competition in the vitally important U.S. market and did not become popular in other countries because of its large size and magnum caliber, forcing the company to discontinue it in 1994.

Other important members of the Llama revolver family include the Scorpio and Piccolo models. These small revolvers with their two-inch barrels closely resemble Smith & Wesson's short-barreled Model 10 in size, appearance and features. Lacking the adjustable sights, ventilated sight rib and heavy barrel underlug of the Martial and Comanche revolvers, these models feature instead low-profile fixed sights and a plain two-inch barrel. For added concealment, both guns favor a rounded (rather than a square) butt profile on the underside of the grip. Introduced in 1991, the Scorpio remains one of Gabilondo's most popular models overseas, although it is not sold in the United States at this writing. Unlike Astra's smallest revolvers—the Cadix and 680 type *(see Chapter 8)*—the Scorpio and Piccolo hold six shots in the cylinder (instead of only five) and are easier to shoot, but at the price of increased size and weight. Llama-Gabilondo still keeps the all-steel Scorpio, which weights 29 ounces unloaded, in production, but has quit making the 23-ounce, alloy-framed Piccolo model.

In view of the safety requirements set forth by the U.S. Gun Control Act of 1968, all but the earliest Llama-brand revolvers employ the clever and innovative method of placing the hammer

The Llama Comanche IV (or Super Comanche) was necessarily large and heavy in order to accommodate the powerful .44 Magnum round safely.

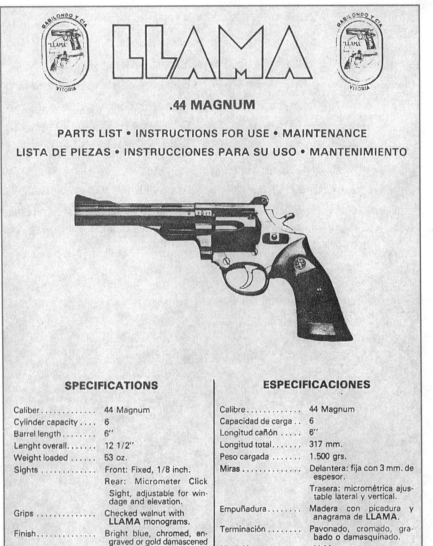

# LLAMA

### .44 MAGNUM

**PARTS LIST • INSTRUCTIONS FOR USE • MAINTENANCE**
**LISTA DE PIEZAS • INSTRUCCIONES PARA SU USO • MANTENIMIENTO**

| SPECIFICATIONS | |
| --- | --- |
| Caliber | 44 Magnum |
| Cylinder capacity | 6 |
| Barrel length | 6'' |
| Lenght overall | 12 1/2'' |
| Weight loaded | 53 oz. |
| Sights | Front: Fixed, 1/8 inch. Rear: Micrometer Click Sight, adjustable for windage and elevation. |
| Grips | Checked walnut with LLAMA monograms. |
| Finish | Bright blue, chromed, engraved or gold damascened |
| Ammunition | .44 Magnum |

| ESPECIFICACIONES | |
| --- | --- |
| Calibre | 44 Magnum |
| Capacidad de carga | 6 |
| Longitud cañón | 6'' |
| Longitud total | 317 mm. |
| Peso cargada | 1.500 grs. |
| Miras | Delantera: fija con 3 mm. de espesor. Trasera: micrométrica ajustable lateral y vertical. |
| Empuñadura | Madera con picadura y anagrama de LLAMA. |
| Terminación | Pavonado, cromado, grabado o damasquinado. |
| Munición | .44 Magnum |

**LLAMA-GABILONDO Y CIA, S.A.** • Portal de Gamarra, 50 • Apartado, 290 • Teléfono, 26 24 00
Telegramas, GABILONDOLLAMA • Télex, 35517 LLAMA - E • VITORIA (España)

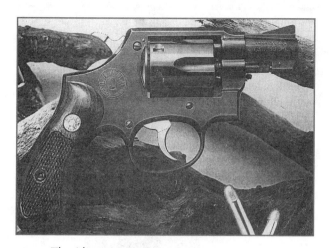

The Llama compact revolver Scorpio resembles the short-barreled, round-butt version of the Smith & Wesson Model 10. An airweight version with aluminum-alloy frame, called the Piccolo, is no longer produced.

on an eccentric cam axis. As a result, the hammer will drop to the level of the firing pin only when the shooter pulls the trigger through a complete double-action cocking stroke or cocks the hammer by thumb for a more precise single-action shot. When the hammer is not cocked, it rests securely against the metal frame slightly above the firing pin, thus ensuring against the possibility of accidental firing. Llama-Gabilondo y Cia has received several safety awards for this system, which it advertises internationally as *"El Revolver Mas Seguro"* ("The Safest Revolver"). Another evidence of this superb attention to detail lies in the adjustable sight found on the larger models: the Martial, the Model 26 and the Comanche. The rear sight, unlike the Smith & Wesson revolvers with their sharp edges, were nicely rounded off on the Llama revolvers to a smooth profile. They were beautifully finished guns, too, their standard bluing job displaying a superior high-polished sheen along with satin chrome, engraved blue, engraved chrome and gold finishes, all available as finish options direct from the factory.

Although these Llama-brand revolves have enjoyed only modest success in the U.S. market, due in part to fierce competition from Charter Arms, Colt, Smith & Wesson and Sturm, Ruger, this well-made line of Spanish

The Llama Omni .45 ACP version, shown here, was an innovative design that included a single-column magazine holding up to seven rounds. It also featured a fully adjustable rear sight.

The compact Mini-max II handles well despite a chunky grip made necessary by fitting 10 rounds of .45 ACP cartridge into the magazine.

The Mini-max, like other pistols based on the Model 1911, has a single-action trigger mechanism, which means its hammer must be cocked before firing. Adding a Swartz firing-pin safety lock makes such "cocked and locked" carry feasible.

Like the Colt Government Model which inspired it, the Micro-max features a plunger tube fixed to the frame, providing enough tension to operate the slide stop (here removed) and the manual safety, visible at the rear of the plunger tube.

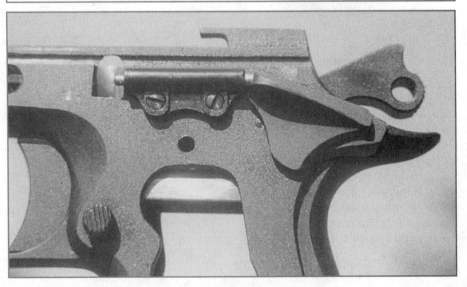

revolvers has proven extraordinarily popular and successful overseas. When a prospective buyer examines these products objectively, with no preconceived notions about "cheap Spanish handguns," the Llama line will stand up to comparisons with any revolvers made anywhere in the world.

# Spanish Armed Forces Pistol Designs

During the late 1970s, Spain's armed forces ordered a new service pistol, with trials lasting into the early 1980s. Llama-Gabilondo's entries in this competition—first the Omni and later the Model 82—represented radical departures from the company's previous work and indicated Gabilondo's willingness to explore new options and new technology. The first Omni, which appeared in 1982, kept its standard tilting-barrel system for locking the breech. Rather than installing a pinned link beneath the barrel (which John M. Browning had designed years earlier for the Colt Model 1911 pistol), Gabilondo turned to a modified system that incorporated a fixed cam beneath the barrel, similar to the FN High Power pistol designed by Browning and introduced in 1935. Aside from this conventional method for locking the breech, virtually every other feature of the Omni demonstrated a fresh, innovative approach to the automatic pistol. The Gabilondo factory paid particular attention to the magazine, which is the heart of any automatic pistol, and came up with three configurations: Omni I was a .45 ACP caliber gun with a seven-round magazine; Omni II a 9mm Parabellum variation with a nine-shot capacity; and the Omni III (also a 9mm), whose 13-round magazine narrowed at the top portion from a double-column width to a single column, allowing the top five rounds to feed straight into the firing chamber

The Gabilondo revolvers utilize a clever safety mechanism that rotates the hammer on an eccentric axis. At rest, the hammer lies directly against the frame, unable to reach the firing pin. Only when the trigger is pulled through does the hammer rotate enough to reach the firing pin.

EXCLUSIVO MECANISMO DE SEGURIDAD EN LOS REVOLVERES LLAMA

EXCLUSIVE SAFETY MECHANISM IN LLAMA REVOLVERS

En la acción de disparo el martillo percutor se desplaza y golpea la aguja percutora en su centro, recobrando la posición inicial de reposo al soltar el disparador.

When firing, the hammer moves and hits the center of the firingpin, returning to the initial uncocked position when the trigger is realeased.

El martillo percutor, en posición de reposo descansa directamente sobre el armazón, desalineado y sin ningún punto de contacto con la aguja percutora.

When the hammer is in the uncocked position it rest directly against the frame, unaligned and without any point of contact with the firing-pin.

A cutaway view of the Model 87 illustrates the compensator assembly attached to the front end of the slide. The Beretta-style breech locking block, visible just above the recoil spring, along with an adjustable overtravel screw on the trigger's trailing edge, are also shown.

flawlessly. The magazine also proved extremely easy to insert into the pistol grip, even in the dark. All the shooter had to do was locate the double-wide opening at the bottom of the grip. The Omni's controls also differed in a subtle way from those used on earlier pistols. For example, the firing pin was made in two pieces forming a ball-and-socket joint. In most pistols the one-piece firing pin is prone to breakage on occasion. Should that happen on the range, it would be difficult to replace without special tools. Even in a pistol with an easily accessible firing pin, such as an M1911, breaking the firing pin while in combat could prove fatal. So confident was Gabilondo with the Omni two-piece firing pin design that it guaranteed the assembly for life.

To ensure optimum trigger pull in both single and double action, the Omni was designed to include dual sear bars—one for single action and the other for double action. In the event a loaded pistol dropped, a firing-pin lock linked to the trigger provided safety. In addition, the manual safety lever, when applied, decocked the hammer mechanically while shielding it from contact with the firing pin. This level of attention to detail was more reminiscent of a Swiss or German design, not a Spanish one. In an attempt to create a gun as user-friendly as possible, Gabilondo even paid considerable attention to the Omni's triggerguard configuration. The front of the triggerguard had a slightly hooked p rotuberance to facilitate the "finger-forward two-handed hold" then in vogue. Moreover, the slightly indented underside of the triggerguard enabled shooters to get a good high grip on the pistol in an attempt to reduce muzzle rise upon firing.

Despite these clever touches and its obvious high quality, the Omni

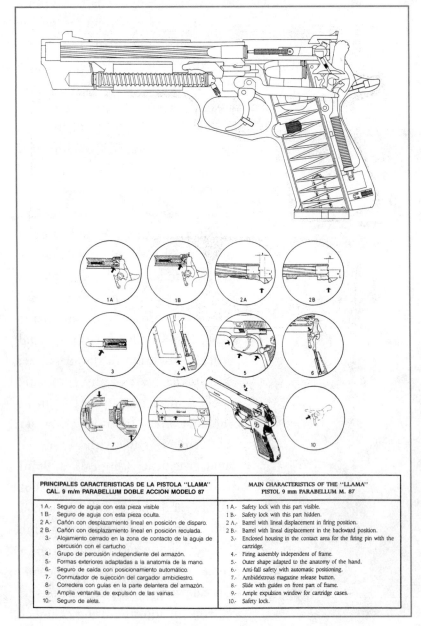

| PRINCIPALES CARACTERISTICAS DE LA PISTOLA ''LLAMA'' CAL. 9 m/m PARABELLUM DOBLE ACCION MODELO 87 | MAIN CHARACTERISTICS OF THE ''LLAMA'' PISTOL 9 mm PARABELLUM M. 87 |
|---|---|
| 1 A.- Seguro de aguja con esta pieza visible | 1 A.- Safety lock with this part visible. |
| 1 B.- Seguro de aguja con esta pieza oculta. | 1 B.- Safety lock with this part hidden. |
| 2 A.- Cañón con desplazamiento lineal en posición de disparo. | 2 A.- Barrel with lineal displacement in firing position. |
| 2 B.- Cañón con desplazamiento lineal en posición reculada. | 2 B.- Barrel with lineal displacement in the backward position. |
| 3.- Alojamiento cerrado en la zona de contacto de la aguja de percusión con el cartucho. | 3.- Enclosed housing in the contact area for the firing pin with the cartridge. |
| 4.- Grupo de percusión independiente del armazón. | 4.- Firing assembly independent of frame. |
| 5.- Formas exteriores adaptadas a la anatomía de la mano. | 5.- Outer shape adapted to the anatomy of the hand. |
| 6.- Seguro de caída con posicionamiento automático. | 6.- Anti-fall safety with automatic positioning. |
| 7.- Conmutador de sujección del cargador ambidiestro. | 7.- Ambidextrous magazine release button. |
| 8.- Corredera con guías en la parte delantera del armazón. | 8.- Slide with guides on front part of frame. |
| 9.- Amplia ventanilla de expulsión de las vainas. | 9.- Ample expulsion window for cartridge cases. |
| 10.- Seguro de aleta. | 10.- Safety lock. |

The Mini-max, upon disassembly, reveals an affinity for the classic Colt Model 1911/Government Model, considered by many to be John M. Browning's greatest invention.

The Micro-max, shown disassembled, strongly resemble the Colt Government Model design without locking ribs atop the barrel—evidence of a straight blowback action.

*Chapter 10*

was not a marketing success. Its strange appearance made it appear too radical and outlandish in the early 1980s, not long before the U.S. armed forces had accepted the Beretta Model 92F as its M9 service pistol, thus opening the door to the wealth of innovative automatic pistol designs emanating from Europe. The M1911 in .45 caliber and its many copies (including Gabilondo's own Llama line) dominated the business. The few police departments and civilian shooters who demanded a double-action model in this caliber were already well served by the superb SIG/Sauer Model P220. Moreover, the Omni was by no means an inexpensive pistol. The suggested retail price in 1983 was $599.95, a daunting figure in those days. As a result, the Omni fell by the wayside with other equally innovative but unappreciated designs of the period, including Steyr's Model GB gas-operated pistol. Understandably discouraged with the Omni's slow sales, Gabilondo ceased production in 1986 and turned its concentration on the Model 82.

Despite the Omni's lack of success, several of its design features were deemed worth preserving and duly appeared in the Llama Model 82. These included the frame contours in general and the shape of the triggerguard in particular. Otherwise, the Model 82 was a departure from the Omni, becoming altogether different from a mechanical point of view. The obvious inspiration for the Model 82 was the Beretta Model 92 service pistol. For example, an oscillating block under the barrel locks and unlocks the breech on the Model 82 in the same manner as the Beretta system. The double-action trigger mechanism on the Model 82 is actuated by a drawbar mounted on the right side of the frame, much like the Beretta. Model 82's high-capacity 15-shot magazine and its loaded-chamber indicator mounted on the extractor are also strongly reminiscent of the Beretta. The equipment used

In Gabilondo's Llama MAX-1 series in 9mm Parabellum (here erroneously referred to as ".9" millimeters), magazine capacity rises to nine rounds, two more than the standard .45 caliber model.

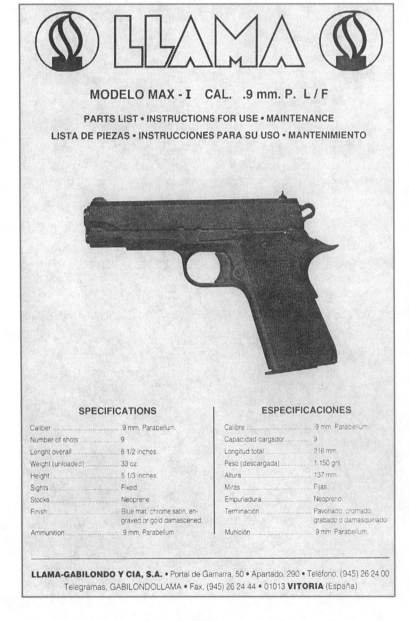

## LLAMA

### MODELO MAX - I  CAL. .9 mm. P. L / F

PARTS LIST • INSTRUCTIONS FOR USE • MAINTENANCE
LISTA DE PIEZAS • INSTRUCCIONES PARA SU USO • MANTENIMIENTO

| SPECIFICATIONS | | ESPECIFICACIONES | |
|---|---|---|---|
| Caliber | .9 mm. Parabellum. | Calibre | 9 mm. Parabellum |
| Number of shots | 9 | Capacidad cargador | 9 |
| Lenght overall | 8 1/2 inches. | Longitud total | 216 mm. |
| Weight (unloaded) | 33 oz. | Peso (descargada) | 1.150 grs. |
| Height | 5 1/3 inches. | Altura | 137 mm. |
| Sights | Fixed. | Miras | Fijas. |
| Stocks | Neoprene. | Empuñadura | Neopreno. |
| Finish | Blue mat, chrome satin, engraved or gold damascened. | Terminación | Pavonado, cromado, grabado o damasquinado. |
| Ammunition | .9 mm. Parabellum. | Munición | 9 mm. Parabellum. |

**LLAMA-GABILONDO Y CIA, S.A.** • Portal de Gamarra, 50 • Apartado, 290 • Teléfono. (945) 26 24 00
Telegramas, GABILONDOLLAMA • Fax, (945) 26 24 44 • 01013 **VITORIA** (España)

in the Model 82 includes ambidextrous safety levers and a reversible magazine release button, features which once again imitate the latest design of the Beretta Model 92. Unlike the Beretta pistol, with its famous open-topped slide configuration inherited from numerous earlier designs, the Model 82 utilizes a stronger, enclosed slide pierced only by an ejection port on the right side. Interestingly, Gabilondo can supply the Model 82 (upon request) with or without a magazine safety. These pistols, which were once sold commercially in the U.S., lack this safety feature; but the Spanish service pistols and Model 82s that were sold to several South American armed forces all have it.

One version of the Llama Mini-max, introduced in late 1995, fires a .45 ACP caliber and uses a 6-shot magazine (it also accepts a slightly longer 7- or 8-shot M1911-type magazine).

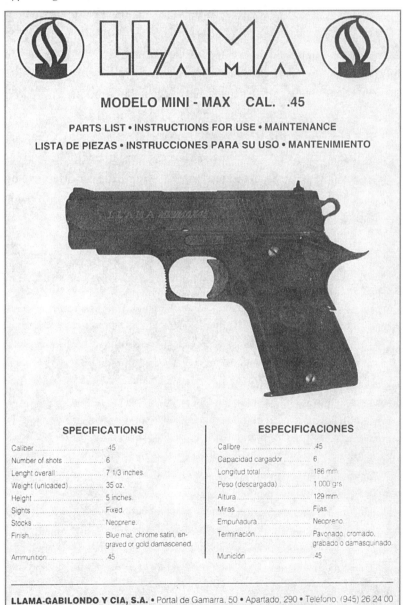

# LLAMA

## MODELO MINI - MAX   CAL.  .45

### PARTS LIST • INSTRUCTIONS FOR USE • MAINTENANCE
### LISTA DE PIEZAS • INSTRUCCIONES PARA SU USO • MANTENIMIENTO

| SPECIFICATIONS | |
|---|---|
| Caliber | .45 |
| Number of shots | 6 |
| Lenght overall | 7 1/3 inches. |
| Weight (unloaded) | 35 oz. |
| Height | 5 inches. |
| Sights | Fixed. |
| Stocks | Neoprene. |
| Finish | Blue mat, chrome satin, engraved or gold damascened. |
| Ammunition | .45 |

| ESPECIFICACIONES | |
|---|---|
| Calibre | .45 |
| Capacidad cargador | 6 |
| Longitud total | 186 mm. |
| Peso (descargada) | 1.000 grs. |
| Altura | 129 mm. |
| Miras | Fijas. |
| Empuñadura | Neopreno. |
| Terminación | Pavonado, cromado, grabado o damasquinado. |
| Munición | .45 |

**LLAMA-GABILONDO Y CIA, S.A.** • Portal de Gamarra, 50 • Apartado, 290 • Teléfono. (945) 26 24 00
Telegramas. GABILONDOLLAMA • Fax. (945) 26 24 44 • 01013 **VITORIA** (España)

The Model 82 went into production in 1986, the same year the Omni died. Gabilondo's vindication for creating these deviations from the M1911-type pistols from the original Llama line finally took place in 1987, when the Spanish armed forces approved the new pistol as their service standard under the designation, *"Modelo M-82 Doble Accion."* With this pistol, Spain entered the ranks of many countries which have abandoned single-action automatic pistols for their troops. While the Model 82 is highly competitive with large-capacity, double-action 9mm service pistols produced in other countries, a few inherent weaknesses lurk in its design. For one, the undersized rear sight hinders rapid acquisition, slowing down accuracy in combat conditions. The reliability of the Model 82 is also suspect when firing certain brands of hollowpoint ammunition (reliability has never been a problem, however, with the high-intensity NATO-spec 9mm ball ammunition used by the Spanish military, for whom Gabilondo designed the Model 82). And, like all high-capacity

The conveniently small size of the Mini-max (top) is apparent when compared to the Astra Model 300 (bottom), another classic small handgun made in Spain.

pistols, the Model 82's grip is fairly large, thus presenting problems for small-statured personnel. This is a large gun, which explains why the *Guardia Civil* decided to retain the compact Star Model BM for issue in situations where concealed carry were required.

With the Model 82 solidly established, thanks to the Spanish Army order, the Gabilondo firm next sought to capitalize on the superb accuracy potential of this powerful pistol by introducing an even better shooter: the Model 87. Basically a Model 82, it had a longer barrel, plus a compensator, more muzzle weight, better adjustable target sights, and a smoother trigger pull (with an overtravel stop on the trigger's trailing edge). It also had a manual safety lever mounted on the left side of the frame, supplementing the slide-mounted decocking type and extended safety, slide stop and magazine release controls. With its two-tone finish—a blued slide mated to a bright, nickel-plated frame—the Model 87 made a strikingly attractive pistol.

This Stoeger ad from the late 1980s lists many desirable features of the Model 87. It also lists other Llama-brand automatic pistols and revolvers then available from Stoeger.

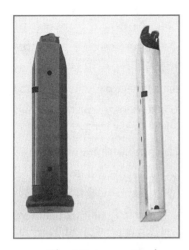

The Mini-max II's double-column magazine (left) holds 10 rounds, compared to the seven-round capacity single-column magazine found in Colt's Government Model or Model 1911 (right).

Although the Models 82 and 87 remain in production and are highly regarded by firearms experts, neither one enjoyed any real success in the U.S. The price of a Model 82 started at $750 in 1988 and rose to $975 by 1993. While firearms evaluators noted its reliability and impressive accuracy, they also expressed sticker shock. The widely available Beretta Model 92F offered all the same features as the Llama Model 82 but at a significantly lower price. The Model 87 had the same problem, retailing for $1,450, although several reviewers noted that with its many built-in features this pistol (at the factory) would cost far more if installed on a standard pistol by a custom gunsmith. Nevertheless, the glowing reviews of these two models proved insufficient to overcome their perceived shortcomings among American shooters.

# Recent Developments

With the decision by Stoeger in 1994 to drop the Llama line, a new importer—SGS Importers International, Inc. (Wanamassa, NJ)—became Llama's U.S. agent. This company (now called Import Sports, Inc.) has helped Gabilondo to revamp its automatic pistol offerings, bringing them more in tune with U.S. marketing trends. With these small but important changes, the revitalized Llama line, while still retaining the desirable features of the classic M1911, was thoroughly modernized, making it a much stronger competitor. Due to the vagaries of U.S. politics, however, the first collaboration between Import Sports and Llama-Gabilondo y Cia

The Mini-max II (top) is not the smallest 10-shot .45 caliber pistol available. Para-Ordnance's P10.45 has that honor. Still, it's a small pistol as shown by comparison with the Llama .380 caliber Micro-max.

*Chapter 10*

The Micro-max (top) is a small pistol built on the order of the Colt .380 pocket pistol. The double-action Pony is shown at bottom for comparison purposes.

almost ended in disaster. Noting the success of the Para-Ordnance .45 caliber pistols—a combination of the Model 1911-type slide with an enlarged frame and high-capacity, 12-shot magazine—Gabilondo decided to make its own version of this innovative design. The result was the Model IX-C, which came on line in 1994. A large pistol, it measured 8½" overall with a 5⅛" barrel. Its height was 5⁹/₁₆" and width was 1⅝". Its weight (unloaded) came to 44 ounces, five ounces more than a standard seven-shot Colt Government Model.

One of the features of the Llama IX-C was the "Swartz safety," a feature Colt had incorporated into its Government Model pistols during the late 1930s. Gabilondo wanted to create a version that was immune to accidental discharges when dropped. The Swartz safety system was designed to solve that problem. It featured a plunger that blocked the firing pin's forward travel until the grip safety was squeezed firmly. This raised a rod (called the firing pin safety actuator), which pushed the plunger out of the firing pin's path. The pistol could then be fired. So long as there was no tension on the grip safety, the actuator rod was released. A small coil spring located beneath the rear sight pushed the plunger down into the locking position, immobilizing the firing pin and preventing the pistol

Gabilondo has revived the clever Swartz safety, used briefly on Colt Government Model pistols back in the 1930s. A rod—moving vertically—is located in the right rear portion of the frame, near the hammer. With the grip safety at rest, this rod lies down in the tunnel (as shown), preventing the firing pin from moving by means of a plunger located in the slide between the firing pin and hammer.

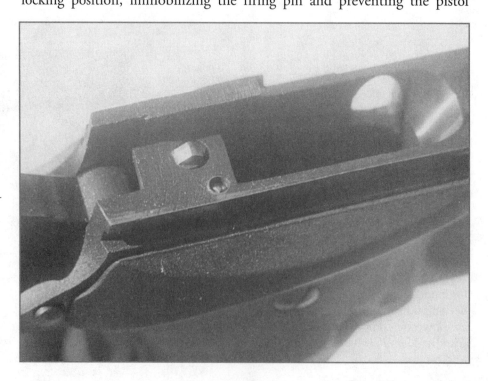

When the grip safety is depressed, it causes the Swartz safety rod to rise out of the frame, pushing the plunger in the slide away from the firing pin. The hammer now has a clear path to the firing pin once the trigger is pulled.

When using the Swartz safety system, shooters must avoid squeezing the grip safety when removing the slide from the frame during disassembly. Otherwise, the rod will rise into the path of the slide and prevent separation of the slide from the frame. The same caution applies when reassembling the pistol, as shown. As it rises out of its well in the frame, the safety rod prevents the slide from returning to its rearmost position.

Llama pistols made by Gabilondo bear a coded serial-number sequence. The last two digits indicate the year of production. In this case, 97 refers to 1997.

*Chapter 10*

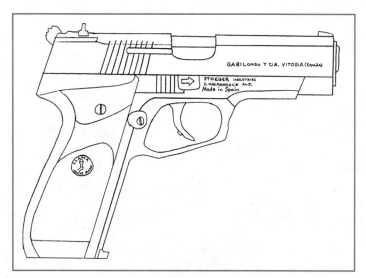

from being fired. Unlike many other modern safety systems, the Swartz system did not interfere with trigger pull and was endorsed by the U.S. Bureau of Alcohol, Tobacco and Firearms (BATF).

Like all Llama-series pistols, the Model IX-C retains its exposed extractor rather than implementing the concealed model used in the Colt M1911-type pistol design. Because it adopted the squared-off, wide-style Para-Ordnance frame, along with its thick checkered neoprene grip pieces, the Model IX-C has an unusually bulky grip. This made the pistol comfortable to shoot, even for shooters unused to the .45 ACP cartridge, but it also caused handling difficulties for most shooters. The IX-C grip does, however, include a semi-arched mainspring housing, which represents a compromise between the straight mainspring housing of the original M1911 and the arched mainspring housing of the later M1911A1. The IX-C's wide grip may make it impossible to take full advantage of this feature, but the semi-arched mainspring housing does seem to please almost everyone who handles on of these pistols. A review in *American Rifleman* (October 1994) noted that, while the Model IX-C magazine was almost identical in appearance to the Para-Ordnance type, it was not interchangeable. Nevertheless, the IX-C's resemblance to the Para-Ordnance pistol is glaringly obvious. For all that, the suggested retail price of the IX-C

The Llama Omni also appeared in a 9mm Parabellum version that incorporated a double-column magazine holding up to 13 rounds. Note the takedown pin (marked with an arrow) to the left of the importer's address on the frame. To remove this pin, the pistol had to be unloaded and the latch pushed to the rear behind the pin.

Llama's MAX-1, in production since 1995, has a standard 7-shot M1911-type magazine. Features of this pistol include its "semi-arched" mainspring housing, extended beavertail grip safety, and exposed extractor (not visible). The variant shown is the full-sized model measuring 8.5 inches in length, similar to the Colt Government Model. (Photograph courtesy of Import Sports.)

The Mini-max departs from M1911 practice by eliminating the separate muzzle bushing and slightly flaring the muzzle end of the barrel. It also adds a removable cylindrical steel plug, closing the gap between muzzle and recoil spring housing.

(around $400) compares favorable with the Para-Ordnance pistol ($750), making the Llama IX-C a formidable competitor among shooters who desire a high-capacity pistol but who are distrustful of the 9mm Parabellum, .38 Super Automatic or .40 S&W calibers, which these pistols mostly use.

Unfortunately, Gabilondo's introduction of the Llama Model IX-C pistol in mid-1994 came at the worst possible time. For in September of that year, the U.S. Congress passed the Crime Bill, which limited the magazine capacity of all new self-loading weapons to a maximum of 10 rounds. This required a revision of the Model IX-C's magazine design, reducing capacity by two rounds. Following the lead of the MAX-1 *(see below)*, Gabilondo also modified the IX-C's hammer design, from a spur configuration to a rounded style. This change, along with a switch to a widened "beavertail" type of grip safety, has made the Model IX-C an easier gun to shoot. It has eliminated any possibility of the slide or hammer pinching the shooter's hand under full recoil. Llama has since introduced a Model IX-D, which uses the same magazine but has a shorter barrel (4¹/₄") and a shorter slide, reducing the overall length to 7⁷/₈" and dropping the unloaded weight to 39 ounces (the same as a standard Colt Government Model).

Gabilondo's next project (in cooperation with SGS/Import Sports) was the MAX-1 pistol, the company's equivalent to the Colt Government Model. Its slide design eliminated the raised rib (sometime ventilated, sometimes solid) on which the earlier M1911-type pistol sights were placed. The MAX-1 retains the Model IX-C's checkered neoprene grips,

Gabilondo hopes its Mini-max (top) will become as successful as its famous Ruby model (bottom) of World War I fame.

*Chapter 10*

but with a slimmer frame that holds a maximum of seven rounds in .45 ACP caliber or nine rounds of 9mm. The semi-arched mainspring housing on the IX-C has also been retained, offering a grip likely to please fans of the original M1911, with its straight mainspring housing, and the M1911A1's arched mainspring housing. The MAX-1 became the first Llama-brand pistol to incorporate a rounded hammer and beavertail grip safety (later used on the Model IX-C and the Mini-max covered below). It also featured a slightly extended slide stop, which made it easier for shooters to actuate than the slide stop on a standard Model 1911 pistol—while adding little or nothing to the pistol's bulk.

The MAX-1 remains a formidable competitor in the active market for M1911-type pistols. It has also benefited from the U.S. ban on Chinese gun imports, making it potentially the heir apparent to Norinco's "Model of the 1911," which was establishing itself at the time as one of the most popular low-cost M1911 clones in the crowded U.S. market. A report in *American Rifleman* magazine (June 1995) states:

*The Max-1 represents a big step toward making the Llama iteration of the M1911 more than just a footnote. A bit more effort to make it accept standard accessories and popular aftermarket replacement parts would put it quite on a plane with the other clones, and its good value for a very low price would make it an especially attractive choice.*

After introducing the Colt Government Model-sized Max-1, Gabilondo followed quickly with the small MAX-1 C/F or MAX-1 Compact. Mechanically identical to the MAX-1, the MAX-1 Compact is slightly shorter (7⁷/₈""compared to 8¹/₂") and two ounces lighter (34 ounces compared to 36 ounces). Magazine capacity is the same (seven rounds in .45 ACP and nine rounds in 9mm). In late 1995 Llama-Gabilondo and Import Sports brought out what many consider the best Model 1911-type Llama pistol ever: the Llama Mini-max. Produced in a choice of three calibers—9mm Parabellum (capacity of eight rounds), .40 S&W (capacity seven rounds), or .45 ACP (capacity six rounds)—this versatile and powerful pistol befits its name: Mini-max, meaning "Minimum size/Maximum firepower." The Mini-Max's dimensions are quite small, similar to those of the earlier Star Models PD or Firestar *(see Chapter 11)*. The Mini-max offers these specifications: **Overall Length:** 7.3 "; **Barrel Length:** 3.7"; **Width:** 1.4"; **Height:** 5.1"; **Weight:** 35 ounces (unloaded). The Mini-max's modest size suits it well for concealed carry in an inside-the-waistband or shoulder holster. Its other features include all of the evolutionary improvements made in the previous Gabilondo models, plus some additional changes made especially for this model, all of which are improvements on the basic

The Mini-max uses a 6-shot magazine, but it can also accept a slightly longer 7- or 8-shot M1911-type magazine (shown in a stainless steel version).

Model 1911 design. These Mini-max innovations include an extended, flared "beavertail"-type safety, rounded hammer, exposed pivoting extractor, 3-dot sights (the front "dot" is actually a rectangle), soft checkered neoprene grips, extended slide release, the Swartz safety *(see above)*, and a squared, slightly recurved triggerguard (to facilitate two-handed shooting). A wide choice of calibers and finishes are available, including matte blue, satin chrome, dural-tone and stainless steel. Unlike any previous Llama pistol, the muzzle end of the Mini-max indicates a considerable departure from M1911 practice. By slightly flaring the muzzle end of the barrel, and by adding a removable cylindrical steel plug to close the gap between the muzzle and the recoil spring housing, Gabilondo has, for the first time in a Llama-brand pistol, eliminated the separate muzzle bushing of the M1911 series. This innovation makes disassembly for cleaning and maintenance easier than that of any previous Llama pistol (or of the M1911 itself).

Llama-Gabilondo y Cia has in the past earned a reputation for making its guns out of steel that was not sufficiently hardened or was otherwise improperly heat-treated, causing the guns to show signs of excessive wear

The Mini-max (top) is about the same size and weight as Star's Firestar pistol (bottom), which also emanates from Spain. Made completely from steel, both pistols are significantly heavier than the classic Star Model PD, the first truly compact factory .45 pistol.

The Mini-max, which lacks ambidextrous controls, has an exposed extractor (shown), a long-standing departure from M1911 practice.

A 7- or 8-shot M1911-type magazine protrudes slightly from the bottom of the Mini-max's grip.

after firing only a few hundred rounds. With the introduction of the Mini-max, Gabilondo began extensive advertising of its "upgraded new steel design." Based on the test firing of over 1,000 rounds by the author, there was no discernible metal wear and no loss of performance, either in reliability or in accuracy. The only weak point seemed to be the dull military-blue finish, which wore rapidly on the high edges of the pistol. What features of the M1911 have been retained in the Mini-max are as important as what has changed. Like its illustrious predecessor, the Mini-max remains an extremely ergonomic combat pistol. Moreover, it can use the same magazines made for the Model 1911 or Government Model pistols. Such magazines, which hold one or two extra rounds of ammunition, are of necessity slightly longer than the Mini-max magazine and therefore they protrude slightly from the bottom of the grip. Still, such interchangeability of magazines is a desirable feature primarily because of the widespread availability of the M1911 magazines.

A review in the June 1996 issue of *American Rifleman* reported testing of the Mini-max as having mediocre accuracy, occasional reliability problems, and a tendency to throw empty cartridge cases into the shooter's face. However, the writer's own testing of a Mini-max pistol in a .45 caliber version, similar to that tested by the *American Rifleman*, did not reveal any such problems. Indeed, our tests demonstrated excellent accuracy for a defensive pistol and near-perfect reliability after a single jam in the first magazine. The Mini-max is undeniably a fine pistol for self-defense—its primary mission—and a pistol capable of serious competition in the growing U.S. market for compact handguns with power. To make it even more attractive, the Mini-max is significantly less expensive than Star's competing Firestar, which is the closest equivalent in features, size and performance. Moreover, the Mini-max's similarity in handling to the world-famous Model 1911 can only work to this little powerhouse's benefit.

In 1997 Llama announced the Mini-max II, a high-capacity version of the Mini-max. Broadly similar in concept to the excellent Para-Ordnance P12.45, the Mini-max II incorporates a thicker grip frame than the original version, enabling its double-column magazine to hold up to 12 rounds in its overseas version. As with other guns imported into the U.S. since 1995, however, the Mini-max II is limited to a maximum capacity of 10 rounds. Like the standard Mini-max, the slightly thicker Mini-max II is available in 9mm Parabellum and .40 S&W calibers in addition to the original .45 ACP caliber. At the same time, Llama also introduced the updated "Llama Micro-max." Following its debut in 1997, the most obvious departures from the basic Model III-A design are a rounded hammer and a matte black finish, both inspired by the Mini-max. Like the Model III-A, the Micro-max is made in .380 caliber solely for the U.S. market.

Having finally achieved a major Spanish government contract with the armed forces acceptance of the Model 82 pistol back in 1987, Llama-Gabilondo's future seems assured. Its line of Llama revolvers remains highly regarded in Europe, and its M1911-style MAX-1, Mini-max and Micro-max are well-timed to exploit commercial sales in the all-important U.S. market. Though sometimes erroneously regarded as the worst of the three surviving Spanish handgun firms, Llama-Gabilondo is in reality a very innovative firm producing a wide variety of quality handguns.

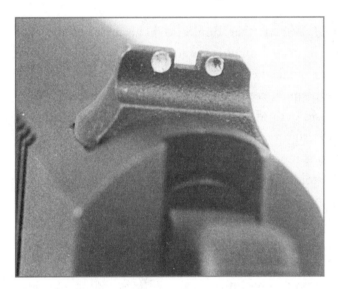

The Mini-max, like many other handguns of recent manufacture, uses a three-dot sighting system. The rear sight (shown) has two flanking dots.

# Chapter 11

## Bonifacio Echeverria (Star) Since 1945

n the years since World War II, Star Bonifacio Echeverria has become one of the world's most respected manufacturers of automatic pistols. The company has continued to make both full-sized service models for military and police use along with small, concealable models for self-defense, creating best-sellers and classic designs in both categories. While the original inspiration for postwar design remained the U.S. Model 1911, Star has in recent years switched to a modification of the Czech Model 75 (CZ-75) design. Sales of Star pistols have attained worldwide distribution thanks to a happy combination of excellent design, reasonable prices, and top-quality materials and manufacturing.

Except for improved disassembly procedures, the various "Super" model Star pistols resembled their earlier counterparts. The example is a 9mm Parabellum Model B Super, but the company also built "Super" series pistols in five other calibers.

## Model A Super

The Model A went through a minor redesign in 1946, adding a loaded-chamber indicator and an ingenious disassembly catch located on the right side of the frame. When rotated half a turn, this catch, which was connected to a link beneath the barrel, tipped the link forward. The slide could then be drawn forward easily off the frame. The resulting pistol—called the Super A or Model A Super—remained in production until 1989 without ever completely supplanting the standard Model A, which actually stayed in production for several years after Star had discontinued the Super A. Because it chambered the 9mm Largo cartridge, the Model A Super was used during the postwar years as a Spanish service pistol and was not finally released from reserve stocks until 1995-96.

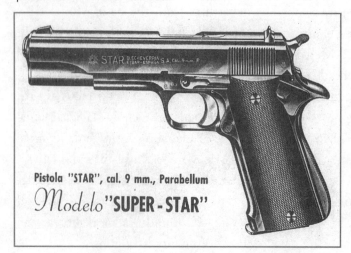

Pistola "STAR", cal. 9 mm., Parabellum
Modelo "SUPER - STAR"

The disassembly of a Star Super-series pistol begins by removing the magazine.

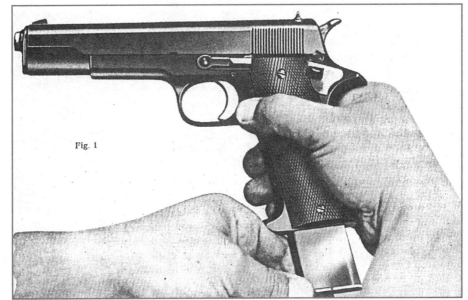
Fig. 1

After removing the magazine, the slide is drawn back to unload the firing chamber and verify that it is empty. The disassembly latch is then rotated down on the right side of the frame and then forward.

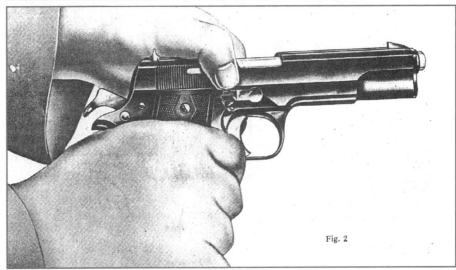
Fig. 2

The disassembly latch (on the right side of the frame) is pushed all the way forward to the point where it stops against an abutment on the frame. The barrel cam is now disengaged from the slide stop shaft.

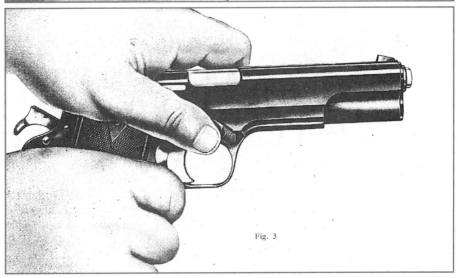
Fig. 3

*Chapter 11*

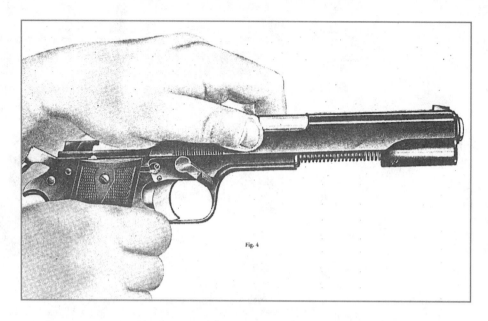

Fig. 4

## Model B and Model B Super

Star's success with the Model B continued after World War II and became, along with Unceta's Astra Model 600 *(see Chapter 7)*, a favorite of West German police forces in the early 1950s. The South African army also bought large numbers of the Model B, not replacing them in front-line service until the late 1980s. Many other countries bought these pistols as substitutes for their armed forces. While playing second fiddle may sound ignominious, it proved a surprisingly lucrative business for Star, which sold hundreds of thousands of Model Bs that way. By the time Echeverria ceased production in 1975, this model had become the favorite of many knowledgeable pistol shooters. Fast-handling and stunningly accurate, it remains an excellent choice for self-defense.

In 1946, Star's Model B Super (9mm Parabellum) was accepted by Spain's armed forces to replace the Model 1921 (Astra M400) pistol. This version differed from the original Model B with a new disassembly system. It was available for commercial sale as well, although it never became quite as popular as the original Model B. That same year, Star Bonifacio Echeverria introduced its Model P (.45 ACP). Similar in appearance, it was slightly larger in order to accommodate the larger cartridge and a 7-round detach-

The Star Model 31 can be fired double action from the hammer-down position, or by cocking the hammer for a lighter single-action first shot (as shown).

able box magazine. The Model P saw widespread service with Spanish and West German police forces in addition to lucrative commercial sales, enough to remain in production until 1975.

## Small Caliber Models (1946-1991)

The Model F series of .22 caliber target pistols made its first appearance in 1942. Because of wartime demands upon Star's manufacturing capacity, however, the company did not make these precision shooting pistols in large numbers until after the war. The Model F, which was manufactured from 1942 to 1967, featured a four-inch barrel, blued finish, fixed sight and checkered plastic grips. Star also altered the basic Model F design into a number of variations and slight modifications, including the Model FS (1942-67), which had a six-inch barrel and adjustable sights. Star also made a special pistol optimized for international shooting competition, called the Model F Olympic Rapid Fire, which fired the .22 Short cartridge and used a muzzle brake to reduce recoil to a minimum. It also had a seven-inch barrel, a special lightweight slide (made from an aluminum alloy), and provisions on the front of the frame for detachable muzzle weights. This pistol proved unique to all other Model F variants firing .22 Long Rifle cartridges and using 10-shot detachable box magazines. The Model FR, which replaced the Model F in 1967 and remained in production until 1972, featured a slide hold-open latch on the left side of the frame. The top left side of the frame was relieved to clear the latch, but otherwise it was

The elegant little Model DK was widely regarded as one of Star's most attractive pistols. Too small to meet the U.S. minimum for imported pistols, it has become a collector's item in America.

The right-side view of a Model DK indicates that this M1911-type pistol, like other Star and Llama-brand pistols based on that illustrious ancestor, has an exposed extractor designed to simplify manufacture.

The Model DK, like the much larger Colt Model 1911, has a locked breech and features a Colt-style muzzle bushing.

mechanically identical to the Model F. Another version—the FRS—was a Model FR with a six-inch barrel and came with a choice of blued or chrome-plated finish. Still another variant—the FM (which replaced the FR in 1973)—had a heavier frame but was otherwise identical.

Star's Model I series in .32 and .380 calibers (see also Chapter 3) had earlier enjoyed some success in police and military service. In the early 1950s, Star sought to recapture some of its past glory with a slightly modified version, the Model IR. Identical mechanically to the prewar Model I, its contoured barrel featured flat sides, and its left grip had an integral thumbrest molded in. The IR enjoyed some success, but it was soon eclipsed by the Model S series, whose resemblance to the well-respected Colt Model 1911 gave it a marketing advantage over the odd-looking IR. Between 1941 and 1965, the Models S and SI, which replaced and supplanted the H- and I-series guns, were also produced in .32 (SI) and .380 (S) calibers. Bearing a strong resemblance to a miniaturized Colt Model 1911, the Model S saw extensive police service in Spain. The Model S appears frequently in the U.S., mostly because Interarms imported a large quantity of factory-reconditioned Model S pistols between 1989 and 1991. Interestingly, Star refinished some of these used pistols with its own silver-colored Starvel (polish chrome) finish, which was better suited to civilian handguns than as a service pistol.

The Model DK (or "Starfire" as it's known in the U.S.) first appeared in 1957. Its numerous features included a curved rear gripstrap, an aluminum-alloy frame (which kept unloaded weight down to less than 15 ounces), and a safety catch on the frame's left rear, much like Colt M1911. An excellent concealment-type pistol with good power for its small size and weight, the Starfire proved quite popular. When importation into the U.S. ended in 1968, production continued for the foreign market. Eventually, the pistol's design did migrate to the U.S. because the Gun Control Act forbade the *import* of small pistols, not their *manufacture*—or even their assembly—in a domestic facility using imported parts. Initially,

The Model DK, known also as the "Starfire," should not be confused with the "Firestar," a slightly larger pistol.

Colt expressed an interest in the design, commissioning the Garcia Corporation, then the importers of Star pistols from Spain, to make a .380-caliber Starfire-type pistol, later called the Colt Pony. Garcia's subsidiary —the Firearms International plant (Accokeek, Maryland)—made a small batch of about 50 pistols, but Colt turned them down, claiming dissatisfaction with their quality. Colt later developed its own .380-caliber M1911 look-alike pistol, the Colt 380 Government Model, in 1983. Garcia then arranged to import Starfire components from Spain for assembly in the Firearms International plant (production was later taken over completely in the U.S.). Advertised as the Firearms International (FI) Model D, the pistol was made there from 1974 until 1977, after which the Iver Johnson company acquired Firearms International's tooling and reintroduced the little .380 in 1985, calling it the X-300 Pony. This model remained in production until 1986, then disappeared for a time when Iver Johnson fell upon hard times. It was reintroduced in 1990, then went out of production around 1993, apparently for the last time.

## Models BM and BKM

Star's Model BKM pistol made its debut in the early 1970s. Also called the Star Starlight, it was identical to the Model B mechanically but considerably shorter in length (seven inches overall with a barrel length of four inches). Its unloaded weight, thanks to a lightweight aluminum alloy frame,

Colt's .380 Government Model is one of several pistols whose design was inspired by the Starfire. (Photo courtesy of Colt)

*Chapter 11*

The Star Model BM appeared in 1970 as a radically downsized Model B. Echeverria made it in 9mm Parabellum caliber only. It served widely in Spain's Guardia Civil and was sold extensively in the commercial market. The light BKM model was identical except for its airweight aluminum-alloy frame (instead of steel).

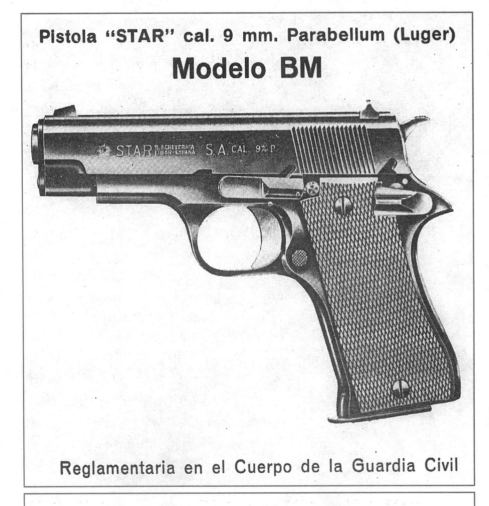

**Pistola "STAR" cal. 9 mm. Parabellum (Luger)**

# Modelo BM

**Reglamentaria en el Cuerpo de la Guardia Civil**

Fig. 1    Fig. 2

Fig. 3    Fig. 4

Unlike the Model 1911 which inspired it, the BM's manual safety was locked on, whether the hammer was at full cock (Figure 1) or uncocked (Figure 4). Figure 3 shows the hammer in its half-cocked position (a safety setting meant solely to prevent the gun from firing should a thumb slip off the hammer when cocking the pistol).

was only 26 ounces. A heavier (35 oz.) all-steel version, the BM, appeared in 1976 and remained appreciably shorter than the parent Model B. The Model BM saw considerable military and police service and remains popular with Spanish forces for concealed carry.

While closely based on the Colt M1911A1, the Star BKM and BM pistols dropped the grip safety. The Star pistols normally had a blued finish, but late in the production run the chrome Starvel finish also appeared. Checkered wooden grips were standard, but Pachmayr made a set of wraparound rubber grips for this series. The controls on the BKM/BM handle the same as the Colt M1911A1 Government Model, making these compact Spanish guns excellent smaller understudies for the Government Model. This similarity to the classic Colt design—coupled with greater concealability—did much to popularize the Star pistols. Regrettably, Star ceased production of the BK and BKM, along with the similar Model PD (see below), in order to concentrate on production of the Firestar pistol.

Because of the alloy-framed PD's impressive recoil, shooters some-times opted for a recoil-absorbing neoprene grip from Pachmayr (bottom). The Colt Double Eagle Compact's double-action pistol (top) owes its existence, at least indirectly, to the market for concealable .45 caliber pistols created by the PD.

## *Model PD*

As its designation indicates, the Star Model PD, despite its strong simi-larity to the 9mm BKM/BM, fired the .45 ACP caliber cartridge. Holding up to six rounds, the PD was a remarkably compact pistol despite the large, powerful cartridge it fired. Its specifications included the following: **Overall Length:** 7.5"; **Barrel Length:** 4.0"; **Height:** 5.0"; **Width:** 1.3"; **Weight (unloaded):** 25 oz. Introduced in 1975, the PD inspired the current generation of small .45 caliber pistols. And, while it is regrettably now out of produc-tion, this model remains one of the finest compact .45 ACP pistols on the market. Created with the input of American pistol authority Pete Dickey, a long-

Later PDs (bottom) featured a recurved triggerguard and fre-quently sported a chromed Starvel finish. The Springfield Armory Compact .45 (top) was one of many portable and con-cealable .45 caliber pistols inspired by the innovative PD.

time contributor to *American Rifleman* magazine, the PD became a cult favorite, especially after it received the approval of Jeff Cooper, an even more highly regarded expert in the field.

Mechanically the PD is quite similar to the Model 1911, which it also resembled closely in external appearance. Echeverria did, however, make some minor changes in the interests of design simplification and reduction in size and weight. To hold down the latter, an alloy frame was used, producing a stiff recoil but at the same time making the little pistol even more concealable. The PD's breech-locking mechanism is a slight modification from the short-recoil system found in the Colt M1911/Government Model. The PD's modified barrel has only a single locking lug atop the barrel, but its function is unimpaired. The thumb safety acts like the Colt's, its grip safety having been omitted in favor of a magazine safety. The PD design includes an adjustable rear sight (not necessary on a pistol intended for short-range defensive shooting) in an effort to gain points with the BATF (exportation to the United States). The sights on all but the latest models were slightly undersized.

Unfortunately, the quality of materials and workmanship on the PD is notoriously spotty, varying from only fair to extremely good, depending on the quality-control exercised at the Star plant at any particular time. For example, the Star Bonifacio Echeverria Company made most of its PDs with a blued finish, but late in its production run the Starvel chrome finish was also used. Checkered walnut grips came standard on the PD, but Pachmayr made an excellent set of wraparound rubber grips for less recoil, which is occasionally encountered on the PDs. Star dropped the PD from its line in 1991 to concentrate on Firestar production in three different calibers, rationalizing this move by concentrating on a single family of compact pistols. Still, many shooters regret the demise of the famous PD, as well as the similar 9mm BKM and BM.

Pistols imported by Interarms in 1989 included the Model BM, BKM, PD, 30 and 30PK. The Firestar appeared a year later, at first only in 9mm. Eventually, it supplanted the BM/BKM/PD line. (Drawings courtesy of Interarms)

REORDER ADDITIONAL SHEETS FROM:

**INTERARMS**
10 PRINCE STREET
ALEXANDRIA, VA 22313

**Star Pistols**

Model BKM & BM

Model BKM & BM

Model 30M & 30PK

Model 30M & 30PK

Model BM
Chrome

Model BM
Chrome

Model PD

Model PD

The .45 ACP caliber Star Model PD, introduced in 1975, strongly resembles the Model BKM in size, but its grip is thicker because of the larger cartridge it used. Note also the optional extended magazine, which not only added to the magazine capacity but also improved the grip for large-handed shooters.

The Model PD, unlike the BKM, had a stepped-down slide (just ahead of the ejection port). Note also the exposed extractor behind the ejection port.

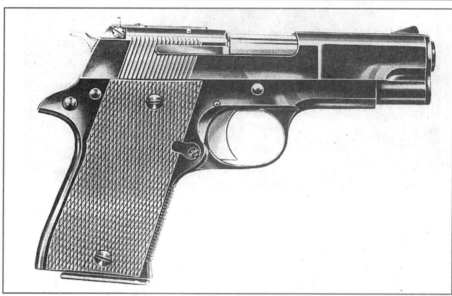

Star's "Starlite," a tiny .25 caliber pistol, is one of several Echeverria models never to have been exported to the U.S. by Spain. Their small size did not meet the import requirements set down in 1968.

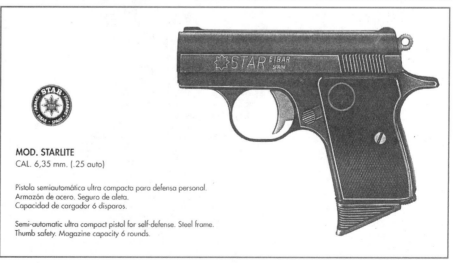

**MOD. STARLITE**
CAL. 6,35 mm. (.25 auto)

Pistola semiautomática ultra compacta para defensa personal.
Armazón de acero. Seguro de aleta.
Capacidad de cargador 6 disparos.

Semi-automatic ultra compact pistol for self-defense. Steel frame.
Thumb safety. Magazine capacity 6 rounds.

The Star Model 31 disassembles much like any other automatic pistols based on the short-recoil system developed by John M. Browning with his Model 1911 and High Power pistols. Disassembly instructions for this and other important Spanish pistols are covered in an appendix to this book.

# *Model 28*

Beginning in the late 1970s, Star's Model 28 (along with Astra's A-80 and Gabilondo y Cia's Llama Omni) was determined to become Spain's next service pistol. Spanish military and police orders were substantial, while business in South American (notably Peru) and South Africa was flourishing. Like many successful designs, the large double-action Model 28 copied several useful features from a variety of sources. Its design closely follows that of the Czech-designed CZ Model 75, especially with its slide-to-frame relationship and double-action trigger linkage. The Model 28, whose smooth trigger pull is directly attributable to the CZ-75, also employed a packaged, modular hammer lockwork based on those found in the Tokarev TT-33 and SIG P-210 service pistols. In addition to the hammer itself, this module includes the same cocking lever, sear, ejector and disconnector (which allows only one shot for each pull on the trigger).

The Model 28 is by no means a slavish copy of foreign designs, however. Echeverria made several changes designed to suit Spain's military needs more closely. For example, its one-piece, checkered plastic grip makes the pistol surprisingly comfortable to handle and fire. The grip is not held in place by screws; in fact, nowhere in this model's construction are there any screws at all. The extended tang at the top rear area

The author fired this five-shot offhand group of 1.5 inches at 25 feet using the Star Model 31.

of the grip protects the shooter's hand from injury caused by contact with the recoiling slide or hammer—a painful encounter experienced all too frequently with some models of automatic pistols. The safety arrangements on the Model 28 are also quite different from those found on other service pistols. Its slide-mounted ambidextrous safety, when pushed down to its safe setting (with the hammer cocked), does not automatically drop the hammer, as in a Walther or Smith & Wesson automatic pistol. Instead, when applying the safety on the Model 28, the path of the hammer to the firing pin is blocked, pushing it forward out of the hammer's reach. This feature allows shooters to carry the Model 28 cocked and locked should a single-action first shot be desired. There's also the option of lowering the hammer (once the safety lever is in the safe setting) by pulling the trigger.

**MOD. MEGASTAR 45**
CAL. 45 ACP

Pistola semiautomática de Doble Acción.
Armazón de acero. Percutor abatible desde la aleta del seguro.
Seguros: Doble de aguja percutora, cargador y cierre.
Alta capacidad de cargador.

Semi-automatic Double Action pistol.
Steel frame. Hammer decocking from thumb safety.
Firing pin safety plus firing pin block, magazine safety.
High magazine capacity.

The huge Megastar resembles an overgrown Firestar, but it reverts to a double-action trigger like the Model 28-series pistols which inspired the Firestar's design. Offered originally in both 45 ACP and 10mm Auto, the .45 is the only one that lasted.

Pushing the safety up and forward removes the block, allowing a double-action first shot to be fired, followed by single-action shots once the recoiling slide has cocked the hammer. The overall result of these unoriginal but useful features and innovations is a strong, well-built handgun suitable for civilians and the military alike.

Prior to its testing by the Spanish armed forces and subsequent entrance into the commercial market in 1983, the Model 28 competed in a service pistol trial sponsored in 1979 by the United States Air Force. The winner of this test could well anticipate orders for up to 200,000 pistols, so Echeverria's interest in competing is understandable. Other European pistols sent to the Air Force for testing included Beretta's Model 92S, the FN High Power, Fast Action and Double Action pistols, and Heckler &

The Firestar (bottom) owes many of its design features to the Model 30 (top). The Firestar shown is the M-43 model in 9mm Parabellum caliber. Note the recessed slide, a feature not found on bulkier .40 and .45 caliber variants.

Koch's Model P9S and VP-70 pistols. U.S. entrants included Colt's experimental design, the SSP, and Smith & Wesson's Model 459, the U.S.-built Model 1911A1 automatic pistol and the Smith & Wesson Model 15 revolver (since the last two guns listed were already in service, the Air Force wanted to see if any new designs brought with them enough increase in performance or efficiency to justify adoption).

Despite its advanced design and excellent workmanship, tests conducted on the Model 28 were disastrous. Accuracy was judged "marginal," both in firing from a rest and in freehand firing. The pistol also failed harsh environmental testing; but most damning of all was the pistol's reliability. Out of 5,526 rounds fired in endurance testing, the sample Model 28 pistols failed to feed, fire or extract an incredible 1,142 times. These dismal results amounted to an average of one failure for every five rounds fired! In other tests, however, the Model 28 demonstrated commendable accuracy and reliability. Heckler & Koch's otherwise ultra-reliable VP-70 also performed poorly in the same test, with 127 failures to feed, fire or extract out of 771 tries. Most likely this problem was actually ammunition-related, what with the manufacture of 9mm Parabellum in the U.S. at its nadir in those days. The only ammunition used in this set of U.S.

Another test firing by the author using a Model 31 produced this five-shot offhand group measuring only 1.8 inches across at a distance of 50 feet.

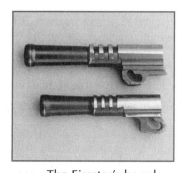

The Firestar's barrel (bottom), while closely resembling that of the Model 31 (top), is shorter. Its unlocking cam is also positioned differently. While the two guns share many similarities in their design, major parts cannot be interchanged.

Air Force trials was made by Smith & Wesson, which was at the time still producing ammunition. By European standards, the S&W ammunition was slightly underpowered compared to the Parabellum P08 ("Luger") pistol and many other European designs. The Star Model 28 worked best with high-intensity ammunition loaded up to NATO standards. Conversely, American ammunition manufacturers, with an eye on possible product liability lawsuits, often download ammunition from its "hottest" specifications to avoid blowing up old guns. This practice is what apparently led to the abysmal performances of the Model 28 at the U.S. Air Force tests. Later, in 1984, Star—through its longtime North American agent, Interarms—introduced the Model 28 into the American market. There it became firmly established as a solid, reliable performer until it was replaced in 1985 by the improved Model 30.

# Model 30M

One of the few complaints with the Model 28 concerned its slide serrations, which helped to pull back the slide prior to loading the firing chamber and to cock the hammer as well. These striations were set so far back on the slide, however, that the manual safety levers covered them to such an extent that shooters had no decent grip with which to work the slide. In answer to this objection, Bonifacio Echeverria placed the serrations on its new Model 30M further forward on the slide. The company also made slight improvements to the extractor to improve its reliability. Aside from these slight changes, the company retained the legendary accuracy and reliability of the Model 28. So impressed were the

The .45 caliber Firestar M-45 produced this five-shot offhand group measuring 1.1 inches across from a distance of 25 feet.

Spanish armed forces with the Model 30 that they awarded Echeverria with two important contracts. In 1990, the *Guardia Civil* adopted the Model 30M, featuring a steel frame, while the Spanish *Policía National* (National Police) ordered a smaller, lighter version, called the Model 30PK. The latter version was shorter than the standard model

*Chapter 11*

The Firestar's controls are designed for snag-free carry and convenient operation. Note the smooth contours of the rear sight and slide serrations. The manual safety, while positioned low to the frame (to reduce width), is large and checkered for quick, positive operation.

(7.6 inches overall compared to 8.1 inches for the 30M), and lighter (30 ounces as opposed to 40 ounces for the Model 30M with its steel frame). Both of these models are good shooters, with the heavier 30M promising less recoil. The alloy-framed PK, however, was really no problem in this respect, thanks to a substantial grip that spread the recoil over a wide area.

In 1990, the Model 30 was replaced by the Star Model 31 for commercial sale. The standard Model 31 (also known as the Model 31M) still boasts its all-steel construction, while the alloy-framed Model 31PK is lighter by 10 ounces. A shortened version of the Model 31M makes it a handier gun to fire than the earlier Models 28 or 30. Mechanically, however, all these pistols are nearly identical and all use the same operating controls and procedures. Echeverria makes the Model 31 series in a matte blue finish or a proprietary finish, called Starvel, a matte chrome finish that strongly resembles stainless steel and is both durable and attractive. Echeverria uses Starvel on its new-production pistols as well as on models reworked at its factory. Occasionally, former military or police pistols, such as the 9mm Model B and .380 Model S, receive this deluxe treatment as part of the refurbishing process.

Small-arms experts around the world highly regard all variations of the Model 28 line. Guns of this type have sold widely and have proven their efficiency in a number of countries. Regrettably, passage of the U.S. Crime Bill in late 1994 has stopped importation of Model 28, 30 and 31 pistols to this country. Even the PK versions of these pistols are quite large, having

The Star Firestar (bottom) reverts to a single-action mechanism reminiscent of the company's older pistols, such as the Model B (top). The goal was to miniaturize the pistol for concealed carry.

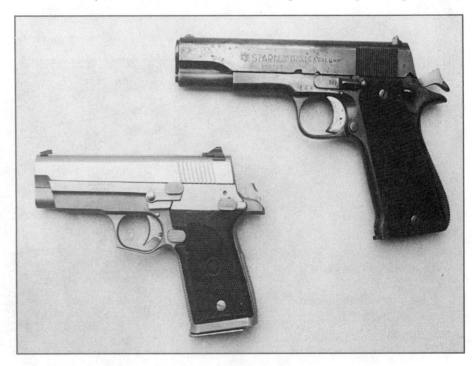

The Ultrastar's controls are mounted low, giving it sleek, smooth contours. Combined with its lightweight polymer frame, the pistol's concealability is enhanced.

been designed around their 15-shot magazines. This feature may make them easy to shoot, but it also reduces their appeal in a U.S. market limited to pistols holding no more than 10 rounds in their magazines.

# *Firestar*

Star Bonifacio Echeverria's introduction in 1990 of the Firestar M-43 in 9mm Parabellum caliber helped mark in large part the modern era of compact self-defense handguns in serious calibers. Its specifications are as follows: **Capacity:** 7 rounds; **Overall Length:** 6.5"; **Barrel Length:** 3.4"; **Height:** 4.7"; **Width:** 1.25". Only its weight—30 ounces (unloaded)—is excessive for a deep concealment handgun.

Mechanically, the Firestar is the same as a Model 28, 30 or 31 with a CZ-75-type breech-locking mechanism scaled down to the smallest size possible. The Firestar slide sits inside of, rather than atop, the frame. But to make the Firestar especially compact, Star uses a single-action trigger mechanism instead of the bulkier double-action trigger found on the full-sized CZ clones. The Firestar, like other Star pistols, comes in either a matte blue finish or in Starvel's silver-colored, hard chrome finish. Checkered soft rubber grips are standard and do not lend themselves to replacement, although some shooters supplement them with rubber slip-on grip sleeves. The Firestar's controls feature manual safety levers placed ambidextrously on both sides of the frame. The sights are designed for rapid acquisition. A modern firing-pin lock, which can be deactivated only by pulling the trigger through its entire travel, makes this pistol one of the better types to

Echeverria's efforts to shrink the Firestar to concealable dimensions have been successful. Even the largest version, the .45 caliber variant (top), is only slightly larger than the Walther PPK (bottom), considered by many to be the ultimate concealment pistol.

*Chapter 11*

carry in the cocked and locked mode of operation. Aggressive checkering of the front and rear gripstraps provide a firm, positive hold. The long grip tang (another featured copied from Star's full-sized Model 28-series pistols) helps prevent pinched hands caused by the hammer being cocked as the slide makes its rearward recoil stroke. On the negative side, the Firestar's magazine release doesn't drop the magazine completely clear of the gun; and the magazine safety, which prevents the gun from firing with the magazine removed, displeases many shooters.

Accuracy and reliability with the Firestar is surprisingly good, especially considering the gun's small size. Oddly, Star has never offered a lightweight version of the standard 7-shot Firestar with an aluminum-alloy frame, even after so equipping its high-capacity Firestar Plus (see below). Star's M-40 Firestar in .40 S&W caliber (introduced in 1991) is the same size as the

The Ultrastar's construction features a polymer frame. It derives a removable backstrap and hammer module and CZ-75-style slide from earlier Star models.

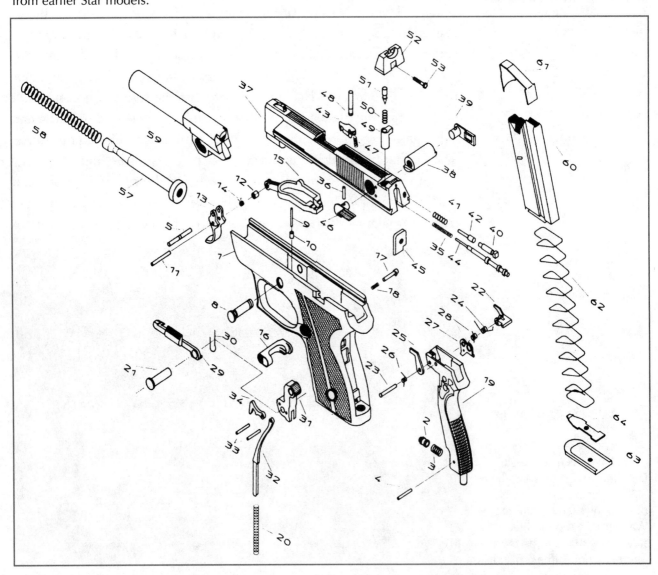

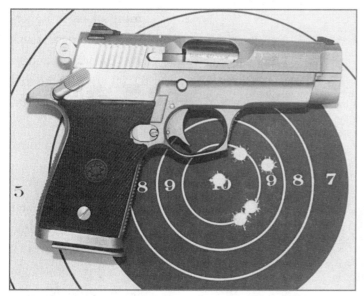

The Firestar in .40 S&W caliber is a surprisingly accurate pistol considering its small size. The author fired this five-shot off-hand group measuring 1.2 inches across from a distance of 25 feet using a chrome-plated (Starvel) model. Left-handers especially appreciate the Firestar's ambidextrous manual safety, which is shown in the "safe" position.

9mm M-43 version. The M-40, however, holds one less round in its magazine (a maximum of six). The slide contours are also slightly heavier than the 9mm version. Considering its size, the Model M-40 is a remarkably powerful pistol, placing it in the same range as the Smith & Wesson Chiefs Special/Walther PPK.

The .45 ACP caliber Star Firestar M-45, which dates from 1992, is Star Bonifacio Echeverria's replacement for its famous Model PD. It holds up to six rounds in the magazine and is, by virtue of its larger cartridge, slightly larger than the aforementioned M-43 and M-40 pistols. Still, M-45 remains a small pistol, as the following specifications indicate: **Overall Length:** 6.9"; **Barrel Length:** 3.6"; **Height:** 4.9"; **Width:** 1.3"; **Weight** (unloaded): 35 ounces. A compact .45 caliber pistol like this one appeals strongly to shooters who prefer the .45 over the 9mm (and other smaller calibers). Adding to its versatility, a seven-shot extension magazine is also available as an option, offering a fully grip for shooters with large hands at only a slight loss of concealability.

Perhaps the least attractive of the entire Firestar line is the Firestar Plus, an interesting but not altogether successful attempt to turn the Firestar into a high-capacity model. Interarms introduced it to the North American market in June 1994 amid much fanfare. Working against the Firestar Plus

The Ultrastar first appeared in 9mm Parabellum in 1994 and in .40 S&W caliber a year later.

*Chapter 11*

The Megastar proved reasonably accurate, as those results indicate. It also handled well despite its size, with careful design and attention to detail making the difference.

was the timing of its introduction, just before the high-capacity magazine ban was passed in September 1994. Chambered originally in 9mm Parabellum caliber only, this pistol had a high-capacity magazine holding up to 13 rounds. Within a year after its arrival, however, Star was forced to offer the Firestar Plus with a magazine holding a maximum of 10 rounds. Unfortunately, this gun's awkwardly enlarged grip does not make a good 10-round pistol. Moreover, it loses much of the original Firestar's good concealability. There is, though, one highly desirable feature in its design: a lightweight aluminum-alloy frame. In general, the Firestar line offers a relatively small handgun in one of three popular handgun calibers widely regarded as capable of serious self-defense.

## Megastar

Star Bonifacio Echeverria announced its enormous Megastar pistol in 1992, with a 10mm version following a year later. Originally offered in .45 ACP caliber, it held up to 12 rounds. When it was reduced to a 10-round magazine for U.S. importation in 1995, the Megastar quickly fell out of favor and was discontinued from the company line. In any event, the Megastar was heavily influenced by the company's earlier pistols, all based on the CZ-75. The Megastar's specifications are indeed impressive: **Barrel Length:** 4.56"; **Height:** 5.8"; **Width:** 1.4"; **Weight** (unloaded): 48 ounces. Although Star tried to compensate for its bulk by rounding and smoothing all sharp corners, its size made the Megastar unsuitable for all but those with the largest hands.

Still, the Megastar's size did confer some positive features. Its hefty construction made it extraordinarily rugged, while its weight reduced recoil. With its excellent sights and smooth trigger pull, the Megastar shot surprisingly well considering its bulk. Its safety mechanisms include an automatic internal firing pin block that is released only when the trigger is pulled rearward at the precise moment the pistol is fired. Typical of Star, a magazine disconnect safety is also standard. The ambidextrous manual safety lever offers several choices. Pushed down to the safe position, a white dot is exposed. The safety lever locks the firing pin and retracts it into the slide, so that even if the hammer should fall while it's cocked, it cannot reach the firing pin. Placing the safety on safe does not lower the hammer automatically; but after pushing the safety lever down to safe, the hammer is lowered in one of two ways: by pulling the trigger or by pushing the safety lever further down. The Megastar's manual safety lever moves up and back to fire, exposing a red dot. The location of the safety lever well back on the slide, combined with the Megastar's awkward size, all conspire to force shooters to shift these guns in their shooting hands prior to firing the pistol.

The Megastar appeared either in a standard blued or Starvel hard chrome finish. The grips were checkered black plastic. Checkering also appeared on the front and rear gripstraps, as well as on the front of the triggerguard—in the style of the time—for those shooters who place the index finger on their support hand forward. Fit and finish were superb, and the Megastar's sleek lines and smooth contours aroused much admiration.

# Ultrastar

The Ultrastar, introduced in 1994 in 9mm Parabellum caliber and in .40 S&W caliber a year later, represents Echeverria's attempt to establish itself at the forefront of innovative pistol design and manufacture. While it

The Ultrastar can be quite accurate. The author shot this 1.5-inch, five-shot off-hand group from 25 feet.

retained the company's M-30/Firestar series' method of setting the slide into the frame—rather than having the slide sit atop the frame—the Ultrastar departed from its past by choosing a polymer frame. Other modern innovations include a double-action trigger mechanism, ambidextrous manual safety, large combat sights (with three-dot highlight) and, despite its compact dimensions, a nine-shot magazine. Interarms' press release, dated early 1994, made much of the new model's advanced features, as follows:

*Here at last is the one you've been waiting for! The Ultrastar is a compact double-action pistol chambered for 9mm Parabellum and features an All-New Polymer Frame. The new Ultrastar incorporates the design refinements requested by real professionals…a slim profile, lightweight (sic), and first shot double-action speed second to none. Other features include a triple-dot sight system, a windage adjustable rear sight, ambidextrous three-position manual safety including decocker, all steel internal mechanism, an all-steel barrel and slide mounted on rails inside the frame and supplied with two magazines.*

Small and light enough for easy concealment, the Ultrastar is nevertheless easy to shoot, thanks to its substantial grip. As a result, the gun is comfortable to fire and more accurate than many competing compact models. While not especially popular in the U.S., the Ultrastar sells quite well elsewhere.

In summation, Star Bonifacio Echeverria's many excellent postwar pistol designs have made some of its products the most sought after of all Spanish handgun manufacturers. The many excellent Star pistols in recent years have continued the company's fine reputation, offering top value and good design at highly competitive prices.

The Firestar's manual safety can be applied even with its hammer in the uncocked position.

# Chapter 12

## The Spanish Handgun Collector

panish automatic pistols and revolvers have a rich and interesting history, making them fertile ground for collectors, both beginning and advanced. Having been used in most of the major wars of the 20th century, Spanish handguns have played an important role in world history. Because of their widespread use and generally low cost, these pistols have become widely distributed; indeed, collectors who travel to any extent are likely to encounter Spanish-made handguns more often than most other types. Even the wealthiest and most ambitious collectors will never run out of interesting variations. On the other hand, the beginning collector of modest means can also uncover Spanish pistols that are much easier on the wallet than virtually any other type of pistol.

As we have observed in the earlier chapters of this book, Astra Unceta y Cia, Llama Gabilondo y Cia and Star Bonifacio Echeverria have all, since the end of World War II, joined the ranks of the world's most respected manufacturers of automatic pistols (and, in the cases of Astra and Llama, of revolvers as well). These three companies make a wide variety of handgun models in various sizes to suit the full range of handgun needs, including military and police service, civilian self-defense, and sporting and competition use. One would be hard-pressed not to find a Spanish-made pistol, past or present, that failed to perform as needed—and usually for a lower price than other brands require. Since the mid-1980s many armed forces, including those of several Central and South American countries, as well as Spain's own military, have sold large numbers of military pistols of Spanish make. Some are only in good to fair

Condition is everything in collection. Any parts breakage on an old handgun should be noted. It should make you think twice before buying, or at the least enable you to negotiate a lower price. Note the broken extractor star on this Garate, Anitua y Cia .455 caliber revolver.

shape, generating little interest among collectors, while notably the ex-Portuguese Navy's Astra Model 600s are in excellent condition. These guns generally sell for much less than comparable models made in the U.S. or in parts of Europe.

Where are the best places to find Spanish pistols? In gun stores, for starters. Such pistols often show up there, while others come from people who simply want a newer gun to replace an old Spanish model that has been in the family for many years. It's surprising how many interesting guns have turned up that way. Buyers may also advertise for Spanish pistols in newspapers, although doing so may weaken the buyer's bargaining position (advertising usually emphasizes the desirability of such handguns to potential buyers). Ads in specialty magazines, such as *Gun List* (700 East State Street, Iola, WI 54945) and *Shotgun News* (P.O. Box 669, Hastings, NE 68902), are also helpful. For example, *Gun List* emphasizes mostly single guns for sale by individuals, while the emphasis at *Shotgun News* leans toward large quantities of guns sold by businesses. A considerable overlap exists, however.

In the author's experience, the best sources for buyers interested in all types of guns—especially out-of-production guns—are at the gun shows, which advertise their arrival in newspapers, in *Gun List*, on television and in *The American Rifleman* (the NRA magazine). One advantage of a gun show is the opportunity to see a variety of gun owners and dealers at one time. Those buyers and sellers typically rent table space wherever a show is

held. These shows generally run a day or two, usually over a weekend. Those who plan to buy should attend a show either at the very beginning of the show—before the goods have been picked over—or a few hours before the show folds up, when owners are anxious to make a sale at a reasonable price. The risk in waiting, of course, is that somebody else may have already picked up the gun you wanted. But in the case of a gun that hasn't been sold an hour or two before the show ends, the buyer should be in an excellent bargaining position.

One of the most attractive aspects of shopping for older Spanish guns is that they are poorly researched and, as a result, their prices are fluid. A buyer is much more likely to find a price followed by "OBO" (Or Best Offer) on an old Spanish automatic pistol than on virtually any other

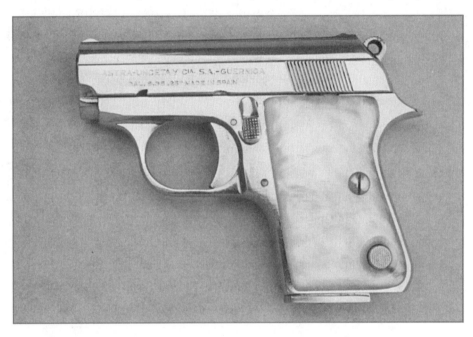

The fancier the finish—when applied at the factory—the scarcer the gun and the more it's worth. This Astra Model 2000 displays an optional chrome plating with mother-of-pearl grips.

handgun. Because of the generally low esteem in which shooters hold Spanish handguns—particularly most of the older models—it's a good chance that buyers can bargain and dicker until they get a price reduction. In general, Spanish guns do not sell as well as the best-known American, British, French, German and Italian brands. This may reduce the investment value of Spanish guns, but it also makes them ideal for collectors on a tight budget.

Most old guns in mint or near-perfect condition command a premium over guns with worn or reblued finishes. Most legitimate gun collectors are scrupulous enough not to attempt passing off a reblued gun as a mint collector's piece. But a few dishonest types may try to take advantage of an unwary buyer. Fortunately, one can usually tell the difference between the

*Chapter 12*

two. If the letters and markings on the slide—particularly the smaller ones—look blurred or partially obliterated, chances are the gun has been reblued. Another clue that a gun has been reblued is rust pitting with a blued color rather than the usual red-oxide tint. As a general rule of thumb, rebluing reduces a gun's value by about 50% compared to an unissued version of the same model in mint condition. Sometimes the reduction in value is even greater, especially if the gun represents an especially rare or desirable model. Collectors usually shy away from any pistol or revolver not in the same condition in which it left the factory. Therefore, any aftermarket changes or additions—including, of course, rebluing or other refinishing operations—reduce a gun's value as a collector's item, even if such alterations enhance its function or operation. A gun with no inherent collector's value, but one that may produce good results on a firing range or a hunt, is called a "shooter." Such pieces have little or no special value to a collector.

Any documentary evidence that ties a gun to a person or historical event is bound to increase its historical interest and its value to a collector. An obvious example is the "Capture Paper" issued to U.S. veterans as they return home with weapons acquired during war. In the same light, the wise speculator in firearms always makes it a point to save all the factory literature and packaging that came with the gun (the latter is surprisingly scarce, since new owners usually throw away the box in which their guns arrived). A factory manual or an original cardboard pistol box from the 1920s or 1930s can be exceedingly hard to come by. Upon purchasing a new hand-

gun, only time will tell if it becomes a classic and commands a premium among collectors in the years to come. Those who buy a new handgun for investment purposes are forewarned against taking more than a token test-firing. In fact, when buying a handgun for investment purposes, the less shooting the better.

# The Parts Situation

The overwhelming number of guns covered in this book have been out of production for decades. Like other mechanical devices, handguns wear out, particularly military or police guns that have been subjected to rough use. For these reasons, collectors may find guns that are in bad shape, with worn, broken or missing parts. Fortunately, the replacement parts situation for many Spanish pistols has improved dramatically in recent years. The Gun Parts Corporation (GPC, William's Lane, West Hurley, NY 12491) is a good place to start looking for replacement parts for Spanish handguns—indeed, for guns of any nationality. When writing GPC, be brief and concise in stating your needs. Sometimes a drawing or photograph of the gun or part in question will help clarify your situation. GPC also works with Triple K (see below) in supplying spare and replacement magazine, and with Sile, Inc. (see below) in supplying reproduction hard rubber stocks made to fit old and out-of-production Spanish pistols.

Missing parts, such as the manual safety on this Llama Model IV, are a bane to collectors. They raise genuine safety concerns as well.

Federal Arms Corporation of America (7928 University Avenue, Fridley, MN 55432) has since 1996 become a leader in accessories for the fine Astra Model 400 and Star Models A and B and Super A and B model pistols. Accessories offered by Federal include high-quality replacement barrels for the Astra Model 400 and Star Models A and Super A in alternate calibers for drop-in caliber conversions from 9mm Largo to 9mm Parabellum. The conversion process is as easy as field-stripping a pistol and swapping barrels. This author has used the Astra Model 400 9mm Parabellum conversion barrel and found it extremely efficient, with no other modifications required to make the pistol function perfectly with 9mm Parabellum rounds. The existing magazine and recoil spring, while they are made to function specifically with the 9mm Largo cartridge, also work fine with the 9mm Parabellum cartridge. In addition to these excellent new barrels, Federal Arms offers replacement wooden grips for the Star pistols of Model 1911 type, including the Models A, B, Super A and Super B.

Triple K Manufacturing Company (2222 Commercial Street, San Diego, CA 92113) stocks a huge assortment of automatic pistol magazines. Although the company already makes magazines for literally thousands of different types of automatic pistols, it is always looking for that large group of automatic pistols for which it has not made replacement magazine in the past. Triple K's search has included many of the Spanish automatic pistol models covered in earlier chapters of this book. Those who own a Spanish automatic pistol may therefore be in position to sell it to Triple K, or let them borrow it (in which case they will provide two free magazines for

🌸 Any genuine handgun accessories, such as an original holster and spare magazines, enhance the handgun's value to collectors.

the pistol and return it within a few weeks). While researching this book, the author received magazines for three Spanish pistols in this manner. The best procedure is to check with the company before sending them your gun. They will in turn respond in writing and explain the arrangements. Triple K's *Encyclopedia and Magazine Reference Catalog for Auto Loading Guns* is a good source of general information on automatic pistols. It also identifies those guns for which Triple K already has magazines in stock. The company also stocks a large assortment of grips, which it obtains from Sile, Inc. Conn. (998 N. Colony Road, Meriden, CT 06450). This company is an original source for reproduction hard rubber stocks. Another large grip-manufacturing company is Vintage Industries, Inc. (781 Big Tree

Drive, Longwood, FL 32750), which has on hand a large collection of grips for vintage pistols and revolvers (they also make replacement grips upon request).

## Testing Old Handguns

Having warned readers that "the less shooting, the better," I know full well that the temptation to ignore that advice may prove irresistible. We all love shooting—and weren't guns, after all, made for that purpose? With that in mind, the following suggestions for shooting will hopefully make the experience as safe as possible for all concerned—including those old guns.

First, of course, make sure the gun isn't loaded. That may sound condescending, but the longer I'm in this business the more carelessness I've observed. Next, *point the muzzle in a safe direction* and remove the magazine (if a pistol) or open the cylinder (if a revolver) to check the action. Remember, with an automatic pistol you first remove the magazine; only then do you pull back the slide to empty the firing chamber. In disassembling the weapon, follow any directions that may be available for this operation. The appendix to this book contains disassembly directions for some of the more common Spanish types, including the Browning Model 1903 copies ("Ruby" or "Eibar" pistols in 6.45mm/.25 ACP and 7.65mm/.32 ACP), Astra Model 400 series, Colt Model 1911 copies (includes many Llama and Star models), Astra Model 900, Star Firestar and other pistols of CZ-75 type

(Star Models 28, 30, 31; Astra Models A-70 and A-75), and Astra A-80 series (SIG P220 clones). Other books on firearms disassembly are available; and don't forget that the company which made your out-of-production gun originally may still be in business. In that case, a letter or phone call will probably produce an owner's manual (or photocopy) within a few days, and usually free of charge. It's always a good idea also to have any old weapon looked over and approved by a gunsmith before firing it.

Having disassembled the weapon, it must be cleaned thoroughly. Look inside the barrel. How does the rifling look? Is the bore shiny or rusted? You want the barrel—particularly the bore—to be in the best shape possible, for it's the piston of this internal-combustion engine that makes it a handgun. How do the lockwork and firing mechanism look? Are any internal parts missing, rusted or otherwise non-functional? Now is the time to arrange for their replacement. Assuming everything is in order, lightly oil the parts that rub against each other during operation. These include the barrel-to-barrel bushing interface and the area where the slide sits on the frame (a little oil goes a long way, so be careful). Having oiled the working parts and reassem-

One cannot overstate the enjoyment a collector or shooter receives from firing a well-made antique pistol. But one must follow wise precautions to avoid damage to property, death or injury.

bled the handgun, press the trigger, as if in the act of shooting, but without any ammunition. Does the trigger mechanism work smoothly and consistently? And how about the manual safety? Does it block the hammer, lock the trigger, or otherwise prevent the gun from firing effectively? If the safety mechanism is missing, worn or broken, there's a good chance some damage has been done to the sear or other parts of the firing mechanism. In that case, the gun probably won't fire at all, or it may fire unpredictably, perhaps even fully automatically. This can pose a grave risk of danger to you and any innocent bystanders.

If everything proves to be in order, it's time to take the gun to the range. When looking for suitable ammunition, make sure you have the right caliber for your gun. Spanish guns marked "9mm" are often 9mm Short (i.e., 9x17mm or .380 ACP) or 9mm Largo (9x23mm), rather than 9mm Parabellum (9x19mm). Using the wrong ammunition is a great way to damage your gun, not to mention injuring or even killing yourself.

Having determined the right caliber for your handgun, it's time to choose the right kind of ammunition. Is it high-pressure +P or +P+? For example, in an elderly Star Model B or Llama Model XI "Especial," high-pressure 9mm Parabellum ammunition is definitely *out*. For any 9mm Largo pistol, Winchester's 9x23mm high-performance ammunition released in 1996 is also *out*. The latter was not a replacement Largo round at all, but rather a new high-performance cartridge for Colt Model 1911 pistols with customized barrels. As a general rule, choose only standard-pressure ammunition for such aged weapons. Reloads of unknown composition are out. In fact, unless you are a highly experienced reloader, it's wise to avoid reloads entirely when test-firing an old handgun, especially for the first time. Factory ammunition from a reputable manufacturer is loaded to the highest standards and under the strictest quality control. This applies especially to the older calibers that have been around for a long time. Experienced reloaders should insist on using their own homemade ammunition.

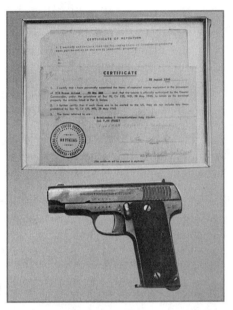

Any historical documentation, such as this authentic capture document (issued by the U.S. Army for this Ruby pistol in 1945), adds to the value of a firearm, tying it to a particular historical period.

Then, armed with a reputable loading manual, start at the low end of the loading chart for any given cartridge. Eye and ear protection is a must. Modern or even brand-new guns have been known to blow up in their owner's hands. How much more might an old gun—especially some Spanish wartime piece of questionable metallurgy—disintegrate at the moment of truth? In that event, your eyes must be protected. The same applies to your ears. All guns make loud noises, so be sure to protect yourself.

Now that you're ready to shoot, make sure no obstructions lie inside the bore and that it's clean and dry (no oil). Next, load a *single* round into the cylinder or magazine and fire it. Collect the spent cartridge casing and examine it for signs of distress (a split or bulged case may indicate the mechanism is operating under too much pressure). If the case looks abused, stop firing immediately and retire the gun until a gunsmith can check it out. If everything looks fine again, load two to four rounds (not a full magazine) and continue firing. Once the pistol has fired several rounds without doubling or firing fully automatically, it's time to load a complete magazine. After shooting, clean the gun thoroughly and oil it lightly before storing it away. For automatic pistols, remember to check both magazine *and* chamber, in that order). In general, shooting an old Spanish handgun can be lots of fun—but always approach the experience with caution and intelligence.

*Chapter 12*

# In Summation

Regrettably, not all is well in the world of Spanish handgun collection. Even the authoritative *Blue Book of Gun Values* is largely "absent without leave" on the subject beyond the "big three" manufacturers: Astra, Llama and Star. Regrettably, the passage of time has obscured the interesting history of many of these guns and the companies that created them in the hills of northern Spain during the early decades of the 20th century. In any event, collecting Spanish handguns ranks among the most interesting projects involving firearms I've every worked on. These guns are both historically interesting and, for the most part, mechanically sound in design and workmanship. Prices tend to be low, and the variety is great. While collectors are almost certain not to enjoy the rapid appreciation of value they may expect with a collection of, say, German Lugers, P38 pistols or Colt M1911s or Single Action Army revolvers, it's possible to buy many Spanish guns for the price of a single collector-grade Luger or M1911. And who can honestly say that a large, well-coordinated collection of historically significant Spanish handguns in excellent condition won't be worth a great deal more in the years to come?

While we know that a 1920s-vintage Astra Model 300 (bottom) has acquired some collector's value, we cannot say with certainty how much a 1995-vintage Llama Minimax (top) might be worth one day. A wise collector who buys with an eye toward possible future resale should retain any new gun's packaging intact. He'll also minimize firing and other wear and tear on the pistol in an effort to keep it in excellent condition.

# *Appendix I*

## *Slide markings on Ruby-type pistols supplied to the Allied forces during World War I.*

uring World War I, Gabilondo won the French army contract to produce its "Ruby" model pistol. Unable to make the Ruby in the quantities desired, Gabilondo was joined by approximately 50 other manufacturers in Spain to fill orders mostly from the French, but also the Italians and Romanians. Each drawing provides a view of the left side of the slide, which traditionally contains the most information found on an automatic pistol. Where other markings of note exist, they are also mentioned. The most significant of these additional markings is a double letter inside an oval, made at the request of the French following their discovery that the magazines of Ruby-type pistols did not interchange freely among pistols made by different manufacturers. On pistols so marked, the double letter inside an oval appeared on both the left grip tang and on the bottom of the magazine floorplate.

All pistols shown on the following pages hold 9-shot magazines and were made to fire the 7.65mm (.32 ACP) caliber. In general, the pistols of this period (1915-1918) were plain, unadorned models. Slides and frames received a dull military blue finish and grips consisted of simple checkered walnut, there being no time or need to make anything fancier. Such refinements as changes in magazine capacity and elaborate company logos stamped onto slides and hard-rubber grips, as well as other embellishments, came mostly after the war. *(continued on pg. 255)*

**1.** Acha Hermanos, located in the city of Vitoria south of Eibar, called this gun either the Acha or the Model 1916. This, the company's first venture into handgun production, remained on the market until 1922, after which Acha refined its line, bringing out similar models until the early 1930s.

**2.** Aldazabal made several Ruby-type pistols, including both a 7-shot and a 9-shot model. This model was marked AL on the left grip tang, a sure giveaway of its French service.

**3.** During World War I, a group of former Esperanza y Unceta employees formed the company SA Alkartasuna to make pistols for the French. While not one of Gabilondo's original subcontractors, this company is known to have made formal arrangements with Gabilondo to subcontract a portion of the production. Alkartasuna produced an estimated 80,000 pistols for the French. In addition to the version using the standard length barrel, long-barreled models are also known to exist, as are 7-shot compact models. The factory burned down in 1920.

**4.** Berasaluce Arietio-Aurteña of Eibar introduced the "Allies" model in 1916, with production continuing until after the war. A 7-shot model introduced in 1924 was considerably more compact than the full-sized, 9-shot wartime model shown.

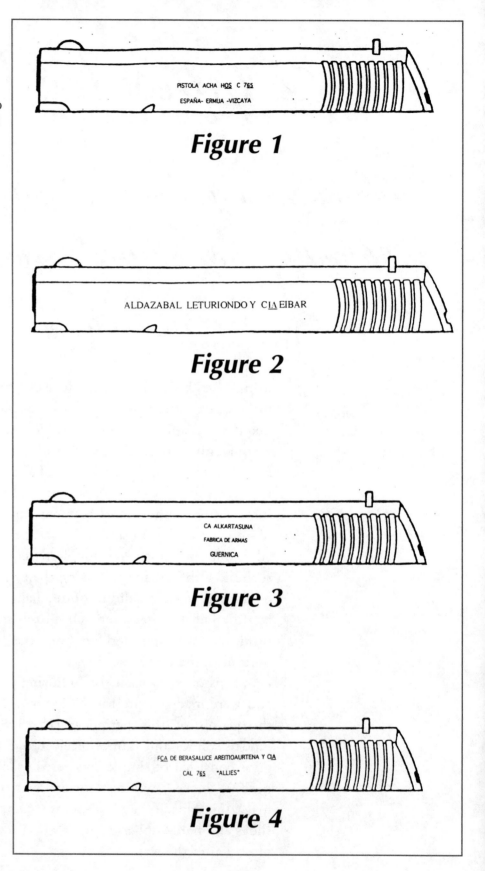

Figure 1

Figure 2

Figure 3

Figure 4

**5.** Gaspar Arizaga's first model appeared late in World War I and was the standard Ruby product (shown). Later, he branched into more innovative designs and acquired a good reputation for quality by Eibar standards. Arizaga remained in business until the Spanish Civil War.

**6.** Arizmendi y Goenaga, one of Eibar's oldest firms, dated from 1886 and lasted until the Spanish Civil War ended operations in 1936. Although the firm specialized in revolvers early on, it produced several Eibar-type automatics even before World War I began. The company quickly joined the quest for French gold, which began with the Ruby's adoption in 1915 by that country.

**7.** A form of the Astra pistol from Esperanza y Unceta, survives to this day as Astra-Unceta y Cia. Along with Gabilondo, the prime contractor (see Figures 19 and 20 below), and Bonifacio Echeverria (see Figure 16), Ruby-type pistols made by Esperanza y Unceta have enjoyed fine reputations for quality among this type of pistol. The company's address, in the city of Guernica, appeared on the opposite (right) side of the slide.

**8.** Azanza y Arrizabalaga's Modelo 1916 is sometimes seen marked AA on the left grip tang. The company also produced the smaller Reims model, in both 6.35mm (.25 ACP) and 7.65mm (.32 ACP) calibers for France in 1914-1915 prior to taking up the manufacture of this larger, standard military model.

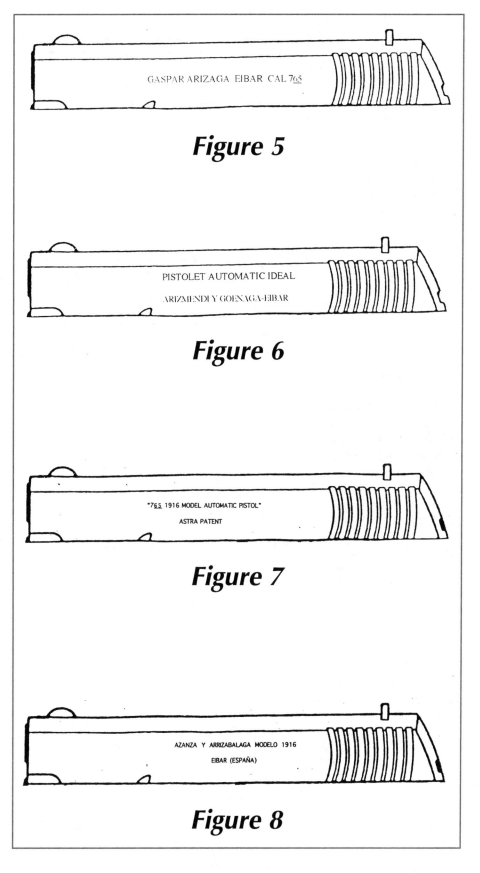

GASPAR ARIZAGA EIBAR CAL 7.65

**Figure 5**

PISTOLET AUTOMATIC IDEAL

ARIZMENDI Y GOENAGA-EIBAR

**Figure 6**

"7.65 1916 MODEL AUTOMATIC PISTOL"

ASTRA PATENT

**Figure 7**

AZANZA Y ARRIZABALAGA MODELO 1916

EIBAR (ESPAÑA)

**Figure 8**

*Appendix 1*

**9.** While not one of Gabilondo's original subcontractors, this company (Beistegui Hermanos) is known to have made formal arrangements with Gabilondo to subcontract a portion of the production. Note the English-language slide markings (cf. Figure 10 below). Also the slide serrations are straight rather than curved, an unusual refinement in pistols of this type.

**10.** An alternative marking can be observed on Beistegui Hermanos pistols (this one uses the Spanish word España for Spain).

**11.** The Bernedo company was formed during World War I specifically to make handguns for the French. Although the company survived the war and introduced an original pistol design of its own in the early 1920s, it failed in the depressed business climate of the late 1920s. In addition to the version using the standard length (ca. 3.5-inch) barrel as shown here, long-barreled models are also known to exist with identical slide markings on the standard-barrel variant shown.

**12.** Blank Slide variants appear from time to time, many with details (i.e., 9-shot magazines, wooden grips) suggesting wartime manufacture. They cannot be traced with certainty to any one gunmaker. Others are marked only "AUTOMATIC PISTOL," again with no clue concerning their manufacturer, while some have a caliber marking on the slide or grips and no other identification. Some also have straight (rather than curved) slide serrations.

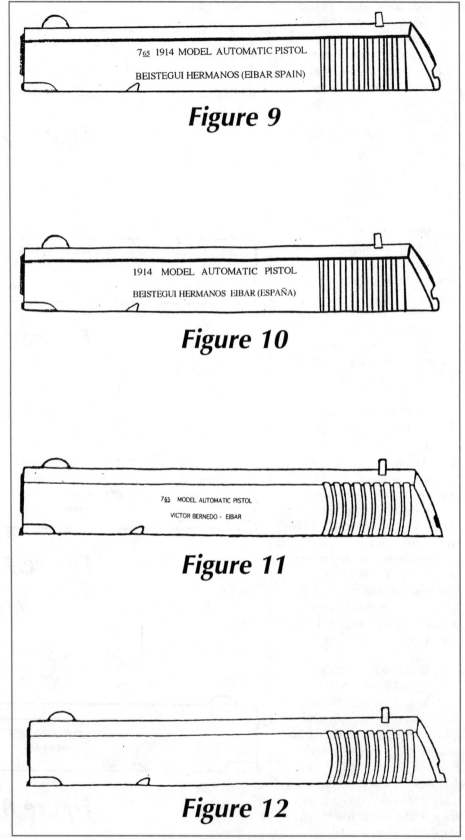

7⅐65 1914 MODEL AUTOMATIC PISTOL

BEISTEGUI HERMANOS (EIBAR SPAIN)

### Figure 9

1914 MODEL AUTOMATIC PISTOL

BEISTEGUI HERMANOS EIBAR (ESPAÑA)

### Figure 10

7⅐65 MODEL AUTOMATIC PISTOL

VICTOR BERNEDO - EIBAR

### Figure 11

### Figure 12

**13.** The Brunswig was another of Esperanza y Unceta's trade names. These pistols sometimes have an "EU" in an oval marking on the left grip tang. Compare with Figures 7 and 18.

**14.** The Cobra was produced by an unknown manufacturer from World War I until the early 1920s. This pistol was sold by Arizmendi, Zulaica y Cia after World War I.

**15.** Echave y Arizmendi, later called "Echasa," was one of only four companies allowed by Francisco Franco's government to remain in the handgun business after 1939, the others being Unceta (Astra), Gabilondo (Llama) and Echeverria (Star).

**16.** Bonifacio Echeverria's Ruby-type pistols are quite scarce, with only an estimated 10,000 made before the company began supplying a pistol of its own design—the Star—to the French. "Izarra" is also a word for "star," but only in the Basque language used in the region around Eibar. Echeverria pistols have one of the best reputations for quality among the Ruby copies. The company survives to this day as Star Bonifacio Echeverria SA. Note this pistol's straight slide serrations. Like the Alkartasuna (Figure 3) and Bernedo (Figure 11) models, the Izarra also sometimes appeared in a long-barreled version.

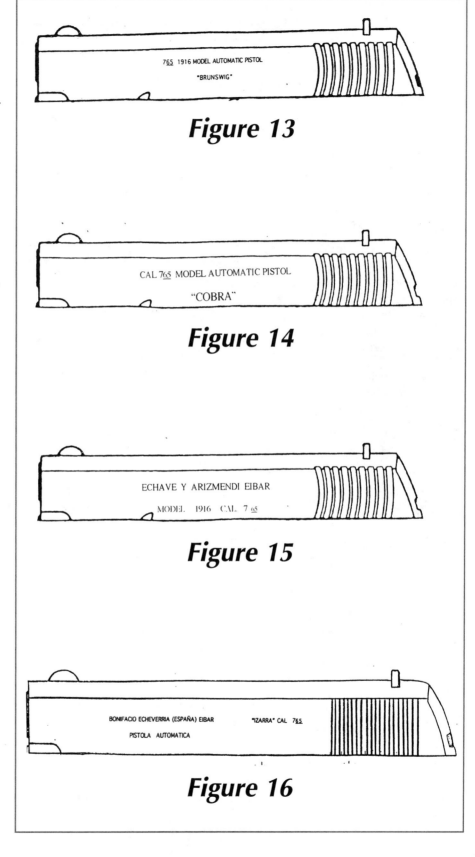

**Figure 13**

**Figure 14**

**Figure 15**

**Figure 16**

**17.** Erquiaga y Cia made the Fiel pistol as a Gabilondo subcontractor during the war. Sales continued for several years after the war, too, and the company added other models to its line before failing in the 1920s.

**18.** This was yet another of Esperanza y Unceta's trade names used in the export business to the French and Italian armed forces in World War I. These pistols also sometimes have an "EU" in an oval marking on the left grip tang and magazine bottom. Esperanza y Unceta produced an estimated total of 150,000 pistols for the French and an unknown, but presumably much smaller, number for the Italians before the war ended.

**19.** Gabilondos y Urresti was the original creator of the 9-shot Ruby model in 1914. Upon re-ceiving the initial French armed forces contract in 1915, it became the prime contractor and most important company in Ruby pistol manufacture. These pistols sometimes have a "GU" in an oval marking on the left grip tang and magazine bottom.

**20.** Sometime after Ruby production began, the slide inscription was changed to reflect the Gab-ilondo firm's relocation to nearby Elgoibar from Eibar. Like the earlier model in the drawing above, these pistols also sometimes have a "GU" in an oval marking on the left grip tang and magazine bottom. The company survives today as "Llama-Gabilondo y Cia."

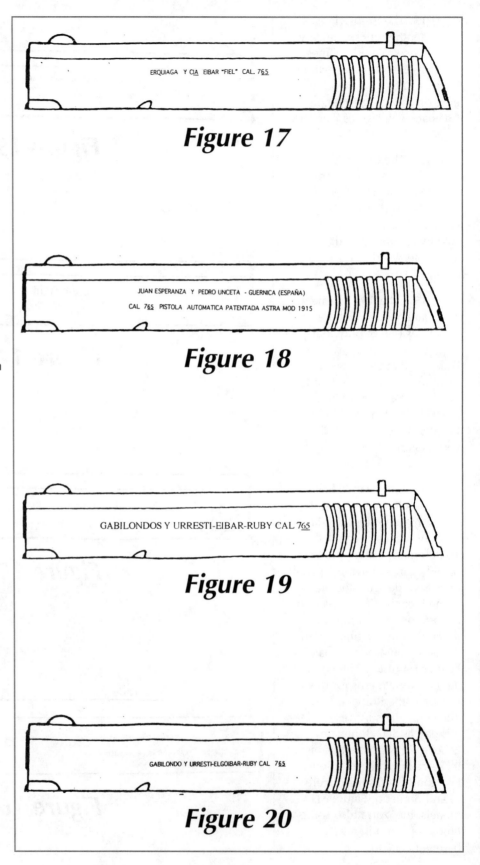

ERQUIAGA Y CIA EIBAR "FIEL" CAL. 7.65

**Figure 17**

JUAN ESPERANZA Y PEDRO UNCETA - GUERNICA (ESPAÑA)
CAL 7.65 PISTOLA AUTOMATICA PATENTADA ASTRA MOD 1915

**Figure 18**

GABILONDOS Y URRESTI-EIBAR-RUBY CAL 7.65

**Figure 19**

GABILONDO Y URRESTI-ELGOIBAR-RUBY CAL 7.65

**Figure 20**

**21.** Sometimes marked with a "GN" in an oval marking on the left grip tang and magazine bottom, this gun came from the same company that created Spain's first workable automatic pistol—the Charola y Anitua of 1897. It also made .455 caliber revolvers for the British military in 1915-1916. Note the straight slide serrations.

**22.** Isidro Gaztañaga's Destroyer model sometimes added "IG" in an oval marking on the left grip tang and magazine bottom. Production began in 1916.

**23.** Hijos de Angel Echeverria was one of four original subcontractors to join Gabilondo early on in making Ruby-type pistols for the French.

**24.** Hijos de Calixto Arrizabalaga produced pistols similar to this one until the Spanish Civil War forced the company out of business.

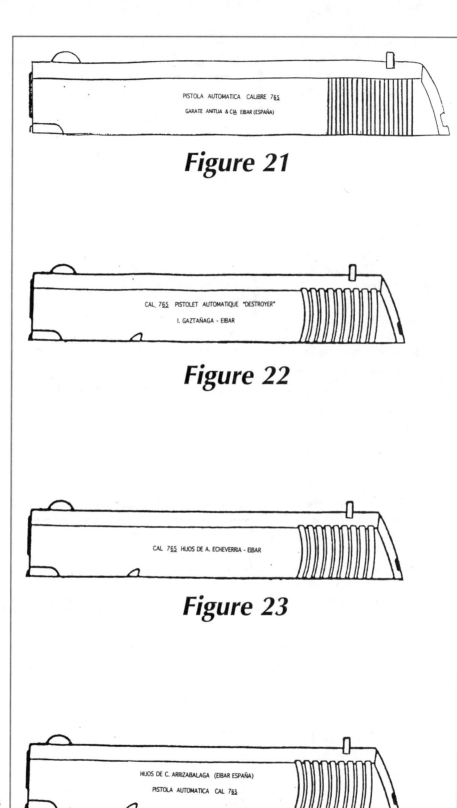

*Figure 21*

*Figure 22*

*Figure 23*

*Figure 24*

*Appendix 1*

**25.** The Imperial made by José Aldazabal is a typical Ruby copy of the World War I period except for its straight slide serrations.

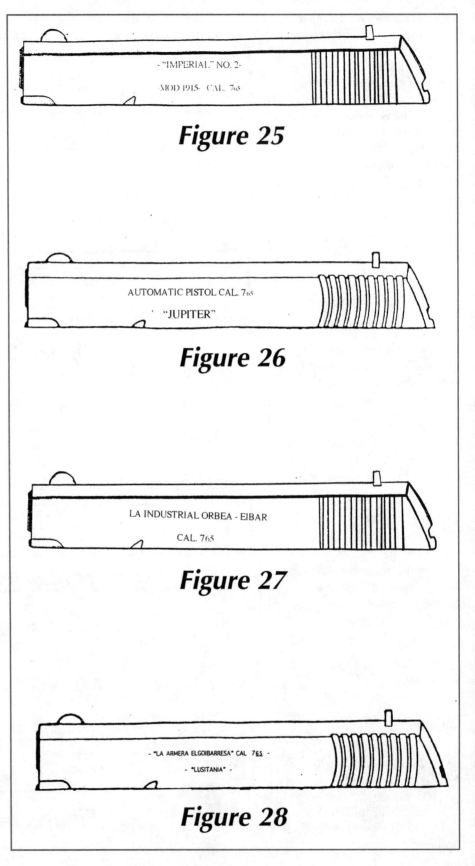

*Figure 25*

**26.** The Jupiter, possibly made by Etxezagarra y Abitua, was sold by Fabrique d'Armes de Guerre de Grande Précision, a Spanish company whose French-language name suggests a Belgian or French origin in hopes of attracting business from customers skeptical of Spanish workmanship.

*Figure 26*

**27.** La Industrial Orbea, one of Spain's oldest gun-manufacturing companies (founded in 1859) produced 10.4mm revolvers for the Italian armed forces along with this French-contract pistol.

*Figure 27*

**28.** La Armera Elgoibarresa was one of the four original subcontractors to Gabilondo early in the making of Ruby-type pistols for the French. As the slide inscription indicates, the company worked out of Elogoibar rather than Eibar.

*Figure 28*

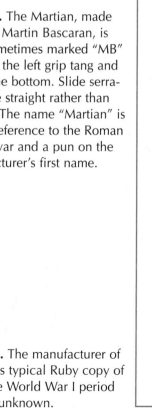

**29.** Modesto Santos was one of the companies formed in Eibar in 1915 to produce pistols for the French. This pistol—Les Ouvriers Réunies—was sold to the French armed forces by a French agent, which explains the choice of French for the slide markings.

**30.** The Liberty was one of several models made for the wartime trade by Retolaza Hermanos. See also Figures 33, 35, 36 and 40.

**31.** The Martian, made by Martin Bascaran, is sometimes marked "MB" on the left grip tang and magazine bottom. Slide serrations are straight rather than curved. The name "Martian" is both a reference to the Roman god of war and a pun on the manufacturer's first name.

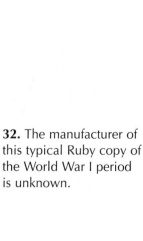

**32.** The manufacturer of this typical Ruby copy of the World War I period is unknown.

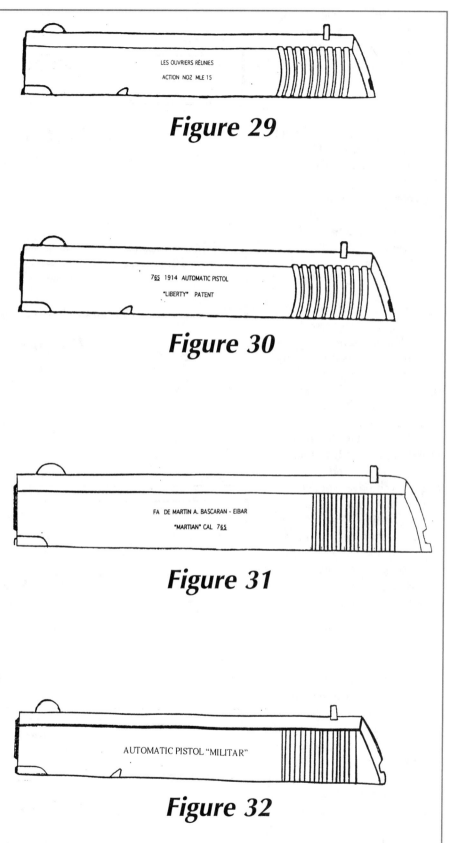

LES OUVRIERS RÉUNIES
ACTION NO2 MLE 15

*Figure 29*

765 1914 AUTOMATIC PISTOL
"LIBERTY" PATENT

*Figure 30*

FA DE MARTIN A. BASCARAN - EIBAR
"MARTIAN" CAL 765

*Figure 31*

AUTOMATIC PISTOL "MILITAR"

*Figure 32*

*Appendix 1*

**33.** This "Military Automatica" pistol represents another product of the Retolaza Hermanos company.

**34.** Still another product of the Retolaza Hermanos company, the Paramount has a dual caliber designation—7.65 and .32—on the slide legend. Slide serrations may be either straight or curved.

**35.** The Regina was one of the pistols made by Gregorio Bolumburu and may be of wartime manufacture. Slide markings of other 9-shot candidate pistols from Bolumburu's firm are as follows: AUTOMATIC PISTOL CAL 7.65 GREGORIO BOLUMBURU, and "BRISTOL." The Bolumburu and the Bristol both have wooden grips similar to those made during wartime. They have straight rather than curved serrations on the rear end of the slide, suggesting more than the usual care was taken to make these pistols.

**36.** The Retolaza, sometimes marked "RH" inside an oval on the left grip tang and at the bottom of the magazine floorplate, may have EIBAR included following the brand name on the slide. Retolaza also sold pistols of this type to the Yugoslav armed forces after the war, marking these with the cyrillic letters "B.T.3." (V.T.Z.).

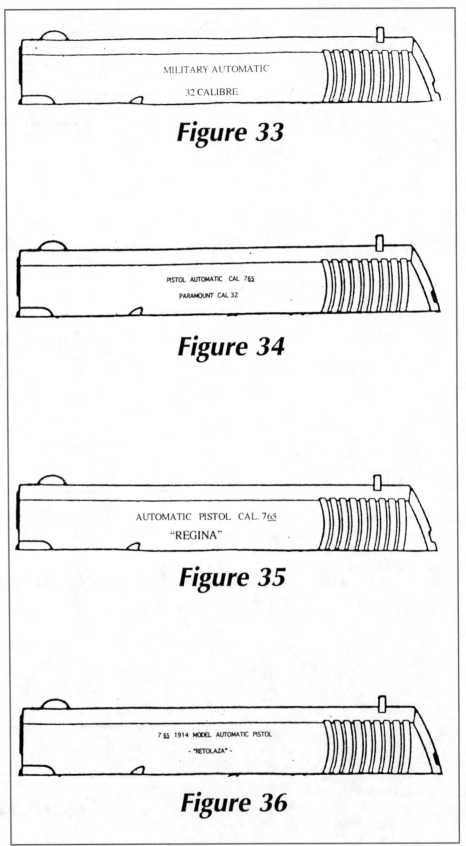

**Figure 33**

**Figure 34**

**Figure 35**

**Figure 36**

**37.** Made by Zulaica y Cia in Eibar, the Royal pistol was sold through a sales agency called SA Royal Vincitor. Compare this model with Figure 46 below.

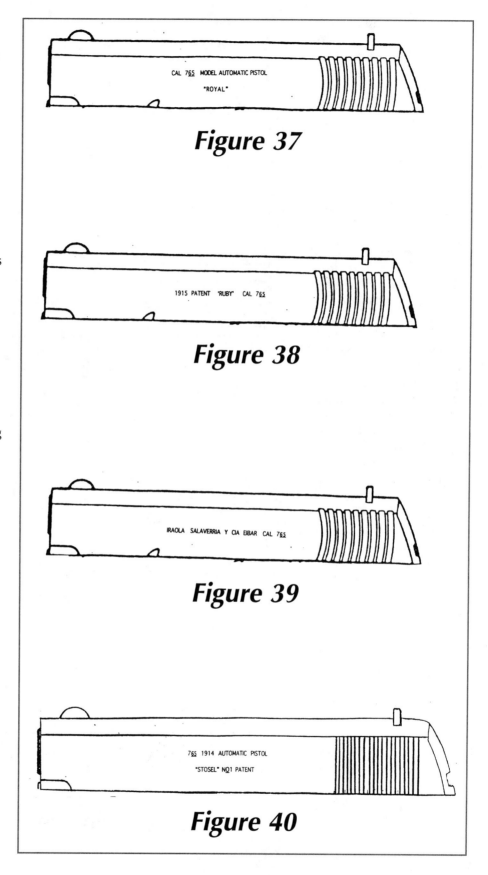

**Figure 37**

**38.** The Ruby is yet another product of the Gabilondo company. Compare it with Figures 19 and 20 above.

**Figure 38**

**39.** This pistol is sometimes marked "IS" in an oval on the left grip tang in addition to the slide markings shown. Iraola Salaverria was one of four original subcontractors who joined Gabilondo early in making Ruby-type pistols for the French. It went out of business around 1921.

**Figure 39**

**40.** The Stosel was named after a Russian general in command of Port Arthur, a city in Manchuria, during the Russo-Japanese War in 1904-1905. This model was yet another Retolaza product. Note the vertical rather than curved slide serrations. Compare with Figures 30, 33, 34 and 36 above.

**Figure 40**

*Appendix 1*

**41.** The Trust is one of many automatic pistols made or marketed by Tomás de Urizar. This model is closely associated with the company's wartime production.

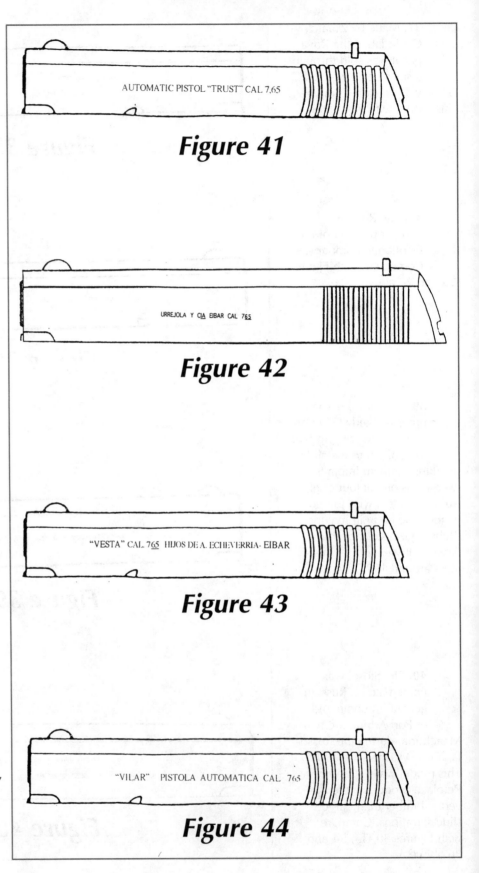

**Figure 41**

**42.** Although the slide serrations on this model made by Urrejola y Cia were the more desireable straight style rather than curved, this pistol had a notorious reputation for poor quality and the firm was out of business by 1925.

**Figure 42**

**43.** The Vesta is an alternate form of the "Hijos de Angel Echeverria" pistol (see Figure 23).

**Figure 43**

**44.** The Vilar is identical, except for slide markings, to the "Liberty" model made by Retolaza Hermanos (see Figure 30). It is probably still another Retolaza product.

**Figure 44**

*Spanish Handguns*

**45.** An alternate form of the Vilar pistol (above), this version has elegant script and vertical slide serrations, the kind of extra effort only rarely lavished on wartime Ruby copies.

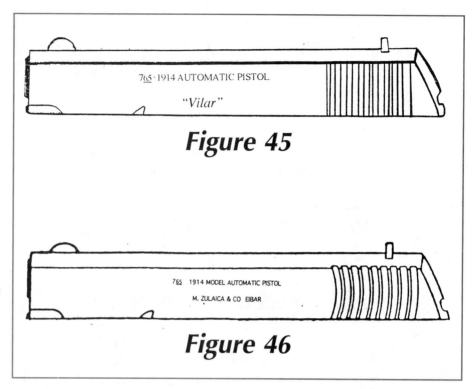

7.65·1914 AUTOMATIC PISTOL

*"Vilar"*

# Figure 45

**46.** M. Zulaico y Cia is marked "ZC" on the left grip tang in addition to the slide markings shown above. Compare with Figure 37.

7.65  1914 MODEL AUTOMATIC PISTOL

M. ZULAICA & CO  EIBAR

# Figure 46

*(continued from pg. 243)*

Guns are listed alphabetically, either by the manufacturer's last name (if known) or by brand name. In some cases, the brand name is used rather than the manufacturer's simply because the brand name is better known. Some slide markings are written in French, in consideration of the large market there, while others are written in Spanish because of their point of origin. Many of the guns listed have slide markings in English, the U.S. having already become, by this time, an important international language of commerce.

This list was assembled through personal observation of extant specimens and from collating lists and examples from a number of sources, both French and English. Spellings on other observed specimens may vary slightly from the examples given here. Some lists, having been drawn up by French researchers, follow French rules of pronunciation; indeed, it is likely that the Spanish manufacturers themselves re-spelled words to suit their customers (e.g., "Victor" for "Vincenzo").

Our knowledge of Ruby-type pistols is constantly evolving. What follows, therefore, is not intended to be the final or ultimate word on the subject. Regrettably, with the passage of time, the loss of many pertinent records, the demise of companies and the deaths of all individuals directly involved, the whole of this complex story can probably never be chronicled.

# *Appendix* II

## *Disassembly Procedures For Selected Spanish Pistols*

## *Disassembly Procedures for a Ruby ("Eibar") Type Pistol*

Ruby-type pistol requires periodic disassembly for a variety of reasons: for cleaning after maintenance, for inspection after storage, for replacement of worn or broken parts, and so on. In general, this type of pistol should be disassembled and cleaned as soon as possible after firing, about once a month when not in use, or on a daily basis when the gun is routinely carried in a holster, or immediately after it has been dropped into water, mud or sand. The Ruby and its many clones are themselves copies of the Browning Model 1903, introduced by John M. Browning in the .32 ACP caliber Colt Model 1903 and the 9mm Browning Long caliber FN Model

A disassembled Ruby-type pistol consists of (top to bottom): slide, barrel, recoil spring and guide rod, frame and magazine. In most Spanish-made Ruby-type pistols copied from the Browning Model 1903 (such as the Tomàs de Urizar "Venus" pistol shown) the manual safety is located on the midpoint of the frame. When applied, it locks the trigger. And, because it holds the slide open, the safety catch also acts as an extra aid in the disassembly process.

To begin unloading the pistol, press the magazine release, then draw the magazine completely away from the bottom of the handle portion of the frame.

1903 (the "Grand Modèle"). Widely copied throughout the world, the Browning Model 1903-type design still appears in many small-frame and medium-frame automatic pistols. Basic field-stripping is quick and easy and can be accomplished without the need for any tools—unless one wishes to remove the grips, in which case a screwdriver is required. The pistol described here as an example of a Ruby-type pistol and is called the "Venus" model, made by Tomàs de Urizar in Spain around 1922.

Before describing the disassembly procedure itself, it's important to learn a few of the terms used in describing a Ruby-type pistol. Please refer to Figures 1 and 2 as these definitions are covered:

• The **slide** is a rectangular steel sleeve surrounding the top and sides of the barrel, which it holds along with a spring and the various parts of the firing mechanism, in position. While the gun is being fired, the slide moves back and forth to operate the loading mechanism. Its rear portion is serrated to help in loading and cocking the pistol.

• The **Frame** or receiver is that portion by which the shooter holds or grips the pistol. The slide moves back and forth on the upper part of the frame.

• The **recoil spring** is a strong coil spring made of tempered steel. It causes the slide and barrel to move forward following the recoil after each shot. In the Venus model, the recoil spring is located in a tunnel drilled into the receiver beneath the barrel.

• A **round** is a complete projectile ready for firing. It consists of a bullet, a gunpowder charge, a primer to ignite the gunpowder charge, and a metal casing that holds the entire assembly together.

With the magazine removed from the frame, draw the slide back as far as it will go, using the serrations at the rear, ejecting any round that may remain in the firing chamber.

**1.** The first step in disassembling any Ruby-type pistol is to remove all ammunition from the magazine and the firing chamber. The magazine is removed by pressing the magazine release, then removing the magazine from the bottom of the handle portion of the frame (see Figures 1 and 3). *Once the*

*Appendix 2*

*magazine has been completely removed from the frame*, draw back the slide, using the serrations at its back end, as far as it will go, ejecting any rounds that may still lie in the firing chamber and the rear end of the barrel (see Figure 4).

**WARNING!** — *Removal of the magazine alone will not make the gun safe! If a round remains in the firing chamber, one shot can still be fired from the pistol, whether intentionally or accidentally. The two steps in the unloading process MUST be taken in the order indicated: first, remove the magazine; and second, draw back the slide. Reversing these two steps will reload the weapon with one round.*

**2.** With the gun now verifiably unloaded (both magazine and firing chamber), draw back the slide again until it locks back into that fully-open position by means of the manual safety (see Figure 5). In the original

With the gun completely unloaded (first the magazine and then the firing chamber), draw the slide back again until it's locked in the fully-open position (using the manual safety). Grasp the barrel by its front end and rotate it about a quarter-turn clockwise until the locking ribs are free of the matching locking recesses machined into the frame.

Once the barrel has been drawn out of the slide, the pistol should be disassembled sufficiently for barrel-cleaning.

If further disassembly is called for, hold the slide firmly against the pressure exerted by the recoil spring and release the manual safety. Then draw the recoil spring assembly out of the frame.

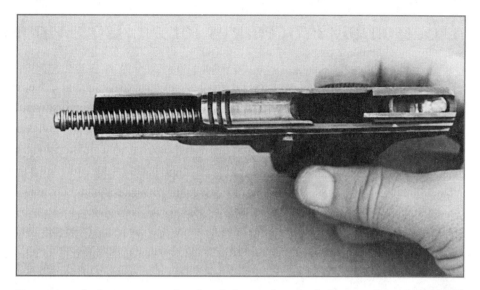

Browning design, a manual safety is located at the left rear of the frame and locks into a notch near the end of the slide. In most other Spanish copies, however, the manual safety is located just above the trigger and locks into a notch at the midpoint of the slide.

**WARNING!** — *If the gun has just been fired, give the barrel time to cool before turning it. If time is short, lock the slide open (using the manual safety) so the barrel can cool from both ends for as long as possible before re-firing. Grasp the barrel with a cloth, if possible, to protect your hand from the heat.*

**3.** Grasp the barrel by the front end and rotate it about a quarter-turn clockwise until the locking ribs (machined into the underside of the barrel) are no longer held by the matching recesses machined into the frame. Now draw the barrel out of the front end of the slide (see Figure 6). In many cases, the pistol, which has been partly disassembled, can now be cleaned.

**4.** If a more complete cleaning is called for, including the breech face in the slide (plus oiling the guide rails for the slide), the procedure is as follows: Hold the slide firmly against the forward pressure exerted by the recoil spring, release the manual safety and ease the slide forward all the way off the front of the frame. Now draw the recoil spring assembly out of the frame (see Figure 7). At this point, the pistol has been disassembled into the following parts: slide, frame, barrel, recoil spring assembly, and magazine (see Figure 2). This is enough disassembly for normal cleaning purposes. If desired, the grips may alsoremoved by first loosening and removing the retaining screw(s) with a screwdriver before lifting out the grip pieces. Reassembly is a straightforward reversal of the above steps. Once the pistol is reassembled, *but before it is loaded,* press the trigger to lower the hammer. This will relieve tension on the mainspring.

# Disassembly Procedures for an Astra Model 400-Type Pistol

An Astra Model 400-type pistol requires periodic disassembly for cleaning, for inspection after storage, and for replacement of worn or broken parts. Ideally, this pistol should be disassembled and cleaned as soon as possible after firing, about once a month when in storage, on a daily basis when the gun has been carried in a holster, or immediately after it has fallen into water, mud or sand. The Astra Model 400-type design, which was introduced in Spain in 1921, is actually a slight modification of the .32 ACP caliber Browning Model 1910 pocket pistol. It was later enlarged, however, to handle the much stronger 9mm Largo cartridge. The Astra Model 400 is found throughout the world, as are its smaller cousins: the Model 300 in .32 ACP or .380 ACP and the Model 600 in 9mm Parabellum caliber. The disassembly procedure for all three models is identical, including the later "tubular" model Astra pistols (e.g., Models 700, 800, 3000 and 4000).

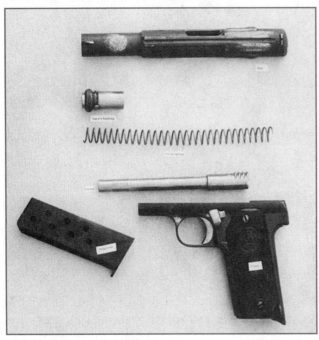

An Astra Model 400-type pistol, when disassembled, consists of the slide, barrel bushing and collar, barrel, recoil spring, frame, manual safety and magazine.

Because these Astra Model 400-type pistols use a blowback (unlocked breech) mechanism, their recoil springs are noticeably more powerful than comparable springs found on locked-breech service pistols in similar calibers. Consequently, even more care is involved in the disassembly and reassembly of these oddly-shaped tubular pistols.

Before beginning with the disassembly itself, note that the terms used in describing the Astra Model 400-type pistol are much the same as the Ruby ("Eibar") type, except that the recoil spring is positioned around the outside of the barrel. Refer to Figures 7 and 8 as you read the following definitions which apply specifically to the Astra pistol.

• The **barrel bushing** is a small round cylinder that fits on the muzzle end of the barrel and holds the recoil spring in place. Because of the strength of this model's recoil spring, the barrel bushing is under tremendous pressure. Behind the barrel bushing is the slightly longer **barrel collar**.

**1.** The first step in disassembling any Astra Model 400-type pistol is to make certain that it is completely unloaded, with all ammunition from both the magazine and the firing chamber removed. To remove the magazine, press the release located at the bottom rear portion of the frame, then draw the magazine completely out of the handle portion of the frame (see Figures 7 and 9). Next, draw the slide back all the way, using the serrations

To unload the pistol, start by pressing the magazine release, then draw the magazine completely out of the bottom part of the frame.

**WARNING!** — *This weapon has a magazine disconnect safety. Assuming everything is in proper working order, removing the magazine will prevent any rounds left in the firing chamber from firing accidentally. However, do not assume that such mechanical features will function correctly. Exercise all cautions while unloading the pistol as if there were no magazine safety. The two step of unloading MUST be carried out in the order indicated.. First, remove the magazine before drawing back the slide. Reversing these two steps will reload the weapon with one round in the firing chamber.*

at the rear. Eject any round that remains in the firing chamber at the rear end of the barrel (see Figure 10).

**2.** With the gun completely unloaded (both magazine and firing chamber), push in the barrel collar with a strong, non-scratching tool. While the barrel collar is depressed, turn the barrel bushing to either side until it unlocks, then EASE the barrel bushing, barrel collar and recoil spring out of the muzzle and set the parts aside (see Figure 11).

With the magazine removed from the frame, draw the slide back to the rear as far as it will go, pulling with the aid of serrations. This procedure will eject any round that may remain in the firing chamber at the end of the barrel. DO NOT RELY ON THE MAGAZINE SAFETY TO KEEP THE GUN FROM FIRING WITH THE MAGAZINE REMOVED.

**WARNING!** — *The barrel bushing, which is under tremendous pressure from the strong recoil spring, must be controlled as it is being turned. Otherwise, it will fly out of the slide with tremendous force. Wear eye protection and point the muzzle away from yourself and any bystanders.*

**3.** Lock the slide open and turn the barrel counter-clockwise, releasing it from its locking lugs in the frame. Move the manual safety lever down and push the slide (with the barrel inside) forward and off the frame (see Figure 12).

**4.** Turn the barrel until the locking ribs (machined on the barrel's underside) are visible on the bottom of the slide, then draw the barrel out of the slide. The pistol is now disassembled into the following parts: slide, barrel

While turning the barrel bushing to either side, push in the barrel collar until it unlocks. Hold the unit firmly against the powerful pressure of the recoil spring while you EASE the barrel bushing, barrel collar and recoil spring out of the muzzle.

bushing, barrel collar, barrel, recoil spring, frame and magazine (see Figure 8). For normal cleaning purpose, the pistol has been disassembled. If desired, the four screws (two on each side of the grip) can be lifted off the grip pieces.

Reassembly is a straightforward reversal of the above steps. Again, because of the great strength of the recoil spring, extreme care is called for when reinstalling the barrel bushing and collar. It's much easier (but never pleasant) to align the locking lugs on these parts with the matching recesses inside the front end of the slide. You can then push the barrel bushing/collar assembly straight onto the slide, turning it so that tension is applied to the recoil spring, which then locks the pieces in place.

After removing the barrel collar, barrel bushing and recoil spring, lock the slide in the locked-open position, turn the barrel counterclockwise (as viewed from the front) until it stops. Push the manual safety lever down and push the slide, with the barrel inside, forward and off the frame.

# Disassembly Procedures for a Colt M1911-Type Pistol

An M1911-type pistol requires periodic disassembly for the following reasons: cleaning after maintenance, inspection after storage, and replacement of worn or broken parts. In general, a Model 1911 (or a pistol similar to it) should be disassembled and cleaned as soon as possible after firing, or about once a month when in storage, or on a daily basis when the gun is carried in a holster, or immediately after it has fallen into water, mud or sand.

An M1911-type pistol is designed to be disassembled without any tools. However, a small adjustable wrench and a screwdriver may come in handy for the second step, which involves removing the barrel bushing and recoil spring plug. Eye protection for every person in the area is also a good idea once the disassembly process has exposed the recoil spring.

Colt M1911-type pistols made in Spain include many Star and Llama models. Most of these strongly resemble the Colt pistol externally and are therefore immediately recognizable to a shooter. The model which deviates most from the Model 1911 in external styling—the Llama Model XI "Especial" (Mugica Model 120—is nevertheless identical in its internal construction and disassembly procedures.

The Llama Model XI M1911-type pistol is shown disassembled.

Figure 2. M1911A1-type pistol (Spanish Llama Model 11) disassembled

*Appendix 2*

The disassembly process, Part 1: remove the magazine.

The following terms are used in describing an M1911-type pistol. Refer also to Figures 13 and 14.

• The **barrel link** is a small metal ring attached to the lower rear end of the barrel.

• The **slide** is a rectangular steel sleeve surrounding the top and sides of the barrel, holding it and its matching spring in position.

• The shooter holds or grips the pistol by the **frame** or **receiver**. The slide moves back and forth on the upper part.

• The **slide stop** consists of an operating lever (by which a shooter locks and unlocks the slide) and a shaft that passes through the frame and holds the barrel link in position. It is manipulated by the shooter in order to hold the slide back in a locked-open position or to close the slide when locked open. The slide stop holds the slide on the frame. Its internal shaft serves as a pivot point for the barrel locking link (which is attached to the bottom rear portion of the barrel).

• The **magazine** of an M1911-type pistol hold up to seven (or eight) .45 caliber cartridges.

• The **barrel bushing** or **muzzle bushing** is a short cylinder that fits on the front end of the slide and barrel.

• The **recoil spring**, made of tempered steel, causes the slide and barrel to move forward following each shot.

• The **recoil spring plug** is a hollow metal cylinder whose front end is held in place beneath the barrel by the barrel bushing.

• The **recoil spring guide rod** is a $1^1/_2$-inch long metal rod attached to the back of the recoil spring. It fits underneath the barrel.

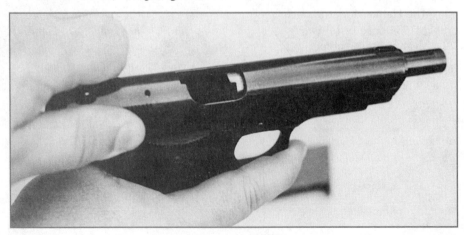

Part 2: To empty the firing chamber, draw the slide back, using the serrations at the rear end.

**1.** The first step in disassembling any M1911-type pistol is to remove all ammunition from the magazine and the firing chamber. To do this, remove the magazine by depressing the release button located on the frame (see Figures 13 and 15). Then draw the slide back as far as possible, ejecting any round that may still be in the firing chamber (see Figure 16).

**WARNING!** — *The unloading process MUST be taken in the order indicated—i.e., removing the magazine and drawing back the slide. Reversing these two steps will reload the weapon with one round, creating a dangerous situation. Removing the magazine alone will not make the gun safe! If a round remains in the firing chamber, one shot can still be fired, whether intentionally or accidentally!*

**2.** With the gun now verifiably unloaded, press in the recoil spring plug and hold it down against pressure exerted by the recoil spring. Rotate the barrel bushing to the right and remove it along with the recoil spring plug. A screwdriver may help to depress the recoil spring plug, and an adjustable wrench will help turn the barrel bushing.

The slide and slide stop must be in correct position, as shown, before the slide stop can be removed.

**3.** Setting aside the barrel bushing and recoil spring plug, draw back the slide, holding it firmly by the serrations at the rear. Pull the slide back until the rearmost notch on the left side of the slide lines up with the projection in the upper right portion of the slide stop (see Figure 17). Hold the slide in that position while preparing for the next step, which is to remove the slide stop.

**4.** Using a screwdriver handle or the bottom of a pistol magazine, push in on the end of the slide stop shaft from the right side of the frame.

Once the slide stop is out of the frame, the slide can be removed from the frame.

**5.** While still holding the slide in position, grasp the slide stop lever from the left side and pull it out of the pistol, from right to left. When the slide stop has emerged completely from the frame, set it aside.

**6.** With the barrel and recoil spring held inside the slide, move the slide forward about two inches, but don't move it all the way off the frame. Hold the slide firmly to prevent loose parts in the recoil spring assembly from falling out and getting lost.

**7.** Ease the slide forward gently until your hand is placed under the recoil spring. Hold the recoil spring against the barrel to prevent parts from falling out. (Figure 18)

**8.** Remove the slide/barrel/recoil spring assembly from the frame, pulling it forward until it leaves the frame. Set the frame aside; it will not be involved in the disassembly process.

**9.** Once the entire slide assembly is off the frame, rotate the guide rod until it has been disengaged from the barrel, then remove it from the back end of the recoil spring. Remove the recoil spring from the slide by pulling it rearward.

**10.** Tilt the barrel link forward until it lies flat against the barrel. Pull the barrel forward and out of the slide (see Figures 19). The pistol should now be divided into the following pieces:

- *slide*
- *barrel*
- *bushing*
- *barrel*

- *recoil spring*
- *recoil spring plug*
- *recoil spring*
- *guide rod*

- *slide stop*
- *frame*
- *magazine*

Tilt the barrel link forward until it lies flat against the barrel. Then pull the barrel forward and out the front of the slide.

# Disassembly Procedures for an Astra Model 900-Type Pistol

[First, review the general instructions for Astra Model 400-type pistol.] The Astra Model 900-type design was introduced in Spain in 1927. It is a major modification of the 7.63mm caliber Mauser Model 1896 pistol/carbine, which it resembles externally. Its internal mechanism and disassembly procedures are entirely different. Though not produced in the enormous numbers of its Mauser competitor, the Astra Model 900 and its six related Models—901, 902, 903, 904, E and F—were highly regarded in their day and are still in evidence all over the world, especially in China and other parts of Asia, the Middle East, Central and South America, Germany, Spain and the United States.

The disassembly procedure for all seven Model 900-type pistols is identical, except that the Models 900, 901 and 902 have fixed magazines integral to the frame, while the Models 903, 904, E and F all use detachable magazines.

The following terms are used in describing an Astra Model 900-type pistol. Refer to Figure 20.

• The **barrel extension** is a large rectangular steel component that is attached permanently to the rear end of the barrel, where the internal parts of the firing mechanism are held in position.

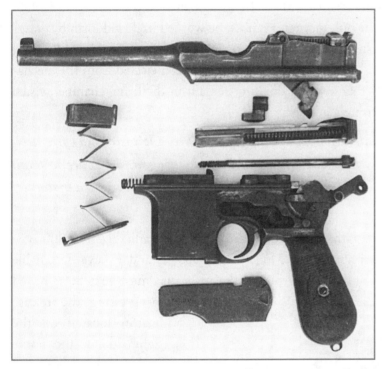

An Astra Model 900 pistol disassembles into the following parts (top to bottom): barrel/barrel extension assembly, bolt, firing pin, frame, removable sideplate and, in front of the frame, the magazine floorplate and spring/follower assembly. Pistols from the Model 903 on use a detachable magazine box instead of the fixed type shown here.

• The **bolt** is a hollow piece of steel that moves inside the barrel extension to cock the hammer. It also loads the firing chamber and contains the firing pin and spring. It also extracts empty cartridge casings from the firing chamber after firing.

• The **magazines** found on the Models 900, 901 and 902 are fixed to the frame, while the Models 903, 904, E and F magazines are detachable units.

• In Model 900-type pistols, the **recoil spring** is located within the bolt assembly, inside the barrel extension at the rear of the frame.

• The **removable sideplate** is a flat piece of steel on the frame's left side. It slides rearward off the frame to expose the pistol's internal firing mechanism, or lockwork.

• The frame **crossbolts** are two large pins, rectangular in shape. The forward piece, found just above the trigger, holds the barrel extension on the

Once the gun has been completely unloaded (both magazine and firing chamber), push the small spring-loaded button at the bottom of the magazine floorplate (Models 900, 901 and 902). While keeping this button depressed, slide the magazine floorplate off (toward the front), being careful to control the leaf-shaped magazine spring and its follower.

frame. The other cross bolt, located above the wooden grips at the rear of the frame, holds the sideplate in place.

• The **bolt retainer** is an L-shaped steel piece which holds the bolt and recoil spring in place within the barrel extension.

**1.** The first step in disassembling any Astra Model 900-type pistol is to make certain it is completely unloaded by removing all ammunition from the magazine and the firing chamber. To unload the fixed internal magazines used in the Models 900, 901 and 902, the bolt mechanism must be worked back and forth by grasping its cocking handles and pulling them toward the rear repeatedly until the bolt remains open, the last round having been ejected from the mechanism. To verify that a round does not remain in the firing chamber, visual inspection is strongly advised.

**WARNING!** — *If handled carelessly during the unloading procedure, the pistol may fire accidentally. Always keep your finger away from the trigger while unloading, and be sure to point the gun in a safe direction so that even if it should discharge, the bullet will not strike a bystander or destroy valuable property.*

In contrast to the procedure used with the earlier Model 900-type pistols described above, the Models 903, 904, E and F have detachable magazines. To unload these pistols the magazine must first be removed

by pressing the release button located on the right side of the frame slightly ahead of and above the trigger. Then draw the magazine from the bottom of the magazine housing forward of the trigger. Now draw the bolt back as far as it will go, using the cocking handles at the rear, ejecting any last round left in the firing chamber.

Lower the manual safety lever alongside the hammer until its lower edge aligns with a notch on the sideplate (located on the left side of the frame). The sideplate can now slide directly off the left side of the frame without interference.

**2.** Push the small spring-loaded button at the bottom of the magazine floorplate (Models 900, 901 and 902 only) and, while keeping this button depressed, slide the magazine floorplate towards the front. Be careful not to lost control of the leaf-shaped magazine spring and its follower (see Figures 20 and 21).

**3.** Lower the manual safety lever next to the hammer until its bottom edge aligns with a notch on the sideplate (located on the left side of the frame (see Figures 22).

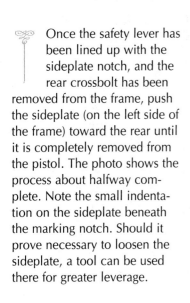

Once the safety lever has been lined up with the sideplate notch, and the rear crossbolt has been removed from the frame, push the sideplate (on the left side of the frame) toward the rear until it is completely removed from the pistol. The photo shows the process about halfway complete. Note the small indentation on the sideplate beneath the marking notch. Should it prove necessary to loosen the sideplate, a tool can be used there for greater leverage.

**4.** Push the barrel/barrel extension slightly to the rear, releasing pressure on the frame crossbolts. At the same time, push the rearmost crossbolt (see Figure 24) from right to left until it is completely out of the frame.

**5.** With the safety lever in position and the rear crossbolt removed, push the sideplate (located on the left side of the frame) toward the rear until it is completely removed from the pistol (Figure 23). If the sideplate is too tight to remove by hand, insert a screwdriver or tool of some kind into the small indentation beneath the marking notch.

**6.** Push the manual safety lever all the way down into the fire position. Then, while pushing the barrel/barrel extension slightly to the rear (releasing pressure on the forward frame crossbolt), push the one remaining (forward) crossbolt (see Figure 24) from right to left until it is completely out of the frame.

**7.** For the third time, push the barrel/barrel extension slightly to the rear, then release it from the frame, lifting it straight up at the point where the frame rails on the slide open up to allow removal of the barrel extension (Figure 23 illustrates how the guide rails are separated). The large steel block controlling the pistol's breech-locking and unlocking mechanism is pinned to the underside of the barrel extension and pivots freely. Do not attempt to remove this locking block, which was pinned onto the barrel extension at the factory.

**8.** Remove the bolt from the barrel and barrel extension by pressing in on the rear portion of the firing pin (using a small screwdriver if necessary).

Rotate the firing pin a quarter turn to the right (clockwise) and remove the firing pin from the rear end of the bolt.

**9.** Push the bolt retainer (on the right side of the barrel extension) forward until it can be lifted out. Pull the bolt and recoil spring to the rear until they've been completely removed from the barrel/barrel extension assembly. The pistol has now been disassembled into the following parts: barrel/barrel extension assembly, bolt, firing pin, frame, removable sideplate and magazine (see Figure 20). Normal cleaning may now proceed. If desired, the grip screw can be removed and lifted from the two wooden grip pieces.

Viewed from the right side of the pistol, the bolt retainer—a large, rectangular piece (top left)—is removed so the bolt can be taken out of the barrel extension. The two frame crossbolts, in turn, allow the removal of the sideplate (left) and the barrel extension (right) from the frame.

When reassembling a Model 900-type pistol, reinsert the bolt and its recoil spring through the rear of the barrel extension. Push in slightly on the recoil spring so the bolt assembly can be placed back into the bolt. Release the pressure on the recoil spring and reinsert the firing pin by lining up its square and rounded sides with the corresponding surfaces at the rear end of the bolt. Push the bolt in about 1/8 of an inch (using a screwdriver) and turn it, locking the pin in place inside the bolt.

Make sure that the locking block (on the underside of the barrel/barrel extension assembly) has been moved as far to the rear as possible. Lower the barrel/barrel extension assembly onto the frame from above, clearing the open spaces in the frame's guide rails. Then, while exerting some pressure rearward on the front of the barrel, replace the forward crossbolt into the frame. After pushing the manual safety lever up a bit to clear the sideplate, slide the sideplate all the way forward onto the frame and reinsert the rear frame crossbolt into the frame. Replace the magazine assembly, lower the hammer and press the trigger (making certain, of course, the gun is unloaded).

# Disassembly Procedures for a CZ Model 75-Type Pistol

A CZ Model 75-type pistol, like the others described above, requires periodic disassembly for cleaning after maintenance, for inspection after storage, and for replacement of worn or broken parts. This pistol should be disassembled and cleaned as soon as possible after firing it, or about once a month when in storage, or on a daily basis when the gun is carried in a holster or has just fallen into water, mud or sand. The CZ-75 design (introduced in Czechoslovakia in the mid 70s) is actually a slight refinement of the FN/Browning Model 1935 or "High Power." It also strongly resembles the disassembly of the SIG P220 (see below). Basic field-stripping, which is quick, convenient and easy, requires no tools, unless the grips are removed, in which case a screwdriver is needed. The pistol used in the following pages is an example of a CZ-75-related model: a Star Firestar M-45 made by Star Bonifacio Echeverria in Spain. Star's Model 28, 30 and 31 pistols, along with the company's Megastar, also have similar disassembly procedures, as do the Astra Models A-70 and A-75.

Once disassembled, a Star Firestar (CZ Model 75-type) pistol breaks down into the following parts: slide, frame, slide stop, magazine and magazine release, and barrel, recoil-spring assembly.

The following are terms used in describing a CZ-75-type pistol. Refer also to Figure 25 and to other terms listed under previous sections (i.e., Ruby-type, Astra Model 400-type, Colt M1911-type and Astra Model 900-type pistols.

• The **slide stop** (see Colt M1911-type).

• The **recoil spring** (see Colt M1911-type, et al). In this model the recoil spring, along with a guide rod, fits into a tunnel drilled into the receiver beneath the barrel.

**1.** When disassembling any CZ-75-type pistol, make certain the gun is completely unloaded, removing all ammunition from the magazine and firing chamber. The magazine is removed first by pressing the magazine release and drawing the magazine out of the bottom of the handle portion (see Figure 26). Then the slide is drawn back, using the serrations at the back end, ejecting any round that might remain in the firing chamber (see Figure 27).

*Appendix 2*

**WARNING!** — *Unloading MUST proceed by first removing the magazine and then drawing back the slide. Reversing these two steps will reload the weapon with one round, creating the same situation described above. Removal of the magazine alone does not make the gun safe! If a round remains in the firing chamber, one shot can still be fired from the pistol, whether intentionally or by accident.*

**2.** With the gun now completely unloaded (both magazine and firing chamber), draw back the slide a fraction of an inch until the two disassembly marks—one on the frame and one on the slide—are aligned. While holding the slide in that position, exert pressure against the forward push of the recoil spring (see Figure 28).

**3.** Continue holding the slide in this position until the disassembly marks on slide and frame are aligned. Next, push the slide stop shaft inward (from the right side of the slide). In some models (including the Firestar used in illustrating this section), merely pushing the slide stop shaft with the fingers will loosen it. Other pistols of the CZ-75 type—notably the CZ-75 itself—may require a tool ( a wooden spoon or the bottom of a pistol magazine) in order to start the slide stop out of the frame. Once that is accomplished, pull the slide stop out from the left side, while continuing to hold the slide slightly to the rear (see Figure 29).

**4.** With the slide stop removed from the frame, draw the slide (with the barrel and recoil spring still inside) off the frame from the front (see Figure 30). After setting the frame aside, the basic disassembly is now complete. Turn the slide assembly upside down and proceed to the next step.

Begin by pressing the magazine release and drawing the magazine completely out of the bottom of the handle portion of the frame.

Draw the slide back as far as possible, aided by the grip serrations at the rear, ejecting any round that may still be in the firing chamber.

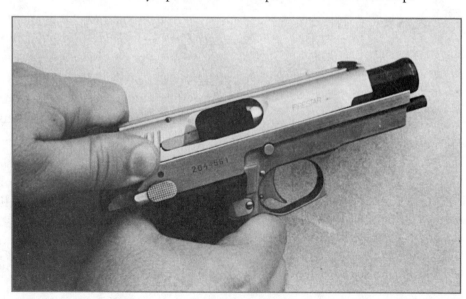

**5.** Press the rear end of the recoil spring guide rod until it can be pulled down and away from the locking cam (see Figure 31). Slowly ease the recoil spring assembly out of the slide (see Figure 32).

 **WARNING!** — *The recoil spring is under strong pressure. It is important to control this pressure by relieving it slowly as the spring is removed. Some kind of eye protection is a good idea—a recoil spring can fly a considerable distance if it's released suddenly and uncontrollably.*

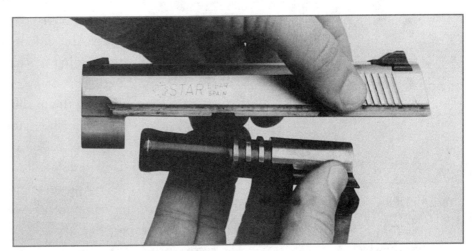

 Draw the barrel down and to the rear until it is completely out of the slide.

**6.** Lower the rear end of the barrel and draw it back away from the slide (see Figures 33 and 34). The pistol has now been disassembled into the following parts: slide, barrel, recoil spring assembly, slide stop, frame, and magazine (see Figure 25). The pistol has now been disassembled far enough for normal cleaning. The grips can be removed, if desired, by loosening and removing the retaining screw(s) with a screwdriver.

# Disassembly Procedures for an Astra A-70 or A-80 Type Pistol

An Astra A-70-type pistol—including both the single action A-70 itself and the similar, but double action A-75—and the Astra A-80-type pistol, which includes the Models A-80, A-90 and A-100 (as well as the later, more compact models A-70 and A-75), are all based on the SIG P220 design. And that design is itself a slight modification of the construction methods pioneered in FN's Browning High Power pistol and later incorporated, with minor changes, into the CZ-75. Any SIG P220-type pistol, like most rugged service pistols, is designed to be quickly and conveniently field-stripped without any tools (a screwdriver, however, is needed for removing the grips, if desired). The pistol used to illustrate these instruction is a Model A-70. Where A-80 disassembly procedures vary, they are noted below.

*Appendix 2*

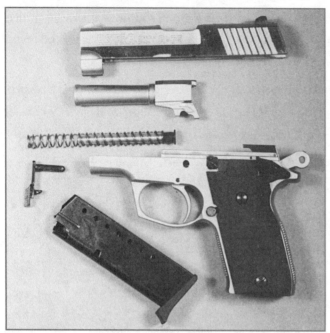

The parts of an Astra A-70 or A-80-type pistol (an A-75 is shown) which are essential to its disassembly include (top to bottom): slide, barrel, recoil spring and guide rod, frame, slide stop and magazine.

Before beginning with the disassembly itself, one needs to know the terms used in describing a pistol of A-70 or A-80 type. Refer to Figure 35 and to similar terms provided previously for other pistols covered in the appendix.

• The **slide** surrounds the top and sides of the barrel, holding it and its accompanying spring, as well as the firing mechanism, in position. During firing, the slide moves back and forth to operate the loading mechanism. Serrations located at the back end of the slide are used for loading and cocking the pistol.

• The **slide stop** can be manipulated to hold the slide back in a locked-open position, or to close the slide if locked open.

• The **disassembly latch** unlocks the mechanism and allows the major components—i.e., the frame and the slide—to be separated from one another.

• The **recoil spring** causes the slide and barrel to move forward following recoil after each shot. In A-70 and A-80-type pistols, the recoil spring is placed around a guide rod, which prevents the spring from kinking.

**1.** Again, the first step in disassembling any A-70 or A-80-type pistol is to make sure it's completely unloaded, removing all ammunition from both the magazine and the firing chamber. The magazine is removed by pressing

After unloading the pistol and with the magazine removed, draw the slide back to the rear, ejecting any round that may still be in the firing chamber. Lock the slide open by pressing upwards on the slide stop.

the magazine release and drawing the magazine from the bottom of the handle portion of the frame. Then draw the slide back as far as possible, using the serrations on the back end of the slide, ejecting any round that may remain in the firing chamber.

**WARNING!** — *Removal of the magazine alone will not make a gun safe! If a round remains in the firing chamber, a shot can still be fired from a pistol, whether intentionally or accidentally! The two steps involved in unloading any automatic pistol MUST be taken in the order indicated, first removing the magazine and then drawing back the slide. Reversing these two steps will reload the weapon with one round, creating a dangerous situation in which a loaded gun can fire a shot.*

*NOTE: Steps 2a, 3a and 4a below apply only to pistols of the A-80 type, including the A-80 itself, plus the A-90 and A-100.*

**2a.** With the gun now completely unloaded (both magazine and firing chamber), hold the pistol in your right hand and, with the left hand, pull the slide all the way back. While still holding the slide back, use the right thumb to push the slide stop up until it holds the slide in the locked-open position (Figure 36).

**3a.** Push the disassembly latch down and forward until its range of motion reaches about 90 degrees. Figure 37 shows the disassembly latch on an A-100 pistol, located just above the trigger on the right side of the frame. The latch points to the rear when in its rest position and with the pistol fully assembled. When in its disassembly position, the latch points almost straight down.

**4a.** Pull the slide back slightly to unlock the slide stop (or press down on the slide stop to unlock it). Then let the slide—with the barrel and recoil spring assembly still attached to it—push the whole slide group completely off the front of the frame. Setting the frame aside, turn the slide upside down (see Step 5 below).

With the slide (on an A-80-type) locked open, push the disassembly latch down (shown just above the trigger pointing to the rear in its assembled position) and forward to its limit of motion, which is about 90 degrees. When properly aligned for disassembly, the latch will point almost straight down, parallel to the trigger.

*NOTE: Steps 2b, 3b and 4b below apply only to the pistols of the A-70 type, including the A-70 itself and the A-75.*

**2b.** Draw the slide back a fraction of an inch until the two disassembly marks, one on the frame and one on the slide, are aligned. Hold the slide in this position, exerting pressure against the forward push of the recoil spring (see Figure 38). *Note; This is identical to the directions for the CZ Model 75 and related pistols, such as the Star Model B (covered above).*

**3b.** Hold the slide in this position until the disassembly marks on slide and frame are aligned, then push inward on the slide stop shaft (on the right side of the slide). In some models, simply pushing the slide stop shaft with the fingers will loosen it, while other pistols may require a tool (a wooden spoon or the bottom of a pistol magazine) to start moving the slide stop out of the frame (see Figure 39).

With an A-70 type pistol, pull the slide back slightly to un-lock the slide stop and align the disassembly notch on the slide with the matching projection on the slide stop.

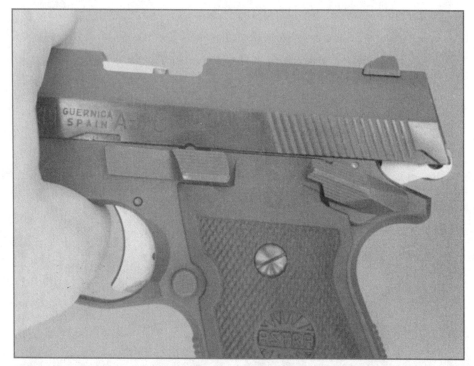

Hold the slide so that the projection on the slide top and the matching notch in the slide remain aligned. Start moving the slide stop out of its seat in the frame by pushing it from right to left.

Remove the slide stop from the frame and push the slide (with the barrel and recoil spring assembly still attached to it) slowly forward.

**4b.** Once the slide stop is partially out of the frame on the right side, pull it out the rest of the way from the left side, still holding the slide slightly to the rear. With the slide stop completely out of the A-70-type pistol, push the slide group forward and off the frame (see Figure 40). Proceed to Step 5 below.

*NOTE: The remaining steps apply to pistols of both A-70 and A-80 type.*

**WARNING! —** *The recoil spring, which operates under strong pressure, must be controlled by relieving the pressure slowly. Eye protection is a good idea, for a recoil spring can fly a considerable distance when released suddenly and uncontrollably.*

6. Lower the rear end of the barrel and draw it to the rear and out of the slide. The pistol has now been disassembled into the following

parts: slide, barrel, recoil spring assembly, frame, and magazine (see Figure 35). Normal cleaning may now proceed. If desired, remove the grips by loosening and removing the retaining screws (two screws on each side on all A-70 and A-80-type pistols). Reassembly is a straightforward reversal of the above steps.

Keep pushing the slide/barrel/recoil spring assembly toward the front until it has been pushed completely off the frame. Finish disassembly by compressing the recoil spring and removing the spring, followed by the barrel until both are clear of the slide.

# *Appendix III*

## *Spanish Pistols Markings*

### *Proofmarks*

This Alkartasuna 7-shot 7.65mm (.32 ACP) pocket model pistol, made before 1923, has no proofmarks at all, only a circular marking (a company logo) on the grip tang.

**S**pain took longer to establish national proofing laws and standards for firearms than some of the other important firearms producing nations, notably Austria, Belgium, France, Germany and Great Britain. Although Spain began proofmarking shotguns in 1910, it was not until July 18, 1923—almost five years after World War I ended—that Spain's first proofing system for its automatic pistols and revolvers came into use. The first Spanish handgun proofmark, known as the "rampant lion," actually took two slightly different forms. In one version, the entire lion, including its head, appeared with a left profile, while in another the lion's head was twisted to its left side so that, while the animal's body still appeared in left profile, viewers now saw the right side of its head. In addition, during the period 1923-1927 the initials "P.V." were used before being replaced by the year code (see below). In any event, the rampant lion proofmark remained in force until December 14, 1929.

The second Spanish handgun proof took the form of a flaming bomb. Introduced on December 14, 1929, this mark remains in use. Its round, old-style bomb has a letter "P" in its center (for pistols) or a letter "R" (for revolvers). To pass the proof test, an automatic pistol must fire two proof loads, each of which develops 30 percent more than normal maximum operating pressure. This is followed by two more shots at normal powder levels to determine whether the self-loading mechanism is functioning properly. For a revolver, where reloading takes place by means of the turning cylinder (which the shooter controls with his trigger finger), over-pressure loads are used.

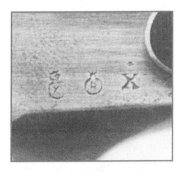

A Star Model B of 1952 proofing (code letter "X") includes the triad of proofs, albeit in a different arrangement than the Astra pistols.

Another pair of marks, called "admission proofs," appear on Spanish handguns submitted to the official Spanish government proofhouse in Eibar after December 14, 1929. From December 14, 1929 to July 9, 1931, this admission proof resembled a crown atop a shield marked with a letter "X" at its center. After that, the crown (representing the Spanish monarchy) was suppressed in favor of a knight's helmeted head, although the shield with the letter "X" remained the same, as it does to the present. All proofing of handguns in Spain still occurs in the city of Eibar at the *Banco Oficial de Pruebas* (Official Proofhouse).

# Year Codes

As in several other nations, notably Germany and Italy, Spain adopted a coding system in 1927 indicating the year in which a gun was submitted to the proofhouse for testing. The code progresses as follows:

This 1946-dated Llama "Especial" has the triad of proofs, but only two items—the year code "Q" and the admission to proof symbol—appear side by side on the frame. The flaming bomb definitive proofmarks, which appear on the slide and triggerguard, are not visible.

| | | |
|---|---|---|
| A, 1927 | X, 1952 | V1, 1977 |
| B, 1928 | Y, 1953 | X1, 1978 |
| C, 1929 | Z, 1954 | Y1, 1979 |
| CH, 1930 | A1, 1955 | Z1, 1980 |
| D, 1931 | B1, 1956 | A2, 1981 |
| E, 1932 | C1, 1957 | B2, 1982 |
| F, 1933 | D1, 1958 | C2, 1983 |
| G, 1934 | E1, 1959 | D2, 1984 |
| H, 1935 | F1, 1960 | E2, 1985 |
| I, 1936 | G1, 1961 | F2, 1986 |
| J, 1937 | H1, 1962 | G2, 1987 |
| K, 1938 | I1, 1963 | H2, 1988 |
| L, 1939 | J1, 1964 | I2, 1989 |
| LL, 1940 | K1, 1965 | J2, 1990 |
| M, 1941 | L1, 1966 | K2, 1991 |
| N, 1942 | M1, 1967 | L2, 1992 |
| Ñ, 1943 | N1, 1968 | M2, 1993 |
| O, 1944 | Ñ1, 1969 | N2, 1994 |
| P, 1945 | O1, 1970 | Ñ2, 1995 |
| Q, 1946 | P1, 1971 | O2, 1996 |
| R, 1947 | Q1, 1972 | P2, 1997 |
| S, 1948 | R1, 1973 | Q2, 1998 |
| T, 1949 | S1, 1974 | R2, 1999 |
| U, 1950 | T1, 1975 | S2, 2000 |
| V, 1951 | U1, 1976 | |

**NOTE:** *The year codes indicated above usually appear with an asterisk(\*) above the letter or letters. The Spanish government is expected to keep this system, or perhaps some slight variation thereof, in effect for the foreseeable future.*

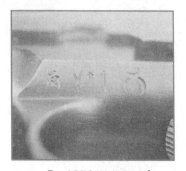

By 1979 (year code "Y1"), when Gabilondo made this Llama Model X-A .32 ACP caliber automatic pistol, the definitive proofmark no longer had a "P" or an "R" marking to distinguish between pistols and revolvers. Note that the proofmarks appear conspicuously on the outer surface of this pistol.

This coding system indicated only the year in which the gun was submitted for proofing, which is not necessarily the same as its year of manufacture. Generally, the two years are either the same or at least very close; after all, a company is in business to make a profit and cannot sit on unsold merchandise for an extended period of time—but there are exceptions. One occurs when a company's handgun is ready for market late in the year but hasn't made it to the proofhouse until early the next year. Perhaps the most remarkable exception occurs with some pistols made in 1936 at the beginning of the Spanish Civil War. These guns did not receive proofmarks until things began to return to normal around 1940. With guns of dubious or changing legal status, moreover, the gap between the date of manufacturing and proofmarking sometimes stretched from months into years. A notable example of this would be the selective-fire versions of the Astra Model 900 line—i.e., the Models 902, 903, F and E—which awaited government permission to be sold or exported on a case-by-case basis. This procedure extended from the establishment of the Republican arms commission in 1931 until the last of these models was sold in 1960.

Proofmark, year code and admission proof were usually placed close together somewhere on the frame (in automatic pistols) or barrel (in revolvers), thus creating a three-mark system, or triad, which on early pistols appeared prominently on the frame of automatic pistols or the barrel of revolvers. Since the mid-1960s, these marks have usually been

This .45 ACP caliber Star Firestar M-45 has the year code L2 (for 1992) together with the admission to proof and definitive proof symbol. All have been stamped inside the magazine well, making them invisible to casual inspection (in accordance with modern fashion).

An early Astra Model 400 (1924 production) features the company's sunburst emblem, with ASTRA in the center and the letters "E" and "U" (for Esperanza y Unceta) above and below the ASTRA inscription.

By 1944, when Unceta y Cia made this Astra Model 600, the company logo had changed. The new letters were "U" on top and "C" on the bottom (for Unceta y Cia). The modern Astra logo has eliminated the letters at the top and bottom of the sunburst.

From the 1950s to the 1980s, Gabilondo y Cia adopted a symbol that included the brand name (in this case "RUBY") with a star above and a star below, all placed in a circular medallion attached to the grip.

placed internally underneath a grip piece or stock so as not to mar the gun's appearance. For this reason, guns whose production runs spanned this period—such as the Astra Models 2000 (Cub) and 4000 (Falcon)—bear an exposed triad in early production and a concealed triad in later production. All Spanish handguns of current manufacture continue to use the triad, but its location is concealed under the left grip or inside the magazine well, where a casual observer is unlikely to notice it.

# Spanish Military Markings

Since the early days of the 20th century, Spanish gunmakers have used special markings on handguns destined for armed forces use. The first military acceptance stamp took the form of a letter "Y" inside a circle. This stamp was applied both during the monarchy (until 1931) and during the Republican regime (1931-1939). The second military acceptance stamp, adopted by Franco's government, took the form of a round, flaming bomb, similar in appearance to the one described above in the proofmarks section, but with the letter "I" in the center. This stamp first appeared in the latter stages of the Spanish Civil War.

Some units of Spain's armed forces have had their own special markings. The paramilitary *Guardia Civil* often used the intertwined letters "GC" in elaborate and elegant script beneath a crown marked on the slides of its pistols. Others meant for naval service featured a crossed-anchor emblem, while the *Carabineros* frequently had their pistols marked with a crown-and-sunburst crest. The air force, in addition, marked some of its pistols with a crowned and winged propeller emblem (see Chapter 4 for illustrations of these various armed forces markings).

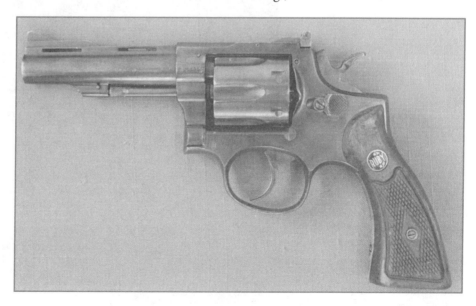

In order to observe the triad of proofs on this Llama Minimax dated 1995 (N2), the left grip must first be removed.

During the 1970s and 1980s, the Llama trademark changed to a hand holding a torch, as it appears on a 7.65mm (.32 ACP) Model X-A pistol of 1979 manufacture.

Pistols delivered directly to the armed forces did not require the usual commercial proofmarks described above. The military acceptance stamp, which involved the armed forces' own testing and inspection procedures, was considered rigorous enough. Nevertheless, commercially-marked guns sometimes ended up in the government arms system, notably the Astra Model 901 and 902 selective-fire machine pistols (taken by the Republican government in 1931), the many Astra Model 300 compact pistols, and the Llama Model IV 9mm Largo pistols that were pressed into standardized use with the *Guardia Civil* during the 1930s.

# Company Markings

Some of the early company markings found on Spanish handguns were gaudy in the extreme. For example, the early postwar "Apache" .25ACP caliber Browning-style pistol (made by Ojanguren y Vidosa) included the likeness of a Parisian hoodlum gang member, complete with beret, impressed into its checkered hard-rubber grips. The similar "Colonial" pistol featured a troll's face on the grips above the word COLONIAL. The Model "Cow-Bow" (also a .25 ACP caliber Browning clone) showed a mounted cowboy, his rifle held overhead at arm's length, on the grips over the words COW BOY. Many other Spanish handgun manufacturers also marked their pistols and revolvers with fancy logos. The Urizar company's dragon motif, which appeared on many of its automatic pistols, is probably the most distinctive and certainly the best known of the pre-Civil War trademarks. In some cases, the combination of a company emblem with its brand name and other markings made for an almost repulsive display. The

The current Llama symbol is a stylized torch as shown on a .45 ACP caliber Minimax pistol made in 1995.

Gabilondo began its Llama pistol line in 1931 with a sequential numbering system that was separate from previous Gabilondo pistols, such as the Ruby. By 1946, when the company built this Model XI "Especial," the Llama serial range had exceeded 113,000 pistols.

The last two digits of the numbering system currently in use in Spain indicate the year of manufacture, in this case 1995.

"Looking Glass" .25 caliber Browning-style pistol made by Acha Hermanos is one particularly unattractive example. At the top of this model's tiny grip appeared an intertwined "AHC" (for Acha Hermanos y Cia). Beneath the company trademark appeared the words "LOOK-ING GLASS" inside a banner, while below that was a person's head in profile inside an oval representing a mirror. Finally, near the bottom of the grip, the AHC logo was repeated. Acha Hermanos somehow managed to fit all of this garish decoration onto one grip piece for a tiny 6-shot .25 caliber pistol. In what has to be considered a miracle of manufacturing, the company somehow managed for find a blank space in which to put a grip screw.

In some cases the logos favored by most Spanish manufacturers undoubtedly conveyed a darker purpose, that of confusing the casual buyer into thinking he had purchased a gun made by a respected foreign manufacturer. Particularly noticeable in this regard were the revolvers of Suinaga y Aramperri and Orbea Hermanos, whose fancy company logos bore a remarkably close resemblance to the distinctive Smith & Wesson trademark. Among automatic pistols, the "Super Destroyer" model, a Walther PP lookalike made by Gaztañaga, Trocaola y Cia, displayed the name of the pistol within a Walther-style banner on the grip, thereby confusing the buyer into thinking he had a genuine Walther PP on his hands.

Fortunately, most Spanish manufacturers, including those that survive to this day, have kept such deceptive practices to a minimum. Unceta y Cia, maker of the Astra line of automatic pistols and revolvers, long ago settled on a sunburst emblem around the word ASTRA, originally with a letter "E" at the top and a "U" at the bottom in honor of the firm's founders, Esperanza and Unceta. After Señor Esperanza left the partnership in 1936, the company logo gradually evolved into the letter "U" at the top and "C: at the bottom (for Unceta y Cia). These letters were deleted from the company logo, however, during the mid- to late 1960s. Another marking

*Firestar M-45, serial number 2044561, from 1992.*

Star Firestar M-45
Federal "American Eagle" 230 gr
50' off hand

sometimes used on pistols made by Unceta prior to 1927 is the word "Hope," which appears on some early Model 200, 300, 400 and 900 pistols as well as on the Model 700 pistols (which were made in 1927 but had undoubtedly been marked before Esperanza left the company in 1926). "Hope" is the English translation of the Spanish name "Esperanza," hence its presence on pistols manufactured prior to 1926—as well as its disappearance soon afterwards.

Although Gabilondo originated the Llama line of automatic pistols and revolvers in 1931, its pistols made prior to World War II had no distinctive company logo. The slide had only the company name, address, caliber and "LLAMA" markings (the grips, being made of wood, discouraged carving). Once the export business picked up following the war, Gabilondo began to develop distinctive trademark emblems, which it placed on all its pistol grips. The first such emblem, which appeared around 1954, consisted of the word LLAMA with one small star above it and another small one below. For its "Ruby" line of low-cost revolvers, Gabilondo used the same two-star marking but substituted the word RUBY for LLAMA. The next grip emblem—a hand holding a torch—proved remarkably long-lived, remaining in use until the early 1990s, when the current emblem (a torch with no hand) came into use.

Bonifacio Echeverria, which made the Star automatic pistol line, settled on a star emblem early in the company's history, registering it as a trademark in 1919 and staying with it ever since. The only difference between the current emblem and its original counterpart, one that was introduced with the 9mm Firestar Model 1990, has no rays emanating from it.

# Numbering Systems

## CAMPO-GIRO

| MODELS | SERIAL NUMBERS |
| --- | --- |
| Model 1913/16 | 1-13625 |
| Model 400 or Model 1921 | 1-105275 |
| Model 600 | 1-59400 |
| Model 700 | 1-20 |
| Model 800 prototype series | 1-30 |
| Model 900 series (Models 900-904, Models E, F) | 1-34336 |
| Model 2000 Cub in .22 Short caliber | 50,001 |
| Model 200 as produced for Colt | ICC-85600CC |

In 1983, a 6.35mm (.25 ACP) caliber Model 2000 was given the serial number 1317025, after which the company introduced its current system, which combines a letter prefix with a 4-digit serial number. The first pistol numbered under this new system was a Model 4000 Falcon, serial number A0001.

Llama pistols began their sequential numbering system in 1931 separate from that of previous Gabilondo pistols. By 1946 the Llama serial range had surpassed 113,000 for the company's large-frame pistols (the small-frame Llama pistols were in a different series than the larger ones). Conversely, Star Bonifacio Echeverria began its production with separate

The early Star logo, used from 1919 to 1990, was a six-pointed star, from which rays emanated (as shown on this 9mm Parabellum Model B pistol from 1952).

*Appendix 3*

serial numbers for each model up until World War I. It then settled on a sequential serial numbering system in which each pistol received a serial number based on the date on which it was produced regardless of model or caliber. Star stayed with this sequential serial numbering system throughout the company's production until 1995, when a law was passed in Spain requiring all serial numbers on Spanish pistols to adopt a new system, which worked as follows:

• *The first two digits represent the company's assigned manufacturing number; i.e., Llama-Gabilondo's assigned number is 07, while Star's is 51.*

• *The next two digits cite product identification; i.e., 04 refers to a pistol.*

• *The next five digits identify each pistol's serial number, resetting to 00001 at the beginning of each year.*

• *The last two digits are the year code; i.e., 95 for 1995, 96 for 1996, 97 for 1997, and so on (some Star pistols made in 1995 have only the last two sets of numbers, i.e., the 5-digit serial number and the 2-digit year code).*

## Some Unusual Markings Worth Noting

Unusual—and uniquely Spanish in origin—are the "assembly numbers" that appear on various pistol parts (usually the slide, barrel and frame). These are observable only when the weapons are disassembled. Factory workers applied these parts in an effort to keep those components (to be used in the same pistol) together. The numbers bear no relation to the serial number eventually assigned to the pistol. At one time it was commonly felt that assembly numbers were a relic of the distant past, when Spanish factories farmed out the construction of handgun components to numerous workshops in and around the Basque towns, but such numbers have been seen (by the author and others) on pistols of recent manufacture as well.

The current Star logo, introduced with the Firestar model in 1990, is an eight-pointed star without rays.

Another interesting inscription on Spanish pistols is "MADE IN SPAIN." As the fortunes of Spanish pistols have risen and fallen, this marking has represented either a mark of quality or a sign of shame, more often the latter. Hence the inscription often appears in an inconspicuous part of the frame that is unlikely to be seen without a diligent search.

In 1933, Unceta received an unusual request from Japan for 900 Astra Model 900 pistols to be stamped (in Chinese characters) "Made in Japan" on the left side of the frames for eventual sale in China. The factory, always willing to fill special orders, duly performed this operation, even though what it said was patently untrue. The guns were, after all, made in Spain. Japan's only role was the exportation of the guns into China. Astra Model 900s bearing this inscription had serial numbers 27000-27899 and were made between 1933 and 1934.

German markings on Spanish pistols during World War II included *Waffenamt* numbers on some Star Model B and Astra Model 300 and 600 pistols. The *Waffenamt* (German for "Weapons Office"), a civil service unit

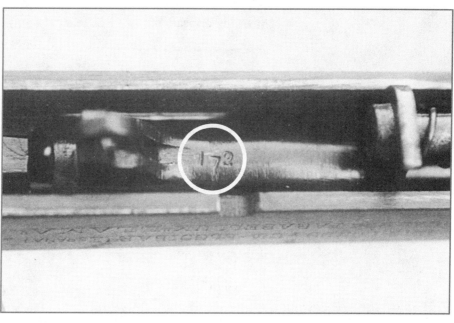

A 9mm Parabellum caliber Llama Model XI "Especial" pistol bears the assembly number "172" stamp on its barrel.

of the Nazi German government, was based in various cities where firearms were manufactured or imported. Their job was to determine whether military small arms were suitable for use by the German armed forces. Upon passing the necessary inspections, these weapons received the *Waffenamt* stamp, consisting (in the case of Spanish pistols accepted into Germany's armed forces) of a WaA 251 (Astra Model 300 in 9mm Short [.380 ACP] only) or WaAD20 (Astra Model 600 and Star Model B). The *Waffenamt* stamp appeared on each pistol's right grip tang. Interestingly, those Astra Model 400 and 900-series pistols known to have been used by German forces have no official German markings at all. The Germans apparently trusted the Spanish proofmark system by this time, and the orders involved were relatively small (only 1,050 Model 900s, 2,004 Model 903s and 4,000 Model 400s).

Another German mark applied to some Spanish handguns was the Geco commercial mark, consisting of a large capital letter "G: with "eco" in smaller, lower-case letters on the same line. "Geco" is a German acronym for the Gustav Genschow Company of Hamburg, a major ammunition manufacturer and commercial importer of firearms before, during and after World War II. Before then, Geco imported and sold large numbers of Spanish-made concealed-hammer revolvers made by Francisco Arizmendi. And during the period 1933-1945, the company imported both Astra and Llama automatic pistols into Germany. Hitler's regime approved of sales of such guns for private purchase both by armed forces personnel and by civilians who had "legitimate reasons" for owning handguns. This generally applied to civilians who worked in some capacity for the Nazis. The Geco marking appears on the right rear grip tang of pistols imported under these

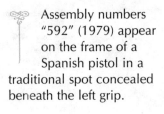 Assembly numbers "592" (1979) appear on the frame of a Spanish pistol in a traditional spot concealed beneath the left grip.

conditions. Two Spanish-made pistols which received the Geco stamp during World War II were the 6.35mm (.25 ACP) caliber Astra Model 200 and the 7.65mm (.32 ACP) caliber Llama Model I pistol.

Special markings, if genuine, may add to the collector and investment value of Spanish pistols and will certainly add to a given pistol's historical interest. However, as in all collecting, the prospective buyer must beware of the possibility of forgeries, particularly among former Nazi-era firearms whose sellers demand exorbitant prices. Would-be buyers of what are purportedly rare or unusual Spanish pistols would be wise to research such matters beforehand and perhaps seek professional appraisals before making any commitments.

# *Appendix IV*

## *Ammunition for Spanish Handguns*

pain's handgun manufacturers have done little in the way of developing their own ammunition, preferring instead to use sources already established in the marketplace. This decision demonstrates good business sense on the part of the Spanish handgun makers, who are better known for refining existing designs over innovation. *[All dimensions, characteristics and specifications included on the following pages are approximations only.]*

## 5mm Charola y Anitua (5mm Clement)

This cartridge was introduced in 1897 along with the first automatic pistol ever made in Spain (see Chapter 1). It got an immediate boost when Belgian inventor Clement chambered his automatic pistol design for it. Both the Charola y Anitua pistol and the Clement cartridge developed a broad distribution, particularly in Europe, early in the 20th century.

Being much larger than the .25 ACP, this cartridge called for a larger pistol, with only a marginal increase in power. Because of this combination—a large cartridge and large pistol, plus a limited level of stopping power—the 5mm Clement never attained the backing of a major company, hence it never received the widespread popularity of the .25 ACP. As a result, the 5mm Charola y Anitua cartridge is exceedingly scarce today.

### SPECIFICATIONS

| | |
|---|---|
| *Case Length* | 0.71″ |
| *Overall Cartridge Length* (including bullet) | 1.01″ |
| *Bullet Diameter* | .202″ (5.1mm) |
| *Bullet Weight* | 36 grains |
| *Muzzle Velocity* | 1030 fps (36-grain bullet) |
| *Muzzle Energy* | 78 foot/pounds |

# 5.5mm Velo Dog

Introduced in 1894 (along with a revolver of the same name made by Galand of Paris and Belgium), this small cartridge became highly popular in a variety of revolvers, including Galand's compact, lightweight pocket model with folding trigger. Galand made its original "Velo Dog" revolver for bicyclists to use on excursions into the countryside where wild dogs roamed. Spanish manufacturers quickly seized on the new Velo Dog ammunition and produced many revolvers in this caliber prior to 1936.

Handguns made in Spain for the 5.5mm Velo Dog cartridge included numerous copies of the Velo Dog revolver made by several Spanish companies between the late 1890s and the mid-1920s. Not counting the many FN Model 1903 and 1906 copies, Spanish manufacturers copied Galand's Velo Dog revolver more than any other type of handgun.

## SPECIFICATIONS

| | |
|---|---|
| *Cartridge Case Length* | 1.12″ |
| *Overall Cartridge Length* | 1.35″ |
| *Bullet Diameter* | .225″ (5.71mm) |
| *Bullet Weight* | 45 grains (standard full metal jacketed configuration) |
| *Muzzle Energy* | 42 foot/pounds (European loadings equal 650 fps.) |
| *Muzzle Velocity* | 750 fps (55 fp in the Remington loading) |

*Note: The 5.5mm Velo Dog round only was slightly less powerful than the .22 Long Rifle and .25 ACP rounds (see below)*

# 5.6mm/.22 Short, Long and Long Rifle

The oldest cartridge in continuous production, the .22 Short dates from 1857 when Smith & Wesson perfected this round. Its primer was contained in a raised flange that encircled the rear end of the cartridge casing. The first gun to use this innovative round was Smith & Wesson's First Model (or Model 1) revolver, which proved highly popular during the American Civil War (1861-1865), thanks to a combination of compact size and self-contained, waterproof ammunition.

Originally a blackpowder cartridge, the **.22 Short** has used smokeless powder since the early 1890s. The switch to noncorrosive priming began in 1927, and the first high-velocity .22 Short cartridge came along in 1930. Muzzle velocities in handgun-length barrels using .22 Short rounds range from about 865 fps for standard velocity rounds to 1,035 fps for high-velocity rounds. The usual bullet weight for the .22 Short is 29 grains for the solid bullet and 27 grains in the hollowpoint configuration.

The 6.35mm/.25 ACP has proven highly popular in small automatic pistols, such as the Astra Model 2000, which has been in continuous production for more than 40 years.

The .22 Long round, which made its debut in 1871, has a slightly longer case than the .22 Short, and it's topped by the same 29-grain bullet. This is a less versatile round than either the .22 Short or .22 Long Rifle (see below), but it remains in production.

Introduced in 1887 by the Stevens gun company, the **.22 Long Rifle** round uses the 22 Long's slightly extended case, plus a longer 40-grain bullet. An inexpensive rimfire round, the .22 Long Rifle is extremely popular among recreational shooters. It's useful also at close ranges against some species of small game and varmints. It has been used with much success as well in silenced or suppressed weapons for quiet recreational shooting, game poaching and military operations. The .22 Long Rifle generally uses a 40-grain lead bullet—although slightly lighter bullets, including hollowpoints, are also available. Muzzle velocities vary widely, with some rounds being supersonic at 1,300 (high velocity) to 1600 (hyper velocity) fps. The original black powder 1880s-vintage .22 Long rifle left the muzzle at around 1,150 feet per second.

Despite their small size, these .22 rimfire rounds are surprisingly deadly. In some countries, more people die yearly as a result of wounds received from these diminutive rounds than from all other rounds combined. Moreover, animals as large as deer and mountain lion have been brought down routinely with them. Spanish manufacturers have, in fact, produced many .22 caliber handguns over the years. Automatic pistols made for the .22 include the Echasa, the Astra Model 5000 (Constable), the Star Model F, the Llama Model XV, and numerous others. Revolvers have included the Astra Cadix and several Llama models, including the Model XXVI currently in production.

# 6.35mm Browning/.15 ACP (1905-present)

FN introduced this tiny round in 1906 for use in the FN Model 1906 pistol designed by John Browning. Colt introduced it to the U.S. market in 1908 in its similar Vest Pocket Model. The **6.35mm Browning** cartridge became known in the U.S. as the .25 ACP (Automatic Colt Pistol) from the date of its first appearance in this country. Since then, the round has seen worldwide use, becoming the round of choice for hundreds of brands of automatic pistols. While a low-powered round, it is highly useful in small pistols, offering a slightly shorter overall length, more reliable feeding, and more certain primer ignition than the .22 Long Rifle rimfire round mentioned above. In fact, Browning himself developed this round specifically because he did not trust the older .22 Short or .22 Long Rifle, with their rimfire ignition method and wide-rimmed cartridge cases, to feed an automatic pistol reliably. Events have in many instances proved him right.

Specialty rounds, such as Hornady XTP hollowpoints and MagSafe ammunition, use lighter bullets driven to significantly higher velocities—and, in some scenarios, offer better stopping power. In any configuration, the 6.35mm/.25 ACP is an anemic performer even under the best of circumstances; however, it does offer shooters a small, light handgun that can accompany its owner almost everywhere. Obviously, having a .25 caliber handgun is better than having no weapon at all—and in most cases of civilian self-defense, where no shots are usually fired at all, the mere presence of a gun has caused a would-be predator to reconsider his attack plan and seek out unarmed prey instead.

Literally scores of different Spanish handguns have used the 6.45mm Browning/.25 ACP round. Prior to 1936, most of these guns were FN Model 1906 copies (see Chapter 5), but since then .25 caliber pistols have appeared in greater variety. Some well-known recent models include Astra's Model 2000 (or Cub) and Star's Model CU (or Starlet).

## SPECIFICATIONS

| | |
|---|---|
| *Muzzle Velocity* | 810 fps (with a 50-grain bullet) |
| *Cartridge Case Length* | 0.62″ |
| *Overall Cartridge Length* | 0.9″ (22.8mm) |
| *Bullet Diameter* | .251″ (6.38mm) |
| *Bullet Weight* | 50 grains (standard full metal jacketed configuration) |
| *Muzzle Energy* | 65-73 foot/pound range (with conventional jacketed bullet) |

# .32 S&W

Introduced in 1878 with the Model 1½ revolver by Smith & Wesson, the .32 S&W cartridge soon became highly popular in a variety of small revolvers made by a wide range of manufacturers. Prior to the development of small automatic pistols firing the .25 ACP and the .32 ACP (see below) the .32 S&W became the most common round for small, lightweight handguns—usually revolvers—intended for personal protection.

Spanish handguns made for the .32 S&W cartridge have included several copies of Smith & Wesson's hinged-frame revolvers, both the spur-hammer and concealed-hammer (i.e., "hammerless") types, none of which remained in production past 1936. The Astra Cadix, a side-opening revolver, chambered this caliber briefly in the late 1950s and early 1960s.

## SPECIFICATIONS

| | |
|---|---|
| *Case Length* | 0.61″ |
| *Overall Cartridge Length* | 0.92″ |
| *Bullet Diameter* | .312″ |
| *Bullet Weight* | 85 Grains (with the standard lead bullet) |
| *Muzzle Energy* | 97 foot/pounds |

# .32 S&W Long

Introduced in 1903 with Smith & Wesson's First Model Hand Ejector revolver, the .32 S&W Long cartridge quickly became popular among police forces in the U.S. and, to a lesser extent, in Europe.

## SPECIFICATIONS

| | |
|---|---|
| *Cartridge Case Length* | 0.93″ |
| *Overall Length* | 1.27″ |
| *Bullet Diameter* | .312″ |
| *Bullet Weight* | 98 grains (standard factory configuration) |
| *Muzzle Energy* | 132 foot/pounds |

*[Note: Any revolver made to fire the .32 S&W Long will also fire the .32 S&W cartridge.]*

# .32 Long Colt

Introduced in 1875 with Colt's New Line revolvers, the .32 Long Colt began as a blackpowder cartridge. Ironically, it proved more popular in Europe than in America, where it originated. Similar rounds from Smith & Wesson (see above) quickly eclipsed it.

Spanish handguns made for the .32 Long Colt cartridge included various copies of the Smith & Wesson M&P Model, notably the Oscillante model by Antonio Errasti, plus several Colt copies by T.A.C. (Trocaola, Aranzabal y Cia) of Eibar.

## SPECIFICATIONS

| | |
|---|---|
| *Cartridge Case Length* | 0.92″ |
| *Overall Cartridge Length* | 1.26″ |
| *Bullet Diameter* | .313″ |
| *Bullet Weight* | 82 grains (standard factory configuration) |
| *Muzzle Velocity* | 790 fps/114 foot/pounds |

# .32-20 WCF (Winchester Center Fire)

Introduced in 1882 with the Winchester Model 73 lever-action rifle, this cartridge also became popular (in downloaded form) in a number of contemporary revolvers. The heavier bullet are better suited to revolvers, downloaded to provide a muzzle velocity of only 850-950 feet per second, with resultant muzzle energy figures of 185-250 foot/pounds. In addition to the dangers of using overloaded ammunition and the hazards to life, limb and equipment that are entailed, the .32-20 WCF requires an unusually long chamber by revolver standards. For use in a handgun, this cartridge offers nothing that more modern cartridges can't do in a smaller, more efficient package. Spanish handguns made for the .32-20 WCF cartridge included the T.A.C. Model 333, which is a long-barreled copy of the Smith & Wesson Hand Ejector revolver.

## SPECIFICATIONS

| | |
|---|---|
| *Cartridge Case Length* | 1.32″ |
| *Bullet Diameter* | .312″ |
| *Overall Cartridge Length* | 1.59″ |
| *Bullet Diameter* | .312 |
| *Bullet Weight* | 80 to 115 grains |

# 7.62mm Nagant

Introduced in 1895 with the Model 1895 revolver (made originally by Nagant of Liège, Belgium, and later licensed to Czarist Russia), the Nagant round is similar to the .32-20 WCF (see above). The Model 1895 is best known for its interesting feature of camming the cylinder forward when the hammer is cocked in order to effect a gas seal. Much of the ammunition in this caliber, therefore, has the bullet completely seated inside the case mouth (most revolvers made in this caliber, though, lacked the gas-seal

The following rounds have seen wide use in Spanish handguns (left to right): 5.6mm/.22 Long Rifle; 6.35mm Browning/.25 ACP; .32 Smith & Wesson; 7.65mm Browning/.32 ACP; 9mm Browning Short/.380 ACP; 9mm Parabellum; 7.63mm/.30 Mauser; 7.62 Nagant/3-line Russian; 9mm Bergmann-Bayard/Largo; .40 S&W; .45 ACP;.455 Webley.

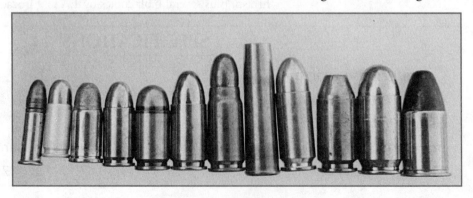

feature). Spanish manufacturers quickly seized on this caliber, producing many revolvers that resembled the Russian service revolver (but without the gas-seal feature) prior to 1936.

Spanish handguns made for the 7.62mm Nagant cartridge included the Nagant-type revolvers of Francisco Arizmendi y Goenaga and the later "Nagan" model of Francisco Arizmendi y Cia, both of which were fair- to moderate-quality revolvers. None, however, copied the gas-seal mechanism of the Russian M1895 variation, using instead a simpler fixed cylinder with no provision for fore-and-aft movement.

---

## SPECIFICATIONS

| | |
|---|---|
| ***Bullet Diameter*** | .295″ |
| ***Bullet Weight*** | 108 grains |
| ***Muzzle Velocity*** | 725 fps (rising to about 1100 fps in the Russian gas-seal revolvers) |
| ***Muzzle Energy*** | 125 foot/pounds |

---

# 7.65mm Browning/.32 ACP (1899-present)

First introduced in 1899 in the FN Model 1900 pistol, the 7.65mm Browning/.32 ACP cartridge has become one of the world's top automatic pistol rounds. Even now new handguns are being designed and built to use this excellent cartridge, which offers good power for a small round. Considered a low-powered round in the U.S., it has proven quite popular in Europe, Africa and Asia for police and even military pistols. The recent development of relatively compact 9mm Parabellum caliber pistols—such as the SIG P225 and Walther P5—has significantly eroded this once-flourishing market. It is at its best in pocket-sized pistols for personal protection, including Walther's Model 3, the various 6- and 7-shot Spanish "Ruby" clones, and the contemporary LWS-32 Seecamp and Beretta Model 3032 Tomcat. It has also seen extensive use in larger guns, such as the Ruby made for military service.

Specialty rounds, such as MagSafe ammunition, are available, using lighter bullets at significantly higher velocities. Muzzle energies for standard cartridges using FMJ bullets are in the 129-145 foot/pound range. The modern Winchester Silvertip loading, which has proven highly effective as an antipersonnel round, fires a 60-grain hollowpoint bullet at a muzzle velocity of 970 feet per second, making possible an expansion of the bullet in living tissue. Since an expanding bullet is more likely to strike a vital area than a bullet that passes straight through and fails to expand, such a feature serves those who demand maximum stopping power from an inherently weak pistol round. Other specialty rounds—notably

Glaser Safety Slugs and MagSafe Ammo Company's "Undercover" round—are even more effective at short distances.

The 7.65mm Browning/.32 ACP offers considerably more killing or wounding power than either the .22 Long Rifle or 6.35mm Browning/.25 ACP rounds. A modern high-tech frangible or hollowpoint bullet coupled with a small pistol makes a potent, concealable combination. Spanish handguns made to fire the 7.65mm Browning/.32 ACP included the many "Ruby" clones of the FN Model 1903 and, more recently, the Echasa Model Fast, the Llama Model 1, the Star Model H and the Astra Models 300,3000 and Constable. In current production, Spanish pistols using this caliber include the Llama Model X and the Astra Models A-60 and Falcon. Regrettably, modern Spanish pistols in this caliber are rarely imported into the U.S.

## SPECIFICATIONS

| | |
|---|---|
| *Cartridge Case Length* | 0.68″ (17mm) |
| *Overall Cartridge Length* | 1.03″ (24.9mm) |
| *Bullet Diameter* | .309″ (7.849mm) |
| *Bullet Weight* | 71 grains (standard full metal jacketed configuration) |
| *Muzzle Velocities* | from 905 to 960 fps for conventional rounds |

# *8mm Lebel*

Introduced in France in 1892 for the service revolver adopted by France's armed forces (and used until 1945 by the French military), this long-lived cartridge served with the French police even longer and still shows up in former French colonies. Gun manufacturers in Belgium and Spain also took up the round and made revolvers to fire it.

Numerous Spanish revolvers, including enlarged Velo-Dog patterns, appeared in this round in the period prior to World War I. But the most famous revolvers chambered in this manner were models made for French military service during that war. These included revolvers copied from Colt's swinging-cylinder models and Smith & Wesson's Hand Ejector/Military & Police design.

## SPECIFICATIONS

| | |
|---|---|
| *Cartridge Case Length* | 1.07″ (25mm) |
| *Overall Cartridge Length* | 1.44″ |
| *Bullet Diameter* | .323″ (8.204mm) |
| *Bullet Weight* | 102 grains (standard factory configuration) |
| *Muzzle Velocity* | 625 fps |
| *Muzzle Energy* | 104 foot/pounds |

# 7.63mm Mauser/.30 Mauser (1896-present)

First developed by Hugo Borchardt in 1893 for his automatic pistol, and an ancestor of the Parabellum (Luger) pistol, the 7.63mm round became famous from 1896 on when the Mauser company used it as the standard round for the famous Model 1896 or "Broomhandle" pistol. In response to the widespread distribution of this model, the .30 Mauser round later formed the basis of the Soviet 7.62mm pistol and submachine-gun cartridge and has experienced widespread use throughout Europe and Asia, and to a lesser extent the Middle East, Central and South America. The .30 Mauser is today an obsolescent round, although at least one manufacturer (Fiocchi of Italy) continues to make high-quality modern ammunition in this caliber, thanks to the large number of surplus guns still in circulation. Communist China and some Eastern European countries still have the similar 7.62mm Soviet-era pistol round in production.

Stopping power is low by modern standards because these lightweight bullets tend to overpenetrate and are thus unlikely to expand in flesh. Muzzle energies for standard cartridges using FMJ bullets are in the 129-145 foot/pound range. Use of the .30 Mauser cartridge in Spanish handguns included most Mauser clones, including the Astra Model 900 series pistol-carbines and those made by the Beistegui Hermanos firm. These weapons became widely distributed in the Americas, Europe and Asia, especially China, giving the Mauser company some fierce competition. In addition, Astra experimented with a small number of Model 1921/Model 400 pistols in this caliber.

Although Spain came late to the 9mm Parabellum cartridge, combat experience with pistols like the Star Model B (shown) convinced Spanish manufacturers that this round had a bright future. Soon after Echeverria introduced the Model B, Astra and Gabilondo followed suit with 9mm Parabellum pistols of their own.

## SPECIFICATIONS

| | |
|---|---|
| *Cartridge Case Length* | 0.99" (25mm) |
| *Overall Cartridge Length* | 1.36" |
| *Bullet Diameter* | .308" (7.823mm) |
| *Bullet Weight* | 86 grains (standard full metal jacketed configuration) |
| *Muzzle Velocity* | 1600 fps (for flat trajectory and good accuracy at extended ranges of 300-400 meters) |

# 7.65mm Parabellum/.30 Luger (1900-present)

Deutsche Waffen-und Munitionsfabriken (DWM) developed the 7.65mm Parabellum/.30 Luger cartridge for the Borchardt/Luger-designed Model 1900 Parabellum pistol. It was the first Luger pistol to see official military service (as adopted by the Swiss armed forces). Unlike previous cartridges described for Browning-designed pistols, the 7.65mm Parabellum/.30 Luger cartridge develops high pressures in the firing chamber. As a result, it generally requires a breech-locking mechanism in a pistol made to fire it. Because of the locked-breech design, pistols using the 7.65mm Parabellum/.30 Luger cartridge tend to be of full-sized military type.

The 7.65mm/.32 ACP cartridge has proven popular both as a military and police round in service pistols, including the 9-shot Victor Bernedo model (top) of World War I vintage, and in pocket pistols for civilian self-protection similar to the 6-shot "Venus" (below).

Interestingly, the 7.65mm Parabellum/.30 Luger round uses a bottle-necked cartridge casing; i.e., the case mouth is necked down to accept a considerably narrow bullet. The muzzle velocity is approximately 1220 fps for conventional rounds with the 93-grain standard full metal jacketed bullet, producing a muzzle energy of 305 foot/pounds. When comparing the 7.65mm Parabellum/.30 Luger round with the 9mm Parabellum/Luger round (see below), the former offers no real advantage. Its primary advantage lies in places where the more popular and widespread 9mm Parabellum is forbidden. Due to a general lack of interest in the 7.65mm Parabellum/.30 Luger in the U.S., no specialty rounds are presently available.

With the development of the 9mm Parabellum cartridge (see below), it became apparent that the 7.65mm Parabellum/.30 Luger cartridge would become extinct. But such has not been the case. While the smaller cartridge is rarely encountered in the U.S., and no pistols in this caliber have ever been mass-produced here, the 7.65mm Parabellum/30 Luger retains a small following in Europe, where it had been used both as a pistol and a submachine-gun round. Pistols so chambered are easy to convert to (and from) the much more popular 9mm Parabellum round. In most cases only a barrel change is required, because the magazine works well with either caliber (in most cases, moreover, the recoil spring also is interchangeable). Thus, in places where the 9mm Parabellum is restricted by law, such as in post-World War I Germany (and now in Italy and Brazil), the 7.65mm Parabellum/.30 Luger cartridge has enjoyed its greatest popularity. Many famous 9mm pistols (other than the Parabellum or Luger pistol), including the FN High Power, the Beretta Model 92, the SIG P210, and several Walther designs (the P38 and P5, among others) have all been made for the 7.65mm Parabellum/.30 Luger caliber. Spanish pistols made for this round are scarce in the U.S., but Spanish manufacturers have made 9mm Parabellum pistols for sale in Italy, Brazil and other countries where civilian shooters are not allowed to own 9mm Parabellum pistols.

## SPECIFICATIONS

| | |
|---|---|
| *Cartridge Case Length* | 0.75 (21.5mm) |
| *Overall Cartridge Length* | 1.15" |
| *Bullet Diameter* | .308" |
| *Bullet Weight* | 93 grains (standard full metal jacketed configuration) |

# .38 S&W

Introduced in 1877 by Smith & Wesson, and used with many of that company's break-open, hinged-frame revolvers (notably the world-famous Safety Hammerless or "Lemon Squeezer" design made in this caliber and in the smaller .32 S&W covered above), the .38 S&W became highly popular in a variety of revolvers, including compact, lightweight pocket models and full-sized revolvers made for military and police service.

Spanish manufacturers have produced many revolvers in the .38 S&W caliber. Prior to the Spanish Civil War, they included both hinged-frame and side-opening Smith & Wesson copies. Spanish handguns made for the .38 S&W cartridge, however, have since 1945 been side-opening revolvers exclusively.

## SPECIFICATIONS

| | |
|---|---|
| *Cartridge Case Length* | 0.78" |
| *Overall Cartridge Length* | 1.20" |
| *Bullet Diameter* | .359" |
| *Bullet Weight* | 145 grains |
| *Muzzle Velocity* | 700 fps (standard factory loading) |
| *Muzzle Energy* | 173 foot/pounds |

*Appendix 4*

# .38 Long Colt

Introduced in 1875 and used with several revolvers by Colt, the .38 Long Colt round became popular after the U.S. armed forces adopted it in 1892. Although the U.S. military soon dropped it as a result of less than positive results under combat experience in the Philippines during the early years of the 20th century, but by then the .38 Long Colt had already caught on and was widely copied.

Spanish handguns made for the .38 Long Colt cartridge included a number of side-opening revolvers produced mostly during the pre-Spanish Civil War period, in both Colt (Army Special) and Smith & Wesson (Hand Ejector; Military & Police) styles. Ojanguren y Marcaido made both Colt and Smith & Wesson copies in this caliber, while other S&W revolver copies in .38 Long Colt caliber were made by Garate, Anitua y Cia, Guisasola, Orbea Hermanos and Suinaga y Aramperri. A more recent model in .38 Long Colt caliber was the Ruby Extra Model 12, made by Llama-Gabolindo.

## SPECIFICATIONS

| | |
|---|---|
| **Cartridge Case Length** | 1.03″ |
| **Overall Cartridge Length** | 1.32″ |
| **Bullet Diameter** | .357″ |
| **Bullet Weight** | 150 grains |
| **Muzzle Velocity** | 770 fps (standard factory loading) |
| **Muzzle Energy** | 195 foot/pounds |

# 9mm Browning Corto or Kurz (Short)/.380 ACP (1908-present)

First introduced in 1908, this became the last of the automatic pistol cartridges invented by John Browning. Due to its slightly greater power compared to the .32 ACP (see above), the .380 has enjoyed more use as a military round, as compared to personal protection. But the increase in power necessitates an increase in size as well. Therefore, compared to .32 caliber pistols, .380 pistols must be at least slightly larger or they must sacrifice one round of ammunition capacity.

The specialty rounds, such as MagSafe ammunition, use lighter bullets at significantly higher velocities. Comparing the 9mm Browning Short/.380 ACP round with the 7.65mm Browning/.32 ACP round (see above) the .380 obviously lends more power to the .32 in a pistol of the same size (at the cost, however, of increase recoil and possibly a reduction in magazine capacity of one round or more). At one time, the 9mm Short/.380 ACP round represented the practical upper limit of what a small, unlocked-breech (blowback) pistol could safely handle. In Spain, this cartridge has been popular, although not as much so as pistols chambered for the slightly smaller 7.65mm Browning/.32 ACP round (see above). Older (pre-1936) Spanish handguns firing the 9mm Browning Short/.380 ACP include the Handy Model 1917, the Astra Model 300, the Llama Model 2 and the Star Models HN and IN. More recent models include the Llama Models 3 (III) and 3A (IIIA), the Star Models DK (Starfire) and SI, and the Astra Models 4000 (Falcon), 5000 (Constable) and A-60.

---

## SPECIFICATIONS

| | |
|---|---|
| *Cartridge Case Length* | 0.68″ (17.1mm) |
| *Overall Cartridge Length* | 0.98″ (24.9mm) |
| *Bullet Diameter* | .356″ (9.04mm) |
| *Bullet Weight* | 95 grains (standard full metal jacketed configuration) |
| *Muzzle Velocity* | 955 fps (conventional rounds) |
| *Muzzle Energy* | 190 foot/pounds |

---

# 9mm Parabellum/9mm Luger/9x19mm (1902-present)

Introduced in 1902, the 9mm Parabellum has, after a very controversial history (see below), become one of the world's premier handgun rounds. Numerous bullet configurations are available, although military organizations generally limit themselves to bullets with a full metal jacket. Consequently, the muzzle velocity of 9mm Parabellum/Luger rounds varies from subsonic speeds of approx. 950 to 1500 fps. Because of the many velocity/bullet weight combinations, muzzle energy is generally about 350 foot/pounds from a pistol-length barrel, making it a powerful round by pistol standards. Developments in modern ammunition have greatly improved the stopping power and lethality of the 9mm round.

The 9mm Parabellum or Luger cartridge is a high-pressure, high-intensity round packing an impressive amount of energy into a small space, thereby making it highly efficient. However, it does fire a small bullet, which has always proven a handicap by comparison with the larger .45 ACP pistol round. Recent efforts have concentrated on harnessing the inherently high energy levels of the 9mm Parabellum, opening the bullet into a wider,

*Appendix 4*

flatter shape upon impact, thereby making a bigger bullet out of a small one. Despite fierce opposition, the 9mm Parabellum remains a solidly established military, police and civilian handgun (and submachine gun) round.

One disadvantage of this round centers on the high pressures developed in the firing chamber of firearms designed to use it. This creates some problems for designers who attempted to create a durable, lightweight pistol that was safe for this high-intensity round. Another shortcoming of the 9mm Parabellum is that found in military ammunition with fully-jacketed bullets. Here the bullet tends to over-penetrate, going straight through an enemy without stopping him. While modern hollowpoint bullets go far toward solving this problem, such ammunition is not available to most armed forces because of international conventions governing warfare. This over-penetration factor, which is hardly unique to the 9mm Parabellum, is shared by the 7.65mm Parabellum (.30 Luger), 7.63mm (.30 Mauser) and most other small-diameter, high-speed pistol cartridges.

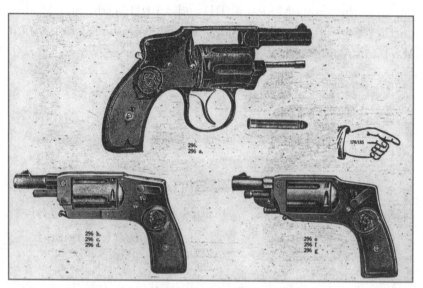

The 1911 ALFA catalog (published in Germany by the A.L. Frank Company) shows a "L'Eclair" model by Garate, Anitua y Cia (note the GAC monogram on the grip) at the top, along with the long Velo-Dog cartridge. The L'Eclair was of a rather standard configuration, with a fixed triggerguard, while the folding-trigger revolvers (shown below) were more typical of the Velo-Dog line. While the folding-trigger revolvers shown are "Arminius" models manufactured in Germany, Spanish manufacturers also made many such guns.

Today, the 9mm Parabellum is probably the world's most prolific handgun and submachine gun cartridge for military and police use; and yet it took several years past its beginnings in 1902 to spread much beyond its native Germany. In the mid-1930s, the 9mm Parabellum round began to proliferate as manufacturers throughout Europe discovered its capabilities. The first Spanish handgun to use the 9mm Parabellum round—Echeverria's Star Model B—appeared in 1933. Three excellent new handguns appeared in 1935, all chambered for the 9mm Parabellum: FN of Belgium's Browning High Power, Poland's VIS (or Radom) pistol, and Finland's Lahti. Widespread use of this cartridge in submachine guns, from the MP-18 of World War I onward, helped establish the 9mm Parabellum as an international standard.

During World War II, the extensive use of weapons by the Germans—the Luger, the Walther P38 and the Erma MP40 "Schmeisser" submachine gun—spread the cartridge even further throughout Europe. The British adopted the Sten gun in 9mm Parabellum caliber in 1940 and ordered Inglis High Power pistols (copies of the FN Browning weapon) in 1944-45 prior to standardizing the 9mm pistol in 1957. France, Italy, Switzerland

and Austria all converted their military pistol and submachine gun armories over to 9mm Parabellum weapons in the 1950s, as did a number of other countries in Asia, Africa and the Americas. Spain officially began the switch from 9mm Largo (see below) to the 9mm Parabellum in 1946, adopting the army's Super B pistol.

Following the notorious Black September raid by the Palestinians against the Israeli athletic delegation at the Munich Olympics in 1872, the West German government sought improved armament for its police, trading in most of their underpowered .32 caliber pistols for three pistols in 9mm Parabellum caliber: the SIG P225, the Walther P5, and the Heckler & Koch PSP or P7M8. All three pistols, in the interest of compactness, used small 8-shot magazines, and all were widely distributed outside of Germany.

Spain also sought a modern 9mm handgun with which to re-equip its armed forces, making Spain's pistol firms compete for the sale. This led to the development in the late 1970s and early 1980s of Star's Model 28, Gabilondo's Llama Omni and Model 82, and Astra Unceta y Cia's Model A-80. One feature of these Spanish guns (not part of the German P5-P7 series) was a large-capacity magazine, inspired by FN's High Power, Beretta's Model 92 and other foreign pistols. The Spanish guns used 15-round magazines for the most part.

Despite the fact that the competing (and somewhat similar) 9mm Largo cartridge (see below) distracted the Spanish armed forces from manufacturing 9mm Parabellum caliber pistols for decades, the lure of overseas markets proved irresistible in time. By the early 1930s, Star Bonifacio Echeverria was producing the Model B in this caliber, followed in 1936 by Gabilondo (the Llama Model XI) and in 1943 by Unceta y Cia (the Astra Model 600). Since then, Spanish manufacturers have made numerous handguns for this highly popular 9mm Parabellum cartridge, including the Llama Model 82 and Star Model 31, along with various pistols intended for export, such as the Firestar, Minimax, A-75 and A-100. In addition, Unceta makes the Astra police Model 357 revolver, which is available with a spare cylinder for conversion to the 9mm cartridge, and Echeverria (Star).

## SPECIFICATIONS

| | |
|---|---|
| *Cartridge Case Length* | 0.76″ (19.1mm) |
| *Overall Cartridge Length* | 1.16″ (29.6mm) |
| *Bullet Diameter* | .355″ (9.017mm) |
| *Bullet Weights* | 86 to 158 grains |

# 9mm Largo/9mm Bergmann-Bayard (1896-present)

First developed by Louis Schmeisser, a talented firearms designer who worked for the Theodor Bergmann Company in Germany, the 9mm Bergmann #6A round was first designed in 1903 for the "Mars" automatic pistol (see Chapter 1). The adoption of the Mars pistol by Spain and later by Denmark assured survival of the 9mm Bergmann-Bayard cartridge.

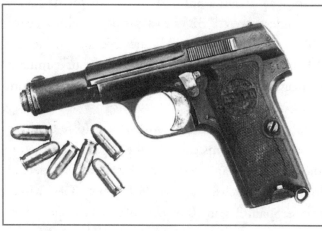

Because Spain stuck with this round the longest, it is today often known by its Spanish name: *9mm Largo.*

Unlike the 9mm Parabellum, whose case is slightly tapered from bottom to top, the 9mm Bergmann-Bayard/Largo round has a straight-sided case, with the same width at the top as at the bottom. These dissimilarities make it extremely unwise to fire 9mm Parabellum ammunition in 9mm Largo pistols—including the Astra Model 400 with its so-called "tolerant" chambers—as a regular practice. The widespread availability of the proper ammunition, the slight but significant differences between the two types of 9mm cartridge, and the advanced age of the guns involved, all of these factors make the use of correct ammunition a virtual necessity for those who want to live to a ripe old age.

Unceta made the Astra Model 300 in both 7.65mm/.32 ACP form and in 9mm Short/.380 ACP (shown). The two rounds are virtually identical in rim width, allowing easy conversion to the fatter, more powerful .380 round. Nevertheless, the more accurate and reliable .32 ACP remains more popular in Europe.

As a military and police handgun cartridge, the 9mm Bergmann-Bayard/Largo round flourished in Spanish official service for many decades. It was used in the Campo-Giro, Model 1921 (Astra Model 400), Star Model A, Jo-Lo-Ar, Llama Model IV and Super Star (Model 1946). Spanish handguns intended for commercial sale using the 9mm Largo cartridge have included all of the above pistols plus some Mauser clones, most notably the Astra Model F series pistol-carbine.

## SPECIFICATIONS

| | |
|---|---|
| *Cartridge Case Length* | 0.91" (25mm) |
| *Overall Cartridge Length* | 1.32" (24.9mm) |
| *Bullet Diameter* | .355" |
| *Bullet Weight* | 125 grains (standard full metal jacketed military configuration) |
| *Muzzle Velocity* | 1120 fps |
| *Muzzle Energy* | 352 foot/pounds |

# .38 Super

Colt introduced the .38 Super round in 1929 for a variation of its Model 1911 automatic pistol. Though less powerful than the .45 ACP usually encountered in the M1911, the .38 Super is a flat-shooting cartridge with good accuracy potential and, when used with suitable modern hollowpoint bullets, is capable of rugged service among military and police forces in addition to civilian self-defense.

The figures below are somewhat better than those cited for the 9mm Parabellum. The slight increase in power, plus the .38 Super's lack of official adoption make the .38 Super popular in places where military rounds are prohibited or restricted for civilian use. The cartridge has long been popular in Mexico, Central and South America, where Spanish gunmakers have serviced the trade with pistols similar to the Colt Model 1911 (but much less costly), such as the Llama "Extra" or Model VIII. Some enthusiasts also fire the round in the Astra Model 400, but they should realize how unwise this is considering the slight dimensional differences between it and the standard 9mm Largo cartridge.

## SPECIFICATIONS

| | |
|---|---|
| **Cartridge Case Length** | 0.90" (25mm) |
| **Overall Cartridge Length** | 1.28" (24.9mm) |
| **Bullet Diameter** | .358" |
| **Bullet Weight** | 115 or 130 grains (both standard full metal jacketed and antipersonnel hollowpoint configurations are available) |
| **Muzzle Velocity** | 1275 fps (with 130-grain bullet) and 1300 fps (with 115-grain bullet) |
| **Muzzle Energy** | 468 and 431 foot/pounds, respectively |

# .38 (S&W) Special

Introduced in 1899 with Smith & Wesson's Military & Police model revolver, this versatile round has become highly popular in a wide variety of revolvers, both compact pocket models and larger service models. In the latter, such as those made by Smith & Wesson on its medium ("K") frame, the .38 Special is easy to shoot, has light recoil, and is quite accurate. In a small, lightweight revolver, such as the Astra Cadix or Smith & Wesson "J" frame, the .38 Special offers a more powerful package for its length and weight than is possible with an automatic pistol. Spanish manufacturers have made—and still do—many revolvers in .38 Special caliber.

Spanish handguns made for the .38 Special cartridge have included many pre-Civil War revolvers, mostly of Smith & Wesson M&P type and a few Colt copies. Since the war ended in 1939, both Astra and Gabilondo have made .38 Special revolvers.

## SPECIFICATIONS

| | |
|---|---|
| *Cartridge Case Length* | 1.16" |
| *Overall Cartridge Length* | 1.55" |
| *Bullet Diameter* | .357" |
| *Bullet Weight* | 130 grains (110-, 125-, 150- and 158-grain bullets are also common) |
| *Muzzle Velocity* | 130-grain military jacketed (ball) loading=950 fps |
| *Muzzle Energy* | 260 foot/pounds |

*[Note: The .38 Special cartridge is longer than the earlier .38 S&W round and also uses a bullet with a smaller diameter; hence the two rounds are not interchangeable. With a 158-grain lead bullet (favored by civilians and police), muzzle velocity drops to 860 fps and muzzle energy rises to 262 foot/pounds.]*

# .357 Magnum

Developed in 1935 (by lengthening the cartridge case of the .38 Special revolver round by 1/8" to 1.29"), the .357 Magnum became one of the best handgun cartridges for hunting and self-protection ever developed. A .357 Magnum cartridge will not fit in a revolver made to fire the .38 Special: an important safety feature. But a .357 Magnum revolver will fire .38 Special rounds, which some shooters prefer. Because of its introduction prior to Spain's Civil War, which began in 1936, no cheap pot-metal guns of Spanish manufacture exist. Considering the .357's power and high operating velocities and chamber pressures, that is good news. Spanish revolvers chambered for the .357 Magnum round include Astra's Model 357 and Llama's Comanche, both well-made, sturdy guns capable of handling this high-intensity round.

## SPECIFICATIONS

| | |
|---|---|
| *Overall Cartridge Length* | 1.51" (case length plus exposed portion of the bullet) |
| *Bullet Diameter* | .357" |
| *Muzzle Velocity* | 1450 fps (with 125-grain bullet or 1235 fps with 158-grain bullet) |
| *Muzzle Energy* | 583 fpe and 535 fpe, respectively |

# .40 S&W (1990-present)

First introduced in 1990, the .40 S&W became an important police round in the United States within the remarkable short span of five years. The characteristics of this round include a muzzle velocity of approximately 985 fps with a 180-grain bullet. An alternative loading, developed about a year later and preferred by many combat handgun authorities, drives a lighter 155-grain bullet at a higher muzzle velocity (about 1140 fps). The .40 S&W has been used primarily in police work (especially in the United

The adoption of the 9mm Bergmann-Bayard/Largo cartridge by Spain's armed forces in the early years of the 20th century assured longevity for this round in Spain. The pistol shown is an Astra Model 1921 (Model 400). It was only Spain's second service pistol to use the 9mm Bergmann-Bayard/Largo round.

States) and as a self-defense caliber for civilian use (mostly in the U.S. as well). Its rise to prominence has been rapid, representing as it does a useful middle ground between the 9mm Parabellum and the .45 ACP cartridges, and yet significantly more powerful than the .38 Special and 9mm.

At this writing most of the world's largest handgun manufacturers have chambered at least one automatic pistol for the .40 S&W round. Because the round is usable with a 9mm-sized extractor, ejector and breech face, the chief design advantage of the .40 S&W over the 9mm is its ability to offer big-bore performance in a medium-sized pistol These include Star's Firestar M-40 and the Astra Models A-75 and A-100. And, beginning in 1995, Llama-Gabilondo also began production of several Model 1911-type pistols—the MAX-I and the Minimax—in .40 S&W caliber.

# 10.4mm Italian

Beginning in 1874 and up until 1945, the 10.4mm round saw extended service with the Italian armed forces in their Model 1874 and Model 1889 revolvers, a remarkably long life span for a service cartridge. Similar in performance and dimensions to early Smith & Wesson .44 caliber efforts, this is an effective round for use in medium-sized revolvers. Spanish handguns made for the 10.4mm Italian cartridge have included copies of the "Bodeo" Italian service revolver (made during World War I) and hinged-frame Smith & Wesson revolver copies made during the same time period for use by Italian armed forces (see also Chapter 2).

## SPECIFICATIONS

| | |
|---|---|
| *Cartridge Case Length* | 0.89″ |
| *Overall Cartridge Length* | 1.25″ |
| *Bullet Diameter* | .422″ (10.72mm) |
| *Bullet Weight* | 177 grains (both black and smokeless powder rounds have been used) |
| *Muzzle Velocities* | 735 fps to 810 fps (with a switch in powders) |

# .41 Magnum

Introduced in 1964 with the Smith & Wesson Model 57 revolver, the .41 Magnum holds considerable promise, both for police officers and civilian self-defense and hunting enthusiasts, but to date it has largely failed to live up to its promise. Because of its sometimes violent recoil, even with comparatively mild service loadings, the .41 Magnum cartridge is rarely used in police revolvers, while most hunters favor the .44 Magnum—even though the .41 offers almost the same performance level of the .44 with less blast and recoil.

While it is a versatile and useful round in some applications, the .41 Magnum has been struggling to survive since its inception. Sensing this, the Spanish revolver manufacturers have put little effort into it (the only Spanish handgun made for the .41 Magnum cartridge has been Astra's Magnum revolver).

With modern expanding hollowpoint bullets, such as the Winchester Silvertip (left), the 7.65mm/.32 ACP is far more effective at stopping an attacker than with traditional full metal jacketed (FM) or ball ammunition. The same holds true for the 9mm Short/.380 ACP (right) and 9mm Parabellum as well.

## SPECIFICATIONS
........................................

| | |
|---|---|
| *Cartridge Case Length* | 1.28″ |
| *Overall Cartridge Length* | 1.58″ |
| *Bullet Diameter* | .410″ |
| *Bullet Weight* | 210 grains |
| *Muzzle Velocity* | 1150 fps |
| *Muzzle Energy* | 515 foot/pounds |

*[Note: A much hotter hunting load using a 210 soft-point bullet at a muzzle velocity of 1500 fps produces a muzzle energy of about 1049 foot/pounds, albeit at a cost of greatly increased recoil.]*

# .44 Russian

The .44 Russian was introduced in 1870 with the single-action Smith & Wesson Russian Model revolver for sales to the Russian army and, beginning in 1878, the round was sold commercially in the United States and Western Europe beginning in 1878. The round became popular in a variety of revolvers, including models from manufacturers in the U.S., Germany and Belgium as well as in Spain. For a handgun round, the .44 Russian was powerful by the standards of its day and also inherently highly accurate. Owing to its popularity in the U.S., Europe and the Americas, Spanish manufacturers made several large revolver models in .,44 Russian caliber prior to 1936 and they sold widely. Others have included several hinged-frame Model 1880 Smith & Wesson Double Action copies, notably the Orbea Hermanos and Trocaola, Aranzabal y Cia models that became popular in the South American trade prior to World War I.

## SPECIFICATIONS
........................................

| | |
|---|---|
| *Cartridge Case Length* | 0.97″ |
| *Overall Cartridge Length* | 1.43″ |
| *Bullet Diameter* | .429″ |
| *Bullet Weight* | 246 grains |
| *Muzzle Velocity* | 770 fps |
| *Muzzle Energy* | 324 foot/pounds |

# .44-40 Winchester

Introduced in 1873 with the Winchester lever-action rifle, the .44-40 was soon offered in a variety of rifles and revolvers, including the Colt Single Action Army. A good all-purpose round, the .44-40 has proved useful against game animals and for self-defense, its popularity spreading quickly to Mexico and Central and South America. In Spain, a close copy of the Winchester Model 92 lever-action rifle became quite popular for use by police and Guardia Civil. As a result, Spanish manufacturers made several large revolver models in this caliber prior to 1936. Made obsolete in rifles by the .30-30 and in revolvers by the .357, .41 and .44 Magnums, collector arms in the .44-40 caliber remain popular. Navy Arms and others in the business continue to make replicas of historical guns chambered for the round.

More powerful loads are possible for strongly-built rifles, but shooters using old-style lever-action rifles are well advised to stick to revolver-strength loadings. The original Model 1873 Winchester and many of its replicas had brass frames, for instance, which are inherently less strong than steel frames.

The most significant Spanish handgun made for the .44-40 cartridge was the large Smith & Wesson-type of top-break revolver made by Orbea Hermanos. This proved especially popular in the South American gun trade, which flourished from the late 1880s until the worldwide recession of the late 1920s. The coming of the Spanish Civil War in 1936 virtually ended Spanish production of revolvers in the .44-40 caliber.

## SPECIFICATIONS

| | |
|---|---|
| *Cartridge Case Length* | 1.31" |
| *Overall Cartridge Length* | 1.55" |
| *Bullet Diameter* | .427" |
| *Bullet Weight* | 200 grains |
| *Muzzle Velocity* | 775 fps |
| *Muzzle Energy* | 270 foot/pounds |

# .44 (S&W) Special

Introduced in 1907 as a more suitable round than the .44 Russian (see above) for use with the new smokeless powders, the .44 Special has been used both in large and small revolvers. Having been created in the first place by lengthening the .44 Russian case slightly, any revolver made to fire the .44 Special can fire .44 Russian ammunition (the reverse in not true, however).

Spanish handguns made for the .44 Special cartridge are quite rare, the most important among them being a Smith & Wesson M&P copy with side-opening cylinder. Made by Trocaola, Aranzabal y Cia, the barrel of this model had a somewhat misleading inscription: CAS.44 SPECIAL AND U.S. SER-VICE CTG." While no modern Spanish revolvers are specifically made to fire the .44 Special, the modern Astra and Llama revolvers chambered for the .44 Magnum cartridge (see below) can handle the shorter .44 Special rounds.

## SPECIFICATIONS

| | |
|---|---|
| *Cartridge Case Length* | 1.16" |
| *Overall Cartridge Length* | 1.62" |
| *Bullet Diameter* | .429" |
| *Bullet Weight* | 246 grains |
| *Muzzle Velocity* | 755 fps |
| *Muzzle Energy* | 311 foot/pounds |

# .45 ACP (1905-present)

In addition to his pioneering and seminal work with early automatic pistols, U.S. inventor John Moses Browning made tremendous advances in pistol cartridges. Four of the world's most popular ones—the .25 ACP, .32 ACP, .380 ACP and .45 ACP—all owe their existence at least in part to Browning's efforts. Having designed the ammunition, he then proceeded to design the pistol mechanisms around them, leading to the creation of firearms as durable as the cartridges themselves.

One of Browning's most famous handgun/ammunition combinations—the Model 1911 pistol with the .45 ACP cartridge—remains in many minds the ultimate combat handgun system. The M1911 pistol, by the way, while it popularized the .45 ACP round, was not the first handgun to use this powerful cartridge; in fact, the Colt Model 1905 was the first pistol to fire the .45 ACP. Colt did offer the Model 1905 to the U.S. Army and to the commercial market, but success was limited. Acting on advice from Army testers, though, Browning and Colt gradually refined the Model 1905's design until it evolved into the fabulously successful Model 1911. Similar to the 9mm Parabellum covered above, the .45 ACP round has seen extensive use both in handguns and in submachine guns. Since the .45 ACP bullet weighs twice as much as the 9mm bullet, however, recoil is more than most shooters can handle without extensive training. And, since the velocity of the .45 ACP bullet is much less than the 9mm Parabellum's, the .45 is less accurate at extended ranges. Despite these shortcomings, the .45 ACP, while not as widely distributed as the 9mm Parabellum, remains quite popular and is likely to be found virtually the world over.

Spanish manufacturers, having quickly noticed the great success of the Model 1911 pistol, began the process of copying it immediately following World War I. Handguns of Spanish origin using the .45 ACP cartridge have included a number of models from Llama and Star. In recent years Astra-Unceta y Cia has introduced several .45 caliber models as well.

## SPECIFICATIONS

| | |
|---|---|
| *Cartridge Case Length* | 0.898″ |
| *Overall Cartridge Length* | 1.17″ |
| *Bullet Diameter* | .452″ |
| *Bullet Weight* | 230 grains |
| *Muzzle Velocity* | 855 fps |
| *Muzzle Energy* | 405 foot/pounds |

*[Note: While this offers only slightly more energy than its chief competitor (the 9mm Parabellum), the .45 ACP is a fatter, wider bullet offering more wounding and killing power than the 9mm when fully jacketed (military ball) ammunition is used exclusively.}*

# .455 (Webley) Revolver, Mark II (1897-present)

Adopted by the British armed forces in 1897 and first used in the Webley Mark III, this early smokeless-powder revolver cartridge replaced the 1892-vintage .455 Revolver Mark I cartridge, a blackpowder round. The .455 Revolver Mark II cartridge became famous in both World Wars in the powerful Webley revolvers, particularly the Mark VI. In addition to the Webley revolver, Colt, Smith & Wesson, and several Belgian and Spanish companies made revolvers chambered for this powerful short-range cartridge. Though its use today is limited (no revolver in current production uses it), the .455 Webley Mark II round remains in production due to large numbers of surviving surplus revolvers made to fire it (Webley made over 300,000 Mark VI revolvers between 1915 and 1932). The .455 Webley Mark II acquired a reputation during World Wars I and II as an extremely effective handgun round, with excellent close-range stopping power competitive with that of the .45 ACP. Accuracy at extended ranges, however, is poor.

The most important Spanish handguns using the .455 Webley Mark II cartridge were the two revolvers for which the British armed forces contracted in November 1915; i.e., Garate, Anitua y Cia's "Pistol, Old Pattern, Number 1, Mark 1" and Trocaola, Aranzabal y Cia's "Pistol, Old Pattern, Number 2, Mark I." Other Spanish revolvers in the commercial trade also chambered the .455 round.

## SPECIFICATIONS

| | |
|---|---|
| *Cartridge Case Length* | 0.77″ |
| *Overall Cartridge Length* | 1.23″ |
| *Bullet Diameter* | .454″ |
| *Bullet Weight* | 265 grains |
| *Muzzle Velocities* | 600 fps |
| *Muzzle Energy* | 220 foot/pounds |

# Appendix V

## Dimensions Of Selected Spanish Pistols

| PISTOL | CALIBER/ CAPACITY | TOTAL LENGTH (INCHES) | BARREL LENGTH (INCHES) | WEIGHT (OUNCES) |
|---|---|---|---|---|
| Charola y Anitua | 5mm/6 rds. | 9 | 4 | 20 |
| Campo-Giro | 9mm L/8 rds. | 9.3 | 6.5 | 34 |
| Ruby | .32 ACP/9 rds. | 6.1 | 3.5 | 23 |
| Danton | .32 ACP/8 rds. | 6.1 | 3.4 | 24 |
| Super Destroyer | .32 ACP/8 rds. | 5.7 | 3.2 | 20 |
| Jo-Lo-Ar | .380 ACP/8 rds. | 6.5 | 7.7 | 25 |
| Llama Model I | .32 ACP/8 rds. | 6.3 | 3.7 | 20 |
| Astra M200 | .25 ACP/6 rds. | 4.3 | 2.2 | 11.5 |
| Modelo Militar | 9mm L/8 rds. | 7.9 | 4.8 | 39 |
| Star Model A | 9mm L/8 rds. | 8.3 | 4.9 | 35 |
| Astra M400 | 9mm L/8 rds. | 9.3 | 5.9 | 31 |
| Astra M300 | .32 ACP/7 rds. | 6.3 | 3.9 | 25 |
| Astra M900 | 7.63mm/10 rds. | 11.7 | 5.5 | 51 |
| Astra M901 | 7.63mm/20 rds. | 11.7 | 5.5 | 54 |
| Astra Model F | 9mm L/10 or 20 rds. | 12.2 | 6.3 | 51.3 |
| MM31 | 7.63mm/10 or 20 rds. | 11.7 | 5.5 | 50 |
| Astra M600 | 9mm P/8 rds. | 8 | 5.2 | 32 |
| Star Model B | 9mm P/8 rds. | 8.5 | 4.8 | 38 |
| Astra M2000 | .25 ACP/6 rds. | 4.4 | 2.2 | 12.5 |
| Constable | .380 ACP/7 rds | 6.8 | 3.5 | 24 |
| Astra A-75 | 9mm P/8 rds. | 6.5 | 3.5 | 31 |
| Astra A-100 | 9mm P/17 (10) rds. | 7.5 | 3.8 | 34 |
| Echasa "Fast" | .32 ACP/8 rds. | 6.1 | 3.2 | 25 |
| Lur Panzer | .22LR/10 rds. | 8.8 | 4.1 | 28.3 |
| Llama IIIA | .380 ACP/7 rds. | 6.5 | 3.7 | 23 |
| Omni | 9mm P/13 rds. | 8 | 4.3 | 45 |
| Model 82 | 9mm P/15 rds. | 8.2 | 4.5 | 39 |
| Model 87 | 9mm P/15 rds. | 9.5 | 5.3 | 40 |
| Minimax 45 | .45 ACP/6 rds. | 7.3 | 3.7 | 35 |
| Model B Super | 9mm P/8 rds. | 8.5 | 5.1 | 34 |
| BM/BKM | 9mm P/8 rds. | 7 | 4 | 35/26 |
| Model PD | .45 ACP/6 rds. | 7 | 4 | 26 |
| Model 30 | 9mm P/15 rds. | 8 | 4.3 | 40 |
| Firestar | 9mmP or 40/6 or 7 rds. | 6.5 | 3.4 | 30 |
| Firestar | .45 ACP/6 rds. | 6.9 | 3.6 | 35 |
| Ultrastar | 9mm P/9 rds. | 7 | 3.6 | 26 |

# Bibliography

*American Rifleman.* Assorted articles.

Antaris, Leonardo. *Astra Automatic Pistols.* Sterling, CO: FIRAC Publishing Company, 1988

Ezell, Edward C. *Handguns of the World.* Harrisburg, PA: Stackpole Book, Inc., 1983

Gangarosa, Gene Jr. *Complete Guide to Classic Handguns.* Wayne, NJ:
Stoeger Publishing Company, 1997

Gangarosa, Gene Jr. *Complete Guide to Modern Handguns.* Wayne, NJ:
Stoeger Publishing Company, 1997

Grennell, Dean A. and Wiley Clapp. *The Gun Digest Book of 9mm Handguns.*
Northbrook, IL: DBI Books, Inc., 1986

Hogg, Ian and John Weeks. *Military Small Arms of the 20th Century, 6th ed.*
Northbrook, IL: DBI Books, Inc.

Hogg, Ian and John Weeks. *Pistols of the World, 3rd ed.* Northbrook, IL: DBI Books, Inc. 1992

Olson, John. *Famous Automatic Pistols and Revolvers, vol. 2.* Oakland, NJ: Jolex, Inc.

Steward, James B. "Military Automatic Pistols of Royal Spain." *Guns Illustrated* 1972.
Northbrook, IL: DBI Books, Inc., 1971

Still, Jan. *Axis Pistols.* Marceline, MO: Walsworth Publishing Company, 1989.

Thomas, Hugh. *The Spanish Civil War.* New York: Harper & Row, 1977.

Zhuk, Aleksandr. *The Illustrated Encyclopedia of Handguns.* London: Greenhill Books, Inc., 1995

# Index

Hemingway, Ernest, 123, 124
Hijos de Angel Echeverria y Cia, 27, 249, 254
Hijos de Calixto Arrizabalaga, 249
Hogg, Ian, 6, 25-26, 28, 47, 106

— I —
Ideal pistol, 57
Import Sports, Inc., 203, 207, 208
Indian pistol, 90
Industrial Orbea, La, 250
Interarms, 24, 75, 80, 140, 153, 159, 160, 165, 166,
    168, 169, 232
Iraola Salaverria y Cia, 27
Italian armed forces, 28, 30, 34, 37, 43, 45
Iver Johnson company, 217

— J —
John Jovino company, 163
Jo-Lo-Ar pistol, 51, 55, 57, 60-65, 128

— K —
Kulisch Conversion, 182

— L —
La Lira pistol, 50-52
Llama-Gabilondo y Cia, 17, 48-49, 52, 60, 65-67, 69-
    72, 87, 105, 107, 121, 128, 132, 146, 162,
    184-211, 233, 248, 284
    Comanche line, 190, 193-195
    Martial, 191, 192, 194, 195
    MAX-1 series, 200, 206-208, 211
    Micro-max, 186, 196, 199, 204, 211
    Mini-max, 187, 189, 193, 196, 199, 201-203,
        207-211, 242, 282
    Model III, 184, 185
    Model III-A, 184-186, 188, 211
    Model 8 (VIII), 187-188, 190
    Model 8 (VIII-C), 188
    Model 9 (IX), 188
    Model 9 (IX-A), 188
    Model 9 (IX-B), 189
    Model 9 (IX-C), 204, 206-208
    Model 9 (IX-D), 207
    Model 9 (IX) Especial, 189, 283
    Model 10A (X-A), 185-189, 280
    Model 11 (XI), 263
    Model 11 (XI-B), 191
    Model 11 (XI) Especial, 191, 239, 287
    Model 15 (XV) Especial, 185

    Model 16 (XVI), 185
    Model 17 (XVII) Executive, 186
    Model 18 (XVIII) Executive, 186
    Model 19 (XIX), 185
    Model 26 (XXVI), 193, 195
    Model 82, 197, 200-203
    Model 87, 198, 202-203
    Omni, 195, 197-198, 200, 201, 206, 222
    Piccolo, 194
    Scorpio, 194, 195
Longines pistol, 51, 54
Lovitz, Gene, 64
*Luftwaffe*, 121, 138
Luger pistol, 97, 138, 143, 182
Lur Panzer pistol, 177, 181-183
Lusitania pistol, 27

— M —
Madison pistol, 175, 177, 181
Magazines, 234, 238
Makarov pistol, 133
Mannlicher, 34, 52, 69, 70
    Model 1901, 18
    Model 1905, 50
Manufacture d'Armes de Bayonne (MAB), 181
Marin Bascaran company, 129
Martial revolver, 191, 192, 194, 195
Martin Bascaran company, 251
Mathews, J. Howard, 27
Mauser, Paul von, 101
Mauser-Werke, 7, 111
    Model C.96, 48
    Model 712 (*Schnellfeuerpistole*), 100-102, 141, 142
    Model 1893, 27
    Model 1896 (C/96 or Broomhandle), 7, 9, 12, 53,
55-56, 86, 97, 99, 103, 122-123, 141, 143, 267
MAX-1 series, 200, 206-208, 211
Megastar pistol, 223, 230-231
Merwin, Hulbert & Company, 6
Micro-max pistol, 186, 196, 199, 204, 211
Mini-max pistol, 187, 189, 193, 196, 199, 201-203,
    207-211, 242, 282
Modelo Corzo, 111
Modelo Militar, 35, 69-70, 79, 81, 88, 110, 128
Modesto Santos company, 29, 251
Mondial pistol, 50
Moroccan war, 115
Mugica, José Cruz, 59, 67, 106-107, 109
Mugica Model 105, 185

*Index*